Administering VMware Site Recovery Manager 5.0

VMware Press is the official publisher of VMware books and training materials, which provide guidance on the critical topics facing today's technology professionals and students. Enterprises, as well as small- and medium-sized organizations, adopt virtualization as a more agile way of scaling IT to meet business needs. VMware Press provides proven, technically accurate information that will help them meet their goals for customizing, building, and maintaining their virtual environment.

With books, certification and study guides, video training, and learning tools produced by world-class architects and IT experts, VMware Press helps IT professionals master a diverse range of topics on virtualization and cloud computing and is the official source of reference materials for preparing for the VMware Certified Professional Examination.

VMware Press is also pleased to have localization partners that can publish its products into more than forty-two languages, including, but not limited to, Chinese (Simplified), Chinese (Traditional), French, German, Greek, Hindi, Japanese, Korean, Polish, Russian, and Spanish.

For more information about VMware Press please visit
http://www.vmware.com/go/vmwarepress

Administering VMware Site Recovery Manager 5.0

TECHNOLOGY HANDS-ON

Mike Laverick

vmware® PRESS

Upper Saddle River, NJ • Boston • Indianapolis • San Francisco
New York • Toronto • Montreal • London • Munich • Paris • Madrid
Capetown • Sydney • Tokyo • Singapore • Mexico City

Administering VMware Site Recovery Manager 5.0

Published by Pearson Education, Inc.

Publishing as VMware Press

Warning and Disclaimer

Corporate and Government Sales

VMware Press offers excellent discounts on this book when ordered in quantity for bulk purchases or special sales, which may include electronic versions and/or custom covers and content particular to your business, training goals, marketing focus, and branding interests. For more information, please contact U.S. Corporate and Government Sales, (800) 382-3419, corpsales@pearsontechgroup.com. For sales outside the United States, please contact International Sales, international@pearson.com.

Library of Congress Control Number: 2011919183

ISBN-13: 978-0-321-79992-0
ISBN-10:   0-321-79992-5

Text printed in the United States on recycled paper at RR Donnelley in Crawfordsville, Indiana.
First printing, December 2011

VMWARE PRESS PROGRAM MANAGER
Andrea Eubanks de Jounge

ASSOCIATE PUBLISHER
David Dusthimer

ACQUISITIONS EDITOR
Joan Murray

DEVELOPMENT EDITOR
Susan Zahn

MANAGING EDITOR
John Fuller

FULL-SERVICE PRODUCTION MANAGER
Julie B. Nahil

COPY EDITOR
Audrey Doyle

PROOFREADER
Kelli M. Brooks

INDEXER
Jack Lewis

EDITORIAL ASSISTANT
Vanessa Evans

BOOK DESIGNER
Gary Adair

COMPOSITOR
Kim Arney

This book is dedicated to Carmel—for putting up with me and my endless ramblings about virtualization.

Contents

Preface

This edition of *Administering VMware Site Recovery Manager 5.0* is not only a new edition of this book but one of the first books published by VMware Press.

About This Book

Version 5.0 represents a major milestone in the development of VMware Site Recovery Manager (SRM). The need to write a book on SRM 5.0 seems more pressing than ever because of the many new features and enhancements in this version. I think these enhancements are likely to draw to the product a whole new raft of people who previously may have overlooked it. Welcome to the wonderful world that is Site Recovery Manager!

This is a complete guide to using SRM. The version of both ESX and vCenter that we use in the book is 5.0. This book was tested against the ESX5i release. This is in marked contrast to the first edition of this book and the SRM product where ESXi was not initially supported. In the previous edition of the book I used abstract names for my vCenter structures, literally calling the vCenter in the Protected Site virtualcenterpro-tectedsite.rtfm-ed.co.uk. Later I used two cities in the United Kingdom (London and Reading) to represent a Protected Site and a Recovery Site. This time around I have done much the same thing. But the protected location is New York and the recovery location is New Jersey. I thought that as most of my readers are from the United States, and there isn't a person on the planet who hasn't heard of these locations, people would more quickly latch on to the scenario. Figure P.1 shows my structure, with one domain (corp.com) being used in New York and New Jersey. Each site has its own Microsoft Active Directory domain controller, and there is a router between the sites. Each site

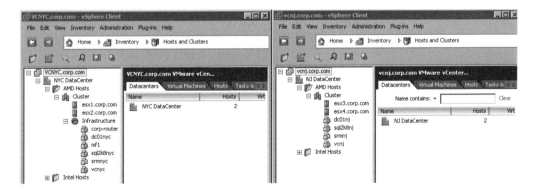

Figure P.1 Two vCenter environments side by side

has its own vCenter, Microsoft SQL Server 2008, and SRM Server. In this case I chose not to use the linked mode feature of vCenter 5; I will introduce that configuration later in the book. I made this decision merely to keep the distinction clear: that I have two separate locations or sites.

You, the Reader

I have a very clear idea of the kind of person reading this book. Ideally, you have been working with VMware vSphere for some time—perhaps you have attended an authorized course in vSphere 4 such as the "Install, Configure and Manage" class, or even the "Fast Track" class. On top of this, perhaps you have pursued VMware Certified Professional (VCP) certification. So, what am I getting at? This is not a dummy's or idiot's guide to SRM. You are going to need some background, or at least read my other guides or books, to get up to speed. Apart from that, I will be gentle with you—assuming that you have forgotten some of the material from those courses, such as VMFS metadata, UUIDs, and VMFS resignaturing, and that you just have a passing understanding of storage replication.

Finally, the use of storage products in this book shouldn't be construed as a recommendation of any particular vendor. I just happened to meet the HP LeftHand Networks guys at VMworld Europe 2008 – Cannes. They very kindly offered to give me two NFR licenses for their storage technologies. The other storage vendors who helped me while I was writing this book have been equally generous. In 2008, both Chad Sakac of EMC and Vaughn Stewart of NetApp arranged for my lab environment to be kitted out in the very latest versions of their CLARiiON/Celerra and NetApp FSA systems. This empowered me to be much more storage-neutral than I was in previous editions of this book. For this version of the book I was fortunate to also add coverage of the Dell EqualLogic system. Toward that end, I would like to thank Dylan Locsin and William Urban of Dell for their support.

What This Book Covers

Here is a quick rundown of what is covered in *Administering VMware Site Recovery Manager 5.0*.

- Chapter 1, Introduction to Site Recovery Manager

    This chapter provides a brief introduction to Site Recovery Manager and discusses some use cases.

- Chapter 2, Getting Started with Dell EqualLogic Replication

  This chapter guides readers through the configuration of replication with Dell EqualLogic arrays, and covers the basic configuration of the ESXi iSCSI initiator.

- Chapter 3, Getting Started with EMC Celerra Replication

  This chapter guides readers through the configuration of replication with EMC Celerra arrays, and covers the basic configuration of the ESXi iSCSI initiator.

- Chapter 4, Getting Started with EMC CLARiiON MirrorView

  This chapter guides readers through the configuration of replication with CLARiiON arrays.

- Chapter 5, Getting Started with the HP StorageWorks P4000 Virtual SAN Appliance with Remote Copy

  This chapter guides readers through the configuration of replication with the HP P4000 VSA, and covers the basic configuration of the ESXi iSCSI initiator.

- Chapter 6, Getting Started with NetApp SnapMirror

  This chapter guides readers through the configuration of NetApp replication arrays, and covers configuration for FC, iSCSI, and NFS.

- Chapter 7, Installing VMware SRM

  This chapter covers the installation of VMware Site Recovery Manager, and details post-configuration steps such as installing an array vendor's Site Recovery Adapter software.

- Chapter 8, Configuring vSphere Replication (Optional)

  This optional chapter details the steps required to configure vSphere Replication (VR).

- Chapter 9, Configuring the Protected Site

  This chapter covers the initial setup of the Protected Site and deals with such steps as pairing the sites, inventory mappings, array manager configuration, and placeholder datastore configuration. It also introduces the concept of the SRM Protection Group.

- Chapter 10, Recovery Site Configuration

  This chapter covers the basic configuration of the Recovery Plan at the Recovery Site.

- Chapter 11, Custom Recovery Plans

   This chapter discusses how Recovery Plans can have very detailed customization designed around a business need. It also explains the use of message prompts, command steps, and the re-IP of virtual machines.

- Chapter 12, Alarms, Exporting History, and Access Control

   This chapter outlines how administrators can configure alarms and alerts to assist in the day-to-day maintenance of SRM. It details the reporting functionality available in the History components. Finally, it covers a basic delegation process to allow others to manage SRM without using built-in permission assignments.

- Chapter 13, Bidirectional Relationships and Shared Site Configurations

   The chapter outlines more complicated SRM relationships where SRM protects VMs at multiple sites.

- Chapter 14, Failover and Failback

   This chapter covers the real execution of a Recovery Plan, rather than merely a test. It details the planned migration and disaster recovery modes, as well as outlining the steps required to failback VMs to their original locale.

- Chapter 15, Scripting Site Recovery

   This chapter covers what to do if Site Recovery Manager is not available. It discusses how to do *manually* everything that Site Recovery Manager automates.

- Chapter 16, Upgrading from SRM 4.1 to SRM 5.0

   This chapter offers a high-level view of how to upgrade SRM 4.1 to SRM 5.0. It also covers upgrading the dependencies that allow SRM 5.0 to function, including upgrading ESX, vCenter, Update Manager, and virtual machines.

Hyperlinks

The Internet is a fantastic resource, as we all know. However, printed hyperlinks are often quite lengthy, are difficult to type correctly, and frequently change. I've created a very simple Web page that contains all the URLs in this book. I will endeavor to keep this page up to date to make life easy for everyone concerned. The single URL you need for all the links and online content is

- www.rtfm-ed.co.uk/srm.html

Please note that depending on when you purchased this book, the location of my resource blog might have changed. Beginning in late January 2012, I should have a new blog for you to access all kinds of virtualization information:

- www.mikelaverick.com

At the time of this writing, there are still a number of storage vendors that have yet to release their supporting software for VMware Site Recovery Manager. My updates on those vendors will be posted to this book's Web page:

- http://informit.com/title/9780321799920

Author Disclaimer

No book on an IT product would be complete without a disclaimer. Here is mine: Although every precaution has been taken in the preparation of this book, the contributors and author assume no responsibility for errors or omissions. Neither is any liability assumed for damages resulting from the use of the information contained herein. Phew, glad that's over with!

Thank you for buying this book. I know I'm not quite James Joyce, but I hope that people find reading this book both entertaining and instructive.

Acknowledgments

Before we move on to Chapter 1, I would like to thank the many people who helped me as I wrote this book. First, I would like to thank Carmel Edwards, my partner. She puts up with my ranting and raving about VMware and virtualization. Carmel is the first to read my work and did the first proofread of the manuscript.

Second, I would like to thank Adam Carter, formerly of HP LeftHand Networks; Chad Sakac of EMC; Vaughn Stewart of NetApp; and Andrew Gilman of Dell. All four individuals were invaluable in allowing me to bounce ideas around and to ask newbie-like questions—regarding not just their technologies, but storage issues in general. If I sound like some kind of storage guru in this book, I have these guys to thank for that. (Actually, I'm not a guru at all, even in terms of VMware products. I can't even stand the use of the word *guru*.) Within EMC, I would like to especially thank Alex Tanner, who is part of "Chad's Army" and was instrumental in getting me set up with the EMC NS-120 systems as well as giving me ongoing help and support as I rewrote the material in the previous edition for use in this edition of the book. I would also like to thank Luke Reed of NetApp who helped in a very similar capacity in updating my storage controllers so that I could use them with the latest version of ONTAP.

Third, I would like to thank Jacob Jenson of the VMware DR/BC Group and the SRM Team generally. I would also like to thank Mornay Van Der Walt of VMware. Mornay is the director for Enterprise & Technical Marketing. I first met Mornay at Cannes in 2008, and he was instrumental in introducing me to the right people when I first took on SRM as a technology. He was also very helpful in assisting me with my more obscure technical questions surrounding the early SRM product without which the idea of writing a book would have been impossible. I would also like to thank Lee Dilworth of VMware in the UK. Lee has been very helpful in my travels with SRM, and it's to him that I direct my emails when even I can't work out what is going on!

I would like to thank Cormac Hogan, Tim Oudin, Craig Waters, and Jeff Drury for their feedback. I'm often asked how much of a technical review books like mine go through. The answer is a great deal—and this review process is often as long as the writing process. People often offer to review my work, but almost never have the time to do it. So I would like to thank these guys for taking the time and giving me their valuable feedback.

About the Author

Mike Laverick is a former VMware instructor with 17 years of experience in technologies such as Novell, Windows, Citrix, and VMware. He has also been involved with the VMware community since 2003. Laverick is a VMware forum moderator and member of the London VMware User Group. Laverick is the man behind the virtualization website and the blog RTFM Education, where he publishes free guides and utilities for VMware customers. Laverick received the VMware vExpert award in 2009, 2010, and 2011.

Since joining TechTarget as a contributor, Laverick has also found the time to run a weekly podcast called, alternately, the *Chinwag* and the *Vendorwag*. Laverick helped found the Irish and Scottish VMware user groups and now regularly speaks at larger regional events organized by the Global VMUG in North America, EMEA, and APAC. Laverick previously published several books on VMware Virtual Infrastructure 3, vSphere 4, Site Recovery Manager, and View.

We Want to Hear from You!

As the reader of this book, *you* are our most important critic and commentator. We value your opinion and want to know what we're doing right, what we could do better, what areas you'd like to see us publish in, and any other words of wisdom you're willing to pass our way.

As an associate publisher for Pearson, I welcome your comments. You can email or write me directly to let me know what you did or didn't like about this book—as well as what we can do to make our books better.

Please note that I cannot help you with technical problems related to the topic of this book. We do have a User Services group, however, where I will forward specific technical questions related to the book.

When you write, please be sure to include this book's title and author as well as your name, email address, and phone number. I will carefully review your comments and share them with the author and editors who worked on the book.

Email: VMwarePress@vmware.com

Mail: David Dusthimer
      Associate Publisher
      Pearson
      800 East 96th Street
      Indianapolis, IN 46240 USA

Chapter 1

Introduction to Site Recovery Manager

Before I embark on the book proper I want to outline some of the new features in SRM. This will be of particular interest to previous users, as well as to new adopters, as they can see how far the product has come since the previous release. I also want to talk about what life was like before SRM was developed. As with all forms of automation, it's sometimes difficult to see the benefits of a technology if you have not experienced what life was like before its onset. I also want at this stage to make it clear what SRM is capable of and what its technical remit is. It's not uncommon for VMware customers to look at other technologies such as vMotion and Fault Tolerance (FT) and attempt to construct a disaster recovery (DR) use case around them. While that is entirely plausible, care must be taken to build solutions that use technologies in ways that have not been tested or are not supported by VMware.

What's New in Site Recovery Manager 5.0

To begin, I would like to flag what's new in the SRM product. This will form the basis of the new content in this book. This information is especially relevant to people who purchased my previous book, as these changes are what made it worthwhile for me to update that book to be compatible with SRM 5.0. In the sections that follow I list what I feel are the major enhancements to the SRM product. I've chosen not to include a change-log-style list of every little modification. Instead, I look at new features that might sway a customer or organization into adopting SRM. These changes address flaws or limitations in the previous product that may have made adopting SRM difficult in the past.

vSphere 5 Compatibility

This might seem like a small matter, but when vSphere 5 was released some of the advanced management systems were quickly compatible with the new platform—a situation that didn't happen with vSphere 4. I think many people underestimate what a huge undertaking from a development perspective vSphere 5 actually is. VMware isn't as big as some of the ISVs it competes with, so it has to be strategic in where it spends its development resources. Saturating the market with product release after product release can alienate customers who feel overwhelmed by too much change too quickly. I would prefer that VMware take its time with product releases and properly QA the software rather than roll out new versions injudiciously. The same people who complained about any delay would complain that it was a rush job had the software been released sooner. Most of the people who seemed to complain the most viciously about the delays in vSphere 4 were contractors whose livelihoods depended on project sign-off; in short, they were often looking out for themselves, not their customers. Most of my big customers didn't have immediate plans for a rollout of vSphere 5 on the day of General Availability (GA), and we all know it takes time and planning to migrate from one version to another of any software. Nonetheless, it seems that's a shake-up in which VMware product management has been effective, with the new release of SRM 5.0 coming in on time at the station.

vSphere Replication

One of the most eagerly anticipated new features of SRM is vSphere Replication (VR). This enables customers to replicate VMs from one location to another using VMware as the primary engine, without the need for third-party storage-array-based replication. VR will be of interest to customers who run vSphere in many branch offices, and yet still need to offer protection to their VMs. I think the biggest target market may well be the SMB sector for whom expensive storage arrays, and even more expensive array-based replication, is perhaps beyond their budget. I wouldn't be surprised to find that the Foundation SKUs reflect this fact and will enable these types of customers to consume SRM in a cost-effective way.

Of course, if you're a large enterprise customer who already enjoys the benefits of EMC MirrorView or NetApp SnapMirror, this enhancement is unlikely to change the way you use SRM. But with that said, I think VR could be of interest to enterprise customers; it will depend on their needs and situations. After all, even in a large enterprise it's unlikely that all sites will be using exactly the same array vendor in both the Protected and Recovery Sites. So there is a use case for VR to enable protection to take place between dissimilar arrays. Additionally, in large environments it may take more time than is desirable for the storage team to enable replication on the right volumes/LUNs, now that VMware admins are empowered to protect their VMs when they see fit.

It's worth saying that VR is protocol-neutral—and that this will be highly attractive to customers migrating from one storage protocol to another—so VR should allow for replication between Fibre Channel and NFS, for example, just like customers can move a VM around with VMware's Storage vMotion regardless of storage protocol type. This is possible because, with VR, all that is seen is a datastore, and the virtual appliance behind VR doesn't interface directly with the storage protocols that the ESX host sees. Instead, the VR appliance communicates to the agent on the ESX host that then transfers data to the VR appliance. This should allow for the protection of VMs, even if local storage is used—and again, this might be very attractive to the SMB market where direct attached storage is more prevalent.

Automated Failback and Reprotect

When SRM was first released it did not come with a failback option. That's not to say failback wasn't possible; it just took a number of steps to complete the process. I've done innumerable failovers and failbacks with SRM 1.0 and 4.0, and once you have done a couple you soon get into the swing of them. Nonetheless, an automated failback process is a feature that SRM customers have had on their wish lists for some time. Instructions to manage the storage arrays are encoded in what VMware calls Site Recovery Adapters (SRAs). Previously, the SRA only automated the testing and running of SRM's Recovery Plans. But now the SRAs support the instructions required to carry out a failback routine. Prior to this, the administrator had to use the storage vendor's management tools to manage replication paths.

Additionally, SRM 5.0 ships with a process that VMware is calling Reprotect Mode. Prior to the reprotect feature it was up to the administrator to clear out stale objects in the vCenter inventory and re-create objects such as Protection Groups and Recovery Plans. The new reprotect feature goes a long way toward speeding up the failback process. With this improvement you can see VMware is making the VM more portable than ever before.

Most VMware customers are used to being able to move VMs from one physical server to another with vMotion within the site, and an increasing number would like to extend this portability to their remote locations. This is currently possible with long-distance live migrate technologies from the likes of EMC and NetApp, but these require specialized technologies that are distance-limited and bandwidth-thirsty and so are limited to top-end customers. With an effective planned migration from SRM and a reprotect process, customers would be able to move VMs around from site to site. Clearly, the direction VMware is taking is more driven toward managing the complete lifecycle of a VM, and that includes the fact that datacenter relocations are part of our daily lives.

VM Dependencies

One of the annoyances of SRM 1.0 and 4.0 was the lack of a grouping mechanism for VMs. In previous releases all protected VMs were added to a list, and each one had to be moved by hand to a series of categories: High, Low, or Normal. There wasn't really a way to create objects that would show the relationships between VMs, or groupings. The new VM Dependencies feature will allow customers to more effectively show the relationships between VMs from a service perspective. In this respect we should be able to configure SRM in such a way that it reflects the way most enterprises categorize the applications and services they provide by tiers. In addition to the dependencies feature, SRM now has five levels of priority order rather than the previous High, Low, and Normal levels. You might find that, given the complexity of your requirements, these offer all the functionality you need.

Improved IP Customization

Another great area of improvement comes in the management of IP addresses. In most cases you will find that two different sites will have entirely different IP subnet ranges. According to VMware research, nearly 40% of SRM customers are forced to re-IP their VMs. Sadly, it's a minority of customers who have, or can get approval for, a "stretched VLAN" configuration where both sites believe they make up the same continuous network, despite being in entirely different geographies. One method of making sure that VMs with a 10.x.y.z address continue to function in a 192.168.1.x network is to adopt the use of Network Address Translation (NAT) technologies, such that VMs need not have their IP address changed at all.

Of course, SRM has always offered a way to change the IP address of Windows and Linux guests using the Guest Customization feature with vCenter. Guest Customization is normally used in the deployment of new VMs to ensure that they have unique hostnames and IP addresses when they have been cloned from a template. In SRM 1.0 and 4.0, it was used merely to change the IP address of the VM. Early in SRM a command-line utility, dr-ip-exporter, was created to allow the administrator to create many guest customizations in a bulk way using a .csv file to store the specific IP details. While this process worked, it wasn't easy to see that the original IP address was related to the recovery IP address. And, of course, when you came to carry out a failback process all the VMs would need to have their IP addresses changed back to the original from the Protected Site. For Windows guests the process was particularly slow, as Microsoft Sysprep was used to trigger the re-IP process. With this new release of SRM we have a much better method of handling the whole re-IP process—which will be neater and quicker and will hold all the parameters within a single dialog box on the properties of the VM. Rather than using Microsoft Sysprep to change the IP address of the VM, much faster scripting technologies like PowerShell, WMI, and VBScript can be used. In the longer term, VMware remains committed to investing in technologies both internally and with its key partners. That could mean there will be no need to re-IP the guest operating system in the future.

A Brief History of Life before VMware SRM

To really appreciate the impact of VMware's SRM, it's worth it to pause for a moment to think about what life was like before virtualization and before VMware SRM was released. Until virtualization became popular, conventional DR meant dedicating physical equipment at the DR location on a one-to-one basis. So, for every business-critical server or service there was a duplicate at the DR location. By its nature, this was expensive and difficult to manage—the servers were only there as standbys waiting to be used if a disaster happened. For people who lacked those resources internally, it meant hiring out rack space at a commercial location, and if that included servers as well, that often meant the hardware being used was completely different from that at the physical location. Although DR is likely to remain a costly management headache, virtualization goes a long way toward reducing the financial and administrative penalties of DR planning. In the main, virtual machines are cheaper than physical machines. We can have many instances of software—Windows, for example—running on one piece of hardware, reducing the amount of rack space required for a DR location. We no longer need to worry about dissimilar hardware; as long as the hardware at the DR location supports VMware ESX, our precious time can be dedicated to getting the services we support up and running in the shortest time possible.

One of the most common things I've heard in courses and at conferences from people who are new to virtualization is, among other things:

> We're going to try virtualization in our DR location, before rolling it out into production.

This is often used as a cautious approach by businesses that are adopting virtualization technologies for the first time. Whenever this is said to me I always tell the individual concerned to think about the consequences of what he's saying. In my view, once you go down the road of virtualizing your DR, it is almost inevitable that you will want to virtualize your production systems. This is the case for two main reasons. First, you will be so impressed and convinced by the merits of virtualization anyway that you will want to do it. Second, and more important in the context of this book, is that if your production environment is not already virtualized how are you going to keep your DR locations synchronized with the primary location?

There are currently a couple of ways to achieve this. You could rely solely on conventional backup and restore, but that won't be very slick or very quick. A better alternative might be to use some kind of physical to virtual conversion (P2V) technology. In recent years many of the P2V providers, such as Novell and Leostream, have repositioned their offerings as "availability tools," the idea being that you use P2V software to keep the production environment synchronized with the DR location. These technologies do work, and there will be some merits to adopting this strategy—say, for services that must, for whatever reason, remain on a physical host at the "primary" location. But generally I am skeptical about this approach. I subscribe to the view that you should use the right tools for the right job; never use a wrench to do the work of a hammer. From its very inception and design you will discover flaws and problems—because you are using a tool for a purpose for which it was never designed. For me, P2V is P2V; it isn't about DR, although it can be reengineered to do this task. I guess the proof is in the quality of the reengineering. In the ideal VMware world, every workload would be virtualized. In 2010 we reached a tipping point where more new servers were virtual machines than physical machines. However, in terms of percentage it is still the case that, on average, only 30% of most people's infrastructure has been virtualized. So, at least for the mid-term, we will still need to think about how physical servers are incorporated into a virtualized DR plan.

Another approach to this problem has been to virtualize production systems before you virtualize the DR location. By doing this you merely have to use your storage vendor's replication or snapshot technology to pipe the data files that make up a virtual machine (VMX, VMDK, NVRAM, log, Snapshot, and/or swap files) to the DR location. Although this approach is much neater, this in itself introduces a number of problems, not least of which is getting up to speed with your storage vendor's replication technology and ensuring that enough bandwidth is available from the Protected Site to the Recovery Site to make it workable. Additionally, this introduces a management issue. In the large corporations the guys who manage SRM may not necessarily be the guys who manage the storage layer. So a great deal of liaising, and sometimes cajoling, would have to take place to make these two teams speak and interact with each other effectively.

But putting these very important storage considerations to one side for the moment, a lot of work would still need to be done at the virtualization layer to make this sing. These "replicated" virtual machines need to be "registered" on an ESX host at the Recovery Site, and associated with the correct folder, network, and resource pool at the destination. They must be contained within some kind of management system on which to be powered, such as vCenter. And to power on the virtual machine, the metadata held within the VMX file might need to be modified by hand for each and every virtual machine. Once powered on (in the right order), their IP configuration might need modification. Although some of this could be scripted, it would take a great deal of time to create and verify those scripts. Additionally, as your production environment started to evolve, those scripts would need constant maintenance and revalidation. For organizations that make hundreds of virtual machines a month, this can quickly become unmanageable. It's worth saying that if your organization has already invested a lot of time in scripting this process and making a bespoke solution, you might find that SRM does not meet all your needs. This is a kind of truism. Any bespoke system created internally is always going to be more finely tuned to the business's requirements. The problem then becomes maintaining it, testing it, and proving to auditors that it works reliably.

It was within this context that VMware engineers began working on the first release of SRM. They had a lofty goal: to create a push-button, automated DR system to simplify the process greatly. Personally, when I compare it to alternatives that came before it, I'm convinced that out of the plethora of management tools added to the VMware stable in recent years VMware SRM is the one with the clearest agenda and remit. People understand and appreciate its significance and importance. At last we can finally use the term *virtualizing DR* without it actually being a throwaway marketing term.

If you want to learn more about this manual DR, VMware has written a VM book about virtualizing DR that is called *A Practical Guide to Business Continuity & Disaster Recovery with VMware Infrastructure*. It is free and available online here:

> www.vmware.com/files/pdf/practical_guide_bcdr_vmb.pdf

I recommend reading this guide, perhaps before reading this book. It has a much broader brief than mine, which is narrowly focused on the SRM product.

What Is Not a DR Technology?

In my time of using VMware technologies, various features have come along which people often either confuse for or try to engineer into being a DR technology—in other words, they try to make a technology do something it wasn't originally designed to do. Personally, I'm in favor of using the right tools for the right job. Let's take each of these technologies in turn and try to make a case for their use in DR.

vMotion

In my early days of using VMware I would often hear my clients say they intended to use vMotion as part of their DR plan. Most of them understood that such a statement could only be valid if the outage was in the category of a planned DR event such as a power outage or the demolition of a nearby building. Increasingly, VMware and the network and storage vendors have been postulating the concept of long-distance vMotion for some time. In fact, one of the contributors to this book, Chad Sakac of EMC, had a session at

VMworld San Francisco 2009 about this topic. Technically, it is possible to do vMotion across large distances, but the technical challenges are not to be underestimated or taken lightly given the requirements of vMotion for shared storage and shared networking. We will no doubt get there in the end; it's the next logical step, especially if we want to see the move from an internal cloud to an external cloud become as easy as moving a VM from one ESX host in a blade enclosure to another. Currently, to do this you must shut down your VMs and cold-migrate them to your public cloud provider.

But putting all this aside, I think it's important to say that VMware has never claimed that vMotion constitutes a DR technology, despite the FUD that emanates from its competitors. As an indication of how misunderstood both vMotion and the concept of what constitutes a DR location are, one of these clients said to me that he could carry vMotion from his Protected Site to his Recovery Site. I asked him how far away the DR location was. He said it was a few hundred feet away. This kind of wonky thinking and misunderstanding will not get you very far down the road of an auditable and effective DR plan. The real usage of vMotion *currently* is being able to claim a maintenance window on an ESX host without affecting the uptime of the VMs within a site. Once coupled with VMware's Distributed Resource Scheduler (DRS) technology, vMotion also becomes an effective performance optimization technology. Going forward, it may indeed be easier to carry out a long-distance vMotion of VMs to avoid an impending disaster, but much will depend on the distance and scope of the disaster itself. Other things to consider are the number of VMs that must be moved, and the time it takes to complete that operation in an orderly and graceful manner.

VMware HA Clusters

Occasionally, customers have asked me about the possibility of using VMware HA technology across two sites. Essentially, they are describing a "stretched cluster" concept. This is certainly possible, but it suffers from the technical challenges that confront geo-based vMotion: access to shared storage and shared networking. There are certainly storage vendors that will be happy to assist you in achieving this configuration; examples include NetApp with its MetroCluster and EMC with its VPLEX technology. The operative word here is *metro*. This type of clustering is often limited by distance (say, from one part of a city to another). So, as in my anecdote about my client, the distances involved may be too narrow to be regarded as a true DR location. When VMware designed HA, its goal was to be able to restart VMs on another ESX host. Its primary goal was merely to "protect" VMs from a failed ESX host, which is far from being a DR goal. HA was, in part, VMware's first attempt to address the "eggs in one basket" anxiety that came with many of the server consolidation projects we worked on in the early part of the past decade. Again, VMware has never made claims that HA clusters constitute a DR solution. Fundamentally, HA lacks the bits and pieces to make it work as a DR technology. For example, unlike

SRM, there is really no way to order its power-on events or to halt a power-on event to allow manual operator intervention, and it doesn't contain a scripting component to allow you to automate residual reconfiguration when the VM gets started at the other site. The other concern I have with this is when customers try to combine technologies in a way that is not endorsed or QA'd by the vendor. For example, some folks think about overlaying a stretched VMware HA cluster on top of their SRM deployment. The theory is that they can get the best of both worlds. The trouble is the requirements of stretched VMware HA and SRM are at odds with each other. In SRM the architecture demands two separate vCenters managing distinct ESX hosts. In contrast, VMware HA requires that the two or more hosts that make up an HA cluster be managed by just one vCenter. Now, I dare say that with a little bit of planning and forethought this configuration could be engineered. But remember, the real usage of VMware HA is to restart VMs when an ESX host fails within a site—something that most people would not regard as a DR event.

VMware Fault Tolerance

VMware Fault Tolerance (FT) was a new feature of vSphere 4. It allowed for a primary VM on one host to be "mirrored" on a secondary ESX host. Everything that happens on the primary VM is replayed in "lockstep" with the secondary VM on the different ESX host. In the event of an ESX host outage, the secondary VM will immediately take over the primary's role. A modern CPU chipset is required to provide this functionality, together with two 1GB vmnics dedicated to the FT Logging network that is used to send the lockstep data to the secondary VM. FT scales to allow for up to four primary VMs and four secondary VMs on the ESX host, and when it was first released it was limited to VMs with just one vCPU. VMware FT is really an extension of VMware HA (in fact, FT requires HA to be enabled on the cluster) that offers much better availability than HA, because there is no "restart" of the VM. As with HA, VMware FT has quite high requirements, as well as shared networking and shared storage—along with additional requirements such as bandwidth and network redundancy. Critically, FT requires very low-latency links to maintain the lockstep functionality, and in most environments it will be cost-prohibitive to provide the bandwidth to protect the same number of VMs that SRM currently protects. The real usage of VMware FT is to provide a much better level of availability to a select number of VMs within a site than currently offered by VMware HA.

Scalability for the Cloud

As with all VMware products, each new release introduces increases in scalability. Quite often these enhancements are overlooked by industry analysts, which is rather disappointing. Early versions of SRM allowed you to protect a few hundred VMs, and SRM 4.0 allowed the administrator to protect up to 1,000 VMs per instance of SRM. That forced some large-scale customers to create "pods" of SRM configurations in order to protect the many thousands of VMs that they had. With SRM 5.0, the scalability numbers have jumped yet again. A single SRM 5.0 instance can protect up to 1,000 VMs, and can run up to 30 individual Recovery Plans at any one time. This compares very favorably to only being able to protect up to 1,000 VMs and run just three Recovery Plans in the previous release. Such advancements are absolutely critical to the long-term integration of SRM into cloud automation products, such as VMware's own vCloud Director. Without that scale it would be difficult to leverage the economies of scale that cloud computing brings, while still offering the protection that production and Tier 1 applications would inevitably demand.

What Is VMware SRM?

Currently, SRM is a DR automation tool. It automates the testing and invocation of disaster recovery (DR), or as it is now called in the preferred parlance of the day, "business continuity" (BC), of virtual machines. Actually, it's more complicated than that. For many, DR is a procedural event. A disaster occurs and steps are required to get the business functional and up and running again. On the other hand, BC is more a strategic event, which is concerned with the long-term prospects of the business post-disaster, and it should include a plan for how the business might one day return to the primary site or carry on in another location entirely. Someone could write an entire book on this topic; indeed, books have been written along these lines, so I do not intend to ramble on about recovery time objectives (RTOs), recovery point objectives (RPOs), and maximum tolerable downtimes (MTDs)—that's not really the subject of this book. In a nutshell, VMware SRM isn't a "silver bullet" for DR or BC, but a tool that facilitates those decision processes planned way before the disaster occurred. After all, your environment may only be 20% or 30% virtualized, and there will be important physical servers to consider as well.

This book is about how to get up and running with VMware's SRM. I started this section with the word *currently*. Whenever I do that, I'm giving you a hint that either technology will change or I believe it will. Personally, I think VMware's long-term strategy will be to lose the "R" in SRM and for the product to evolve into a Site Management utility. This will enable people to move VMs from the internal/private cloud to an external/ public cloud. It might also assist in datacenter moves from one geographical location to another—for example, because a lease on the datacenter might expire, and either it can't be renewed or it is too expensive to renew.

With VMware SRM, if you lose your primary or Protected Site the goal is to be able to go to the secondary or Recovery Site: Click a button and find your VMs being powered on at the Recovery Site. To achieve this, your third-party storage vendor must provide an engine for replicating your VMs from the Protected Site to the Recovery Site—and your storage vendor will also provide a Site Recovery Adapter (SRA) which is installed on your SRM server.

As replication or snapshots are an absolute requirement for SRM to work, I felt it was a good idea to begin by covering a couple of different storage arrays from the SRM perspective. This will give you a basic run-through on how to get the storage replication or snapshot piece working—especially if you are like me and you would not classify yourself as a storage expert. This book does not constitute a replacement for good training and education in these technologies, ideally coming directly from the storage array vendor. If you are already confident with your particular vendor's storage array replication or snapshot features you could decide to skip ahead to Chapter 7, Installing VMware SRM. Alternatively, if you're an SMB/SME or you are working in your own home lab, you may not have the luxury of access to array-based replication. If this is the case, I would heartily recommend that you skip ahead to Chapter 8, Configuring vSphere Replication (Optional).

In terms of the initial setup, I will deliberately keep it simple, starting with a single LUN/volume replicated to another array. However, later on I will change the configuration so that I have multiple LUNs/volumes with virtual machines that have virtual disks on those LUNs. Clearly, managing replication frequency will be important. If we have multiple VMDK files on multiple LUNs/volumes, the parts of the VM could easily become unsynchronized or even missed altogether in the replication strategy, thus creating half-baked, half-complete VMs at the DR location. Additionally, at a VMware ESX host level, if you use VMFS extents but fail to include all the LUNs/volumes that make up those extents, the extent will be broken at the recovery location and the files making up the VM will be corrupted. So, how you use LUNs and where you store your VMs can be more complicated than this simple example will first allow. This doesn't even take into account the fact that different virtual disks that make up a VM can be located on different LUNs/volumes with radically divergent I/O capabilities. Our focus is on VMware SRM, not storage. However, with this said, a well-thought-out storage and replication structure is fundamental to an implementation of SRM.

What about File Level Consistency?

One question you will (and should) ask is what level of consistency will the recovery have? This is very easy to answer: the same level of consistency had you not virtualized your DR. Through the storage layer we could be replicating the virtual machines from one site to another synchronously. This means the data held at both sites is going to be of a very high quality. However, what is not being synchronized is the memory state of your servers at the production location. This means if a real disaster occurs, that memory state will be lost. So, whatever happens there will be some kind of data loss, unless your storage vendor has a way to "quiesce" the applications and services inside your virtual machine.

So, although you may well be able to power on virtual machines in a recovery location, you *may* still need to use your application vendor's tools to repair these systems from this "crash-consistent" state; indeed, if these vendor tools fail you may be forced to repair the systems with something called a backup. With applications such as Microsoft SQL and Exchange this could potentially take a long time, depending on whether the data is inconsistent and on the quantity to be checked and then repaired. You should really factor this issue into your recovery time objectives. The first thing to ensure in your DR plan is that you have an effective backup and restore strategy to handle possible data corruption and virus attacks. If you rely totally on data replication you might find that you're bitten by the old IT adage of "Garbage in equals garbage out."

Principles of Storage Management and Replication

In Chapter 2, Getting Started with Dell EqualLogic Replication, I will document in detail a series of different storage systems. Before I do that, I want to write very briefly and generically about how the vendors handle storage management, and how they commonly manage duplication of data from one location to another. By necessity, the following section will be very vanilla and not vendor-specific.

When I started writing the first edition of this book I had some very ambitious (perhaps outlandish) hopes that I would be able to cover the basic configuration of every storage vendor and explain how to get VMware's SRM communicating with them. However, after a short time I recognized how unfeasible and unrealistic this ambition was! After all, this is a book about VMware's SRM—storage *and* replication (not just storage) is an absolute requirement for VMware's SRM to function, so I would feel it remiss of me not to at least outline some basic concepts and caveats for those for whom storage is not their daily meat and drink.

Caveat #1: All Storage Management Systems Are the Same

I know this is a very sweeping statement that my storage vendor friends would widely disagree with. But in essence, all storage management systems are the same; it's just that storage vendors confuse the hell out of everyone (and me in particular) by using their own vendor-specific terms. The storage vendors have never gotten together and agreed on terms. So, what some vendors call a storage group, others call a device group and yet others call a volume group. Likewise, for some a volume is a LUN, but for others volumes are collections of LUNs.

Indeed, some storage vendors think the word *LUN* is some kind of dirty word, and storage teams will look at you like you are from Planet Zog if you use the word *LUN*. In short, download the documentation from your storage vendor, and immerse yourself in the company's terms and language so that they become almost second nature to you. This will stop you from feeling confused, and will reduce the number of times you put your foot in inappropriate places when discussing data replication concerns with your storage guys.

Caveat #2: All Storage Vendors Sell Replication

All storage vendors sell replication. In fact, they may well support three different types, and a fourth legacy type that they inherited from a previous development or acquisition—and oh, they will have their own unique trademarked product names! Some vendors will not implement or support *all* their types of replication with VMware SRM; therefore, you may have a license for replication type A, but your vendor only supports types B, C, and D. This may force you to upgrade your licenses, firmware, and management systems to support either type B, C, or D. Indeed, in some cases you may need a combination of features, forcing you to buy types B and C or C and D. In fairness to the storage vendors, as SRM has matured you will find that many vendors support all the different types of replication, and this has mainly been triggered by responding to competitors that do as well.

In a nutshell, it could cost you money to switch to the right type of replication. Alternatively, you might find that although the type of replication you have is supported, it isn't the most efficient from an I/O or storage capacity perspective. A good example of this situation is with EMC's CLARiiON systems. On the CLARiiON system you can use a replication technology called MirrorView. In 2008, MirrorView was supported by EMC with VMware's SRM, but only in an asynchronous mode, not in a synchronous mode. However, by the end of 2008 this support changed. This was significant to EMC customers because of the practical limits imposed by synchronous replication. Although synchronous replication is highly desirable, it is frequently limited by the distance between the Protected and Recovery Sites. In short, the Recovery Site is perhaps too close to the Protected Site to be regarded as a true DR location. At the upper level, synchronous replication's maximum distance is in the range of 400–450 kilometers (248.5–280 miles); however, in practice the real-world distances can be as small as 50–60 kilometers (31–37 miles). The upshot of this limitation is that without asynchronous replication it becomes increasingly difficult to class the Recovery Site as a genuine DR location. Distance is clearly relative; in the United States these limitations become especially significant as the recent hurricanes have demonstrated, but in my postage-stamp-sized country they are perhaps less pressing!

If you're looking for another example of these vendor-specific support differences, HP EVAs are supported with SRM; however, you must have licenses for HP's Business Copy feature and its Continuous Access technology for this feature and technology to function properly. The Business Copy license is only used when snapshots are created while testing an SRM Recovery Plan. The Continuous Access license enables the replication of what HP rather confusingly calls vdisks in the storage groups.

Caveat #3: Read the Manual

Storage management systems have lots of "containers" which hold other containers and so on. This means the system can be very flexibly managed. You can think of this as being a bit like Microsoft's rich and varied group structure options in Active Directory. Beware that sometimes this means storage replication is limited to a particular type of container or level. This means you or your storage team has to very carefully determine how you will group your LUNs to ensure that you only replicate what you need to and that your replication process doesn't, in itself, cause corruption by mismatched replication schedules. Critically, some storage vendors have *very* specific requirements about the relationships among these various containers when used with VMware SRM. Additionally, some storage vendors impose naming requirements for the names of these objects and snapshots. If you deviate from these recommendations you might find that you can't even get SRM to communicate with your storage correctly. In a nutshell, it's a combination of the right type of replication and the right management structures that will make it work—and you can only know that by consulting the documentation provided by your storage vendor. In short, RTFM!

Now that we have these caveats in place, I want to map out the structures of how most storage vendors' systems work, and then outline some storage planning considerations. I will initially use non-vendor-specific terms. Figure 1.1 is a diagram of a storage array that contains many drives.

Here is an explanation of the callouts in the figure.

A This is the array you are using. Whether this is Fibre Channel, iSCSI, or NFS isn't dreadfully important in this case.

B This shows that even before allowing access, many storage vendors allow disks in the array to be grouped. For example, NetApp refers to this grouping as a disk aggregate, and this is often your first opportunity to set a default RAID level.

c This is another group, referred to by some vendors as a storage group, device group, or volume group.

D Within these groups we can have blocks of storage, and most vendors do call these LUNs. With some vendors they stop at this point, and replication is enabled at

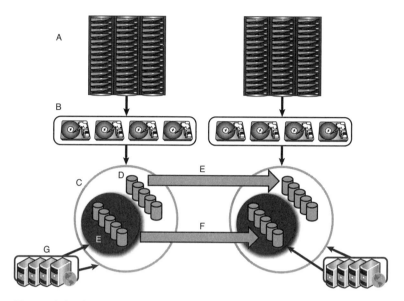

Figure 1.1   A storage array with many groupings

group type C indicated by arrow E. In this case every LUN within this group is replicated to the other array—and if this was incorrectly planned you might find LUNs that did not need replicating were being unnecessarily duplicated to the recovery location, wasting valuable bandwidth and space.

E Many vendors allow LUNs/volumes to be replicated from one location to another, each with its own independent schedule. This offers complete flexibility, but there is the danger of inconsistencies occurring between the data sets.

F Some storage vendors allow for another subgroup. These are sometimes referred to as recovery groups, protected groups, contingency groups, or consistency groups. In this case only LUNs contained in group E are replicated to the other array. LUNs not included in subgroup E are not replicated. If you like, group C is the rule, but group E represents an exception to the rule.

G This is a group of ESX hosts that allow access to either group C or group E, depending on what the array vendor supports. These ESX hosts will be added to group G by either the Fibre Channel WWN, iSCSI IQN, or IP address or hostname. The vendors that develop their SRA (software that allows SRM to communicate to the storage layer) to work with VMware's SRM often have their own rules and regulations about the creation of these groupings; for instance, they may state that no group E can be a member of more than one group C at any time. This can result in the SRA failing to return all the LUNs expected back to the ESX hosts. Some vendors' SRAs automatically allow the hosts to access the replicated LUNs/volumes at the Recovery Site array and others do not—and you may have to allocate these units of storage to the ESX host prior to doing any testing.

This grouping structure can have some important consequences. A good example of this is when you place virtual machines on multiple LUNs. This is a recommendation by VMware generally for performance reasons, as it can allow different spindles and RAID levels to be adopted. If it is incorrectly planned, you could cause corruption of the virtual machines.

In this case, I have created a simple model where there is just one storage array at one location. Of course, in a large corporate environment it is very unlikely that multiple arrays exist offering multiple disk layers with variable qualities of disk IOPS. Frequently, these multiple arrays themselves can be grouped together to create a collection of arrays that can be managed as one unit. A good example of this is the Dell EqualLogic Group Manager in which the first array creates a group to which many arrays can be added. In the Dell EqualLogic SRA configuration the "Group IP" is used as opposed to a specific IP address of a particular array.

In Figure 1.2 the two virtual disks that make up the virtual machine (SCSI 0:0 and SCSI 0:1) have been split across two LUNs in two different groups. The schedule for one group has a latency of 15 minutes, whereas the other has no latency at all. In this case, we could potentially get a corruption of log files, date stamps, and file creation as the virtual machines' operating system would not be recovered at the same state as the file data.

We can see another example of this in Figure 1.3 if you choose to use VMFS extents. As you may know, this ESX has the capability to add space to a VMFS volume that is either running out of capacity or breaking through the 2TB limitation on the maximum size of a single VMFS volume. This is achieved by "spanning" a VMFS volume across multiple blocks of storage or LUNs. Although in ESX 5 the maximum size for a single VMFS version 5 volume has increased, you might still have extents created from previous installations of ESX.

In this case, the problem is being caused by not storing the virtual machine on two separate LUNs in two separate groups. The impression from the vSphere client would be that the virtual machine is being stored at one VMFS datastore. Unless you were looking very closely at the storage section of the vSphere client you might not notice that the virtual machines' files were being spanned across two LUNs in two different groups. This wouldn't just cause a problem with the virtual machine; more seriously it would completely undermine the integrity of the VMFS extent. This being said, VMFS extents are generally

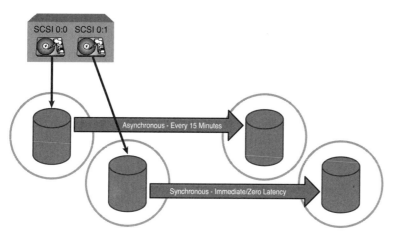

Figure 1.2   A VM with multiple virtual disks (SCSI 0:0 and SCSI 0:1) stored on multiple datastores, each with a different replication frequency

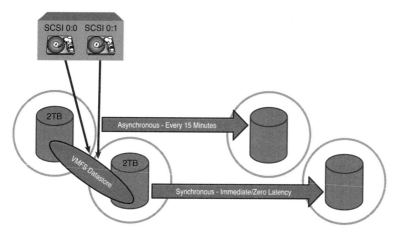

Figure 1.3   In this scenario the two virtual disks are held on a VMFS extent.

frowned upon by the VMware community at large, but they are occasionally used as a temporary band-aid to fix a problem in the short term. I would ask you this question: How often in IT does a band-aid remain in place to fix something weeks, months, or years beyond the time frame we originally agreed? However, I do recognize that some folks are given such small volume sizes by their storage teams that they have no option but to use extents in this manner. This is often caused by quite harsh policies imposed by the storage team in an effort to save space. The reality is that if the storage admins only give you 50GB LUNs, you find yourself asking for ten of them, to create a 500GB extent! If you do, then fair enough, but please give due diligence to making sure all the LUNs that comprise a VMFS extent are being replicated. My only message is to proceed with caution; otherwise, catastrophic situations could occur. This lack of awareness could mean you create an extent, which includes a LUN, which isn't even being replicated. The result would be a corrupted VMFS volume at the destination. Of course, if you are using the new VR technology this issue is significantly diminished, and indeed the complexity around having to use extents could be mitigated by adopting VR in this scenario.

Clearly, there will be times when you feel pulled in two directions. For ultimate flexibility, one group with one LUN allows you to control the replication cycles. First, if you intend to take this strategy, beware of virtual machine files spanned across multiple LUNs and VMFS extents, because different replication cycles would cause corruption. Beware also that the people using the vSphere—say, your average server guy who only knows how to make a new virtual machine—may have little awareness of the replication structure under-neath. Second, if you go for many LUNs being contained in a single group, beware that this offers less flexibility; if you're not careful you may include LUNs which do not need replicating or limit your capacity to replicate at the frequency you need.

These storage management issues are going to be a tough nut to crack, because no one strategy will suit everyone. But I imagine some organizations could have three groups, which are designed for replication in mind: One might use synchronous replication, and the other two might have intervals of 30 minutes and 60 minutes; the frequency depends greatly on your recovery point objectives. This organization would then create virtual machines on the right VMFS volumes that are being replicated with the right frequency suited for their recovery needs. I think enforcing this strategy would be tricky. How would our virtual machine administrators know the correct VMFS volumes to create the virtual machines? Fortunately, in vSphere we are able to create folders that contain volumes and set permissions on those. It is possible to guide the people who create VMFS volumes to store them in the correct locations.

One method would be to create storage groups in the array management software that is mapped to different virtual machines and their functionality. The VMFS volume names would reflect their different purposes. Additionally, in the VMware SRM we can create Protection Groups that could map directly to these VMFS volumes and their storage groups in the array. The simple diagram in Figure 1.4 illustrates this proposed approach.

In this case, I could have two Protection Groups in VMware SRM: one for the boot/data VMFS volumes for Exchange, and one for the boot/data VMFS for SQL. This would also allow for three types of SRM Recovery Plans: a Recovery Plan to failover just Exchange, a Recovery Plan to failover just SQL, and a Recovery Plan to failover all the virtual machines.

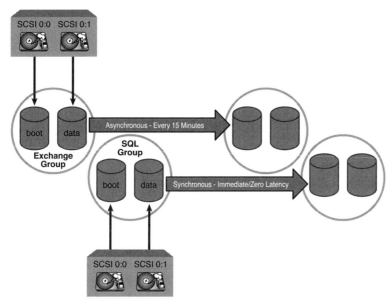

Figure 1.4   Protection Groups approach

Summary

Well, that's it for this brief introduction to SRM. Before we dive into SRM, I want to spend the next five chapters looking at the configuration of this very same storage layer, to make sure it is fit for use with the SRM product. I will cover each vendor alphabetically (EMC, HP, NetApp) to avoid being accused of vendor bias. In time I hope that other vendors will step forward to add additional PDFs to cover the configuration of their storage systems too. Please don't see these chapters as utterly definitive guides to these storage vendors' systems. This is an SRM book after all, and the emphasis is squarely on SRM. If you are comfortable with your particular storage vendor's replication technologies you could bypass the next few chapters and head directly to Chapter 6, Getting Started with NetApp SnapMirror. Alternatively, you could jump to the chapter that reflects your storage array and then head off to Chapter 7. I don't expect you to read the next four chapters unless you're a consultant who needs to be familiar with as many different types of replication as possible, or you're a masochist. (With that said, some folks say that being a consultant and being a masochist are much the same thing…)

Chapter 2

Getting Started with Dell EqualLogic Replication

In this chapter you will learn the basics of how to configure replication with Dell Equal-Logic. The chapter is not intended to be the definitive last word on all the best practices or caveats associated with the procedures outlined. Instead, it's intended to be a quick-start guide outlining the minimum requirements for testing and running a Recovery Plan with SRM; for your particular requirements, you should at all times consult further documentation from Dell, and if you have them, your storage teams. Additionally, I've chosen to cover configuration of the VMware iSCSI initiator to more closely align the tasks carried out in the storage layer with the ESX host itself.

Before I begin, I want to clearly describe my physical configuration. It's not my intention to endorse a particular configuration, but rather to provide some background that will clarify the step-by-step processes I'll be documenting. I have two EqualLogic systems in my rack, each in its own "group." In the real world you would likely have many arrays in each group—and a group for each site where you have EqualLogic arrays. In my Protected Site, I have an EqualLogic PS6000XV which has sixteen 15k SAS drives, and a PS4000E which has sixteen SATA drives, and both are configured with the same management system: the EqualLogic Group Manager. Of course, these arrays are available in many different disk configurations to suit users' storage and IOPS needs, including SATA, SAS, and SSD. Apart from the different types of disks in the arrays, the controllers at the back are slightly different from each other with the PS6000 offering more network ports. The PS6010/6510 is available with 10GB interfaces as well. From a networking perspective, the EqualLogic automatically load-balances I/O across the available NICs in the controller, and there is no need to configure any special NIC teaming or NIC bonds as is the case with other systems. On the whole, I find the EqualLogic systems very easy to set up and configure. Figure 2.1 shows the PS4000 at the top and the PS6000 at the bottom. If the

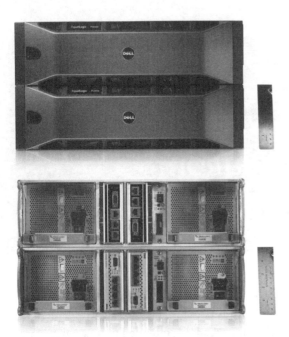

Figure 2.1   The rear of these two Dell EqualLogic systems is color-coded to make them easy to distinguish from the rear of the racks.

figure was in color, you would see that the controls are shown in purple and in green to make the system easy to identify at the back of the rack, with each system offering a rich array of uplink ports and speeds.

In the screen grab of the Group Manager shown in Figure 2.2, you can see that I have two EqualLogic systems. Each member or array has been added into its own group, and

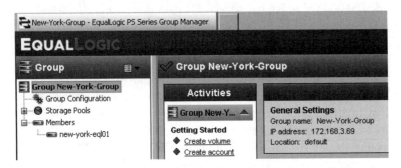

Figure 2.2   A single Dell EqualLogic array (or member) in a single group called "New-York-Group"

of course it's possible to have many members in each group. I configured these group names during a "discovery" process when the arrays were first racked up and powered on using a utility called the Remote Setup Wizard. The Remote Setup Wizard is part of the Host Integration Tools for Windows, and a CLI version is available as part of the Host Integration Tools for Linux. This setup wizard discovers the arrays on the network, and then allows you to set them up with a friendly name and IP address and add them to either a new group or an existing group.

In my configuration I have two members (new-york-eql01 and new-jersey-eql01) that have each been added to their own group (New-York-Group and New-Jersey-Group).

Creating an EqualLogic iSCSI Volume

Creating a new volume accessible to ESXi hosts is a very easy process in the EqualLogic Group Manager. The main step to remember is to enable "multiple access" so that more than one ESXi host can mount and access the volume in question. For some reason, in my work it's the one blindingly obvious step I sometimes forget to perform, perhaps because I'm so overly focused on making sure I input my IQNs correctly. You can kick off the wizard to create a new volume, and see the volume information in detail in the Volumes pane in the Group Manager (see Figure 2.3).

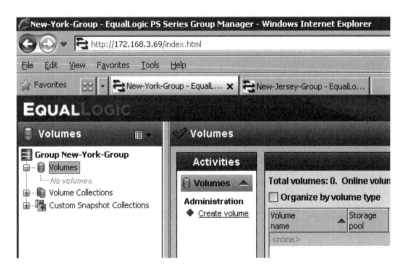

Figure 2.3   Selecting the Volumes node shows existing volumes; selecting "Create volume" lets you carve new chunks of storage to the ESX host

To create a volume, follow these steps.

1. On the Step 1 – Volume Settings page of the wizard (see Figure 2.4), enter a friendly name for the volume and select a storage pool.

   For my volume name I chose "virtualmachines," which perhaps isn't the best naming convention; you might prefer to label your volumes with a convention that allows you to indicate which ESX host cluster has access to the datastore. For the storage pool, in my case there is just one pool, called "default," which contains all my drives, but it is possible to have many storage pools with different RAID levels. It is also possible to have multiple RAID levels within one pool, and this allows the administrator to designate a preference for a volume to reside on a RAID type that's best suited for that application IOPS's demands or resiliency. A recent firmware update from Dell enhanced the EqualLogic array's performance load-balancing algorithms to allow for the automatic placement and relocation of data in volumes within and between EqualLogic arrays. This storage load balancing (conceptually, a storage version of DRS) helps to avoid performance "hits" by redistributing very active data to less heavily used array resources.

2. On the Step 2 – Space page of the wizard (see Figure 2.5), set the size of the volume, and whether it will be fully allocated from the storage pool or thinly provisioned. Also, reserve an allocation of free space for any snapshots you choose to take.

   The allocation here is conservatively set as a default of 100%. Think of this value as just a starting point which you can change at any time. If you create a 500GB LUN, 500GB would be reserved for snapshot data—the configuration assumes that every block might change. You might wish to lower this percentage value to something based on the number of changes you envisage, such as a range from 10% to 30%. It is possible to accept the default at this stage, and change it later once you have a better handle on your storage consumption over time.

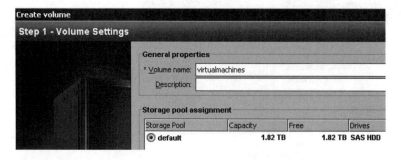

Figure 2.4   Naming a volume and selecting a storage pool

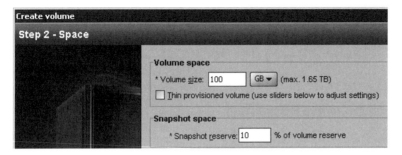

Figure 2.5   EqualLogic has, for some time, supported thin provisioning that can help with volume sizing questions.

Remember, this allocation of snapshot space will not influence your day-to-day usage of VMware SRM. This reservation of snapshot space comes from an allocation that is separate and distinct from that used by VMware SRM. So it's entirely possible to set this as 0% on volumes where you don't envisage yourself creating snapshots of your own, as would be the case with archive or test and development volumes

3. On the Step 3 – iSCSI Access page of the wizard (see Figure 2.6), set the access control for the volume.

   This prevents unauthorized servers from accidentally connecting to a volume intended for another server. You can set this using CHAP, IP address, or iSCSI IQN. In the "Access type" section of the page we are enabling "simultaneous

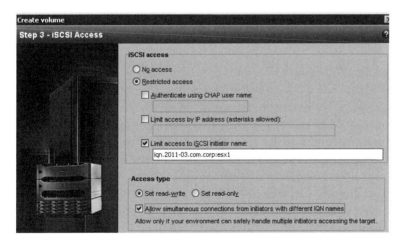

Figure 2.6   Setting the access control to prevent unauthorized servers from accidentally connecting to a volume intended for another server

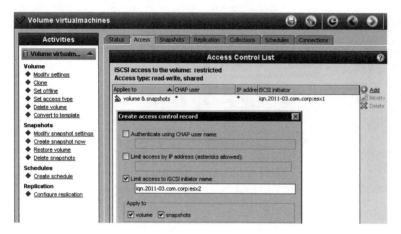

Figure 2.7   As I only have two ESX hosts, it was easy to cut and paste to add the IQNs, and merely adjust the "alias" value after the colon.

connections" on the volume. At this point you can only add one entry at a time, but later on you can add more IQNs to represent your multiple ESXi hosts that will need to access the volume within the VMware HA/DRS cluster.

4. Once the volume is created, use the volume's Access tab and the Add button to add more IQNs/IPs or CHAP usernames representing your ESXi hosts (see Figure 2.7).

Granting ESXi Host Access to the EqualLogic iSCSI Volume

Now that we have created the iSCSI target it's a good idea to enable the software iSCSI target on the ESXi hosts. If you have a dedicated iSCSI hardware adapter you can configure your IP settings and IQN directly on the card. One advantage of this is that if you wipe your ESXi host, your iSCSI settings remain on the card; however, they are quite pricey. Many VMware customers prefer to use the ESXi host's iSCSI software initiator. The iSCSI stack in ESXi 5 has recently been overhauled, and it is now easier to set up and offers better performance. The following instructions explain how to set up the iSCSI stack to connect to the EqualLogic iSCSI volume we just created. Just like with the other storage vendors, it's possible to install EqualLogic's Multipathing Extension Module (MEM) that offers intelligent load balancing across your VMkernel ports for iSCSI.

Before you enable the software initiator/adapter in the ESXi host, you will need to create a VMkernel port group with the correct IP data to communicate to the Equal-

Logic iSCSI volume. Figure 2.8 shows my configuration for esx1 and esx2; notice that the vSwitch has two NICs for fault tolerance. In the figure, I'm using ESXi Standard vSwitches (SvSwitches), but there's nothing to stop you from using Distributed vSwitches (DvSwitches) if you have access to them. Personally, I prefer to reserve the DvSwitch for virtual machine networking, and use the SvSwitch for any ESXi host-specific networking tasks. Remember, ESXi 5 introduced a new iSCSI port-binding policy feature that allows you to confirm that multipathing settings are correct within ESXi 5. In my case, I created a single SvSwitch with two VMkernel ports, each with their own unique IP configuration. On the properties of each port group (IP-Storage1 and IP-Storage2) I modified the NIC teaming policy such that IP-Storage1 had dedicated access to vmnic2 and IP-Storage2 had dedicated access to vmnic3. This configuration allows for true multipathing to the iSCSI volume for both load-balancing and redundancy purposes.

Before configuring the VMware software initiator/adapter, you might wish to confirm that you can communicate with the EqualLogic array by running a simple test using ping and vmkping against the IP address of the group IP address. Additionally, you might wish to confirm that there are no errors or warnings on the VMkernel port groups you intend to use in the iSCSI Port Binding setting of the Port Properties, as shown in Figure 2.9.

In ESXi 5 you should not need to manually open the iSCSI software TCP port on the ESXi firewall. The port number used by iSCSI, which is TCP port 3260, should be automatically opened. However, in previous releases of ESX this sometimes was not done, so I recommend that you confirm that the port is opened, just in case.

1. In vCenter, select the ESXi host and the Configuration tab.

2. In the Software tab, select the Security Profile link.

3. In the Firewall category, click the Properties link.

4. In the Firewall Properties dialog box, open the TCP port (3260) for the Software iSCSI Client (see Figure 2.10).

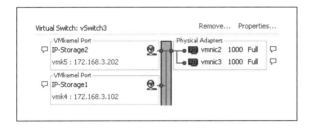

Figure 2.8 In this configuration for esx1 and esx2, the vSwitch has two NICs for fault tolerance.

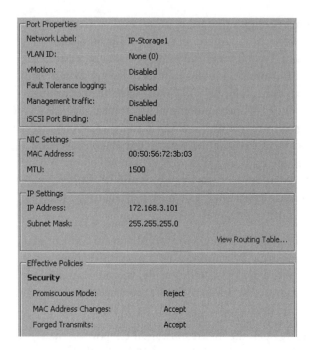

Figure 2.9   iSCSI port binding is enabled due to the correct
configuration of the ESX virtual switch

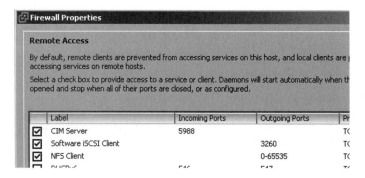

Figure 2.10   By default, ESXi 5 opens iSCSI port 3260 automatically.

5. Add the iSCSI software adapter. In previous releases of ESXi the adapter would be
    generated by default, even if it wasn't needed. The new model for iSCSI on ESXi
    5 allows for better control over its configuration. In the Hardware pane, click the
    Storage Adapters link and then click Add to create the iSCSI software adapter, as
    shown in Figure 2.11.

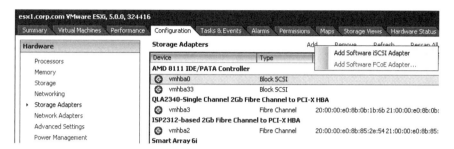

Figure 2.11   In ESXi 5 you must add the iSCSI software adapter. Previously, the "vmhba" alias was created when you enabled the feature.

6. Once the virtual device has been added, you should be able to select it and choose Properties.

7. In the iSCSI Initiator (vmhba34) Properties dialog box click the Configure button; this will allow you to set your own naming convention for the IQN rather than using the auto-generated one from VMware, as shown in Figure 2.12.

8. Bind the virtual device to one of the VMkernel ports on the ESXi host's vSwitch configuration. In my case, I have a VMkernel port named "IP-Storage" which is used for this purpose, as shown in Figure 2.13.

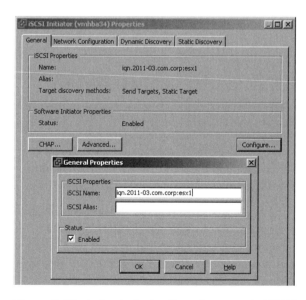

Figure 2.12   Instead of using the auto-generated IQN from VMware, you can use a combination of IP addresses and CHAP.

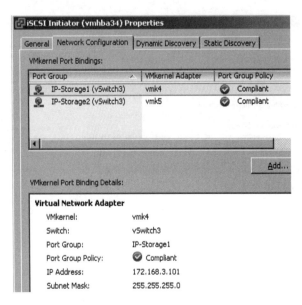

Figure 2.13 The new iSCSI initiator allows you to add VMkernel ports that are compliant with load balancing to enable true multipathing.

9. Select the Dynamic Discovery tab, and click the Add button.

10. Enter the IP address of the iSCSI target that is the EqualLogic group IP address (see Figure 2.14); in my case, this is 172.168.3.69.

11. Click OK.

12. Click Close in the main dialog box; you will be asked if you want to rescan the software iSCSI virtual HBA (in my case, vmhba34). Click Yes. Remember, static discovery is only supported with hardware initiators.

Occasionally, I've noticed that some changes to the software iSCSI initiator after this initial configuration may require a reboot of the ESXi host (see Figure 2.15). So, try to limit your changes where possible, and think through what settings you require up front to avoid this.

Now repeat this setup for the Recovery Site ESXi hosts, changing the IP addresses relative to the location. You might find it useful to create a "test" volume at the Recovery Site to confirm that the iSCSI configuration is valid there. In order for SRM to work with iSCSI you must at least configure the iSCSI initiator, and add an IP address for the storage arrays at the Recovery Site. The SRA within SRM will take care of presenting the storage as Recovery Plans are tested or run.

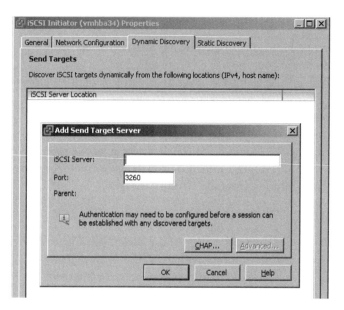

Figure 2.14   Entering the group manager IP address to discover the volumes held on the group members assigned to ESX hosts

Figure 2.15   Because of a configuration change in the ESX iSCSI stack a reboot is required.

Enabling Replication for EqualLogic

Now that we have the ESX hosts accessing a datastore at both locations we can move on to consider enabling replication between the EqualLogic systems. Replication in EqualLogic requires a pairing process where arrays are partnered together; it's not unlike the pairing process you will see in the core SRM product. Once this partnering process has been completed, you can begin the process of adding a replica to a volume. The wizard will automate the process of creating a volume at the destination array configured to receive updates. Once replication is enabled, you can then attach a schedule to the replication object to control when and how frequently replication is allowed.

Configuring Replication Partners

The first stage in setting up replication with EqualLogic involves partnering up your groups. This may already have been carried out in your environment, but I'm going to assume that you have two EqualLogic groups that have never been paired together before. To configure the relationship in the Group Manager select the Replication pane and click the "Configure partner" link to run the configure partner wizard; this wizard initially creates a one-way relationship between two arrays—you will also need to carry out this pairing process in the opposite direction (see Figure 2.16). The pairing up of the group partners is a one-time-only event—as you add more EqualLogic systems or "members" to the group they merely inherit the configuration from the Group Manager.

To configure a replication partner, follow these steps.

1. On the Step 1 – Replication Partner Identification page of the wizard (see Figure 2.17), enter the name of the group in your DR location (in my case, this is New-Jersey-Group) as well as the group IP address used to manage the members contained within the group (in my case, this is 172.168.4.69). It's important to note that these group names are case-sensitive.

Figure 2.16   In the Replication view you trigger the partnering process using the "Configure partner" link.

Figure 2.17   Under "Partner identification" enter the group name and group IP address used at the Recovery Site.

2. On the Step 2 – Contact Information page of the wizard, input your name, email address, and contact numbers as befits your environment. This is not a mandatory requirement and can be bypassed as necessary.

3. On the Step 3 – Authentication page (see Figure 2.18), set the password for the mutual replication between the partners.

4. On the Step 4 – Delegate Space page, it is possible to reserve disk space used on the destination group (in my case, New Jersey) to be used purely for receiving updates from the Protected Site group. Here, I reserved 500GB for this value.

   This Delegate Reservation is intended to offer the storage administrator control over how space is consumed by replication partners. The last scenario we would want is the storage administrator in New York being able to consume disk space for replication purposes in New Jersey in an unchecked manner. You can see such reservations at the storage layer as being similar to the reservation you might make on a VM for memory or CPU space at the VMware layer. The reservation is a guarantee that a minimum amount of resources will be available for a given process. Set it too low and there may not be enough capacity; set it too high and you might waste resources that may have been better allocated elsewhere. Fortunately, if you do set these allocations incorrectly, you can always change them afterward. Remember, in a bidirectional configuration where New York and New Jersey both act as DR locations for each other, you would need a delegate reservation at both sites.

5. Click Finish; you should see that the relationship is listed under Replication Partners (see Figure 2.19). I repeated this configuration on my New-Jersey-Group.

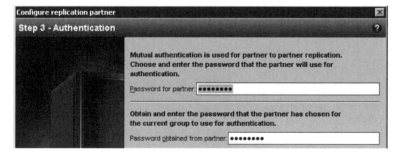

Figure 2.18 Replication uses a shared password model to allow the arrays to authenticate to each other.

Figure 2.19   From the Protected Site in New York I can see the relationship created with New Jersey.

Configuring Replication of the iSCSI Volume

Once the partnership relationships have been established, the next stage is to enable replication for the volume(s) that require it. Again, this is a very simple procedure of selecting the volume in the Volume Activities pane and clicking the "Configure replication" link (see Figure 2.20).

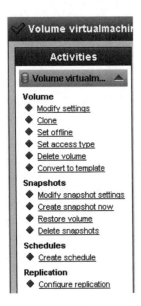

Figure 2.20   The Volume Activities pane shows options such as configuring replication and assigning a schedule to a snapshot or replication process.

To configure replication of the iSCSI volume, follow these steps.

1. On the Step 1 – General Settings page of the wizard (see Figure 2.21), set the percentage values for your replica reserve.

   These two reservations consume space from the Delegate Reservation created earlier when the partnership was first created. Notice how the focus here is the New-Jersey-Group as it will be the destination of any block changes in the volume. The Local Reservation defaults conservatively to 100%. This means if all the blocks changed in a 100GB volume there would be 100GB guaranteed or reserved for those updates. So this "local reserve" is local to the group currently selected. The Remote Reservation is space allocated at the source location and is set to 200%; again, this is a conservative setting which allows for complete duplication of a volume (the 100%) together with an allocation of space should every block change in the volume (the next 100%).

2. On the Step 2 – Advanced Settings page (see Figure 2.22), enable the "Keep failback snapshot" option.

   This is very useful in the context of planned failovers and failbacks with VMware SRM. It allows only the changes accrued while you were running from your Recovery Site to be replicated back to the Protected Site during the failback process. Without it, a complete transfer of all the data would have to be carried out during a

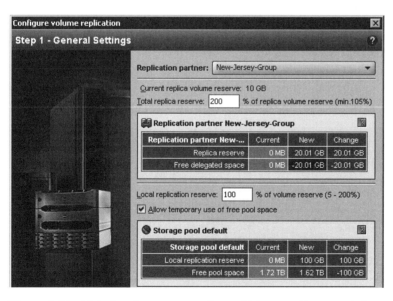

Figure 2.21 Note the storage reservations which control how much free space is assigned to "background" processes in Dell EqualLogic.

Figure 2.22 The "Keep failback snapshot" option accelerates failback; before enabling it, ensure that you have enough free space to hold the data.

failback process. That could be very time-consuming if you had only failed over to the DR location for a few hours or days. Of course, this all assumes that you have enough bandwidth to be able to replicate all your changes back to the Protected Site. If not, EqualLogic offers the Manual File Transfer Utility that allows you to transfer your replication data via removable media—in short, you might find that UPS or FedEx is faster than your network provider.

3. On the Step 3 – Summary page of the wizard (see Figure 2.23), click Finish and you will be asked "Would you like to create a volume replica now?" Selecting Yes automates the process of creating a volume at the destination group to receive updates from the Protected Site group. Select Yes.

There are many places to monitor this initial one-off replication of the volume to the Recovery Site. You can view the status of the replication at the Protected Site array under the Replication pane, and view the status of the Replication Partners by examining the Outbound Replicas node. A similar interface exists on the Recovery Site array listed as an Inbound Replicas node. Additionally, on the properties of the

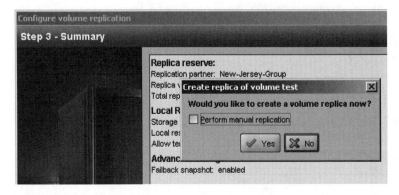

Figure 2.23 Select Yes to create a volume replica; later we will attach a schedule to enable the replication to occur at particular times.

primary volume itself at the Protected Site array, there is a Replication tab that will show statistics (see Figure 2.24). Notice here how no schedule is attached to this replica (that's configured in the next stage); instead, this is where you indicate how frequently the replication will take place.

Configuring a Schedule for Replication

Once a replication object has been created, you must attach a schedule to the process to make sure it repeats at a frequency that befits your recovery point objectives (RPOs) and recovery time objectives (RTOs). This is configured on the properties of the volume, in the Activities pane under the Schedules option (see Figure 2.25).

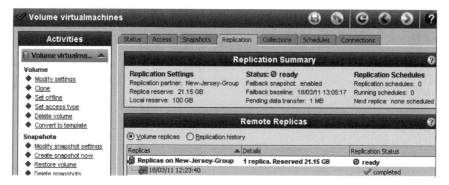

Figure 2.24 The Remote Replicas view will keep a history of each cycle of replication that has occurred.

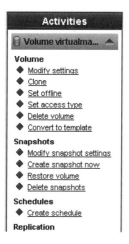

Figure 2.25 EqualLogic separates the creation of the replication job from configuring its frequency.

To configure a schedule for replication, follow these steps.

1. On the Step 1 – Schedule Type page of the wizard (see Figure 2.26) enter a friendly name for the schedule, and select the radio button marked "Replication schedule." Under the "Schedule options" section there are many options. Choose "Daily schedule (run daily at a specified time)," which will allow you to select the frequency and time for when the replication can occur.

2. On the Step 2 – Daily Schedule page of the wizard (see Figure 2.27), configure the start and end dates and start and end times for when the schedule will be running,

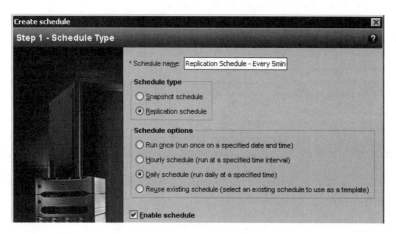

Figure 2.26   Although the radio button states "daily" it is possible to specify schedules that replicate by intervals of one minute.

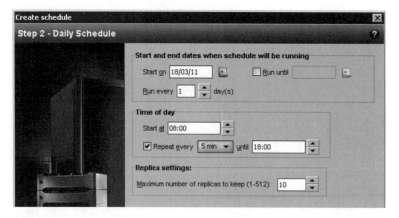

Figure 2.27   Configuring the daily schedule and setting the maximum number of replicas to keep

the frequency with which the schedule will be run, and the maximum number of replicas to keep.

In this sample, replication occurs every day at five-minute intervals during office hours, keeping only the last 50 minutes' worth of information changes. This schedule is only offered as an example of the options available. Configure your schedule relative to your RPO based on the constraints of bandwidth, latency, dropped packets, and amount of data change within a given period.

Once you have configured a schedule, you can save it as a template and then select "Reuse existing schedule" instead of reentering start and end dates and times. In addition, you can modify and delete schedules under the Schedules tab when you select the volume in question. It's also possible to have multiple schedules active on the same volume at the same time if you require such a configuration.

This completes the configuration of the EqualLogic system for VMware SRM. If you monitor the various status windows for replication you should see the schedule building a list of previous replications relative to your schedule.

Using EqualLogic Host Integration for VMware Edition (HIT-VE)

Alongside many other storage vendors EqualLogic has created its own storage management plug-ins for vCenter. Indeed, you might prefer to use these on a daily basis for provisioning volumes since they are often very easy to use and they reduce the number of configuration steps required in the environment. In the context of SRM, they may well speed up the process of initially allocating storage to your ESXi hosts in the Protected Site. Once the volumes are provisioned and presented to the ESXi hosts, it will merely be a case of setting up the appropriate replication relationship. In addition to provisioning new storage, the EqualLogic HIT-VE has the ability to deploy new virtual desktop clones, and allows high-level access to management options previously only available from the Group Manager.

The HIT-VE is a virtual appliance that you can download, import, and power on with the vSphere environment. After the first power on of the virtual appliance, you will complete a series of steps to configure the appliance and "register" the HIT-VE with your vCenter. This process enables the extensions to the vSphere client. Once you open the vSphere client you should see that EqualLogic icons have been added to the Solutions and Applications section of the "home" location in vCenter (see Figure 2.28).

You can log in to the virtual appliance with a username of "root" and a password of "eql"; after you have logged in you should change the password to something more secure and

Solutions and Applications
EqualLogic Datastore Manager
EqualLogic Auto-Snapshot Manager
EqualLogic Virtual Desktop Deployment Utility
Update Manager

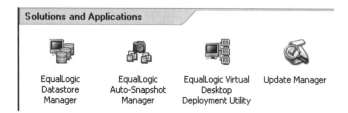

Figure 2.28 The HIT-VE adds multiple icons to the Solutions and Applications section in vCenter.

less in the public domain. At this point, the "Welcome to EqualLogic Host Integration Tools for VMware" script runs, and a numbered menu guides you through the seven core stages for configuring the appliance for vCenter (see Figure 2.29). The virtual appliance ships with two virtual NIC interfaces: The eth0 interface is used to communicate to your management network where your vCenter and ESXi hosts reside, and the eth1 interface is used to communicate discretely with your EqualLogic systems. Steps 4 through 6 are where you inform the appliance of the hostnames, username, and password to communicate to the vCenter, Group Manager, and optionally, one of your VMware View Connection servers. Most of this configuration is very straightforward; there is only one caveat. The authentication to the VMware View server is not allowed using the named "administrator" account, either for the local machine or for the Microsoft Active Directory Domain. You must create an administrator account such as corp\view-admin and delegate

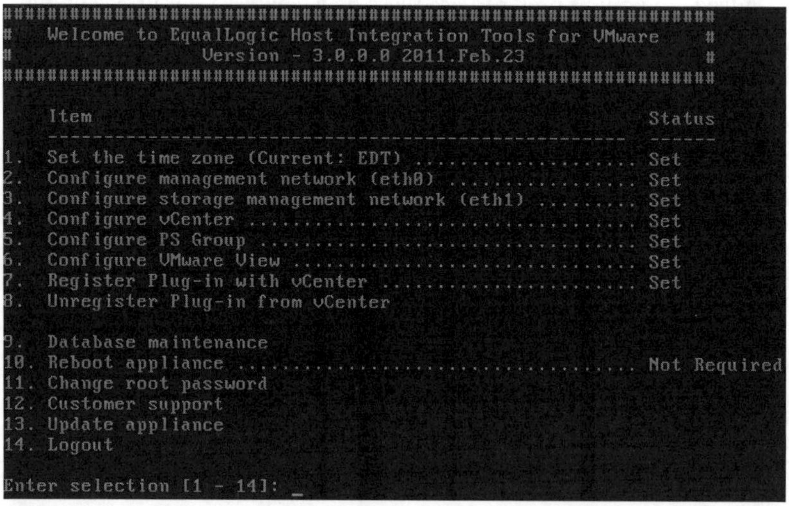

Welcome to EqualLogic Host Integration Tools for VMware
Version - 3.0.0.0 2011.Feb.23
Item
Status
1. Set the time zone (Current: EDT) .... Set
2. Configure management network (eth0) .... Set
3. Configure storage management network (eth1) .... Set
4. Configure vCenter .... Set
5. Configure PS Group .... Set
6. Configure VMware View .... Set
7. Register Plug-in with vCenter .... Set
8. Unregister Plug-in from vCenter
9. Database maintenance
10. Reboot appliance .... Not Required
11. Change root password
12. Customer support
13. Update appliance
14. Logout
Enter selection [1 - 14]: _

Figure 2.29 The script to configure the HIT-VE appliance, and the core stages for configuring the appliance for vCenter

it within the VMware View environment for the HIT-VE to use it. Once steps 4 through 6 have been confirmed, you can then register the plug-ins with vCenter in step 7. After you have completed steps 1 through 7, you can use option 10 to reboot the appliance for these configuration changes to take effect. In the context of VMware SRM, you should configure both the Protected and Recovery Sites with their own HIT-VE virtual appliance to ensure ongoing functionality and expectations should a DR event occur. At the moment you have one HIT-VE virtual appliance per vCenter installation, and it's not possible to have one virtual appliance service the needs of many vCenters, even in a linked mode configuration.

Once this reboot has been completed, you should find, alongside the management icons, a right-click context-sensitive menu on the properties of clusters, datastores, and VM folders (see Figure 2.30).

Once this is correctly configured, it's possible to manage components of the replication relationship, such as schedules of the EqualLogic Auto-Snapshot Manager, directly from vCenter (see Figure 2.31).

If you would like to learn more about the EqualLogic HIT-VE, I recently conducted a survey of storage vendor plug-ins and wrote an extended article about the HIT-VE plug-in on my blog:

www.rtfm-ed.co.uk/2011/03/13/using-dell-equallogic-hit-ve-plug-in/

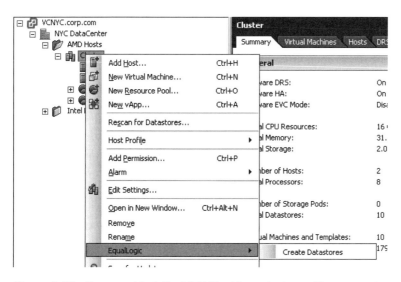

Figure 2.30 Once enabled, the HIT-VE adds context-sensitive menus to various locations in vCenter.

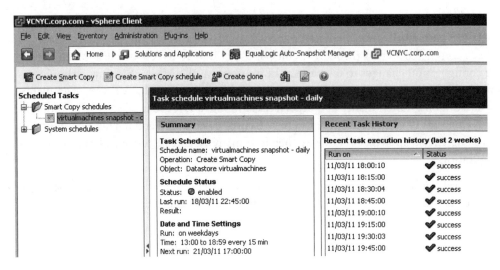

Figure 2.31   You can manage schedules directly from vCenter.

Summary

In this chapter I briefly showed you how to set up Dell EqualLogic replication that is suitable for use with VMware SRM. We configured two EqualLogic systems and then configured them for replication. As I'm sure you have seen it sometimes takes time to create this configuration. It's perhaps salutary to remember that many of the steps you have seen only occur the first time you configure the system after an initial installation. Once your group pairing is in place, you can spend more time consuming the storage you need.

From this point onward, I recommend that you create virtual machines on the VMFS iSCSI LUN on the Protected Site EqualLogic array so that you have some test VMs to use with VMware SRM. SRM is designed to only pick up on LUNs/volumes that are accessible to the ESXi host and contain virtual machine files. In previous releases this was apparently a frequent error message people had with SRM 4.0, but one that I have rarely seen—mainly because I have always ensured that my replicated volumes have virtual machines contained on them. I don't see any point in replicating empty volumes! In SRM the Array Manager Configuration Wizard displays an error if you fail to populate the datastore with virtual machines. In my demonstrations I mainly used virtual disks, but I will be covering RDMs later in this book because it is an extremely popular VMware feature.

Chapter 3

Getting Started with EMC Celerra Replication

In this chapter you will learn the basics of configuring replication with EMC Celerra. This chapter is not intended to be the definitive last word on all the best practices or caveats associated with the procedures outlined. Instead, it's intended to be a quick-start guide outlining the minimum requirements for testing and running a Recovery Plan with SRM; for your particular requirements, you should at all times consult further documentation from EMC and, if you have them, your storage teams. Additionally, I've chosen to cover configuration of the VMware iSCSI initiator to more closely align the tasks carried out in the storage layer of the ESX host itself.

EMC provides both physical and virtual storage appliances in the Fibre Channel market for which it is probably best known. However, like many storage vendors, EMC's systems work with multiple storage protocols and will support iSCSI and NFS connectivity using its Celerra system. This process by which storage is increasingly addressable under any protocol you wish is branded as "Unified Storage" by EMC currently. Like other vendors, EMC does have publicly available virtual appliance versions of its iSCSI/NAS storage systems—specifically, its Celerra system is available as a virtual machine. If you want to learn more about the setup of the Celerra VSA, Cormac Hogan of VMware has written a getting started guide on the Viops.com website. Additionally, the virtualgeek website run by Chad Sakac has a series of blog posts and videos on how to set up the Celerra VSA.

- http://viops.vmware.com/home/docs/DOC-1233

- http://virtualgeek.typepad.com/virtual_geek/2010/09/emc-celerra-vsa-uberv3-dart-60-now-available.html

Before I begin, I want to clearly describe my physical configuration. It's not my intention to endorse a particular configuration, but rather to provide some background that will clarify the step-by-step processes I'll be documenting. I have two EMC systems in my rack: a Celerra NS-20 and a newer Unified Storage EMC NS-120. The NS-120 supports the new VMware features such as VMware Aware Storage APIs (VASA), and the Unisphere management system which closely integrates with VMware such that you can tell a server is running ESX, and you can even inspect the contents of the virtual machine disks that make up the VM.

Both units are remarkably similar in appearance, as you can see in Figure 3.1. Incidentally, both systems are shown here without their accompanying disk shelves.

From the rear, the NS-120 cabling diagram (Figure 3.2) shows you how the system works.

The system is managed by a control station. This is purely a management node, and is not involved in any disk I/O. The Celerra is actually two "blades" which contain the code that allows for the iSCSI/NAS protocol to work. These blades are called Data Movers because they are responsible for moving data between the ESX hosts and the storage layer. The reason there are two is for redundancy. There can be up to eight, and this active/passive model can range from a 1:1 mapping to a 7:1 mapping. They find their storage by being in turn connected to the CLARiiON CX4 or CX3. The complete package when bought together allows for all three protocols (Fibre Channel, iSCSI, and NAS) to be used.

EMC CLARiiON uses a concept called "RAID groups" to describe a collection of disks with certain RAID levels. In my case, RAID group 0 is a collection of drives used by the Celerra host using RAID5. Allocating physical storage to a Celerra system when it has Fibre Channel connectivity to the CLARiiON is not unlike giving any host (ESX, Windows, Linux) access to the storage in a RAID group. You can see the Celerra host registered in the Unisphere management system like any other host (see Figure 3.3); the difference is that the Celerra sees block storage that it can then share using iSCSI, CIFS, and NFS.

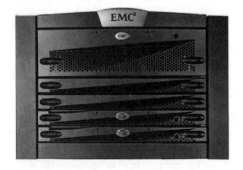 

Figure 3.1 Two generations of EMC equipment, both managed from Unisphere

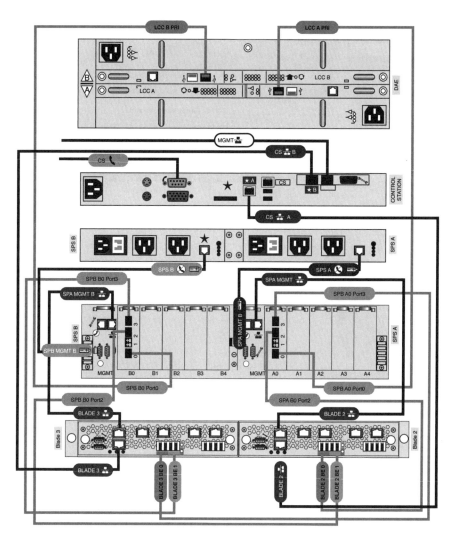

Figure 3.2 NS-120 dual blade copper ports cabling diagram

In the screen grab of the Unisphere management console in Figure 3.4 you can see I have two Celerra systems, which have been connected to an EMC CLARiiON CX3 and CX4, respectively. In this case, new-york-celerra represents the array at the Protected Site (New York) and new-jersey-celerra represents the array at the Recovery Site (New Jersey). I'm going to assume that a similar configuration is already in place in your environment. Figure 3.4 shows all four components within the scope of a single management window. You can add systems to a Unisphere in the domains section of the GUI, using the Add & Remove System link.

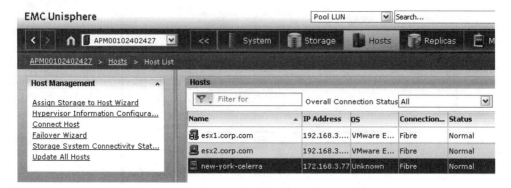

Figure 3.3   The Celerra system could be regarded as just another host in the system as it is registered alongside the ESX hosts.

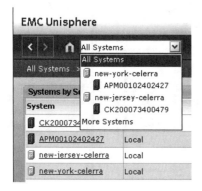

Figure 3.4   From the All Systems pull-down list it is possible to select other arrays to be managed.

Creating an EMC Celerra iSCSI Target

Before you begin, it's worth checking that the Celerra is properly licensed for the features and protocols you want to use. Log in to Unisphere and select the Celerra system from the pull-down list near the "home" area; then select the Celerra system again and click the Manage Licenses link. Figure 3.5 shows the resultant window.

Additionally, you may wish to confirm that the Data Mover has been activated to receive iSCSI communications from the host. You can do this by navigating to the Sharing icon, selecting iSCSI, and clicking the Manage Settings link. Figure 3.6 shows the result.

Once the Celerra is licensed and activated for iSCSI, we can create an iSCSI target. The iSCSI target is the listener (the server) that allows for inbound iSCSI requests from initiators (the client) to be received and processed. Many arrays come already configured

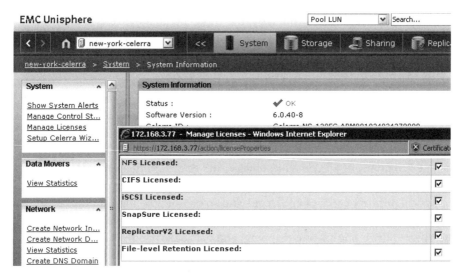

Figure 3.5 Once a Celerra has been selected, you can review its settings from the System Information screen.

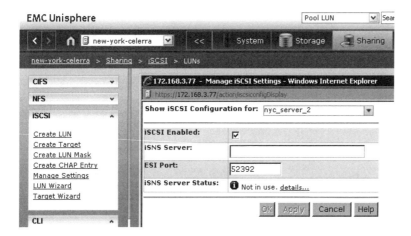

Figure 3.6 For iSCSI requests to be successful, the Data Movers must be listening for those requests.

with an iSCSI target, but with the Celerra you have complete control over defining its properties as you see fit. The Celerra supports many iSCSI targets, each with different aliases, giving a great deal of flexibility.

It's important to know that the Celerra's control station IP address is used solely for management. The I/O generated by ESX hosts reading and writing to a volume will be driven by the Data Mover's interfaces. Similarly, the I/O generated by Celerra replication will be driven by the Data Mover's interfaces. If you are unsure of what IP address the Data Mover's interfaces have, you can see them by clicking the System icon in Unisphere and selecting the Network option in the menu.

As you can see in Figure 3.7, the New York Celerra 172.168.3.75 (Prod_Replication) will be used to drive replication traffic, whereas 172.168.3.76 (Prod_Access) will be used by the ESX hosts to access the iSCSI LUN. Each of these logical IP interfaces is mapped to distinct physical network interfaces named cge0 and cge1. It wouldn't be unusual to have these mapped to different VLANs for security, and to ensure that replication traffic did not interfere with day-to-day production traffic. It is worth pointing out that the devices (the physical network cards of cge0/cge1 and so on) and the logical interfaces (for example, Prod_Replication and Prod_Access) that you build on top of those devices do not necessarily require a one-to-one mapping, and particularly on 10GB devices you could have tens of logical interfaces. In my case, it's just that a simple configuration suits my purposes for demonstration.

The remaining steps in creating an EMC Celerra iSCSI target are as follows.

1. In Unisphere, under the Sharing icon, select the iSCSI option in the menu.

2. In the iSCSI pane, select the Target Wizard link, as shown in Figure 3.8.

   Celerra systems generally come with at least three blades; the first being the control station and the second and third being the Data Movers. Most Celerra systems ship with two Data Mover blades for fault tolerance and redundancy.

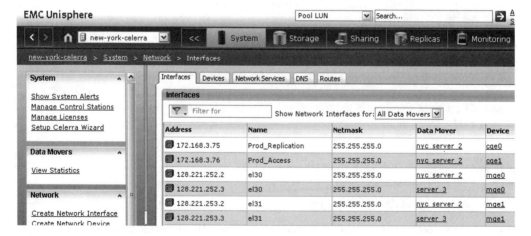

Figure 3.7   The Interfaces tab allows you to view what IP addresses have been allocated.

Figure 3.8 Under the Sharing button, you can select to see the three main file sharing protocols supported by the Celerra, including iSCSI.

3. Click Next in the wizard to select the default Data Mover. In Figure 3.9 you can see that I am selecting the first Data Mover called "nyc_server_2."

4. Enter a unique target alias, such as "new-york-celerra-iscsitarget1"—this is the friendly name by which the iSCSI target will be known in the management tools. By default, if you leave the Auto Generate Target Qualified Name (IQN) option enabled, the system will create for the target an IQN that looks like this:

    iqn.1992-05.com.emc:apm001024024270000-1

Alternatively, you can unselect this option and set your own custom IQN, such as:

    iqn.2009-10.com.corp:new-york-celerra-iscsitarget1

Figure 3.10 shows the former configuration.

Figure 3.9 Selecting the Data Mover that will host the iSCSI target

Figure 3.10 The iSCSI target alias is a soft name presented to hosts connecting to it. The Celerra can support many unique inbound target names.

5. Click the Add button to include the network interfaces used by the Data Mover for iSCSI as you may choose to separate out your CIFS traffic, your NFS traffic, and your iSCSI traffic to take advantage of features such as jumbo frames.

   These network interfaces have IP addresses, and will listen by default on the iSCSI TCP port of 3260 for inbound requests from initiators—in our case, this will be the software iSCSI initiator which is built into ESX. As shown in Figure 3.11, in the dialog box I selected the cge1 interface; if you remember this had the friendly name of "Prod_Access."

6. Click Finish and then click Close.

This wizard essentially automates the process of creating an iSCSI target. We could have created the target manually and modified it at any time by clicking the Sharing icon, selecting iSCSI, and clicking the Targets tab (see Figure 3.12).

IMPORTANT NOTE

You can now repeat this step at the Recovery Site Celerra—in my case, this is New Jersey.

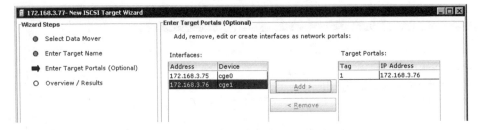

Figure 3.11 The interface using the 172.168.3.76 address which hosts use as the IP to connect to the Celerra system

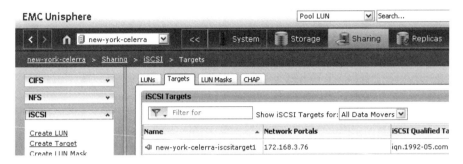

Figure 3.12   Now that a new target has been created it's possible to begin creating iSCSI LUNs.

Granting ESX Host Access to the EMC Celerra iSCSI Target

Now that we have created the iSCSI target it's a good idea to enable the software iSCSI target on the ESX hosts. This means that when we create an iSCSI LUN it will be "preregistered" on the Celerra system, so we will just need to select the iSCSI LUN as the ESX host and grant it access based on the iSCSI IQN we assign to it.

If you have a dedicated iSCSI hardware adapter you can configure your IP settings and IQN directly on the card. One advantage of this is that if you wipe your ESX host, your iSCSI settings remain on the card; however, they are quite pricey. Therefore, many VMware customers prefer to use the ESX host's iSCSI software initiator. The iSCSI stack in ESX 5 has been recently overhauled, and it is now easier to set up and offers better performance. The following instructions explain how to set up the iSCSI stack in ESX 5 to speak to the Celerra iSCSI target we just created.

Before you enable the software initiator/adapter in the ESX host, you will need to create a VMkernel port group with the correct IP data to communicate to the Celerra iSCSI target. Figure 3.13 shows my configuration for esx1 and esx2; notice that the vSwitch has two NICs for fault tolerance. I'm using ESX Standard vSwitches (SvSwitches), but there's nothing stopping you from using a Distributed vSwitch (DvSwitch) if you have access to it. Personally, I prefer to reserve the DvSwitch for virtual machine networking, and use the SvSwitch for any ESX host-specific networking tasks. Remember, ESX 4 introduced a new iSCSI port binding feature that allows you to control multipathing settings. ESX 5 added a port binding policy check which is used to validate your configuration. So, in my case, I created a single SvSwitch with two VMkernel ports, each with its own unique IP configuration. On the properties of each port group (IP-Storage1 and IP-Storage2) I modified the NIC teaming policy such that IP-Storage1 had dedicated access to vmnic2 and

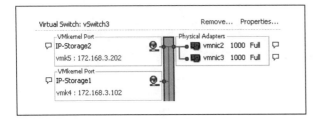

Figure 3.13 In this configuration for esx1 and esx2, the vSwitch has two NICs for fault tolerance.

IP-Storage2 had dedicated access to vmnic3. This iSCSI port binding reflects a continued investment by VMware to improve iSCSI performance made in ESX 4 that allows for true multipathing access to iSCSI volumes for both performance and redundancy that one would normally expect from a Fibre Channel environment.

Before configuring the VMware software initiator/adapter you might wish to confirm that you can communicate with the Celerra by using ping and vmkping against the IP address of the Data Mover. Additionally, you might wish to confirm that there are no errors or warnings on the VMkernel port groups you intend to use in the iSCSI Port Binding setting of the Port Properties (see Figure 3.14).

Port Properties

Network Label:	IP-Storage1
VLAN ID:	None (0)
vMotion:	Disabled
Fault Tolerance logging:	Disabled
Management traffic:	Disabled
iSCSI Port Binding:	Enabled

NIC Settings

MAC Address:	00:50:56:72:3b:03
MTU:	1500

IP Settings

IP Address:	172.168.3.101
Subnet Mask:	255.255.255.0
	View Routing Table...

Effective Policies

Security

Promiscuous Mode:	Reject
MAC Address Changes:	Accept
Forged Transmits:	Accept

Figure 3.14 iSCSI port binding is enabled due to the correct configuration of the ESX virtual switch.

In ESXi 5 you should not need to manually open the iSCSI software TCP port on the ESXi firewall. The port number used by iSCSI, which is TCP port 3260, should be automatically opened. However, in previous releases of ESX this sometimes was not done, so I recommend confirming that the port is opened, just in case.

1. In vCenter, select the ESXi host and then the Configuration Tab.

2. In the Software tab, select the Security Profile link.

3. In the Firewall category, click the Properties link.

4. In the Firewall Properties dialog box (see Figure 3.15) open the TCP port (3260) for the Software iSCSI Client.

5. Add the iSCSI software adapter. In previous releases of ESX this would be generated by default, even if it wasn't needed. The new model for iSCSI on ESX 5 allows for better control over its configuration. In the Hardware pane, click the Storage Adapters link and then click Add to create the iSCSI software adapter (see Figure 3.16).

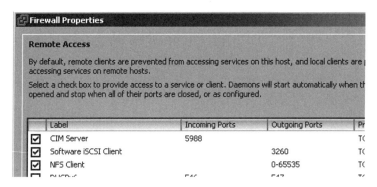

Figure 3.15 By default, ESXi 5 opens iSCSI port 3260 automatically.

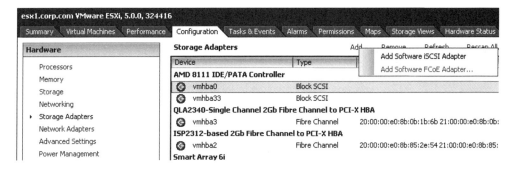

Figure 3.16 In ESXi 5 you must add the iSCSI software adapter. Previously, the "vmhba" alias was created when you enabled the feature.

6. Once the virtual device has been added, you should be able to select it and choose Properties.

7. In the iSCSI Initiator (vmhba34) Properties dialog box, click the Configure button; this will allow you to set your own naming convention for the IQN rather than using the auto-generated one from VMware (see Figure 3.17). Generally I use cut and paste to set this value if I have a small number of hosts, modifying the alias after the colon to ensure its uniqueness.

8. Bind the virtual device to one of the VMkernel ports on the ESX host's vSwitch configuration. I have a port group named "IP-Storage" which is used for this purpose (see Figure 3.18).

9. Select the Dynamic Discovery tab and click the Add button.

10. Enter the IP address of the iSCSI target that is serviced by the two NICs of the Data Mover (see Figure 3.19). In my case, this is 172.168.3.76.

Static discovery is only supported with hardware initiators. Remember, here the IP address of the Celerra iSCSI target is that of the Prod_Access Data Mover interface dedicated to iSCSI traffic (if one has been set up), not the control station which is there purely for management.

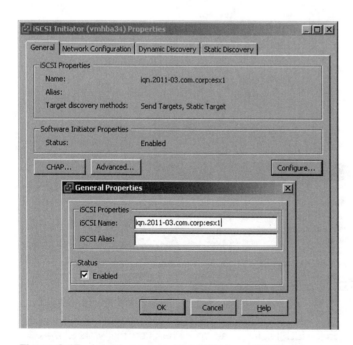

Figure 3.17 Inserting a meaningful IQN for an ESX host

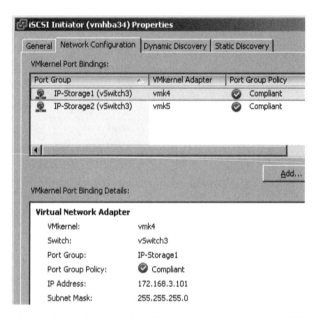

Figure 3.18   The new iSCSI initiator allows you to add VMkernel ports that are compliant with load balancing to enable true multipathing.

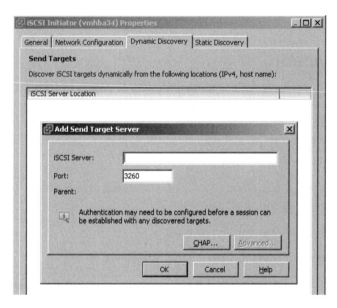

Figure 3.19   Entering the Group Manager IP address to discover the volumes held on the group members assigned to ESX hosts

Figure 3.20 Because of a configuration change
in the ESX iSCSI stack a reboot is required.

11. Click OK.

12. Click Close to close the main dialog box, and you will be asked if you want to rescan
     the software iSCSI virtual HBA (in my case, vmhba34). Click Yes.

Occasionally, I've noticed that some changes to the software iSCSI initiator after this
initial configuration may require a reboot of the ESX host (see Figure 3.20). So, try to
limit your changes where possible, and think through what settings you require up front to
avoid this.

Repeat this setup for the Recovery Site ESX hosts, changing the IP addresses relative to
the location. In order for SRM to work with iSCSI you must at least configure the iSCSI
initiator, and add an IP address for the storage arrays at the Recovery Site. The SRA
within SRM will take care of presenting the storage as Recovery Plans are tested or run.

Creating a New File System

As with other storage vendors, the Celerra system has its own file system within which
LUNs can be created. Often, storage vendors have their own file system to allow for
advanced features such as deduplication and thin provisioning. It is possible to create the
configuration manually, but again, I prefer to use the wizards in the Celerra to guide me
through the process.

1. Open Unisphere on the Protected Site Celerra (New York), and select the Storage
    button, and then the File Systems option.

2. Select the File System Wizard link in the File Systems pane.

3. Click Next in the wizard to select the default Data Mover (see Figure 3.21).

4. Select Storage Pool as the Volume Management Type.

5. Select a Storage Pool; I have just one, clar_r5_performance, with 232,162MB of
    space available (see Figure 3.22).

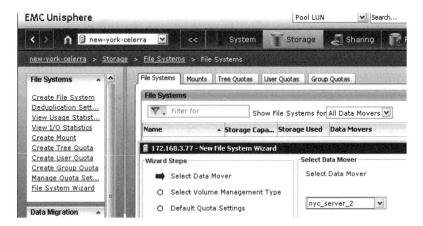

Figure 3.21   Selecting the Data Mover that will be responsible for holding the new file system

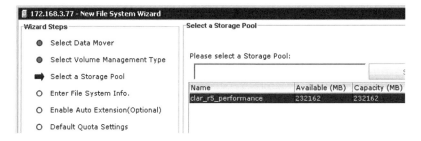

Figure 3.22   The Storage Pool is created within the main Unisphere application and is an allocation of block storage to the Celerra system.

6. Specify a friendly name for the file system you are creating. I used "newyorkcelerraFS1" which is 200GB in size (see Figure 3.23).

   It would be possible for me to make a file system that is almost 1TB in size and then populate it with many iSCSI LUNs. Notice how the value is specified in megabytes. A common mistake I've made is to make tiny file systems and LUNs because I've forgotten the increment is in megabytes and not gigabytes!

7. The rest of the wizard allows for more advanced settings, and you can just accept their defaults. When you're done, click Finish and then click Close.

This wizard essentially automates the process of creating a file system to hold iSCSI LUNs. You can instead create the file system manually, and then modify it at any time by navigating to the File Systems tab (see Figure 3.24).

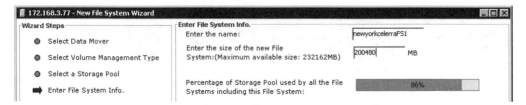

Figure 3.23   Creation of a file system from the raw block storage

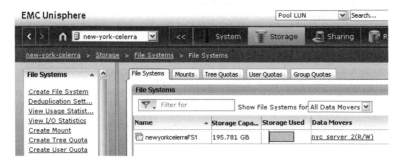

Figure 3.24   The file system can be modified at any time.

IMPORTANT NOTE

You can repeat the previous steps at the Recovery Site Celerra (New Jersey), and adjust your naming convention to reflect the location. However, there is one critical caveat to this: The file system of the Recovery Site needs to be slightly larger to account for the snapshots that are generated by the replication process. How much larger? EMC recommends that if you expect to see a low volume of changes, the file system at the Recovery Site will need to be 20% larger (in my case, 240GB). In the worst-case scenario where you are experiencing a high volume of changes, this can be as high as 150% of reserved space. If you don't reserve space for the snapshot you may receive a "Version Set out of space" error message. The fortunate thing is that if you get this wrong you can increase the size of the file system as required and it doesn't disrupt your production environment. The screen grab in Figure 3.25 shows the file system on the Recovery Site Celerra (New Jersey) as 250GB. It could be made larger using the Extend button. Additionally, you also can specify that the temporary writable snaps (TWS) created at the Recovery Site are created as thin by default, and this could remove some of the space issues.

Figure 3.25   A rather small 250GB file system from which LUNs could be created. In the real world this file system is likely to be much larger.

Creating an iSCSI LUN

In this section I will create an iSCSI LUN. Then I will set up asynchronous replication between the New York Celerra and the New Jersey Celerra using the ReplicatorV2 technology for which I have a license. It is possible to create the configuration manually, but in this case I prefer to use the wizards in the Celerra to guide me through the process.

1. In the Celerra Manager on the Protected Site Celerra (New York) select the Sharing button, and then select the iSCSI option. In the iSCSI pane click the Create LUN link (see Figure 3.26) to start the New iSCSI Lun Wizard.

2. Click Next in the wizard to select the default Data Mover.

3. Click Next to accept the target we created earlier (see Figure 3.27).

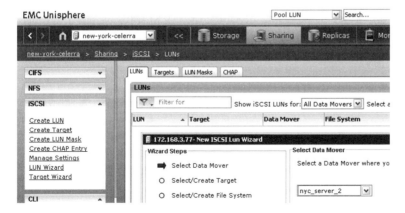

Figure 3.26   You can see which Data Mover will service the request for the iSCSI LUN.

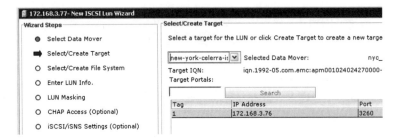

Figure 3.27   The iSCSI target was created earlier in this chapter, so you may have one all ready to use.

4. Select the file system within which the iSCSI LUN will reside.

   In my case, this is the newyorkcelerraFS1 file system that was created in the Creating a New File System section. Notice that although I defined a file system of 200GB, not all of it is available, as some of the space is needed for the file system metadata itself (see Figure 3.28).

5. Set your LUN number; in my case, I chose 100 as the LUN ID with 100GB as its size.

   The Create Multiple LUNs option allows you to create many LUNs in one go that all reside on the same file system, each being the same size. If I did that here they would be 100GB in size (see Figure 3.29).

6. In the LUN Masking part of the wizard, select the option to Enable Multiple Access, and use the Grant button to add the known initiators to the list (see Figure 3.30).

   ESX hosts are already listed here because I enabled the iSCSI software target on the ESX hosts and carried out a rescan. If your ESX hosts are not listed here, you may need to manually add them to the access control list using the Add New button.

Figure 3.28   Celerra systems can support multiple file systems. This file system, invisible to the ESX host, facilitates management of the wider system.

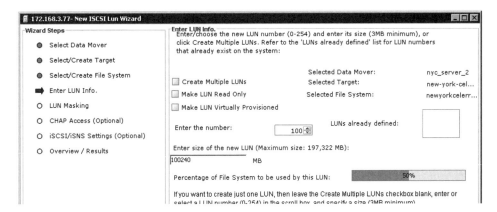

Figure 3.29   A 100GB LUN being created in the 250GB file system. The Make LUN Virtually Provisioned option creates a thinly provisioned LUN.

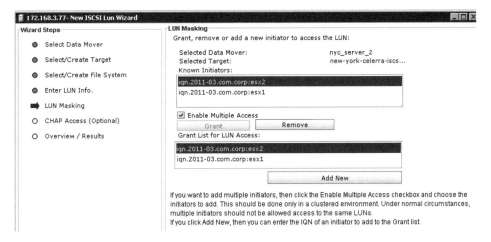

Figure 3.30   Setting up the ESX hosts' iSCSI initiator with the IP of the iSCSI target "registers" them with the Celerra.

7. The CHAP Access dialog box allows you to configure the authentication protocol. Remember, CHAP is optional and not required by the ESX iSCSI initiator. If you do enable it at the iSCSI target you will need to review your configuration at the ESX hosts.

8. Click Finish and then click Close.

This wizard essentially automates the process of creating a LUN and allocating ESX hosts by their IQN to the LUN. You can instead create the LUN manually, and then modify it at any time by navigating to Sharing and selecting iSCSI and then the LUNs tab (see Figure 3.31).

Additionally, if you select the +iSCSI node from the top level, select the Targets tab, right-click the properties of the target, select Properties, and then select the LUN Mask tab, you can see the ESX hosts have been allocated to the LUN.

If you return to the ESX hosts that were allocated to the iSCSI target they should now have the iSCSI LUN available (see Figure 3.32).

Figure 3.31   The 100GB LUN created

Figure 3.32   After a rescan of the ESX hosts, the 100GB LUN appears in the list under the Devices view.

At this stage it would be a very good idea to format the iSCSI LUN with VMFS and populate it with some virtual machines. We can then proceed to replicating the LUN to the Celerra in the Recovery Site.

IMPORTANT NOTE

You can repeat these steps at the Recovery Site Celerra (New Jersey), adjusting your names and IP addresses to reflect the location. When you create the iSCSI LUN, remember to set the LUN to be "read-only," the privilege required at the Recovery Site for LUNs earmarked as the destination for replication (see Figure 3.33). When you run a Recovery Plan in SRM initiating DR for real, the Celerra SRA will automatically promote the LUN and make it read-writable.

There is no need to format the VM's volumes and populate them with VMs; this empty volume created at the Recovery Site will be in receipt of replication updates from the Protected Site Celerra (New York). Additionally, by marking it as a "read-only" LUN you prevent people from accidentally formatting it within the VMware environment at the Recovery Site, as they may mistake it for any area of freely usable disk space.

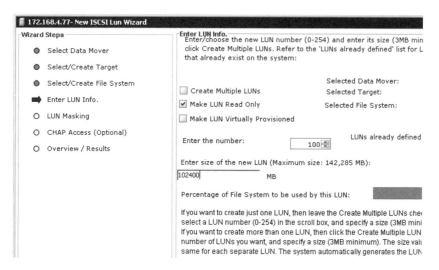

Figure 3.33   The destination LUN required for replication, marked as "read-only"

Configuring Celerra Replication

By now you should have two Celerra systems up and running, each with an iSCSI target, a file system, and an iSCSI LUN. One iSCSI LUN is read-write on the Protected Site Celerra (New York), while the other is read-only on the Recovery Site Celerra (New Jersey). Again, we can use the Replication Wizard to configure replication. Generally, the replication setup is a three-phase process.

1. Create a trust between the Protected Site and Recovery Site Celerras in the form of a shared secret/password.

2. Create a Data Mover interconnect to allow the Celerras to replicate to each other.

3. Enable the replication between the Protected and Recovery Sites.

Before you begin with the wizard you should confirm that the two Celerras can see each other via the cge interface that you intend to use for replication. You can carry out a simple ping test using the Unisphere administration Web pages by selecting the System button, and in the Network pane clicking Run Ping Test. From the corresponding Web page you can select the Data Mover and network interface, and enter the IP address of the replication port on the destination side. In my case, I used the IP address 172.168.3.75 to ping the IP address of 172.168.4.75. Figure 3.34 shows the successful result.

Once you get the successful ping you can proceed to the Replication Wizard.

1. Within Unisphere on the Protected Site Celerra (New York) open the Replicas node and select Replica.

2. Click the Replication Wizard link.

Figure 3.34 From Unisphere it is possible to carry out simple ping tests to confirm that IP communication is available between two arrays.

3. Under Select a Replication Type, select iSCSI LUN (see Figure 3.35).

4. Under Specify Destination Celerra Network Server click the New Destination Celerra button.

5. In the Celerra Network Server Name box shown in Figure 3.36, enter a friendly name to represent the Recovery Site Celerra (New Jersey) and enter the IP address of the control station. Also enter a passphrase which will create a trust between the Protected and Recovery Sites such that they are then able to send data and block updates.

6. Enter the credentials used to authenticate to the Recovery Site Celerra (New Jersey). By default, this should be the "nasadmin" user account and its password.

   Now that the Protected Site Celerra (New York) knows of the Recovery Site Celerra (New Jersey) the next pane in the wizard, Create Peer Celerra Network Server, informs the Recovery Site Celerra of the identity of the Protected Site Celerra (New York). This effectively creates a two-way trust between the two Celerras (see Figure 3.37).

Figure 3.35 Here the type of replication used is iSCSI LUN, valid for the type of storage we are presenting to the ESX host.

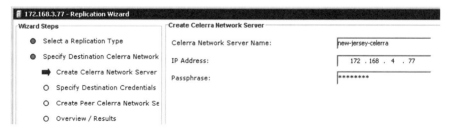

Figure 3.36 Creating a relationship between the 172.168.3.77 and 172.168.4.77 arrays, valid for creating Data Mover interconnects

Figure 3.37   After specifying both peers in the relationship you will be able to pair them together.

7. Click Next, and you will receive a summary of how the systems will be paired together. Click the Submit button, and the Celerras will trust each other with the shared passphrase. You will then be brought back to the beginning of the wizard where you were asked to select a destination Celerra server.

8. Select the Recovery Site Celerra (New Jersey) as shown in Figure 3.38, and click Next.

9. Now that the Celerras are trusted we need to create a Data Mover interconnect that will allow the Data Mover in the Protected Site to send data and block updates to the Recovery Site Celerra (New Jersey). Click the New Interconnect button in the Data Mover Interconnect part of the wizard.

10. Enter a friendly name for the Data Mover interconnect (see Figure 3.39).

   In my case, I called the source (the Protected Site Celerra) interconnect "new-york-celerra1-to-new-jersey-celerra1." Notice how I enabled the advanced settings, so I could select the Prod_Replication interface with the IP address of 172.168.3.75 used by cge0.

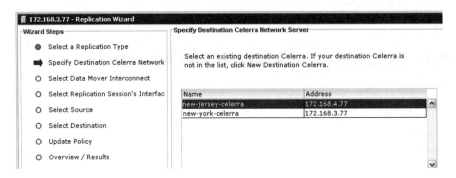

Figure 3.38   Both peers that will be paired together

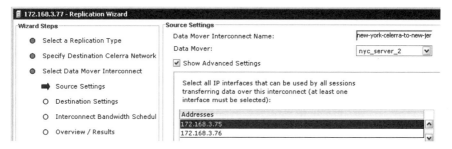

Figure 3.39 Entering a friendly name for the Data Mover interconnect relationship that is being created

11. Under Destination Settings select the IP address used to receive updates from the array at the Protected Site. In my case, I used 172.168.4.75 for the New Jersey Celerra, as shown in Figure 3.40.

12. The Interconnect Bandwidth Schedule (optional) pane allows you to control how much bandwidth to allocate to the replication cycle as well as when replication happens (see Figure 3.41). Set your schedule as you see fit and click Submit to create the Data Mover interconnect.

13. Now that the Data Mover interconnect has been created you can select it in the wizard (see Figure 3.42).

14. In the Select Replication Session's Interface pane you can select which IP address (and therefore which network interface) will take the replication traffic. I selected the 172.168.4.75 address that is dedicated to Prod_Replication on the cge0 interface, as shown in Figure 3.43.

Figure 3.40 Selecting the interface to be used for replication traffic

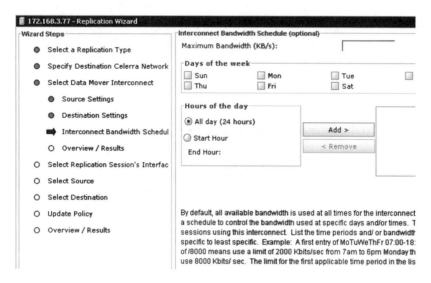

Figure 3.41   Controlling when and at what frequency replication will take place via the Interconnect Bandwidth Schedule

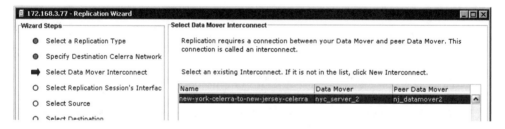

Figure 3.42   Selecting which Data Mover interconnect will be used as the path moving data from one array to another

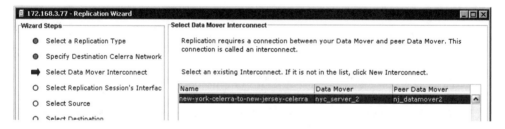

Figure 3.43   The source and destination IP addresses used for the replication traffic

15. Set a friendly replication session name for the session. Additionally, select the iSCSI LUN that you wish to replicate. In my case, this is the 100GB LUN I created earlier. I called mine "new-york-celerra-LUN100" (see Figure 3.44).

16. In the Select Destination pane, select the destination LUN which receives replication updates from the source LUN (see Figure 3.45).

17. The Update Policy pane allows you to configure the tolerance on what happens if replication is unavailable for a period of time. This reflects your RPO. For example, if you select ten minutes, the Recovery Site would be ten minutes behind your Protected Site (see Figure 3.46). It is worth noting that the algorithm that manages this is quite intelligent and will ensure that only the changes needed to

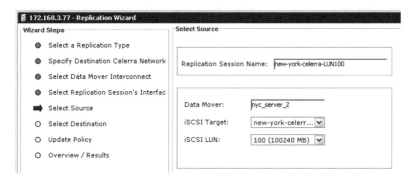

Figure 3.44   Each replication session has a unique session name and allows for session-by-session management controls.

Figure 3.45   Once a source and destination have been configured it is very easy to select them in the wizard.

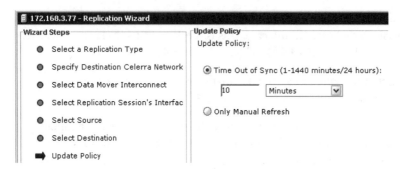

Figure 3.46   Configuring the tolerance on what happens if replication is unavailable for a period of time

keep the DR side within ten minutes of the production side will be replicated across. Figure 3.46 is only an example of the options available. Configure your schedule relative to your RPO based on the constraints of bandwidth, latency, dropped packets, and the amount of data change within a given period.

18. Finally, click Submit, and the replication process will begin.

This wizard essentially automates the manual process of pairing the Celerras together, creating the Data Mover interconnects and the replication session. You can view and modify these entries from the Replication node in the Unisphere administration Web pages. As you gain confidence in using the Unisphere management system you will be able to create these relationships manually. Personally, I like the wizards as they stop me from forgetting critical components.

The Celerra Network Servers tab (see Figure 3.47) is where the control station IP address references are held so that the Protected Site Celerra (New York) knows how to communicate to the Recovery Site Celerra (New Jersey). The DM Interconnects tab shows the network pipe between the two Celerras which is used to transfer replication updates (see Figure 3.48). You can right-click and "validate" these connections, and also modify their properties as you wish.

The Replications tab shows you the replication session created by the wizard; it has buttons that allow you to stop, start, reverse, switch over, and failback the replication relationships (see Figure 3.49).

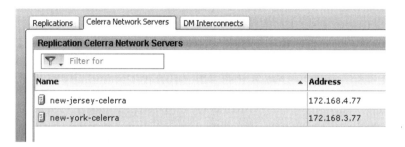

Figure 3.47   The Celerra Network Servers tab, which is where the control station IP address references are held

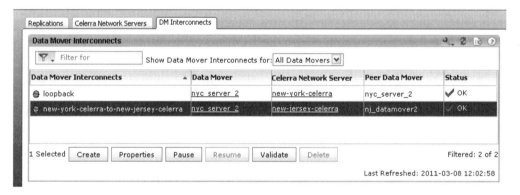

Figure 3.48   The Data Mover interconnect relationship created by the wizard. Click Validate to confirm the interconnect is functioning correctly.

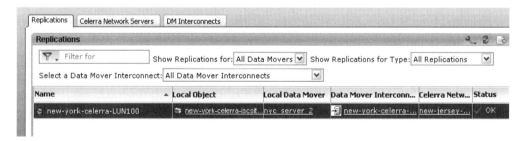

Figure 3.49   The Replications tab, showing the replication session created by the wizard

Summary

In this chapter I briefly showed you how to set up the EMC Celerra iSCSI Replicator which is suitable for use with VMware SRM. We configured two Celerra systems and then configured them for replication. As I'm sure you have seen it takes some time to create this configuration. It's perhaps salutary to remember that many of the steps you have seen only occur the first time you configure the system after an initial installation. Once your targets are created, the file systems and LUNs are created, and replication relationships are in place, then you can spend more of your time consuming the storage.

From this point onward, I recommend that you create virtual machines on the VMFS iSCSI LUN on the Protected Site Celerra so that you have some test VMs to use with VMware SRM. SRM is designed to only pick up on LUNs/volumes that are accessible to the ESX host and contain virtual machine files. In previous releases, if you had a volume that was blank it wouldn't be displayed in the SRM Array Manager Configuration Wizard. The new release warns you if this is the case. This was apparently a popular error people had with SRM 4.0, but one that I rarely saw, mainly because I always ensured that my replicated volumes had virtual machines contained on them. I don't see any point in replicating empty volumes! In SRM 4.0 the Array Manager Configuration Wizard displays an error if you fail to populate the datastore with virtual machines. In my demonstrations I mainly used virtual disks, but I will be covering RDMs later in this book because it is an extremely popular VMware feature.

Chapter 4

Getting Started with EMC CLARiiON MirrorView

In this chapter you will learn the basics of configuring replication with EMC CLARiiON. As with Chapters 2 and 3 which covered Dell EqualLogic and EMC Celerra, this chapter is not intended to be the definitive last word on all the best practices or caveats associated with the procedures outlined. Instead, it's intended to be a quick-start guide outlining the minimum requirements for testing and running a Recovery Plan with SRM; for your particular requirements, you should at all times consult further documentation from EMC and, if you have them, your storage teams. Additionally, I've chosen to cover configuration of the VMware iSCSI initiator to more closely align the tasks carried out in the storage layer of the ESX host itself.

EMC provides both physical and virtual storage appliances in the Fibre Channel market for which it is probably best known. However, like many storage vendors, EMC's systems work with multiple storage protocols and will support iSCSI and NFS connectivity using its Celerra system. Like some other vendors, EMC does have publicly available virtual appliance versions of its iSCSI/NAS storage systems—specifically, its Celerra system is available as a virtual machine. However, at the time of this writing there is no publicly available virtual appliance version of the CLARiiON system.

I have two EMC systems in my rack: a Celerra NS-20 and a newer Unified Storage NS-120. The NS-120 supports the new features from VMware, such as VMware Aware Storage APIs (VASA) and the Unisphere management system which closely integrates with VMware such that you can tell a connected server is running ESX, and you can even inspect the contents of the virtual machine disks that make up the VM. Both units are remarkably similar in appearance, as you can see in Figure 4.1. Incidentally, both systems are shown here without their accompanying disk shelves.

Both the NS-20 and the NS-120 have been added into a domain in the Unisphere management console. In Figure 4.2, which shows the Unisphere management console, you can see that I have two CLARiiON systems. I'm going to assume you already have this configuration in place. If you don't have the two CLARiiON systems listed in the same view, take a look at the domain section of Unisphere, which allows you to configure multi-domain management. Also, I'm going to assume work required at the fabric layer (WWNs and zoning) has already been carried out correctly.

Figure 4.1   Two generations of EMC equipment, shown without their disk shelves

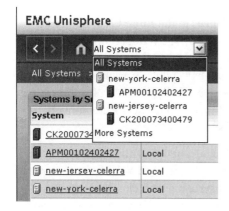

Figure 4.2   From the All Systems pull-down list it is possible to select other arrays from the list to be managed.

In early versions of SRM the EMC CLARiiON SRA required a consistency group for the SRA to work. This is no longer a requirement as of SRM 4.0. Consistency groups are used when you have multiple LUNs to ensure that replication or MirrorView keeps the state of those multiple LUNs in sync. Although consistency groups are no longer a hard requirement, they are a best practice, so I will show you how to create them.

Creating a Reserved LUN Pool

Depending on how your arrays were first set up and configured, you may already have a reserved LUN pool (RLP). This is required specifically for asynchronous replication. The RLP is used for all snaps and so is also required on the DR side at the very least, where snaps are used to present the VMFS volumes to the ESX host during testing mode. You can think of the RLP as an allocation of disk space specifically for the "shipping" of updates from the Protected Site array to the Recovery Site array. The snaps are not really used for "shipping" in the way they are with the Celerra; they are used to preserve a gold copy of the latest confirmed good copy at the DR side (in the event of a partial transfer) and to accumulate the changes that may be written to the production side to blocks in the process of actively being transferred. It is not unusual, in the world of storage arrays, for the vendor to carve out a chunk of storage specifically for sending and receiving updates, as above the RLP is the area where all storage for any type of snapping (for local or remote needs) is drawn. Storage vendors tend to have many different ways of doing this, with some opting to use a percentage of each volume/ LUN reserved for this storage.

The size and number of the RLP depend greatly on the number of changes to the LUN you expect to see between each update. The RLP is also used by SRM during the test phase when a snapshot is engaged on the Recovery Site secondary image (the LUN that receives updates). It may well be the case that an RLP has already been configured in the system; if you are unsure you can check by selecting the array in question in Unisphere, clicking the Replicas icon, choosing Reserved LUN Pool in the menu, and then selecting the Free LUNs tab, as shown in Figure 4.3.

At the same time, you may wish to check if you have the necessary LUNs for the write intent logs (WILs). These LUNs are created in a similar way to the RLP; they are like a transaction log in the system and they help the system to recover from unexpected outages. The WIL is normally a small allocation of storage that is used to hold this logging information.

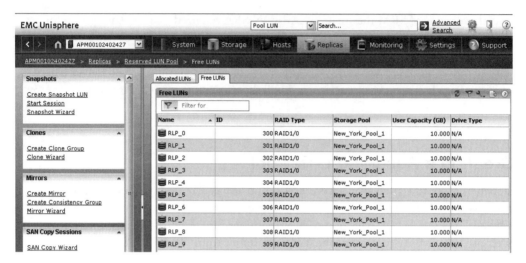

Figure 4.3   The reserved LUN pool on the New York CLARiiON

If your CLARiiON array does not have an RLP, you can easily configure one by following these steps.

1. In Unisphere, select the Storage icon and then select LUNs from the menu.

2. Set a size for the LUN and the number you require—in my case, because my LUNs will be small and updates smaller still, I opted to create ten LUNs of 10GB each (see Figure 4.4). The LUN ID can be safely set to any value beyond what ESX can normally see (LUN 0-255) because the hosts will never interact directly with these volumes.

3. Specify a name for each LUN, such as RLP, and a starting ID, such as 00. This will create a naming convention of RLP_0, RLP_1, and so on.

4. Create the LUNs needed for the WILs.

    In this case, I used a RAID group that was not part of the New York pool—and I allocated disk space just to hold these logs, as shown in Figure 4.5. It is worth noting that WILs which are used to avoid a full mirror resync in the event of a connection failure cannot be currently created in a pool.

5. Click Apply and then Cancel once the LUN creation process has ended.

    Now that we have our required LUNs, we need to allocate these LUNs to the RLP and the WIL, respectively.

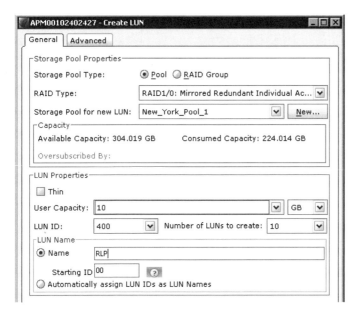

Figure 4.4 In the Create LUN dialog box you can create many LUNs of fixed size. Here I'm creating ten 10GB LUNs with a label of "RLP."

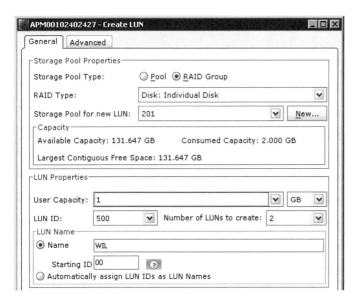

Figure 4.5 Only a small amount of storage is required to hold the WIL.

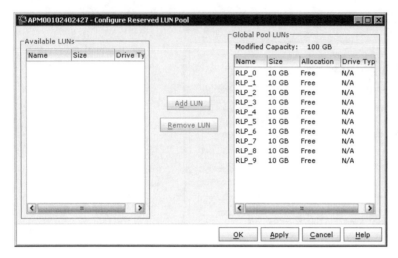

Figure 4.6 Once the LUNs have been created they can be allocated to the reserved LUN pool.

6. Click the Replica icon in Unisphere, select Reserved LUN Pool on the menu, and then click the Configure button. This will allow you to select all the LUNs in the list (RLP_0 to RLP_1) to the Global Pool LUNs list, as shown in Figure 4.6.

7. When you are done, click OK.

8. To allocate the WIL LUNs you just created, click the Configure the Mirror Write Intent Log link in the Configuration and Settings pane.

Creating an EMC LUN

EMC uses a concept called "RAID groups" to describe a collection of disks with a certain RAID level. In my case, RAID group 0 is a collection of drives used by ESX hosts using RAID5. This RAID group has been added to a storage group called "New_York_Cluster1" to be used by various servers in my environment. In this section I will create a LUN in RAID group 0 held in the New_York_Cluster1 storage group. Then I will set up synchronous replication between the New York CLARiiON and the New Jersey CLARiiON using EMC MirrorView technology. Asynchronous replication would be used if your Recovery Site was a long distance away from your Protected Site, and is ideal for most DR environments. Synchronous replication keeps your data in a much better state, but is limited by distance—in practice, around 50–80 kilometers (31–80 miles). Some organizations may deploy synchronous replication to get their data in a good state off-site, and then follow through with asynchronous replication to get the data a suitable distance away from the Protected Site to protect the business from a DR event.

To create an EMC LUN, follow these steps.

1. Open a Web browser to the IP address used to access Unisphere; in my case, this is https://172.168.3.79.

2. Log in with your username and password.

3. Select the CLARiiON array; in my case, this is APM00102402427 (this is the serial number of my CX4).

4. Select the Storage icon, and from the menu that opens, choose LUNs.

5. Click the Create LUN link in the LUNs pane, or click the Create button (see Figure 4.7).

6. In the dialog box that opens, select a free LUN ID number; I used LUN ID 60.

7. Set the LUN size in the User Capacity edit box; I used 100GB.

8. In the LUN Name edit box enter a friendly name. I used LUN_60_100GB_VIRTUALMACHINES, as shown in Figure 4.8.

    This LUN number is not necessarily the LUN ID that will be presented to the ESX host; what's actually presented is a host ID. The LUN number could be 300, but

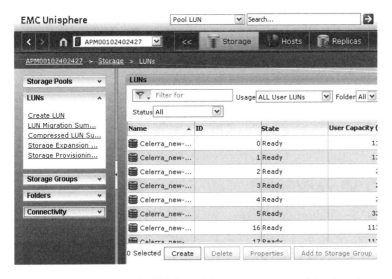

Figure 4.7   The Create LUN link enables you to open a dialog box to create a new datastore for the ESX hosts.

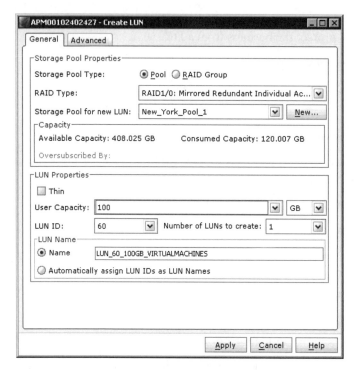

Figure 4.8 A 100GB LUN being created in the New York storage pool

when it's later allocated to the ESX host the administrator can allocate a host ID number residing between the values of 0 and 255 as this is the maximum number of LUNs an ESX host can currently see.

9. Click Apply, and then click the Yes option in the next dialog box that opens to confirm your change. Once the LUN has been created, click OK to confirm the successful operation. The Create LUN dialog box will stay on-screen as it assumes you want to create a number of LUNs of different sizes; once you are done you can click the Cancel button to dismiss it.

Configuring EMC MirrorView

To configure EMC MirrorView, follow these steps.

1. In the LUNs view, right-click the LUN you wish to replicate; in my case, this is LUN_60_100GB_VIRTUALMACHINES.

2. In the menu that opens, select MirrorView and then Create Remote Mirror (see Figure 4.9).

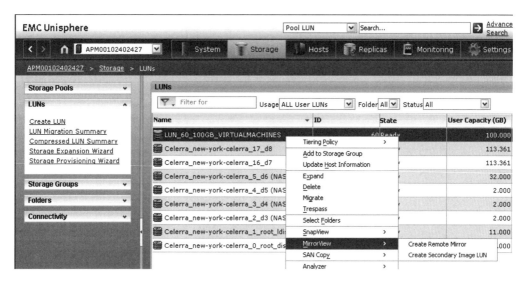

Figure 4.9   Any volume can be right-clicked in this view and enabled for MirrorView.

3. In the dialog box that opens, select Synchronous, and enter a friendly name and then click OK. I named my remote mirror "Replica of LUN60 – Virtual Machines," as shown in Figure 4.10.

   After clicking OK, you will receive the Confirm: Create Remote Mirror dialog box, shown in Figure 4.11. For MirrorView to be successfully set up, a secondary mirror image needs to be created on the Recovery Site (New Jersey). This secondary mirror image is a LUN which is the recipient of updates from the Protected Site array.

   The next step is to create this secondary image LUN in the Recovery Site CLARiiON (New Jersey).

4. Right-click the LUN that was just created, select MirrorView, and this time select the option Create Secondary Image LUN.

   This will open a dialog box that displays the other Recovery Site CLARiiON arrays visible in Unisphere. In this case, Unisphere just selects the next available LUN ID for the secondary mirror. You can see in Figure 4.12 that the CK2000 array is my EMC NS-20 in the New Jersey location.

5. Click OK and confirm the other ancillary dialog boxes. This will create a LUN at the Recovery Site CLARiiON (New Jersey). You can rename it if you wish to make it more meaningful. I called mine "LUN_60_100GB_NYC_VIRTUALMACHINES_ MIRRORVIEW."

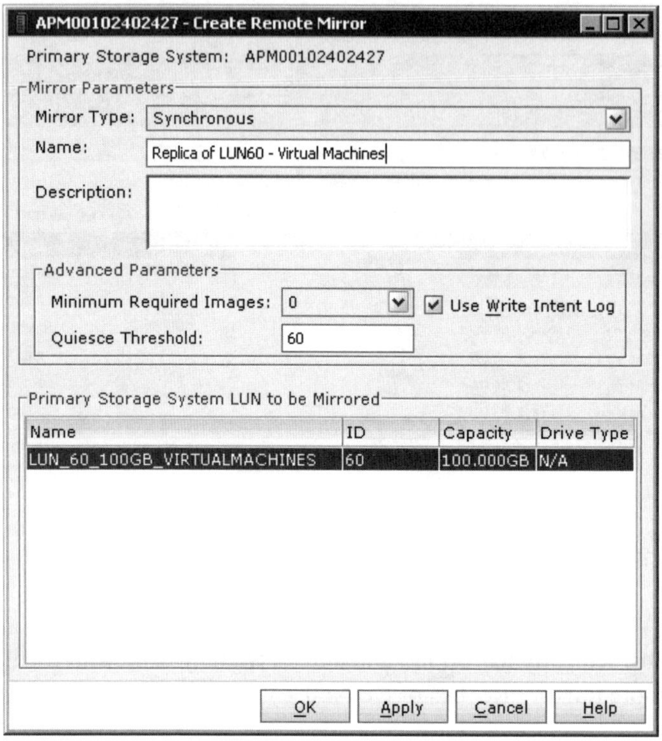

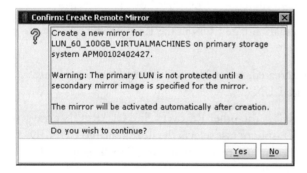

Figure 4.10   Naming the remote mirror

Figure 4.11   A secondary mirror image must be created on the Recovery Site.

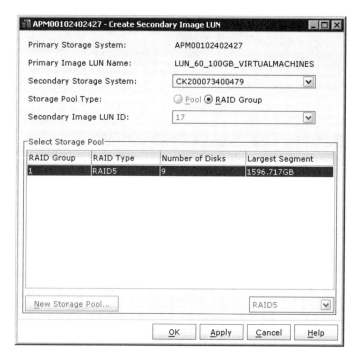

Figure 4.12   The array is CK2000.

6. This new secondary image LUN must be added to the remote mirror created earlier. On the Protected Site CLARiiON (New York) click the Replicas icon, and in the menu that opens select the Mirrors option; this should refresh the display (in my case, it shows "Replica of LUN60 – virtualmachines"). Select Add Secondary Image or click the Add Secondary button, as shown in Figure 4.13.

7. In the corresponding dialog box select the Recovery Site CLARiiON (New Jersey) and expand the +SP A or +SP B to select the secondary image LUN created earlier, as shown in Figure 4.14.

You can reduce the time it takes to synchronize the data by changing the Synchronization Rate to High. This does increase the load on the array, so perhaps if you do change this it's worth changing the setting once the first synchronization has completed. The initial sync required will cause a full synchronization of data from one LUN to another so that both LUNs have the same data state. In my case, because the LUN at the Protected Site is

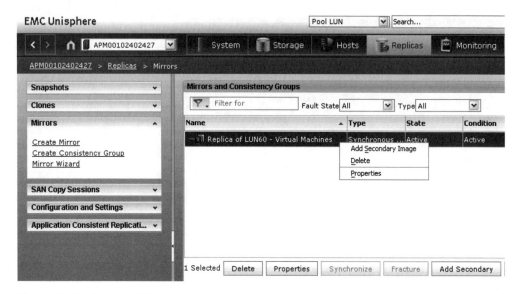

Figure 4.13   Once the MirrorView object is created a secondary image can be added that is the destination volume at the Recovery Site.

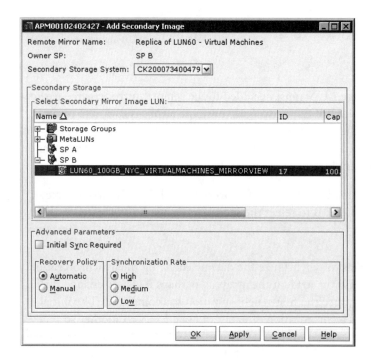

Figure 4.14   The destination LUN at the Recovery Site being used to receive updates from the LUN at the Protected Site

blank, it will save time if I don't enable this option. This option can be useful in a manual failback process if the Protected Site has only been down for a short while during a DR event. There would be little point in carrying out a full sync if the difference between the LUNs was relatively small.

The recovery policy controls what happens if the secondary mirror image is inaccessible. Selecting Automatic forces a resync of the data without the administrator intervening, whereas selecting Manual would require the administrator to manually sync up the LUNs. The synchronization rate controls the speed of writes between the Protected Site CLARiiON (New York) and the Recovery Site CLARiiON (New Jersey). Most customers would choose an automatic reconnection, but for some environments manual is preferred—for example, where network communication fails regularly or on a scheduled basis and the administrator wishes to reestablish communication between the array manually.

Creating a Snapshot for SRM Tests

When testing an SRM Recovery Plan, the replicated secondary mirror LUN—in my case, LUN_60_100GB_NYC_VIRTUALMACHINES_MIRRORVIEW—is not directly mounted and made accessible to the ESX hosts. Instead, a snapshot of the secondary LUN is taken, and this snapshot is presented to the recovery ESX hosts during the test. This allows tests of the Recovery Plan to occur during the day without interrupting normal operations or the synchronous replication between the primary and secondary LUNs. During a test event in SRM the secondary mirror is marked as read-only and is only used to receive updates from the Protected Site array. A MirrorView target is only ever read-only—a promotion strips the flags off if communication still exists with the source array, forcing read-only flags on the source volume.

This snapshot is not created automatically. Instead, it's created manually, and when created it must be named in the correct way for the EMC CLARiiON Site Recovery Adapter (SRA) to locate it. The name of the snapshot must contain the text "VMWARE_SRM_SNAP"—the snapshot does not need to have that test string at the start of the name; it can be anywhere in the body of the snapshot name. This procedure is carried out at both the Protected Site (New York) and the Recovery Site CLARiiON array (New Jersey). This will allow for full tests of the Recovery Plans, runs of the Recovery Plans, and both a test and a run of the failback process. For this reason, EMC recommends that you allocate a snapshot to both the primary and secondary image LUNs so that you can carry out failover and failback procedures with SRM, as well as ensure that you have RLPs set up on both arrays.

To create a snapshot for SRM tests, follow these steps.

1. Within Unisphere on the Recovery Site array (New Jersey) select the secondary image LUN.

2. Right-click the LUN, and from the menu that opens, select SnapView and then Create Snapshot (see Figure 4.15).

3. In the dialog box that opens, enter the name of the snapshot; in my case, this is VMWARE_SRM_SNAP_LUN60 (see Figure 4.16).

It is possible to allocate the snapshot to a storage group, but in this case it is not necessary at this stage. As we discussed earlier, snapshots use an RLP, which you can think of as an allocation of storage purely for snapshots—as they (the snapshots) are not "free." EMC documentation indicates that you should reserve 20% to 30% of the space in the RLP for the snapshot data. So, in my case, the 100GB volume would need around 20–30GB for the RLP. EMC also suggests that snapshots should be used as a method for creating replicas of a production volume where the change rate of data within that production volume does not exceed 20% to 30%. The entirety of the RLP is used for snap data.

Under the Replicas icon, in the Snapshot menu option, you should see a snapshot following the naming convention outlined a moment ago. Notice in Figure 4.17 how the snapshot is currently inactive because it is not in use. During a test of an SRM plan, you would expect this status to change to "Active."

Figure 4.15 Each LUN must be allocated a snapshot. This snapshot is only engaged during a test of a Recovery Plan.

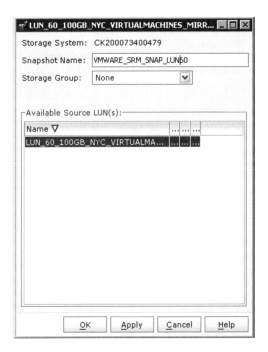

Figure 4.16   The snapshot name being set. The name must contain the text "VMWARE_SRM_SNAP" to work correctly.

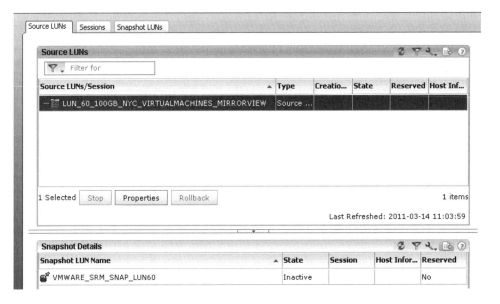

Figure 4.17   The state of the snapshot is "inactive" and changes to an active state when a Recovery Plan is tested.

IMPORTANT NOTE

If you do engage in DR for real, or if you hard-test your plan, you likely will want to test the failback procedure before carrying out failback for real. For this test of failback to be successful you will need a similar snapshot ready at the Protected Site (New York). So repeat this process for the LUN at the Protected Site.

Creating Consistency Groups (Recommended)

Remember that, strictly speaking, the EMC CLARiiON SRA no longer requires consistency groups. However, you may find them useful, especially if you are replicating multiple MirrorView-enabled volumes. Testing has also shown that you are likely to avoid an administrative fractured state on some of your MirrorView volumes when failing back (forcing a full resync) if you use consistency groups.

To create a consistency group, follow these steps.

1. On the protected CLARiiON array (New York) select the Replicas icon, and from the menu that opens, click the Mirrors option.

2. On the right-hand side of the Mirrors pane, click the Create Consistency Group link.

3. Change the Mirror Type to be Synchronous.

4. In the same dialog, enter a friendly name for the group (see Figure 4.18), and then add the remote mirrors from the Available Remote Mirrors list to the Selected Remote Mirrors list and click OK.

This will create a consistency group in the Mirrors view in Unisphere containing, in my case, just one LUN (see Figure 4.19). As my system grows and I create more MirrorView-protected LUNs I could add them to the same consistency group or create different consistency groups for different types of applications. As you will see later, consistency groups map almost directly to the Protection Group object in VMware SRM. After clicking OK, the consistency group will also be created at the Recovery Site CLARiiON (New Jersey).

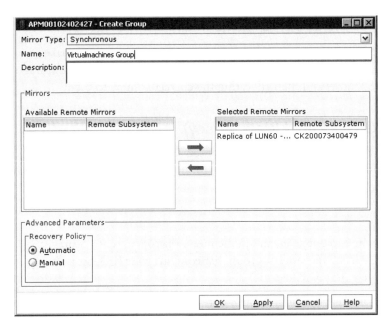

Figure 4.18 Consistency groups can almost mirror SRM Protection Groups, gathering LUNs to ensure predictable replication across multiple LUNs.

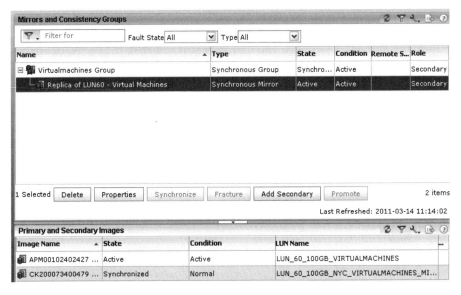

Figure 4.19 Consistency groups enable you to track the LUNs configured for Mirror-View and monitor their state.

Granting ESX Host Access to CLARiiON LUNs

Now that we have created our primary, secondary, and snapshot objects, we can make them available to the ESX hosts. This should be a simple procedure of locating the storage groups that contain the ESX hosts and then allocating the correct volume to them.

At the Recovery Site CLARiiON (New Jersey)

At the Recovery Site, the ESX hosts will need to be granted access to both the MirrorView secondary image LUN and the snapshot created earlier for both tests and runs of the SRM Recovery Plans to work correctly.

To grant this access, follow these steps.

1. In Unisphere, select the Storage icon, and in the menu that opens, click Storage Groups and then right-click the storage group that contains your ESX hosts; in my case, this is called "New_Jersey_Cluster1."

2. Choose Select LUNs in the menu or click the Connect LUNs button (see Figure 4.20).

3. Expand +Snapshots and select the snapshot created earlier; in my case, I called this "VMWARE_SRM_SNAP_LUN60."

4. Expand the +SP A or +SP B and locate the secondary image LUN created earlier.

5. Select the LUN in the list; in my case, I called this "LUN_60_100GB_NYC_ VIRTUALMACHINES_MIRRORVIEW."

6. Scroll down the Selected LUNs list, and under Host ID allocate the LUN number that the ESX hosts will use. In my case, as host ID 60 was available, I used it (see Figure 4.21).

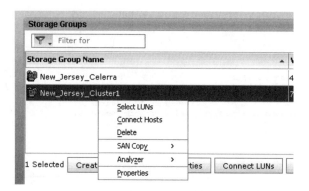

Figure 4.20 At the Recovery Site, the ESX host must be granted rights to the LUNs and snapshot created during the MirrorView configuration.

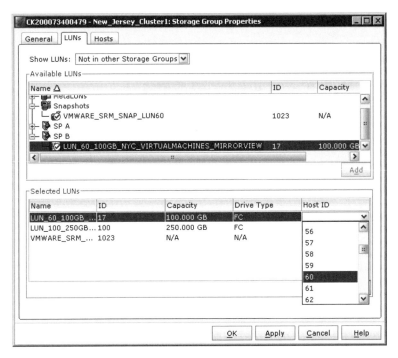

Figure 4.21 Although the LUN ID is 60, the host ID can be any value between 0 and 255.

After clicking OK and confirming the usual Unisphere dialog boxes, you should see the LUN appear in the LUNs list in the storage group (see Figure 4.22). Notice how the description indicates this LUN is merely a secondary copy. The snapshot will only become "active" when you test your Recovery Plans in SRM.

At the Protected Site CLARiiON (New York)

Allocating the LUN and snapshot at the Protected Site is essentially the same process as for the Recovery Site. However, the status labels are different because this LUN is read-writable and is being mirrored to the Recovery Site location.

To allocate the LUN and snapshot follow these steps.

1. In Unisphere, select the Storage icon. In the menu that opens, click Storage Groups, and then right-click the storage group that contains your ESX hosts; in my case, this is called "New_Jersey_Cluster1."

2. Choose Select LUNs in the menu or click the Connect LUNs button.

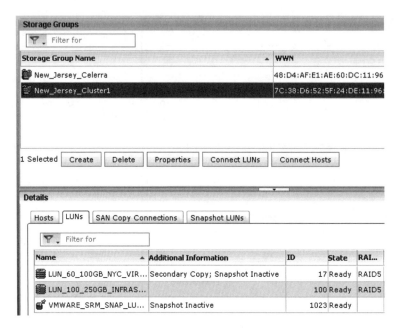

Figure 4.22   Under Additional Information, we can see the LUN is a secondary copy, and the snapshot is inactive.

3. Expand +Snapshots and select the snapshot created earlier. In my case, I called this "VMWARE_SRM_SNAP_LUN60."

4. Expand the +SP A or +SP B and locate the secondary image LUN created earlier.

5. Select the LUN in the list. In my case, I called this "LUN_60_100GB_VIRTUAL-MACHINES."

6. Scroll down the Selected LUNs list, and under Host ID allocate the LUN number that the ESX hosts will use. In my case, as host ID 60 was available, I used it.

After clicking OK and confirming the usual Unisphere dialog boxes, you should see the LUN appear in the LUNs list in the storage group. Notice how the description indicates that this LUN is marked as being "mirrored" (see Figure 4.23).

You should now be able to rescan the ESX hosts in the Protected Site and format this LUN. We can request a rescan of all the affected ESX hosts in the VMware HA/DRS cluster by a single right-click. After the rescan, format the LUN with VMFS and create some virtual machines.

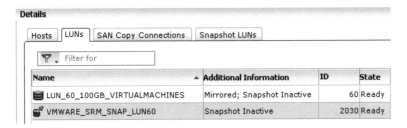

Figure 4.23　At the Protected Site, we see the LUN is mirrored to the Recovery Site.

Using the EMC Virtual Storage Integrator Plug-in (VSI)

Alongside many other storage vendors EMC has created its own storage management plug-ins for vCenter. You might prefer to use these on a daily basis for provisioning LUNs as they are quite easy to use. In the context of SRM, they may speed up the process of initially allocating storage to your ESX hosts in the Protected Site. Once the hosts are provisioned, it will merely be a case of setting up the appropriate MirrorView relationship and snapshot configuration. Who knows; perhaps these plug-ins may be extended to allow configuration of SRM's storage requirements directly from within vSphere. In addition to provisioning new storage, EMC VSI also has enhanced storage views and the ability to create virtual desktops using array-accelerated cloning technologies.

The following components should be installed on your management PC before embarking on an installation of the EMC VSI:

- Unisphere Service Manager

- EMC Solutions Enabler

- RTOOLS software (if you are using EMC's PowerPath technologies)

- The NaviSphere CLI (if you are dealing with a legacy array like my EMC NS-20; the naviseccli is required for all CLARiiONs and will be used by the VNX family as well)

After you install these components and the EMC VSI, when you load the vSphere client you should see an EMC VSI icon in the Solutions and Applications tab with the "home" location (see Figure 4.24).

Figure 4.24   Installing the VSI adds an icon to the Solutions and Applications view in vCenter.

This icon will enable you to configure the plug-in so that it becomes aware of your CLARiiON and Celerra systems. In terms of the CLARiiON, it is merely a case of inputting the IP address of the storage processors (SP A and SP B) on the array together with a username of "nasadmin" and the password that was used when the array was set up (see Figure 4.25); you can set up a similar configuration for any Celerra systems you maintain.

Once correctly configured, the EMC VSI adds a Provision Storage option to the right-click of the VMware cluster and will take you through the process of both creating a LUN on the array and formatting the LUN for VMware's file system VMFS (see Figure 4.26).

If you want to learn more about the EMC VSI, I wrote about its functionality on my blog, RTFM Education:

> www.rtfm-ed.co.uk/2011/03/01/using-the-emc-vsi-plug-in/

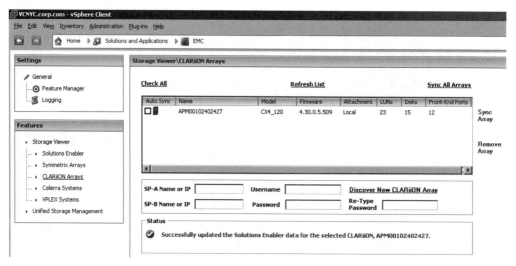

Figure 4.25   Entering the IP addresses of the storage processors, along with a username and password

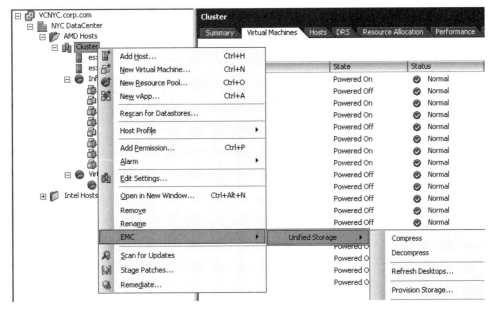

Figure 4.26   VSI adds right-click context-sensitive menus to various parts of vCenter.

Summary

In this chapter I briefly showed you how to set up EMC CLARiiON MirrorView, which is suitable for use with VMware SRM. As I'm sure you have seen it takes some time to create this configuration. It's perhaps salutary to remember that many of the steps you have seen only occur the first time you configure the system after an initial installation. Once your targets are created, your file systems and LUNs are created, and your replication relationships are in place, then you can spend more of your time consuming the storage.

From this point onward, I recommend that you create virtual machines on the VMFS volume so that you have some test VMs to use with VMware SRM. SRM is designed to only pick up on LUNs/volumes that are accessible to the ESX host and contain virtual machine files. In previous releases, if you had a volume that was blank it wouldn't be displayed in the SRM Array Manager Configuration Wizard; the new release warns you if this is the case. This was apparently a popular error people had with SRM 4.0, but one that I rarely saw—mainly because I always ensured my replicated volumes had virtual machines contained on them. I don't see any point in replicating empty volumes! In SRM 4.0 the Array Manager Configuration Wizard displays an error if you fail to populate the datastore with virtual machines. In my demonstrations I mainly used virtual disks, but I will be covering RDMs later in this book because it is an extremely popular VMware feature.

Chapter 5

Getting Started with the HP StorageWorks P4000 Virtual SAN Appliance with Remote Copy

Hewlett-Packard (HP) provides both physical and virtual storage IP-based appliances for the storage market, and in 2009 it acquired Lefthand Networks, a popular iSCSI provider. HP provides a virtual appliance called the StorageWorks P4000 virtual storage appliance (VSA) that is downloadable from the HP website for a 60-day evaluation period. In this respect, the P4000 VSA is ideal for any jobbing server guy to download and play with in conjunction with VMware's SRM—the same applies to EMC's Celerra VSA. If you follow this chapter to the letter you should end up with a structure that looks like the one shown in Figure 5.1 in the VSA's management console, with the friendly names adjusted to suit your own conventions.

In the screen grab of the HP P4000 Centralized Management Console (CMC) shown in Figure 5.1 you can see that I have two VSAs (vsa1.corp.com and vsa2.corp.com), each in its own management group (NYC_Group and NJ_Group). As you can see, I have a volume called "virtualmachines" and it is replicating the data from vsa1 to vsa2 to the volume called "replica_of_virtualmachines." It is a very simple setup indeed, but it is enough to get us started with the SRM product.

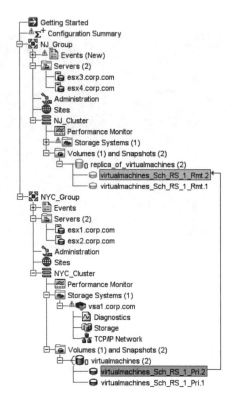

Figure 5.1   Replication of the virtualmachines volume in the NYC_Group
to the replica_of_virtualmachines volume in the NJ_Group

Some Frequently Asked Questions about the HP P4000 VSA

During my time using the HP P4000 VSA, I've been asked a number of questions about the use of these types of VSAs. Generally, the questions focus on scalability and performance issues. There's a natural anxiety and assumption that a VSA will perform less well than a physical array. Of course, much depends on the scalability written into the software. As well, everyone now knows the VM itself presents few limitations in terms of scale and performance; these limitations evaporated some years ago. Nonetheless, that doesn't mean every vendor-provided VSA can take advantage of the VM's capabilities. The following is a list of questions that people in the VMware Community Forums and customers alike have asked me. The answers to these questions should help you with your decision making.

Q1. What are the recommended minimums for memory and CPU?

The minimum requirements are 1GB of RAM and one vCPU offering 2GHz or more of CPU time. Adding more vCPUs does not significantly improve performance, but the more storage you add the more memory you may require.

Q2. Should the VSA be stored on a local VMFS volume or a shared VMFS volume?

This depends entirely on the quality of the storage. If your local storage is faster and offers more redundancy than any remote storage you have, you would use local storage. In some environments, you might prefer to build your VSAs into a cluster, with volumes in that cluster configured with *Network* RAID 10 to protect the storage layer from unexpected outages. The HA capability is in the Network RAID functionality of the volumes. The best practice is not to use VMware HA, but to leverage the VSA functionality at the storage layer using Network RAID. If the VSA is placed on local storage, it effectively makes that local resource behave as network resources available to other hosts and systems on the network. Additionally, it offers replication to local storage where it previously had none.

Q3. VSA is licensed by a MAC address. Should you use a static MAC address?

It is recommended that you use a static MAC address if you decide to purchase the VSA. If you are just evaluating the VSA or simply using it to evaluate SRM a static MAC address is not required, just recommended.

Q4. Can you use vCenter cloning to assist in creating multiple VSAs?

Yes. But the VSA must not be configured or in a management group. If you have procured a licensed version of the VSA be aware that the VMware template deploy process generates a new MAC address for the new VM, and as such it will need licensing or relicensing after being deployed. If you do consider cloning the VSA, I recommend using static MAC addresses to more tightly control the configuration and licensing process.

Q5. Setting up two VSAs in a management group with all the appropriate settings takes some time. Can you use the clone feature in vCenter to reset lab environments?

Yes. Build up the two VSAs to the state you need, and then simply right-click the management group and choose the Shutdown Management Group option. You can then clone, delete, and clone again. You should be careful, as both the cloning and template processes change the MAC address. An alternative to this approach is to learn the HP command-line interface (CLI), which allows you to script this procedure. This is not covered in this book.

Q6. Can you capture the configuration of the VSAs and restore it?

No. You can capture the configuration for support purposes but not for configuration. Working with HP support you can restore your configuration if it has become damaged for some reason. You can back up your configuration to a file, and use this as a method of repairing a lost or damaged configuration. You can do this by right-clicking the group in the management console and selecting the View Management Group configuration, which opens a dialog from which you can save the setup to a .bin file. If you do have a significant number of VSAs to configure, I recommend that you use HP's CLI called the CLiQ. This would allow you to script your configuration. It also would reduce the time required to roll out the appliance, and guarantees consistency of the build from one appliance to another.

Question 6 concludes the frequently asked questions surrounding the VSA. Next, I will take you through the process of downloading, uploading, and configuring the appliance. You should find this to be a relatively easy process. I think the HP VSA has one of the most intuitive setup and configuration routines I've seen.

Downloading and Uploading the VSA

You can download from HP's website a full trial version of the HP P4000 VSA for use with VMware ESX or Microsoft Hyper-V. For obvious reasons, I'm using the ESX version in this book! To download the VSA, go to www.hp.com/go/tryvsa and follow the instructions.

After you unzip the downloaded file, use the "import" feature to upload the file to a datastore in your environment. Personally, I'm trying my best to use the OVF and OVA versions wherever possible. The main reason I am adopting the OVF version is to encourage its use among virtual appliance vendors; when it works, it is a joy to use.

Importing the StorageWorks P4000 VSA

To import the StorageWorks P4000 VSA, follow these steps.

1. To begin, extract the .zip file.

2. Open the vSphere client to your vCenter, and select the ESX host or VMware cluster on which you want the HP VSA to run.

3. In the File menu of the vSphere client, select Deploy OVF Template.

Figure 5.2 shows the page that appears after the administrator selects the "Deploy from a file or URL" radio button and browses to the .ovf file in the extracted .zip file. This should be located in the drive you unzipped it to at the following directory path:

HP_P4000_VSA_Full_Evaluation_Software_for_VMware_ESX_requires_ESX_servers_AX696_10512\Virtual_SAN_Appliance_Trial\Virtual_SAN_Appliance\vsatrial\VSA.ovf

4. Accept the OVF Template details.

5. Accept the End User License Agreement (EULA).

6. Enter a friendly VM name for the appliance, and select a VM folder location to hold it. In my case, I called the appliance "hp-vsa1" and placed it in the Infrastructure folder, as shown in Figure 5.3.

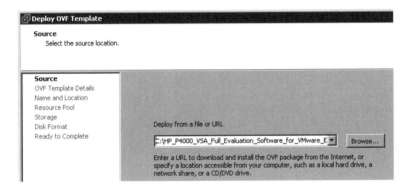

Figure 5.2 Browsing for the VSA's .ovf file

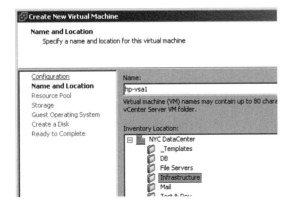

Figure 5.3 Establish a good naming convention for your virtual appliances that matches your organization's naming convention.

7. Select an ESX host or cluster upon which the VSA will run.

8. If you have one, select a resource pool. Figure 5.4 shows the administrator selecting the Infrastructure resource pool.

   Resource pools are not mandatory, and any VM can run just on the DRS cluster (or root resource pool). However, you may find resource pools useful for organizing VMs logically, and ensuring that key VMs are fairly allocating the resources they demand.

9. Select a datastore to hold the VSA's VMX and VMDK files. Figure 5.5 shows the administrator selecting the infrastructureNYC datastore.

   Note that the VSA must reside on a datastore accessible to the host. Remember, while using local storage is cost-effective, you will be unable to use features such as vMotion, DRS, and HA to manage and protect the VSA.

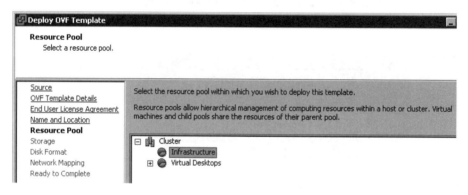

Figure 5.4   Selecting the Infrastructure resource pool

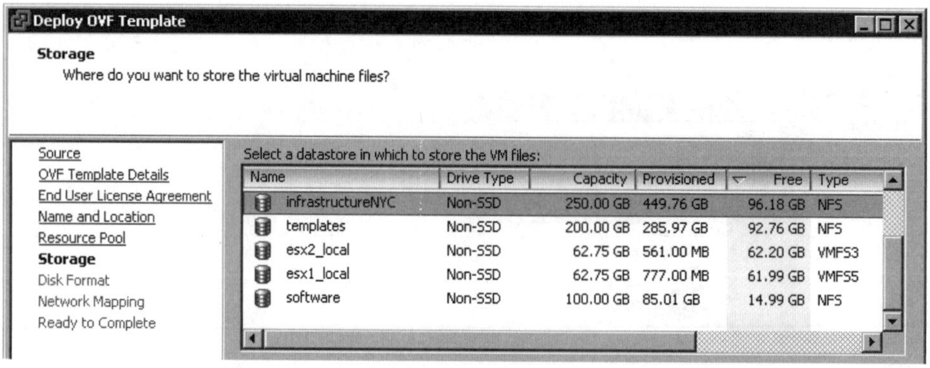

Figure 5.5   Selecting the infrastructureNYC datastore

10. Accept the default for the virtual disk format used.

This first virtual disk essentially contains the system disk of the HP VSA, so it should be safe to use the thin virtual disk format. Later we will add a second virtual disk or RDM to the appliance; this is the storage that will be presented to the ESX host. In that case, you need to be more circumspect about the format and location used from a performance perspective.

11. Select a vSwitch port group for the VSA.

Remember, this network must be accessible to the ESX hosts to allow the software iSCSI stack that exists in ESX to speak to the HP VSA and the iSCSI volumes it presents. Using utilities such as ping and vmkping should allow you to confirm the accessibility of the VSA once its IP configuration has been completed. Incidentally, the port groups (vlan11, vlan12, and vlan13) in Figure 5.6 are port groups on VMware's Distributed vSwitch (DvSwitch). SRM does work with the older Standard vSwitches (SvSwitches), but I thought it would be interesting to use all the Enterprise Plus networking features with SRM in this book. The Virtual Storage Appliance port group is a virtual machine port group on the *same* virtual switch as my VMkernel ports that I created to access IP storage from an ESX host.

Modifying the VSA's Settings and First-Power-On Configuration

Once the VSA has been imported the next step is to power it on for the first time. You must complete a "run once" or post-configuration phase before you can manage the VSA with its companion software.

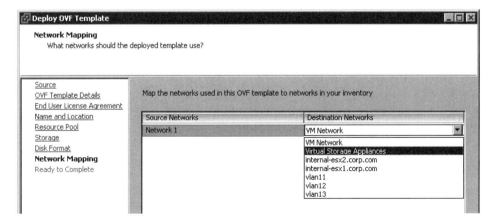

Figure 5.6 Selecting the network port group on a vSphere vSwitch

Adding a Virtual Disk for Storage

The next step is to add a virtual disk or RDM to the HP P4000 VSA. This disk will be a volume presented to your ESX hosts and used to store virtual machines protected by SRM. As such, you will want to make it as big as possible as you will create VMs here. Additionally, it must be located on the SCSI 1:0 controller as shown in Figure 5.7. Note that the HP VSA does support adding more disks to SCSI 1:1, and so on.

Later, when we create volumes in the HP P4000 VSA, you will see that it does support thin provisioning to present a volume of any size you like, even though it does not have the actual disk space at hand. Despite doing this, the larger this second disk is the more space you will have for your virtual machines. The HP VSA can support five virtual disks on SCSI 1: With each virtual disk being a maximum of 2TB, it means one VSA can present up to 10TB of storage. Of course, you will have to review the settings for memory to the HP VSA in order to manage this amount of storage.

Licensing the VSA

Before you power on the VSA for the first time, you might want to consider how the product is licensed should you wish to use VSA beyond the 60-day evaluation period. VSA is licensed by the virtual MAC address of the VM generated by VMware at power on. While this auto-generated MAC address shouldn't change, it can change in some cases where you manually register and unregister a VM from one ESX host to another. Additionally, if you fail to back up the VMX you could lose this information forever. Lastly, if for whatever reason you clone the VSA with a vCenter clone/clone to template facility, a brand-new MAC address is generated at that point. You might prefer to set and record a static MAC address to your VSA (whether you do this will depend on your

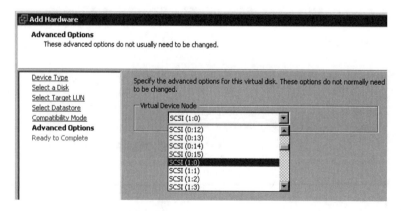

Figure 5.7 The VSA boots from SCSI 0:0, and must have its data held on a second SCSI controller (SCSI 1) to enhance its performance.

circumstances and requirements) in the range provided by VMware. It is possible to set a static MAC address in the GUI, as shown in Figure 5.8, and there is no need to edit the virtual machine's VMX files directly. Just remember to record your static MAC address alongside the VM name, hostname, and IP address.

Whatever you choose, static or dynamic, be sure to make a record of the MAC address so that your license key (if you have purchased one) will be valid if you need to completely rebuild the VSA from scratch. HP recommends a static MAC address.

Primary Configuration of the VSA Host

In this section I will explain the steps involved in the primary configuration of the VSA host. Before we walk through those steps, though, you may want to consider your options for creating your second VSA. Although it doesn't take long to add in the VSA, we currently have a VSA that is in a clean and unconfigured state; to rapidly create a second VSA you could run a vCenter "clone" operation to duplicate the current VSA VM configuration. You can do this even if the VM is located on local storage. HP does not support cloning the VSA once it is in a management group setup with the client console used to manage the system.

The primary configuration involves configuring the hostname and IP settings for the VSA from the VMware Remote Console window. You can navigate this utility through a

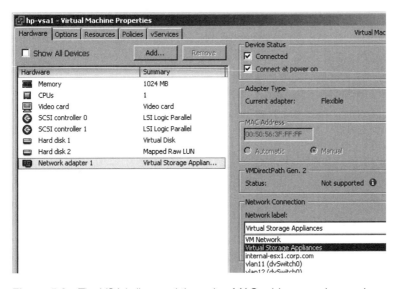

Figure 5.8   The VSA is licensed through a MAC address, and as such the recommendation is to use a static MAC address.

combination of keystrokes such as the Tab key, space bar, and Enter/Return key. It is very simple to use; just stay away from the cursor keys for navigation, as they don't work.

1. Power on both VSA VMs.

2. Open a VMware Remote Console.

3. At the Login prompt, type "start" and press Enter. The VSA presents a blue background with white text. You can navigate around the VSA's console using the Tab and Enter keys.

4. Press Enter at the Login prompt as shown in Figure 5.9.

5. In the menu that appears, select Network TCP/IP Settings and press Enter, as shown in Figure 5.10.

6. Cursor up, and select < eth0 > and press Enter as shown in Figure 5.11. Note that, by default, the HP VSA has (and requires) only a single virtual NIC; the VSA should receive its network redundancy by virtue of a vSphere vSwitch which has multiple, physical vmnics attached to it to create a network team.

7. Change the hostname and set a static IP address.

   When I repeated this process for my second VSA, I set the name to be vsa2.corp. com with an IP address of 172.168.4.99/24 and a default gateway of 172.168.4.1. (A default gateway is optional, but if your VSAs are in two different physical locations, it is likely that you will need to configure routing between the two appliances.)

Figure 5.9   The login option. By default, the "root" account on the HP VSA is blank.

Figure 5.10   The tiered menu system on the HP VSA's console

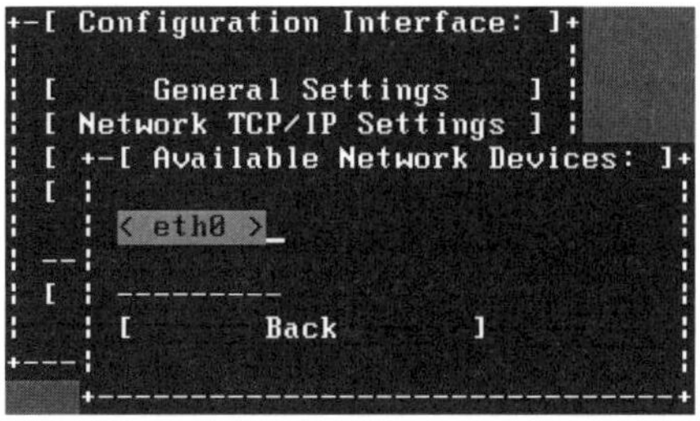

```
+-[ Configuration Interface: ]+
:                              :
: [      General Settings    ] :
: [ Network TCP/IP Settings ] :
: [ +-[ Available Network Devices: ]+
: [ :                              :
:   : < eth0 >_                    :
  --:                              :
: [ : ---------                    :
:   : [       Back        ]        :
+---:                              :
     +----------------------------+
```

Figure 5.11   Select the eth0 interface to configure a static IP address.

Although all my equipment is in the same rack, I've tried to use different IP ranges with routers to give the impression that NYC and NJ represent two distinct sites with different network identities, as shown in Figure 5.12. You can navigate the interface here by using the Tab key on your keyboard.

8. Press Enter to confirm the warning about the restart of networking.

9. Use the Back options to return to the main login page. You might wish to update your DNS configuration to reflect these hostnames and IP addresses so that you can use an FQDN in various HP management tools.

Installing the Management Client

Advanced configuration is performed via the HP CMC. This is a simple application used to configure the VSA (a Linux version is also available). Your PC must have a valid or

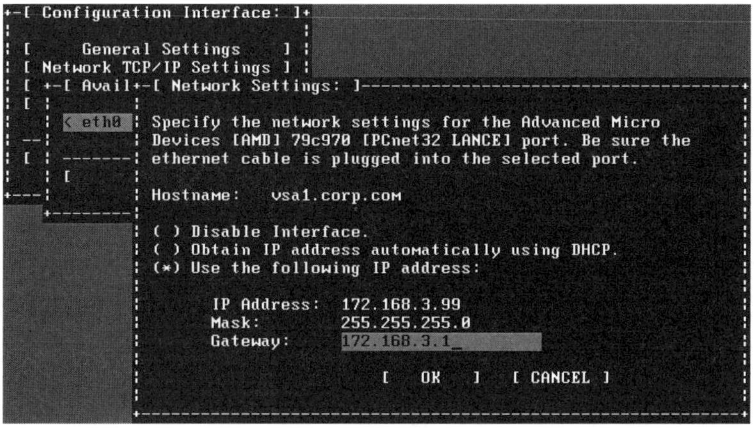

```
+-[ Configuration Interface: ]+
:                              :
: [      General Settings    ] :
: [ Network TCP/IP Settings ] :
: [ +-[ Avail+-[ Network Settings: ]------------------------------+
: [ :       : Specify the network settings for the Advanced Micro :
:   : < eth0 : Devices [AMD] 79c970 [PCnet32 LANCE] port. Be sure the :
  --:        : ethernet cable is plugged into the selected port.   :
: [ : ------ :                                                     :
+---:        : Hostname:   vsa1.corp.com                           :
     +-------:                                                     :
             : ( ) Disable Interface.                              :
             : ( ) Obtain IP address automatically using DHCP.     :
             : (*) Use the following IP address:                   :
             :                                                     :
             :     IP Address:  172.168.3.99                       :
             :     Mask:        255.255.255.0                      :
             :     Gateway:     172.168.3.1_                       :
             :                                                     :
             :            [   OK   ]   [ CANCEL ]                  :
             +-----------------------------------------------------+
```

Figure 5.12   Different IP ranges with routers to give the impression that NYC and NJ represent two distinct sites with different network identities

routable IP address to communicate to the two VSAs. You will find the HP CMC in the directory where you extracted the .zip file from the evaluation page:

HP_P4000_VSA_Full_Evaluation_Software_for_VMware_ESX_
requires_ESX_servers_AX696_10512\Virtual_SAN_Appliance_Trial\
Centralized_Management_Console

I will be using the Windows version of the CMC. Installation is very simple, and isn't worth documenting here; a typical installation should be sufficient for the purposes of this book.

Configuring the VSA (Management Groups, Clusters, and Volumes)

Now that the appliance is operational and accessible, it's possible to use the graphical management console to complete the higher-level configuration of the VSA. This includes adding the VSA into the console, and then configuring it so that it resides in a management group and cluster.

Adding the VSAs to the Management Console

Before you begin, you might as well test that your management PC can actually ping the VSAs. You're not going to get very far in the next step if you can't do this. I repeated this add process so that I have one management console showing two VSAs (vsa1/2) in two different locations.

1. Load the CMC, and the Find Systems Wizard will start.

2. If the VSA is not automatically discovered, you can click the Add button and enter the IP address or hostname of the VSAs, as shown in Figure 5.13.

3. Click OK, and repeat this for any other VSAs you wish to manage.

4. When you're finished click Close.

Adding the VSAs to Management Groups

Each VSA will be in its own management group. During this process, you will be able to set friendly names for the groups and volumes. It clearly makes sense to use names that reflect the purpose of the unit in question, such as the following:

- NYC_Group and NJ_Group
- NYC_Cluster and NJ_Cluster

- Virtual_Machines Volume

- Replica_Of_Virtual_Machines Volume

Of course, it is entirely up to you what naming process you adopt. Just remember that these names are not allowed to contain a space as a character. To add a VSA, follow these steps.

1. In the Getting Started node, click "2. Management Groups, Clusters and Volumes" and then click Next to go to the Welcome page.

2. Choose New Management Group.

3. For the management group name enter something meaningful, such as "NYC_ Group", and select the VSA you wish to add; in my case, this is vsa1.corp.com.

    In a production setup, theoretically you could have five VSAs which replicate to one another asynchronously in the Protected Site and another five VSAs in the Recovery Site that replicate to one another and with the Protection location in an asynchronous manner. Remember, spaces are *not* allowed in the management group name. You can use CamelCase or the underscore character (_) to improve readability, as shown in Figure 5.14.

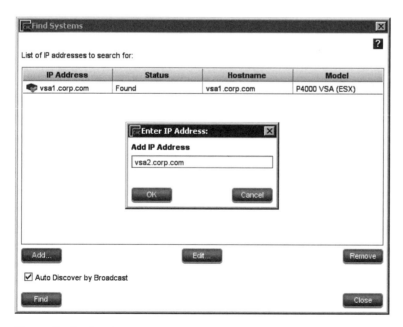

Figure 5.13 For this to work, the hostname must be registered in DNS. Multiple VSAs can be added into the CMC and managed centrally.

Management Groups, Clusters, and Volumes Wizard
Create a Management Group
Name your management group and select storage system
Management Group Name:
NYC_Group
This name cannot be changed
Create management group with storage systems sele
Name
IP Address
Model
vsa1.corp.com
172.168.3.99
P4000 VSA (ESX)
vsa2.corp.com
172.168.4.99
P4000 VSA (ESX)

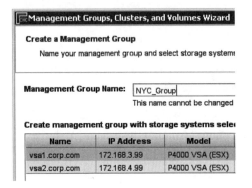

Figure 5.14 Multiple VSAs can be added to a group. In this case, we will have one VSA for each location: NYC and NJ.

4. Set a username and password, as shown in Figure 5.15.

   The username and password are stored in a separate database internal to the VSA. The database is in a proprietary binary format and is copied to all VSAs in the same management group. If you are the forgetful type, you might want to make some record of these values. They are in no way connected to the logins to your vCenter or Active Directory environment.

5. Select the "Manually set time" radio button. As the VSA is a virtual appliance it should receive time updates from the ESX host, which is in turn configured for NTP. To

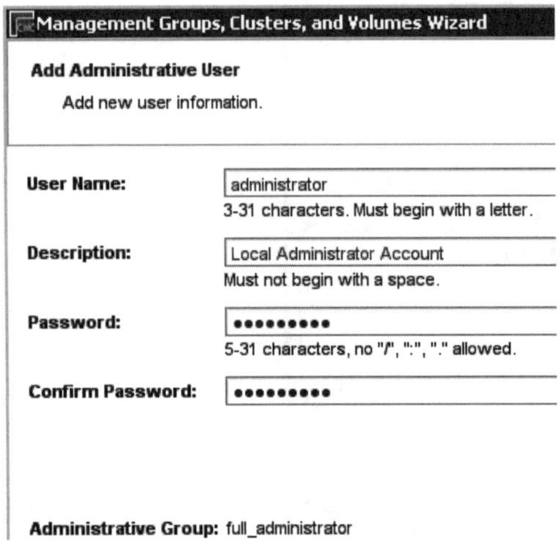

Management Groups, Clusters, and Volumes Wizard
Add Administrative User
Add new user information.
User Name:
administrator
3-31 characters. Must begin with a letter.
Description:
Local Administrator Account
Must not begin with a space.
Password:
5-31 characters, no "/", ":", "." allowed.
Confirm Password:
Administrative Group: full_administrator

Figure 5.15 The HP VSA allows for its own set of user accounts and password for authentication to the group.

enable this I edited the VMX file of my two VSAs and enabled the `tools.syncTime = "TRUE"` option.

6. Configure the email settings as befits your environment.

Creating a Cluster

The next stage of the wizard is to create a cluster. In our case, we will have one VSA in one management group within one cluster and a separate VSA in a different management group within a cluster. The cluster is intended for multiple VSAs within one management group; however, we cannot set up replication or snapshots between two VSAs in different sites without a cluster being created.

1. Choose Standard Cluster.

2. Enter a cluster name, such as NYC_Cluster.

3. Set a virtual IP.

   This is mainly used by clusters when you have two VSAs within the same management group, and, strictly speaking, it isn't required in our case, but it's a best practice to set this now for possible future use. I used my next available IP of 172.168.3.98, as shown in Figure 5.16. When I set the virtual IP on my

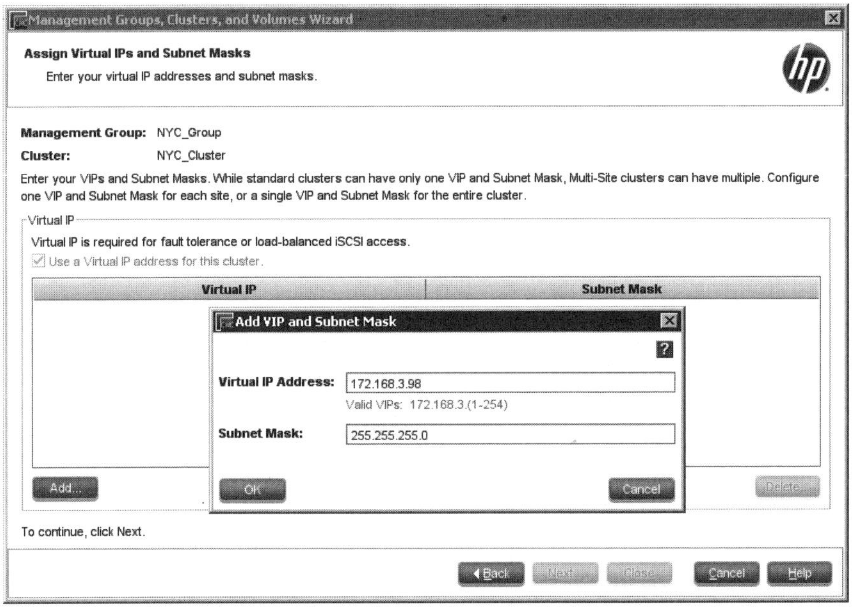

Figure 5.16   Setting a virtual IP

other VSA, I used an IP address of 172.168.4.98. (Virtual IPs are used in the "cluster" configuration of the HP VSA, a setup which is beyond the scope of this book. However, you must supply at least one virtual IP in order to complete the configuration.)

Creating a Volume

The next step in the wizard is to create your first volume. You may skip this stage in the wizard, using the Skip Volume Creation option in the bottom right-hand corner of the page. *Volume* is another word for *LUN*. Whatever word you are familiar with, we are creating a block of storage that is unformatted which could be addressed by another system (in our case, ESX) once formatted files can be created on it. Some storage vendors refer to this process as "creating a file system." This can be a little confusing, as many people associate this with using EXT3, VMFS, or NTFS. A volume or file system is another layer of abstraction between the physical storage and its access by the server. It allows for advanced features such as thin provisioning or virtual storage.

A volume can be either full or thinly provisioned. With thinly provisioned volumes the disk space presented to a server or operating system can be greater than the actual physical storage available. So the volume can be 1TB in size even though you only have 512GB of actual disk space. You might know of this concept as virtual storage, whereby you procure disk space as you need it rather than up front. The downside is that you must really track and trace your actual storage utilization very carefully. You cannot save files in thin air; otherwise, you could wind up looking like Wile E. Coyote running off the edge of a cliff. If you need to, you can switch from full to thin provisioning and back again after you have created the volume.

1. Enter a volume name, such as "virtualmachines".

2. Set the volume size.

3. For the provisioning type, check either Full or Thin.

   As shown in Figure 5.17, I created a volume called "virtualmachines," which is used to store VMs. The size of the "physical" disk is 100GB, but with thin provisioning I could present this storage as though it were a 1TB volume/LUN. (A replication-level option would be used if I were replicating within a management group. In the case of this configuration it is irrelevant because we are replicating between management groups.) The figure shows the creation of the "primary" volume at the Protected Site of NYC. At the Recovery Site, a configuration of "Scheduled Remote Copy" will configure the volume to be marked as "Secondary" and, as such, read-only.

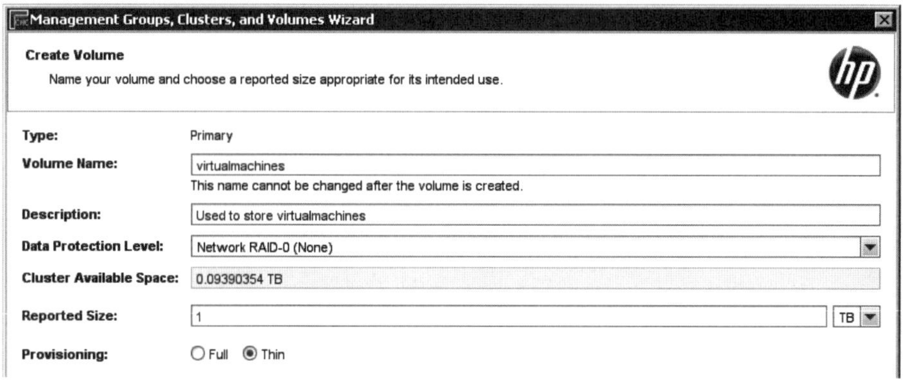

Figure 5.17   Creating the "primary" volume at the Protected Site of NYC

When I repeated this process for vsa2 I selected the Skip Volume Creation option, as when I set up replication between vsa1 and vsa2, and the Replication Wizard will create for me a "remote volume" to accept the updates from vsa1. At the end of some quite lengthy status bars, the management group, cluster, and volume will have been created. Now we must repeat this process for vsa2, but using unique names and IP addresses:

- Management Group Name: NJ_Group

- Cluster Name: NJ_Cluster

- Volume Name: Select Skip Volume Creation

At the end of this process, you should have a view that looks similar to the one shown in Figure 5.18. The small exclamation mark alerts are caused by the HP VSA trying and failing to verify my "dummy" email configuration, and they can be safely ignored.

Licensing the HP VSA

Although the HP VSA is free to evaluate for 60 days without any license key at all, certain advanced features will need a license applied to them to be activated. You can find the Feature Registration tab when you select a VSA from the Storage Node category. License keys are plain text values that can be cut and pasted from the license fulfillment Web page or by using email/fax to submit your HP order number. This window of the interface has a Feature Registration button which, when clicked, will open a dialog box to edit the license key (see Figure 5.19). Remember, license keys are directly related to the MAC address of the VSA. Events that could potentially change the MAC address will result in features not being available to the VSA.

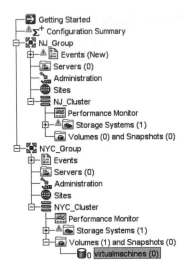

Figure 5.18   The primary volume of "virtualmachines" held in the NYC_ Group. Replication has not been configured to the NJ_Group.

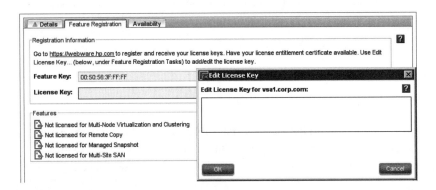

Figure 5.19   The Edit License Key dialog box

Configuring the HP VSA for Replication

It is very easy to set up replication between two VSAs in two different management groups. With the HP VSA we use a scheduled remote snapshot. This allows for asynchronous replication between two VSAs at an interval of 30 minutes or more. A much smaller cycle of replication is supported between two VSAs in the same management group, but this does not work with SRM and was never intended for use across two sites. As with many iSCSI and NFS systems the HP VSA comes with the capability to control the bandwidth consumed by the cycle of replication to prevent this background process from interfering with day-to-day communications.

In the HP VSA the snapshot process begins with a local snapshot at the protected location; once completed, this snapshot is copied to the recovery location. After the first copy, the only data transferred is the changes, or deltas. This is a very common approach with asynchronous replication systems, and you are likely to see a similar approach from other storage vendors that occupy this space. We have a setting to control the retention of this data. We can control how long to retain the snapshot data both at the Protected and Recovery management groups. To do this, follow these steps.

1. In the CMC, expand the group node and cluster nodes to locate your volume in the list.

2. Right-click your volume and, from the context menu that appears, choose New Schedule to Remote Snapshot a Volume, as shown in Figure 5.20.

3. In the Recurrence section of the dialog box set the Recur Every option to be every 30 minutes.

4. Under Primary Snapshot Setup, enable the option to be retained for a maximum of three snapshots.

   It's really up to you how long you keep your snapshots. In this configuration I would have three snapshots in 180 minutes; when the fourth snapshot is taken the oldest one will be purged. The longer you retain your snapshots and the more frequently you take them, the more options exist for data recovery. In the test environment we are configuring you probably won't want to hang on to this data for too long. The more frequently you take snapshots and the longer you retain them the more storage

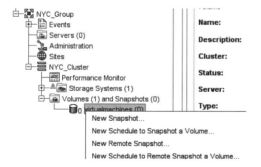

Figure 5.20   The HP VSA presents several options, but only Scheduled Remote Copy is supported with VMware SRM.

space you will require. For testing purposes you might find much less frequent intervals will be appropriate, as you need less space to retain the snapshots, as shown in Figure 5.21.

5. Under Remote Snapshot Setup, make sure the NJ_Group is selected, and then click the New Remote Volume button.

This will start a separate wizard that will create a remote volume on the VSA in the NJ_Group. It will be the recipient of block updates from the other VSA in the NYC_Group.

6. Select the NJ_Group in the Management Groups, Clusters, and Volumes Wizard, and ensure that you select the radio button for Existing Cluster and the radio button to Add a Volume to the Existing Cluster, as shown in Figure 5.22.

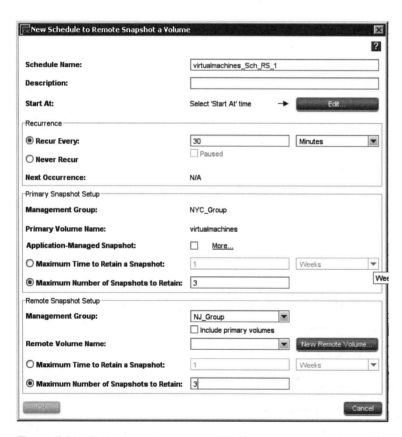

Figure 5.21 Notice how the option to click OK is not yet available. This is often because a "Start at" time has yet to be configured.

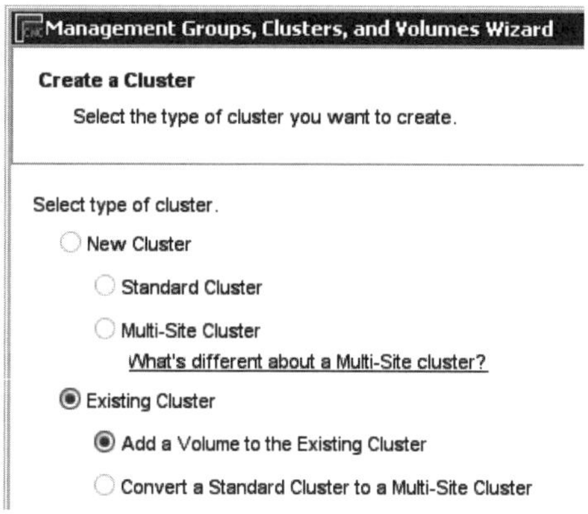

Management Groups, Clusters, and Volumes Wizard

Create a Cluster

Select the type of cluster you want to create.

Select type of cluster.

○ New Cluster

　○ Standard Cluster

　○ Multi-Site Cluster
　　What's different about a Multi-Site cluster?

◉ Existing Cluster

　◉ Add a Volume to the Existing Cluster

　○ Convert a Standard Cluster to a Multi-Site Cluster

Figure 5.22   Adding a new volume to the NJ_Cluster within the existing NJ_Group

7. In the Choose an Existing Cluster part of the wizard, select the cluster at the Recovery Site (in my case, this is the NJ_Cluster).

8. In the Create Volume dialog box, enter a friendly name for the volume, such as "replica_of_virtualmachines" as shown in Figure 5.23. Notice how the type of this volume is not "Primary" but "Remote"—remote volumes are read-only and can only receive updates via the scheduled remote copy process.

9. Click Finish and then click Close.

   At the end of this process the New Schedule to Remote Snapshot a Volume dialog box will have been updated to reflect the creation of the remote volume. However,

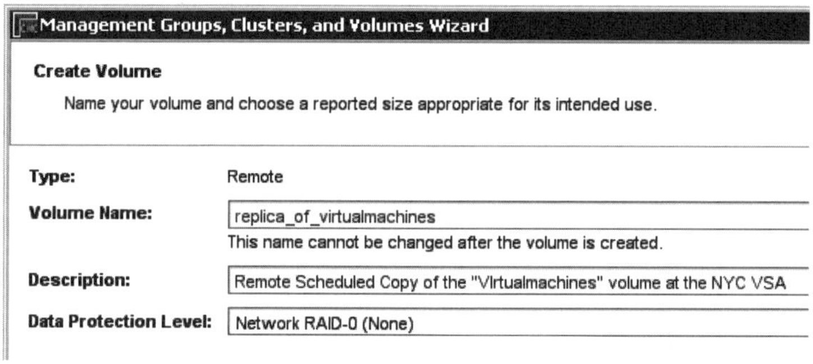

Management Groups, Clusters, and Volumes Wizard

Create Volume

Name your volume and choose a reported size appropriate for its intended use.

Type:	Remote
Volume Name:	replica_of_virtualmachines
	This name cannot be changed after the volume is created.
Description:	Remote Scheduled Copy of the "Virtualmachines" volume at the NYC VSA
Data Protection Level:	Network RAID-0 (None)

Figure 5.23   The naming of your volumes is entirely up to you, but ensure that they are meaningful and easy to recognize in the interface.

you will notice that despite setting all these parameters, the OK button has not been enabled. This is because we have yet to set a start date or time for the first snapshot.

The frequency of the snapshot and the retention values are important. If you create too shallow a replication cycle, as I have done here, you could be midway through a test of your Recovery Plan, only to find the snapshot you are currently working on is purged from the system. In the end, because of lack of storage, I adjusted my frequency to be one hour, as about midway through writing this book I ran out of storage and that was with a system that wasn't generating much in the way of new files or deleting old files. So my schedule is not an indication of what you should set in the real world if you are using HP storage; it's merely a way to get the replication working sufficiently so that you can get started with SRM.

10. In the dialog box next to the Start At time text, click the Edit button, and using the date and time interface, set when you would like the replication/snapshot process to begin.

11. Click OK. If you have not licensed the VSA, this feature will work but only for another 60 days. You may receive warnings about this if you are working with an evaluation version of the VSA.

Monitoring Your Replication/Snapshot

Of course, you will be wondering if your replication/snapshot is working. There are a couple of ways to tell. Expanding the volumes within each management group will expose the snapshots. You might see the actual replication in progress with animated icons as shown in Figure 5.24. After selecting the remote snapshot, you will see a Remote Snapshots tab (see Figure 5.25). This will tell you how much data was transferred and how long the transfer took to complete.

As you can see, my replication cycle is not especially frequent, and because of the retention of the snapshot, you could regard what the HP VSA method of replication offers as a series of "undo" levels. Now, to some degree this is true; if we have three snapshots (Pr1, Pr2, and Pr3), each separated by one hour, we have the ability to go back to the last snapshot and the one created an hour before it. However, most SRAs default to using the most recent snapshot created or to creating a snapshot on-the-fly, so if you wanted to utilize these "levels of undo" you would need to know your storage management tools well enough to replicate an old snapshot to the top of the stack. In other words, Pr1 would become Pr4.

Lastly, it's worth saying that many organizations will want to use synchronous replication where bandwidth and technology allow. This synchronous replication offers the highest level of integrity because it is constantly trying in real time to keep the disk state of the

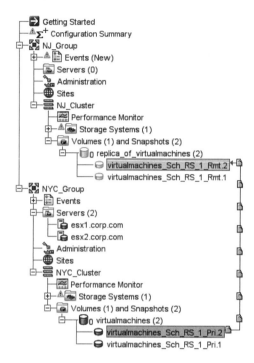

Figure 5.24 The animated view of replication taking place

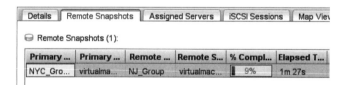

Figure 5.25 The percentage status of the replication job together with the elapsed time since the replication began

Protected Site and Recovery Site together. Often with this form of replication, you are less restricted in the time you can roll back your data. You should know, however, that this functionality is not automated or exposed to the VMware SRM product and was never part of the design. As such, it's a functionality that could only be achieved by manually managing the storage layer. A good example of a storage vendor that offers this level of granular control is EMC, whose RecoverPoint technology allows you to roll back a second-by-second level of the replication cycle. Also remember that this synchronous replication is frequently restricted in distance such that it may be unfeasible given your requirements for a DR location.

Adding ESX Hosts and Allocating Volumes to Them

Clearly, there would be little security if you could just give your ESX hosts an IP address and "point" them at the storage. To allow your ESX hosts access to storage the hosts must be allocated an IQN (iSCSI Qualified Name). The IQN is used within the authentication group to identify an ESX host. In case you have forgotten, the IQN is a convention rather than a hardcoded unique name (unlike the WWNs found on Fibre Channel devices) and takes the format of iqn-date-reverse-fqdn:alias. As a domain name can only be registered once on a particular date (albeit it can be transferred or sold to another organization), it does impose a level of uniqueness fit for its purpose. An example IQN would be:

iqn.2011-03.com.corp:esx1

In this simple setup my ESX hosts are in the NYC site, and they are imaginatively called esx1.corp.com and esx2.corp.com. My other two ESX hosts (yes, you guessed it, esx3 and esx4) are at the NJ site and do not need access to the replicated volume in the NJ_Group management group. When the administrator runs or tests a Recovery Plan within SRM the HP SRA will grant the ESX hosts access to the latest snapshot of replica_of_virtual_ machines, so long as the ESX hosts in the Recovery Site have the iSCSI initiator enabled and the iSCSI Target IP has been configured. For the moment, esx3 and esx4 need no access to the VSAs at all. However, I recommend creating test volumes and ensuring that the ESX hosts in the Recovery Site can successfully connect to the HP VSA, just to be 100% sure that they are configured correctly.

Adding an ESX Host

To add an ESX host, follow these steps.

1. Expand the NYC_Group.

2. Right-click the Servers icon and select New Server.

3. Enter the FQDN of the ESX host as a friendly identifier, as shown in Figure 5.26, and in the edit box under "CHAP not required" enter the IQN of the ESX host. The VSA does support CHAP when used with SRM. But for simplicity, I've chosen not to enable that support here.

Allocating Volumes to ESX Hosts

Now that we have the ESX hosts listed in the HP VSA we can consider giving them access to the virtualmachines volume I created earlier. There are two ways to carry out this task. You can right-click a host and use the Assign and Unassign Volumes and Snapshots menu option. This is useful if you have just one volume you specifically want a host to access.

Figure 5.26   Adding a host to the management system using a friendly name and its iSCSI IQN

Alternatively, the same menu option can be found on the right-click of a volume—this is better for ESX hosts, because in VMware all ESX hosts need access to the same volumes formatted with VMFS for features such as vMotion, DRS, HA, and FT. We'll use that approach here.

1. Right-click the volume; in my case, this is virtualmachines.

2. In the menu that opens, select the Assign and Unassign Volumes and Snapshots option.

3. In the Assign and Unassign Servers dialog box, enable the Assigned option for all ESX hosts in the datacenter/cluster that require access, as shown in Figure 5.27. Click OK.

   When you click OK, you will receive a warning stating that this configuration is only intended for clustered systems or clustered file systems. VMFS is a clustering file system where more than one ESX host can access the volume at the same time without corruption occurring. So it is safe to continue.

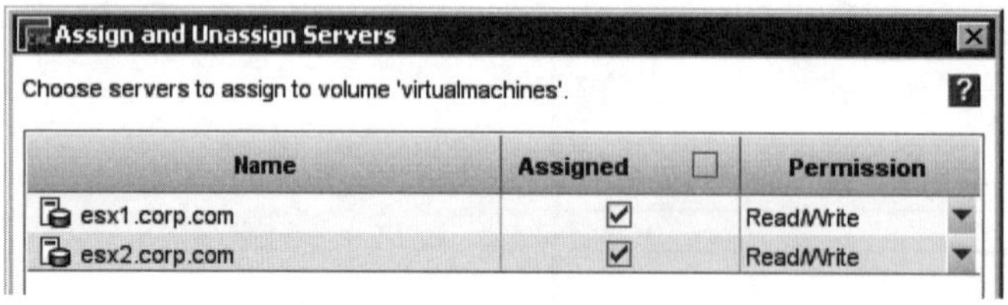

Assign and Unassign Servers   [×]

Choose servers to assign to volume 'virtualmachines'.   [?]

Name	Assigned	☐	Permission
🖫 esx1.corp.com	☑		Read/Write ▼
🖫 esx2.corp.com	☑		Read/Write ▼

Figure 5.27   Once registered with the management console, assigning hosts to datastores is as simple as clicking with the mouse.

For now this completes the configuration of the VSA. All that we need to do is to configure the ESX host connection to the VSA.

Granting ESX Host Access to the HP VSA iSCSI Target

Now that we have created the iSCSI target it's a good idea to enable the software iSCSI target on the ESX hosts.

If you have a dedicated iSCSI hardware adapter you can configure your IP settings and IQN directly on the card. One advantage of this is that if you wipe your ESX host, your iSCSI settings remain on the card; however, they are quite pricey. Therefore, many VMware customers prefer to use the ESX host's iSCSI software initiator. The iSCSI stack in ESX 5 has been recently overhauled, and it is now easier to set up and offers better performance. The following instructions explain how to set up the iSCSI stack to speak to the HP VSA we just created.

Before you enable the software initiator/adapter in the ESX host you will need to create a VMkernel port group with the correct IP data to communicate to the HP P4000 VSA. Figure 5.28 shows my configuration for esx1 and esx2; notice that the vSwitch has two

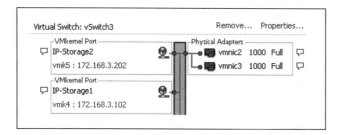

Figure 5.28   Multiple VMkernel ports are only required if you're using multipathing to the iSCSI target. Otherwise, one VMkernel port suffices.

NICs for fault tolerance. In Figure 5.28, I'm using ESX SvSwitches, but there's nothing stopping you from using a DvSwitch if you have access to it. Personally, I prefer to reserve the DvSwitch for virtual machine networking, and use the SvSwitch for any ESX host-specific networking tasks. Remember, ESX 5 introduced a new iSCSI port binding feature that allows you to control multipathing settings within ESX 5. In my case, I created a single SvSwitch with two VMkernel ports, each with its own unique IP configuration, as shown in Figure 5.28. On the properties of each port group (IP-Storage1 and IP-Storage2) I modified the NIC teaming policy such that IP-Storage1 has dedicated access to vmnic2 and IP-Storage2 has dedicated access to vmnic3.

Before proceeding with the configuration of the VMware software initiator/adapter, you might wish to confirm that you can communicate with the HP VSA by using ping and vmkping against the IP address of the Data Mover. Additionally, you might wish to confirm that there are no errors or warnings on the VMkernel port groups you intend to use in the iSCSI Port Binding dialog box, as shown in Figure 5.29.

In ESXi 5 you should not need to manually open the iSCSI software TCP port on the ESXi firewall. The port number used by iSCSI, which is TCP port 3260, should be

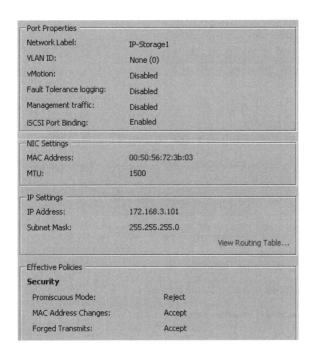

Figure 5.29 With the correct configuration the iSCSI Port Binding policy should switch to an "enabled" status.

automatically opened. However, in previous releases of ESX this sometimes was not done, so I recommend confirming that the port is opened, just in case.

1. In vCenter, select the ESXi host and then the Configuration tab.

2. In the Software tab, select the Security Profile link.

3. On the Firewall category, click the Properties link.

4. In the dialog box that opens, open the TCP port (3260) for the Software iSCSI Client, as shown in Figure 5.30.

   The next step is to add the iSCSI software adapter. In previous releases of ESX this would be generated by default, even if it wasn't required. The new model for iSCSI on ESX 5 allows for better control of its configuration.

5. Click the Storage Adapters link in the Hardware pane, and click Add to create the iSCSI software adapter, as shown in Figure 5.31.

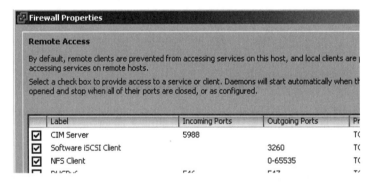

Figure 5.30   Confirming that the Software iSCSI Client port of TCP 3260 is open

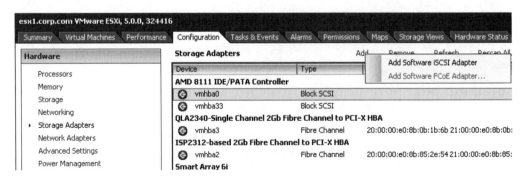

Figure 5.31   Unlike in previous releases, ESXi 5 requires the iSCSI adapter to be added to the host.

6. Once the virtual device has been added, you should be able to select it and choose Properties.

7. In the dialog box that opens, click the Configure button. This will allow you to set your own naming convention for the IQN rather than using the auto-generated one from VMware, as shown in Figure 5.32.

8. The next step is to bind the virtual device to one of the VMkernel ports on the ESX host's vSwitch configuration. In my case, I have a port group named "IP-Storage" which is used for this purpose, as shown in Figure 5.33.

9. Select the Dynamic Discovery tab and click the Add button.

10. Enter the IP address of the iSCSI target in the Add Send Target Server dialog box, as shown in Figure 5.34. In my case, that is serviced by the NIC of the HP VSA of 172.168.3.99.

11. Click OK.

12. Click Close in the main dialog box, and you will be asked if you want to rescan the software iSCSI virtual HBA (in my case, vmhba34). Click Yes.

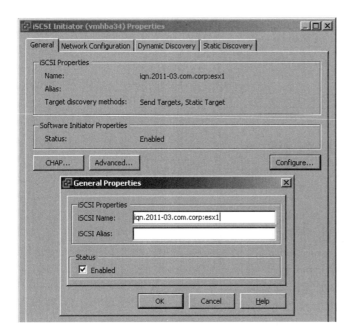

Figure 5.32 While it's not mandatory to change the default IQN, most organizations do prefer to establish their own IQN convention.

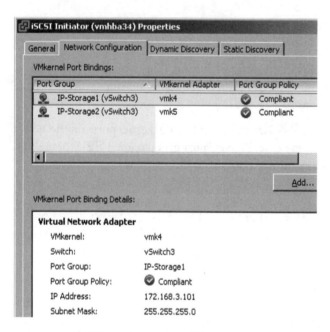

Figure 5.33   VMkernel ports 4 and 5 are compliant and acceptable for use in a multipathing configuration for iSCSI.

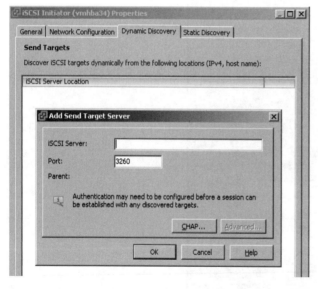

Figure 5.34   Entering the iSCSI target's IP address causes the iSCSI initiator to authenticate to the VSA and request a list of volumes to be returned.

Static discovery is only supported with hardware initiators. Occasionally, I've noticed that some changes to the software iSCSI initiator after this initial configuration may require a reboot of the ESX host, as shown in Figure 5.35. So try to limit your changes where possible, and think through what settings you require up front to avoid this.

Monitoring Your iSCSI Connections

There are many places where you can confirm that you have a valid iSCSI connection. This is important because networks can and do fail. In the first instance, you should be able to see the volume/LUN when you select the virtual iSCSI HBA in the storage adapters in the vSphere client. The properties of the "virtual" HBA—in this case, vmhba32 or vmhba40 (different hosts return a different "virtual" HBA number)—and the Manage Paths dialog box will display a green diamond to indicate a valid connection, together with other meaningful information which will help you identify the volumes returned. However, more specifically you can see the status of your iSCSI connections from the VSA's management console.

1. Expand the NYC_Group.

2. Select the NYC_Cluster.

3. Select the Volumes and Snapshots node.

4. Select the volume in the list and then click the iSCSI Sessions tab.

   In my case, there are four sessions: two for each ESX host, as shown in Figure 5.36. This is because my ESX hosts have two VMkernel ports for IP storage communications, and this allows me to have a true multipathing configuration for the iSCSI storage.

The HP StorageWorks P4000 VSA: Creating a Test Volume at the Recovery Site

I want to confirm that my ESX hosts at the Recovery Site can communicate with my second VSA. To do this I'm going to create and give them access to a blank LUN so that

Figure 5.35 Significant changes to the software iSCSI initiator in ESX can require a reboot to take effect.

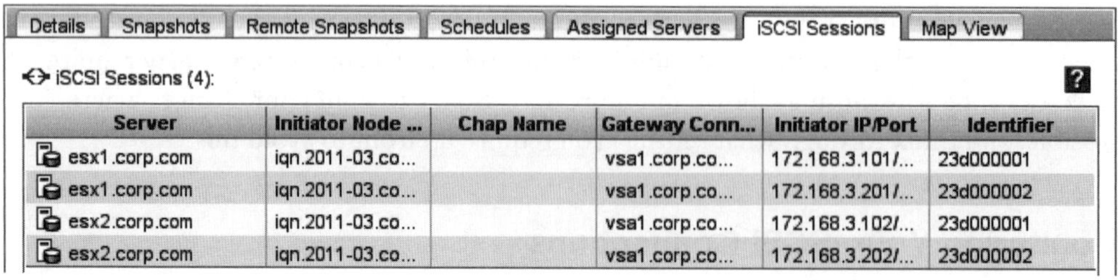

| Details | Snapshots | Remote Snapshots | Schedules | Assigned Servers | iSCSI Sessions | Map View |

iSCSI Sessions (4):

Server	Initiator Node ...	Chap Name	Gateway Conn...	Initiator IP/Port	Identifier
esx1.corp.com	iqn.2011-03.co...		vsa1.corp.co...	172.168.3.101/...	23d000001
esx1.corp.com	iqn.2011-03.co...		vsa1.corp.co...	172.168.3.201/...	23d000002
esx2.corp.com	iqn.2011-03.co...		vsa1.corp.co...	172.168.3.102/...	23d000001
esx2.corp.com	iqn.2011-03.co...		vsa1.corp.co...	172.168.3.202/...	23d000002

Figure 5.36 Multipathing configurations will result in the appearance of multiple sessions to the iSCSI target system.

I am satisfied that they all see this "test" volume. For Recovery Plans to work, the ESX hosts in the Recovery Site (New Jersey) need to be listed in the management system. However, they do not need to be manually assigned access to the replicated volumes; that's something the HP SRA will do automatically whenever we carry out a test or a run of the Recovery Plan. Essentially, the following steps repeat the configuration carried out on the Protected Site (New York), but for a different VSA and different ESX hosts.

1. Open the HP Centralized Management Console.

2. Select the NJ_Group and log on.

3. Expand the Cluster node and the Volumes node.

4. Right-click +Volumes and choose New Volume.

5. In the New Volume dialog box, enter a volume name such as "TestVolume".

6. Enter a volume size, making sure it is more than 2GB. Although we will not be formatting this LUN, ESX itself cannot format a volume that is less than 2GB in size.

   Figure 5.37 shows the result of these steps. Note that hosts in the Recovery Site must be configured with the iSCSI target IP address of the VSA in the site. The SRA will handle the mounting of volumes and authentication requirements.

7. Click OK.

Next you would add your servers to the HP VSA at the Recovery Site, and then assign the volumes to them. These are precisely the same steps I've documented earlier, so I won't repeat them here. At the end of this process, all the ESX hosts in the Recovery Site (New Jersey) should be able to see the TestVolume from the HP VSA.

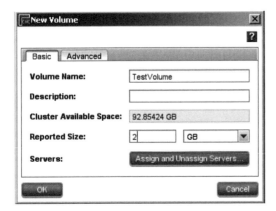

Figure 5.37 Creating a test volume at the Recovery Site

Shutting Down the VSA

It is recommended that you use the VSA management console to take a VSA offline. To do so, follow these steps.

1. Right-click the VSA in the Storage Nodes.

2. In the menu that opens, select Power Off or Reboot.

Alternatively, you can right-click the management group that contains the VSA and select Shutdown from there. This will perform an orderly shutdown of all the VSAs within a management group. Essentially, this places the VSA into a maintenance mode when it is powered on again to prevent data corruption.

Summary

In this chapter I briefly showed you how to set up a 60-day evaluation copy of the virtual appliance that is suitable for use with VMware SRM. We set up two HP P4000 VSAs and then configured them for "Schedule Remote Copy." Lastly, we connected an ESX host to that storage. It's worth saying that once you understand how the VSA works the configuration is much the same for physical P4000 storage arrays.

From this point onward, I recommend that you format the volume/LUN with VMFS and create virtual machines. You might wish to do this so that you have some test VMs to use with VMware SRM. SRM is designed to only pick up on LUNs/volumes that are formatted with VMFS and contain virtual machine files. In previous releases, if you had a VMFS volume that was blank it wouldn't be displayed in the SRM Array Manager Configuration Wizard. This was apparently a frequent error people had with SRM, but one that I rarely saw, mainly because I always ensured that my replicated VMFS volumes had virtual machines contained on them. I don't see any point in replicating empty VMFS volumes! In SRM, the Array Manager Configuration Wizard now displays this error if you fail to populate the datastore with virtual machines. In my demonstrations, I mainly used virtual disks. VMware's RDM feature is fully supported by SRM. I will be covering RDMs later in this book because it is an extremely popular VMware feature.

Since the release of ESX 3.5 and vCenter 2.5, you have been able to relocate the virtual machine swap file (.vswp) onto different datastores, rather than locating it in the default location. A good tip is to relocate the virtual machine's swap file onto shared but not replicated storage. This will reduce the amount of replication bandwidth needed. It does not reduce the amount of disk space used at the Recovery Site, as this will be automatically generated on the storage at the Recovery Site.

Chapter 6

Getting Started with NetApp SnapMirror

In this chapter you will learn the basics of configuring replication with NetApp storage. As with previous chapters, this chapter is not intended to be the definitive last word on all the best practices or caveats associated with the procedures outlined. Instead, it is intended to be a quick-start guide outlining the minimum requirements for testing and running a Recovery Plan with SRM. For your particular requirements, you should at all times consult further documentation from NetApp and, if you have them, your storage teams.

NetApp currently only provides a virtual storage appliance (VSA) or software version of its arrays through OEM solutions with blade server vendors. This is unlike other storage vendors that provide publicly available VSAs for the community with which to test and learn. However, NetApp training course attendees can acquire the NetApp ONTAP Simulator that runs inside a VMware virtual machine. As I have access to the real deal in my lab environment, and since the ONTAP Simulator is not publicly downloadable, I've chosen to not cover the setup of the Simulator. If you do have access to it, Cormac Hogan on the Viops.com website has created a quick guide to getting started with it:

> http://viops.vmware.com/home/docs/DOC-1603

NetApp is probably best known for providing physical storage arrays that offer data deduplication and for advocating the use of NFS with VMware. Actually, NetApp's physical storage appliances are a unified array, which means they support multiple storage protocols including Fibre Channel, Fibre Channel over Ethernet, and iSCSI SANs as well as NFS and SMB (a.k.a. CIFS) NAS connectivity.

At the time of this writing, my sources at NetApp are assuring me that a NetApp simulator should appear sometime after the release of Data ONTAP 8.1. NetApp has made a VSA available via an OEM partner, Fujitsu, which is including it with a new blade chassis. For more details, consult Vaughn Stewart's blog post on the subject:

http://blogs.netapp.com/virtualstorageguy/2010/12/netapp-releases-our-first-virtual-storage-array.html

In 2011, NetApp very kindly updated my lab environment from two NetApp FAS2020 systems to two FAS2040 systems (see Figure 6.1). They are racked up in my collocation facility, and they look very much like two 2U servers with vertically mounted disks behind the bezel. From what I understand, once you know one NetApp filer, you know them all. As such, what we cover in this chapter should apply to all NetApp deployments, large and small. Maybe this is what NetApp means when it says it offers a "unified storage array"?

In the main, I manage the FAS2040 systems using the NetApp System Manager, shown in Figure 6.2. The System Manager application allows you to see all your NetApp systems from one window, and its management console is very friendly. It was recently updated to enable the configuration of SnapMirror replication between multiple arrays. This new version is Web-based (in previous incarnations it was built around the Microsoft

Figure 6.1   A NetApp FAS2040 array

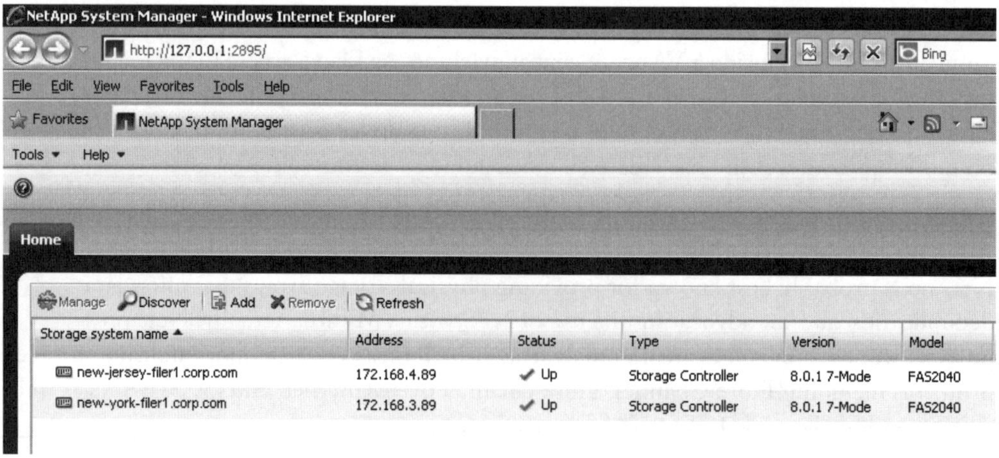

NetApp System Manager - Windows Internet Explorer					
http://127.0.0.1:2895/				Bing	
File Edit View Favorites Tools Help					
Favorites NetApp System Manager					
Tools ▼ Help ▼					
Home					
Manage Discover Add Remove Refresh					
Storage system name ▲	Address	Status	Type	Version	Model
new-jersey-filer1.corp.com	172.168.4.89	✔ Up	Storage Controller	8.0.1 7-Mode	FAS2040
new-york-filer1.corp.com	172.168.3.89	✔ Up	Storage Controller	8.0.1 7-Mode	FAS2040

Figure 6.2   The NetApp System Manager looks set to replace the older FilerView management interface.

Management Console format) and is intended to replace the older FilerView which is a Web-based administration tool natively built into NetApp filers. You can add NetApp filers into the System Manager through the Discover Storage Systems Wizard that scans your IP network ranges, or you can click the Add button to include your arrays based on hostname or IP address.

In Figure 6.2, which is a screen grab of the NetApp System Manager console, you can see that I have two NetApp FAS2040 systems (new-york-filer1.corp.com and new-jersey-filer1.corp.com). I will create a volume called "virtualmachines" on the New York filer and configure it to replicate the data to the New Jersey filer using NetApp SnapMirror. This is a very simple setup indeed, but it is enough to get us started with the SRM product. Later I will cover NetApp support for block-based storage using Fibre Channel and iSCSI. Of course, it's up to you which storage protocol you use, so choose your flavor, and once you're happy, head off to the Configuring NetApp SnapMirror section later in this chapter.

Provisioning NetApp NFS Storage for VMware ESXi

Every NetApp storage system has the ability to serve storage over multiple protocols, so you can attach storage to ESXi/ESXi servers and clusters over NFS, Fibre Channel, FCoE, and iSCSI all from one NetApp box (actually, a LUN can have simultaneous access with FC, FCoE, and iSCSI—that's wild!). To make provisioning a lot faster, NetApp has created a vCenter plug-in called the Virtual Storage Console (VSC) which, in addition to cloning virtual machines, lets you create, resize, and deduplicate datastores and storage volumes, including securing access and setting multipathing policies. Figure 6.3 shows the possible storage options within NetApp with virtualization in mind.

I should point out that NetApp's official stance on this issue is that the VSC is the recommended means for provisioning datastores to vSphere hosts and clusters. I will show you both the manual provisioning process and the automated—and frankly, quite simple—plug-in process.

To begin I will show you how to provision storage the old-fashioned way. The process will be slightly different depending on whether you're provisioning NFS or LUNs, so we'll cover those in separate sections.

In addition to virtual disks, it is possible to provide guest-connected storage directly to a VM via a storage initiator inside the guest OS. This can be accomplished with a software-based initiator for iSCSI LUNs or NFS/SMB network shares over the VM network. Storage presented in this manner is unknown to the VMware Site Recovery Manager, and as such it will not be covered in this book. In addition to these limitations, guest-connected storage requires one to connect the VM network to the storage

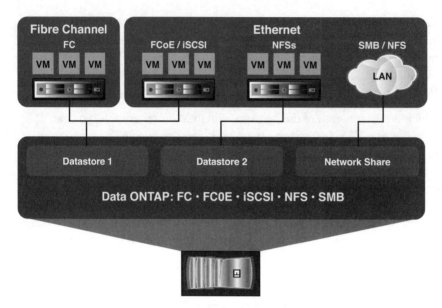

Figure 6.3   The range of different protocols and file systems supported by NetApp

Source: Image by Vaughn Stewart; reprinted with permission from NetApp.

network. For many environments, such a requirement is considered a security risk, and
therefore is not recommended.

Creating a NetApp Volume for NFS

NetApp uses a concept called "aggregates" to describe a collection or pool of physical disk
drives of similar size and speed. The aggregate provides data protection in the form of
RAID-DP, which is configured automatically. In my case, aggr0 is a collection of drives
used to store Data ONTAP, which is the operating system that runs on all NetApp storage
systems. Aggr1 is the remainder of my storage, which I will use to present datastores to the
ESXi hosts in the New York site. To create a datastore you begin by creating a volume,
sometimes referred to as a FlexVol, after you log in to the NetApp System Manager GUI
management tool.

1. Open the NetApp System Manager.

2. Double-click the filer, and log in with the username "root" and your own password.
   In my case, the password is new-york-Filer1.corp.com.

3. Expand the Storage node and select the Volumes icon.

4. Click the Create button. This will open the Create Volume box.

5. Enter the name of the volume. I called mine "vol1_virtualmachines."

6. Select the aggregate that will hold the volume. I selected aggr1.

7. Ensure that the storage type is NAS.

8. The next part of the dialog consists of several options. In my case, I wanted to create a volume that the ESXi host would see as 100GB with 0% reserved on top for temporary snapshot space. The Create Volume dialog box allows you to indicate whether you want to guarantee space for a volume or whether you would like it to be thinly provisioned. The Options tab within the dialog box also allows you to enable data deduplication for the volume, as shown in Figure 6.4. Make your selections as befits your requirements in your environment.

9. Click the Create button to create the volume.

The next step is to give our ESXi hosts rights to the volume. By default, when you create a volume in NetApp it auto-magically makes that volume available using NFS. However, the permissions required to make the volume accessible do need to be modified. As you might know, ESXi hosts must be granted access to the NFS export by their IP address, and they also need "root" access to the NFS export.

We can modify the client permissions to allow the IP addresses used by ESXi hosts in the New York Protected Site. To do this, select the Exports icon, held within the Volumes node. Select the volume to be modified—in my case, vol1_virtualmachines—and click the

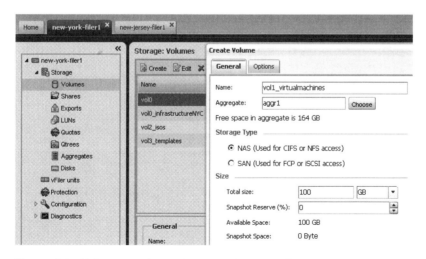

Figure 6.4 Volume creation options available in the Create Volume dialog box

Add button; then enter the IP addresses that reflect your ESXi hosts' VMkernel ports for IP storage. Remember, in the case of ESXi, for an NFS export to be successfully accessed it should be mounted with "root access," so make sure you include these permissions on export, as shown in Figure 6.5.

> **TIP**
>
> Some may find it easier to export the FlexVols created to the IP subnet of the VMkernel ports. This method allows one entry that provides access to all nodes on the storage network. To accomplish this, enter a client address in the following format: 172.168.3.0/24.

This graphical process can become somewhat long-winded if you have lots of volumes and ESXi hosts to manage. You might prefer the command-line options to handle this at the NetApp filer itself. For example, you can create a new volume with the following command:

```
vol create vol1_virtualmachines aggr1 100g
```

Once created, the volume can be "exported" for NFS access and made available to specific IP VMkernel ports within ESXi with this command:

```
exportfs -p rw=172.168.3.101,root=172.168.3.102 /vol/vol1_virtualmachines
```

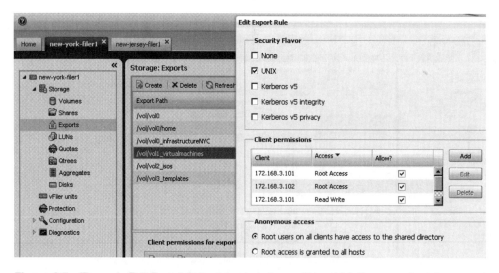

Figure 6.5 The main Edit Export Rule dialog box from within which the correct privileges and rights can be assigned

Or it can be made available to an entire subnet of ESXi hosts with this command:

```
exportfs -p rw=172.168.3.0/24,root=172.168.3.0/24 /vol/vol1_virtualmachines
```

Finally, log in to the filer in the Recovery Site—in my case, this is new-jersey-filer1.corp. com—and repeat this volume creation process. This volume at the Recovery Site will be used to receive updates from the Protected Site NetApp filer (new-york-filer1.corp.com). The only difference in my configuration was that I decided to call the volume "vol1_ replica_of_virtualmachines." This volume at the Recovery Site must be the same size or larger than the volume previously created for SnapMirror to work. So watch out with the MB/GB pull-down lists, as it's quite easy to create a volume that's 100MB, which then cannot receive updates from a volume that's 100GB. It sounds like a pretty idiotic mistake to make, and it's easily corrected by resizing the volume, but you'd be surprised at how easily it occurs. (I know because I have done it quite a few times!) The important thing to remember here is that we only need to set NFS export permissions on the volume in the Protected Site, as the Site Recovery Manager, with the NetApp SRA, will handle setting the export permissions for the SnapMirror destination volume, and will automatically mount the NFS exports whenever you test or run an SRM Recovery Plan.

Granting ESXi Host Access to NetApp NFS Volumes

The next stage is to mount the virtualmachines volume we created on the Protected Site NetApp filer (new-york-filer1). Before you mount an NFS export at the ESXi host you will need to create a VMkernel port group if you have not already done so, configured with the correct IP addresses to communicate to the NetApp filer. Figure 6.6 shows my configuration for ESXi1 and ESXi2; notice that the vSwitch has two NICs for fault tolerance. Before proceeding with the next part of the configuration, you might wish to confirm that you can communicate with the NetApp filer by conducting a simple test using ping and vmkping.

1. In vCenter, select the ESXi host and click the Configuration tab.

2. In the Hardware pane, select the Storage link.

3. Click the Add Storage link in the far right-hand corner.

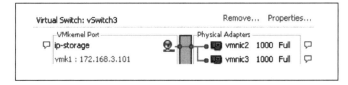

Figure 6.6 VMkernel port with an IP address valid for connecting to the NetApp array on a vSwitch backed by two vmnics for fault tolerance

4. Select Network File System in the dialog box.

5. Enter the IP address or name of the Protected Site filer.

6. Enter the name of the volume using "/vol/" as the prefix. In my case, this is "/vol/vol1_virtualmachines," as shown in Figure 6.7.

   Note that if you have in excess of eight NFS exports to mount you will need to increase the `NFS.MaxVolumes` parameter in the advanced settings. Mounting many NFS exports to many ESX hosts using the GUI is quite tedious and laborious, so you may wish to use a PowerCLI script with a `foreach` loop instead.

7. Enter a friendly datastore name. I used "netapp-virtualmachines."

Although the FQDN would have worked in the Add Storage Wizard, I prefer to use a raw IP address. I've found the mounting and browsing of NFS datastores to be much quicker if I use an IP address instead of an FQDN in the dialog box. Although, quite frankly, this might have more to do with my crazy DNS configurations in my lab environment—within one week, my lab environment can have up to four different identities! From this point onward, I'm sticking with "corp.com." At the end of the day, you may prefer to use specific IP addresses—as the NetApp filer can listen for inbound connections on many interfaces. By using an IP you will be more certain which interface is being used.

The next stage is to configure these NFS volumes to be replicated with SnapMirror. If you know you won't be using another storage protocol with ESXi, such as Fibre Channel and iSCSI, you can skip the next section which explains how to configure these storage types.

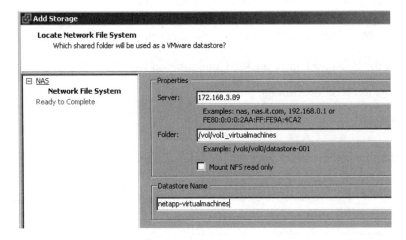

Figure 6.7   Naming the volume

Creating NetApp Volumes for Fibre Channel and iSCSI

Storage presented over Fibre Channel and iSCSI provides block-based access; this means the host will see what appears to be a disk drive and will allow you to use VMware's own file system, VMFS. To achieve this, many storage vendors carve out areas from their physical disk drives into logical units (LUNs). NetApp takes a slightly different approach. Instead, LUNs are created inside flexible volumes, which allows for features such as deduplication to work with LUNs. By default, the iSCSI stack on a NetApp filer is not enabled by default, so I will begin with steps for enabling it.

1. Open the NetApp System Manager and connect to the NetApp filer. Expand the Configuration node, and select the Protocols icon and then the iSCSI icon; then click the Start button to enable the iSCSI service, as shown in Figure 6.8.

    If you wanted to use Fibre Channel connectivity, you would need to start the FCP service that is just below the iSCSI interface in the System Manager. Of course, with the FCP you would have to make sure the appropriate zoning was configured at the FC-switch to allow your ESXi hosts the ability to "see" the NetApp filer with this protocol.

    Before we try to create a new LUN, it's worth setting up the initiator groups that will allow the ESXi hosts access to the LUNs. NetApp allows you to create groups that, in turn, contain either the IQN of each host (if it is the iSCSI protocol) or the WWN (if it is the Fiber Channel protocol).

2. To create these groups select the Storage node, and then select LUNs and the Initiator Groups tab. Click the Create button to create the group and add the appropriate information. Give the group a friendly name, and indicate the system used—in my case, VMware—and the protocol required. Use the Initiators tab to input the IQN or WWN as required, as shown in Figure 6.9. Figure 6.10 shows the IQNs of two ESX hosts: esx1 and esx2.

Figure 6.8 The status of the iSCSI service on a NetApp array

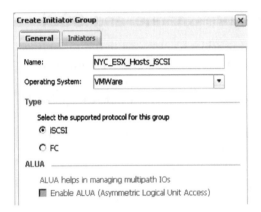

Figure 6.9   The Create Initiator Group dialog box which can be configured to contain either IQN or WWN values

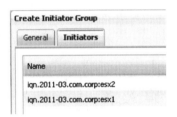

Figure 6.10   The IQNs of two ESX hosts: esx1 and esx2

The next step is to create a LUN to be presented to the ESXi hosts listed in
the initiator group we just created. Remember, in NetApp the LUN resides in
"volumes" to allow for advanced functionality. Fortunately, the Create LUN Wizard
will create both at the same time.

3. Select the Storage node, and then select LUNs and the LUN Management tab; click
   the Create button to start the wizard. Give the LUN a friendly name, set the host
   type, and specify its size, as shown in Figure 6.11. Click Next.

4. Select which aggregate (array of physical disks) to use, and create a new volume for
   the LUN to reside within it, as shown in Figure 6.12.

5. Allocate the new LUN to the appropriate group. In my case, this is the NYC_ESX_
   Hosts_iSCSI group, as shown in Figure 6.13. Click Next and then click Finish; the
   wizard creates the volume and the LUN and allocates the group to the volume.

Now that we've created a LUN and presented it to our ESXi server, we can create a
datastore to use the LUN.

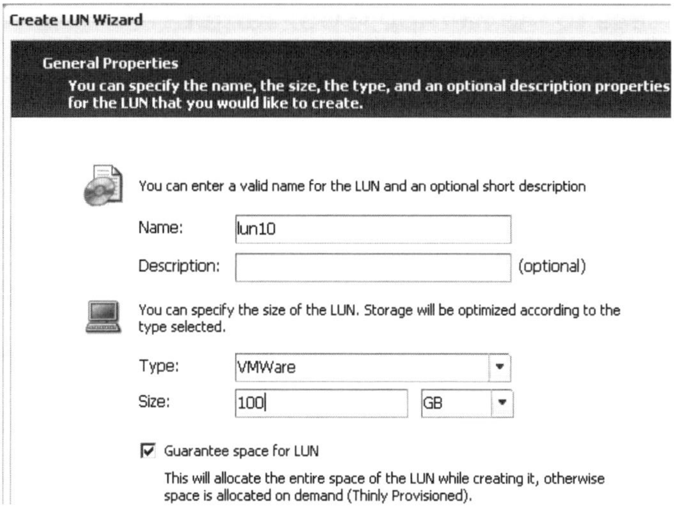

Create LUN Wizard

General Properties
You can specify the name, the size, the type, and an optional description properties for the LUN that you would like to create.

You can enter a valid name for the LUN and an optional short description

Name: lun10

Description: (optional)

You can specify the size of the LUN. Storage will be optimized according to the type selected.

Type: VMWare

Size: 100   GB

☑ Guarantee space for LUN
This will allocate the entire space of the LUN while creating it, otherwise space is allocated on demand (Thinly Provisioned).

Figure 6.11   Creating lun10, at 100GB in size and using a type of "VMware"

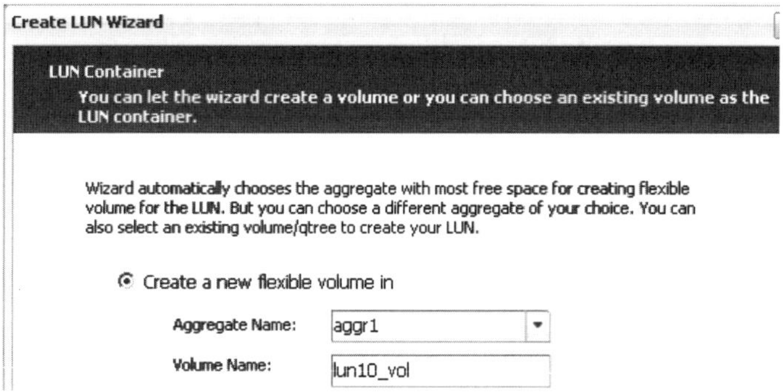

Create LUN Wizard

LUN Container
You can let the wizard create a volume or you can choose an existing volume as the LUN container.

Wizard automatically chooses the aggregate with most free space for creating flexible volume for the LUN. But you can choose a different aggregate of your choice. You can also select an existing volume/qtree to create your LUN.

⊙ Create a new flexible volume in

Aggregate Name: aggr1

Volume Name: lun10_vol

Figure 6.12   Selecting an aggregate and creating a new volume for the LUN to reside within it

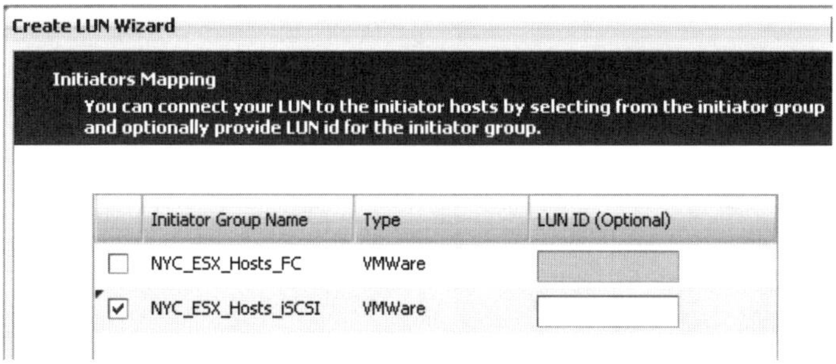

Create LUN Wizard

Initiators Mapping
You can connect your LUN to the initiator hosts by selecting from the initiator group and optionally provide LUN id for the initiator group.

	Initiator Group Name	Type	LUN ID (Optional)
☐	NYC_ESX_Hosts_FC	VMWare	
☑	NYC_ESX_Hosts_iSCSI	VMWare	

Figure 6.13   The LUN being bound to the initiator group created earlier

Granting ESXi Host Access to the NetApp iSCSI Target

Now that we have created the iSCSI LUN it's a good idea to enable the software iSCSI target on the ESXi hosts, and grant the hosts access based on the iSCSI IQN we assign to them. If you have a dedicated iSCSI hardware adapter you can configure your IP settings and IQN directly on the card. One advantage of this is that if you wipe your ESXi host, your iSCSI settings remain on the card; however, they are quite pricey. Therefore, many VMware customers prefer to use the ESXi host's iSCSI software initiator. The iSCSI stack in ESXi 5 was recently overhauled, and it is now easier to set up and offers better performance. The following instructions explain how to set it up to speak to the NetApp iSCSI target we just created.

Before you enable the software initiator/adapter in the ESXi host, you will need to create a VMkernel port group with the correct IP data to communicate to the NetApp iSCSI target. Figure 6.14 shows my configuration for ESXi1 and ESXi2; notice that the vSwitch has two NICs for fault tolerance. In Figure 6.14 I'm using ESXi Standard vSwitches (SvSwitches), but there's nothing stopping you from using a Distributed vSwitch (DvSwitch) if you have access to it. Personally, I prefer to reserve the DvSwitch for virtual machine networking, and use the SvSwitch for any ESXi host-specific networking tasks. Remember, ESXi 5 introduced a new iSCSI port binding feature that allows you to control multipathing settings within ESXi 5. In my case, I created a single SvSwitch with two VMkernel ports each with their own unique IP configuration. On the properties of each port group (IP-Storage1 and IP-Storage2) I modified the NIC teaming policy such that IP-Storage1 has dedicated access to vmnic2 and IP-Storage2 has dedicated access to vmnic3, as shown in Figure 6.14.

Before proceeding with the configuration of the VMware software initiator/adapter, you might wish to confirm that you can communicate with the NetApp product by using ping and vmkping against the IP address you want to use for NFS on the filer. Additionally, you might wish to confirm that there are no errors or warnings on the VMkernel port groups you intend to use in the iSCSI Port Binding dialog box, as shown in Figure 6.15.

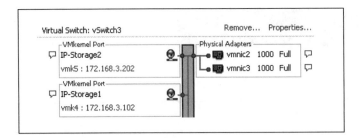

Figure 6.14   The configuration for multipathing for iSCSI connections

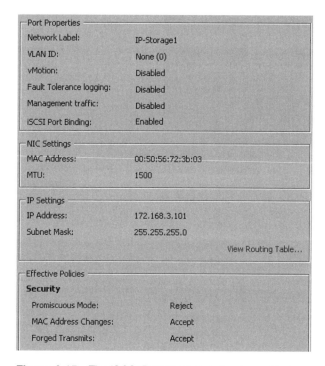

Port Properties
Network Label: IP-Storage1
VLAN ID: None (0)
vMotion: Disabled
Fault Tolerance logging: Disabled
Management traffic: Disabled
iSCSI Port Binding: Enabled

NIC Settings
MAC Address: 00:50:56:72:3b:03
MTU: 1500

IP Settings
IP Address: 172.168.3.101
Subnet Mask: 255.255.255.0
                          View Routing Table...

Effective Policies
Security
  Promiscuous Mode: Reject
  MAC Address Changes: Accept
  Forged Transmits: Accept

Figure 6.15   The iSCSI Port Binding policy is enabled, meaning the host is in a fit state to support iSCSI multipathing.

In ESXi 5 you should not need to manually open the iSCSI software TCP port on the ESXi firewall. The port number used by iSCSI, which is TCP port 3260, should be automatically opened (see Figure 6.16). However, in previous releases of ESX this sometimes was not done, so I recommend confirming that the port is open, just in case.

1. In vCenter, select the ESXi host and then select the Configuration tab.

2. In the Software tab, select the Security Profile link.

3. On the Firewall category, click the Properties link.

4. In the dialog box that opens, open the TCP port (3260) for the iSCSI software client.

   The next step is to add the iSCSI software adapter. In previous releases of ESXi this would be generated by default, even if it wasn't required. The new model for iSCSI on ESXi 5 allows for better control of its configuration.

5. Click the Storage Adapters link in the Hardware pane, and click Add to create the iSCSI software adapter, as shown in Figure 6.17.

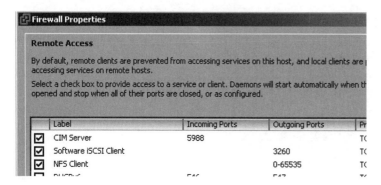

Figure 6.16   By default, ESXi 5 opens iSCSI port 3260 automatically.

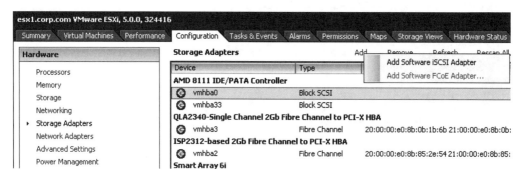

Figure 6.17   In ESXi 5 you must now add a software iSCSI adapter. Previously the "vmhba" alias was created when you enabled the feature.

6. Once the virtual device has been added, you should be able to select it and choose Properties.

7. In the dialog box that opens, click the Configure button. This will allow you to set your own naming convention for the IQN rather than using the auto-generated one from VMware, as shown in Figure 6.18.

8. Bind the virtual device to one of the VMkernel ports on the ESXi host's vSwitch configuration. In my case, I have a port group named "IP-Storage" that is used for this purpose, as shown in Figure 6.19.

9. Select the Dynamic Discovery tab, and click the Add button.

10. Enter the IP address of the iSCSI target (as shown in Figure 6.20) that is serviced by the interface of your NetApp filer—in my case, this is 172.168.3.89.

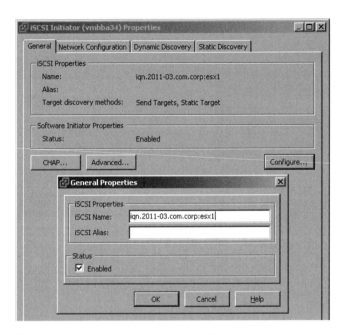

Figure 6.18   Using a combination of IP addresses and CHAP as the main authentication method to the array

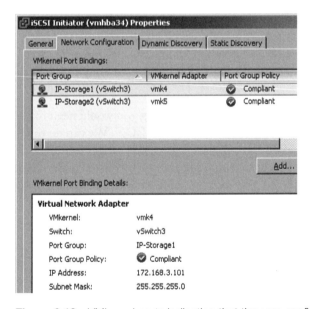

Figure 6.19   VMkernel ports indicating that they are configured correctly for iSCSI multipathing

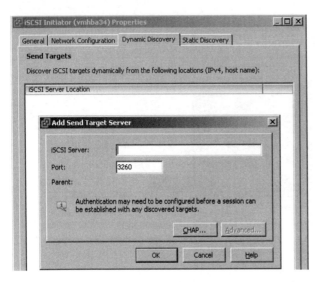

Figure 6.20   The Add Send Target Server dialog box, where you input the IP address of the interface on the array listening for inbound iSCSI connections

11. Click OK.

12. Click Close in the main dialog box. You will be asked if you want to rescan the software iSCSI virtual HBA (in my case, this is vmhba34). Click Yes.

Occasionally, I've noticed that some changes to the software iSCSI initiator after this initial configuration may require a reboot of the ESXi host, as shown in Figure 6.21. So try to limit your changes where possible, and think through what settings you require up front to avoid this.

If you were doing this for the Fibre Channel protocol the first thing you would need to do is to tell the ESXi hosts to rescan their HBAs to detect the new LUN. We can do this from vCenter on the right-click of the cluster. For QLogic HBAs, you might need to rescan a second time before the LUN is detected. You'll see a new LUN listed under the HBA's devices once the rescan has completed. So, once our ESXi server can see our LUN, we can create a new VMFS datastore to use it, as shown in Figure 6.22.

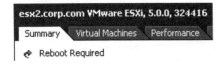

Figure 6.21   Changes to the configuration of the iSCSI initiator can require a reboot to take effect.

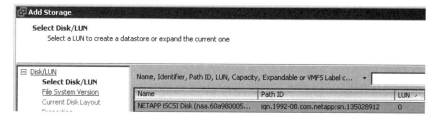

Figure 6.22   The NetApp iSCSI LUN is visible to the ESX host.

Configuring NetApp SnapMirror

SnapMirror is the main data replication feature used with NetApp systems. It can perform synchronous, asynchronous, or semi-synchronous replication in either a Fibre Channel or IP network infrastructure. In this section we will configure SnapMirror to replicate asynchronously between the volumes for NFS and Fibre Channel, which we created earlier on the Protected and Recovery Site filers, but there are a couple of things we need to confirm first.

Confirm IP Visibility (Mandatory) and Name Resolution (Optional)

Before beginning with the setup of replication between the two NetApp filers it's worth confirming that they can see each other through your IP network. I like to enable SSH support on my filers so that I can use PuTTy with them as I do with my ESXi hosts. This means I can carry out interactive commands without resorting to the BMC card. NetApp filers obliviously support the ping command, and using this with both the IP address and the hostname of the Recovery Site NetApp filer (New-Jersey) you can determine whether they can see each other, as well as whether name resolution is correctly configured, as shown in Figure 6.23.

```
172.168.3.89 - PuTTY

login as: root
root@172.168.3.89's password:

new-york-filer1> ping new-jersey-filer1
new-jersey-filer1.corp.com is alive
new-york-filer1>
```

Figure 6.23   Use ping to verify connectivity between your NetApp arrays.

If you fail to receive positive responses in these tests, check out the usual suspects such as your router configuration and IP address. You can check your configuration for DNS under the Configuration node, and the Network and DNS icons, as shown in Figure 6.24.

Enable SnapMirror (Both the Protected and Recovery Filers)

On newly installed NetApp systems, the SnapMirror feature is likely to be disabled. For SnapMirror to function it needs to be licensed and enabled on both systems. You can confirm your licensing status by clicking the Configure link under the SnapMirror node in FilerView. You will need to repeat this task at the Recovery Site NetApp filer (New Jersey) for a new NetApp system.

1. Log in to FilerView by opening a Web browser directly to NetApp's management IP address.

2. Expand the SnapMirror option.

3. Click the Enable/Disable link.

4. Click the Enable SnapMirror button, as shown in Figure 6.25.

Enable Remote Access (Both the Protected and Recovery Filers)

In order for us to configure NetApp SnapMirror we need to allow the filer from the Recovery Site (New Jersey) to access the Protected Site NetApp filer (New York). When we configure this we can use either an IP address or FQDN. Additionally, we can indicate

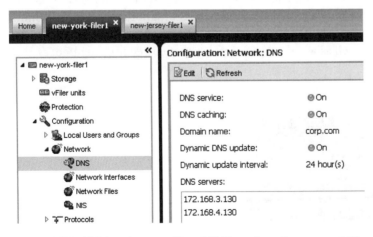

Figure 6.24 Validate that your IP and DNS configurations are valid if you have connectivity problems.

Figure 6.25   Enabling SnapMirror using FilerView

whether the Recovery Site NetApp filer (New Jersey) is allowed remote access to all volumes or just selected ones. In the real world it is highly likely that you would allow remote access in both directions to allow for failover and failback; also, you would do this if your DR strategy had a bidirectional configuration where the New Jersey site was the DR location for New York, and vice versa.

1. Log in to the NetApp System Manager on the Protected Site NetApp filer. In my case, this is new-york-filer1.corp.com.

2. Select the Protection node and then click the Remote Access button, as shown in Figure 6.26.

3. In the Remote Access pop-up window, enter the IP address or name of the Recovery Site NetApp filer (New Jersey) and then click the Add button, as shown in Figure 6.27. You should now be able to browse and direct what volumes the filer in the Recovery Site is able to access.

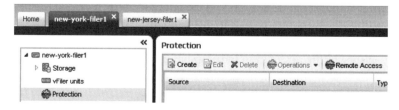

Figure 6.26   Clicking the Remote Access button pairs the two NetApp arrays together.

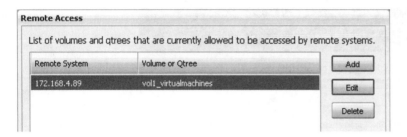

Figure 6.27   Click the Add button in the Remote Access pop-up window to add the volumes that each array will be able to see.

It is possible to add the volume or Qtree by entering in the Edit box the string "All_ volumes", which allows each filer access to all the volumes on the Recovery Site filer. You can now repeat this task at the Recovery Site NetApp filer (New Jersey) to allow the Protected Site access to the Recovery Site's volumes.

TIP

While it is possible to create Qtree–SnapMirror relationships, NetApp does not recommend their use as datastores with VMware. It seems Qtree SnapMirror is not dedupe-enabled as Volume SnapMirror is. This setting can reduce bandwidth requirements considerably. Note that all SnapMirror replications can enable compression for additional bandwidth savings.

Configure SnapMirror on the Recovery Site NetApp Filer (New Jersey)

The next step is to log on to the NetApp filer on the Recovery Site (New Jersey), and enable the replication. We'll need to restrict our destination volume in the Recovery Site so that only SnapMirror can make changes to it. Then we can create the SnapMirror relationship. The important thing to notice here is how the configuration to enable SnapMirror is focused on the Recovery Site filer. Initially, it might feel odd that the SnapMirror configuration is controlled at the Recovery Site NetApp filer (New Jersey), and that in the wizard you specify the destination location before the source location. But if you think about it, in a real DR event the destination location is where you would be managing the storage layer from the DR location.

To enable the replication, follow these steps.

1. In the NetApp System Manager, open a window on the Recovery Site filer. In my case, this is the New Jersey NetApp filer.

2. Expand the Storage node and select the Volumes icon; then locate the destination volumes, right-click, and under the Status menu select the Restrict option, as shown in Figure 6.28.

    This restricted process is required when SnapMirror is being configured and the mirror is being initialized. Once initialization is complete, it will be marked as online.

3. Select the Protection node, and click the Create button to add a new mirror relationship, as shown in Figure 6.29.

Figure 6.28   The volume must be in a restricted mode to allow the initial configuration of SnapMirror to complete.

Figure 6.29   The Protection node on the source NetApp filer in the New Jersey location

4. In the Create Mirror Wizard select the radio button that reads "Select system *<name of your NetApp filer>* as destination system for the new mirror relationship to be created" if it is not already selected (see Figure 6.30).

5. In the System Name and Credentials page of the wizard select the source NetApp filer that will send updates to the Recovery Site, as shown in Figure 6.31.

6. Select the volume at the source location. In my case, this is the New York filer. Using the Browse button you can view the volumes on the filer and select the one you want. In my case, this is vol1_virtualmachines, as shown in Figure 6.32.

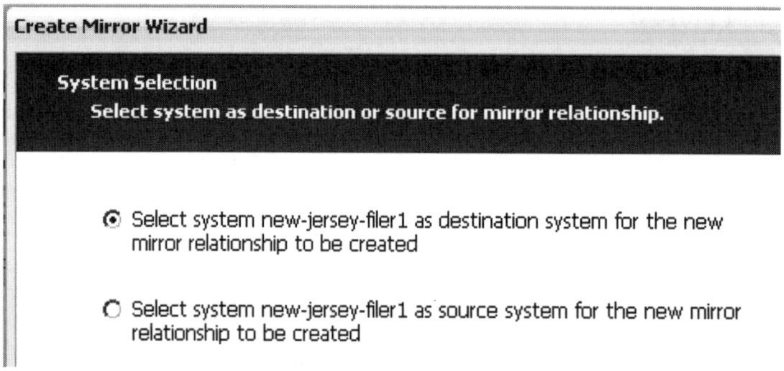

Create Mirror Wizard

System Selection
Select system as destination or source for mirror relationship.

⦿ Select system new-jersey-filer1 as destination system for the new mirror relationship to be created

○ Select system new-jersey-filer1 as source system for the new mirror relationship to be created

Figure 6.30   Selecting the system as the destination for the mirror relationship

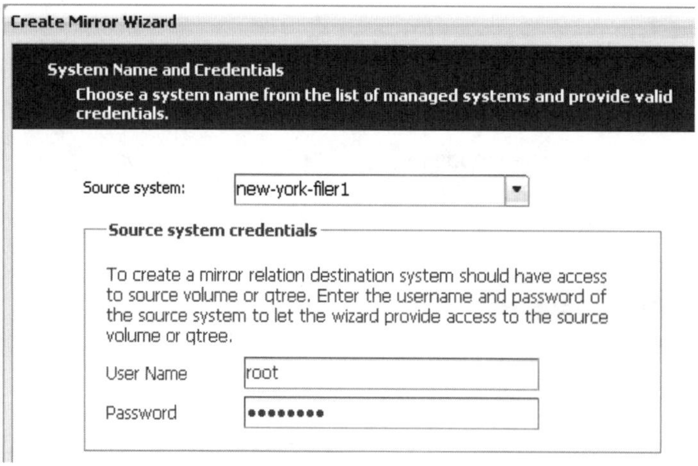

Create Mirror Wizard

System Name and Credentials
Choose a system name from the list of managed systems and provide valid credentials.

Source system: new-york-filer1 ▾

Source system credentials

To create a mirror relation destination system should have access to source volume or qtree. Enter the username and password of the source system to let the wizard provide access to the source volume or qtree.

User Name   root

Password   ••••••••

Figure 6.31   The NetApp System Manager can securely save the root credentials to prevent endless reinput.

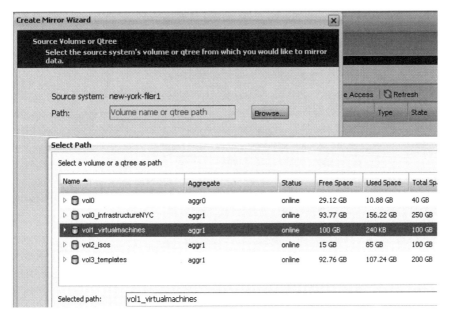

Figure 6.32 Once the volumes are authenticated, the administrator can browse them at the Protected Site and select the one to be mirrored.

7. In the Destination Volume or Qtree Details page of the Create Mirror Wizard, you can select or create the volume at the destination location, as shown in Figure 6.33. In my case, I selected vol1_replica_of_virtualmachines, which I created earlier.

   Notice how the status of the volume is marked as restricted; remember, such volumes must be in this state when configuring SnapMirror for them the first time.

8. Enable the first initialization for SnapMirror and set values for when and how often the replication should take place, as shown in Figure 6.34.

   Clearly, this enables you to control how frequently replication will occur. For DR purposes, you will probably find the daily, weekly, and monthly presets inadequate for your RTO/RPO goals. You might find that using an advanced schedule will allow for great flexibility—replicating or mirroring specific volumes with differing frequencies again based on your RPO/RTO goals. In fact, the interface is just using the "Cron" format, which you may be familiar with from Linux. It is possible to configure the relationship to replicate synchronously or semi-synchronously via the command line.

9. Choose whether to limit the bandwidth available to SnapMirror, or whether to allow unlimited bandwidth, as shown in Figure 6.35.

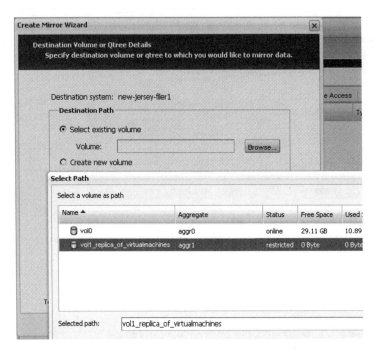

Figure 6.33   Selecting an existing volume as the destination for Snap-Mirror updates. It is possible to create a new volume at this time as well.

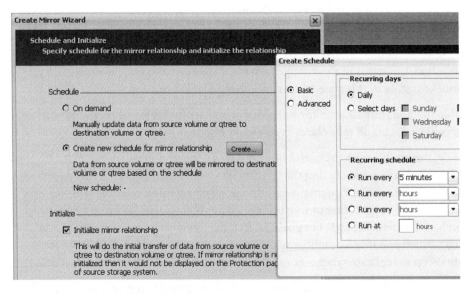

Figure 6.34   Additional options to replicate SnapMirror synchronously are available at the command line.

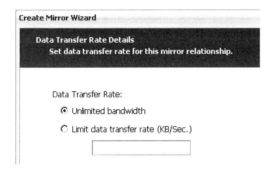

Figure 6.35   NetApp is one of a few vendors that allow you to control both schedule and bandwidth allocations to the SnapMirror process.

In my case bandwidth is not a limitation, but it's important to remember that this factors into your schedule and the number of changes within the cycle to the volume. If you're not careful, you could give SnapMirror a small amount of bandwidth and a very infrequent schedule. In environments where there are many changes in a volume, the replication cycle might never complete. Think of it this way: How would you feel if you were given an excessive amount of work, with no time and insufficient resources? It would leave you with no hope of completing the job by the given deadline.

Introducing the Virtual Storage Console (VSC)

Alongside many other storage vendors NetApp has created its own storage management plug-ins for vCenter. As stated at the beginning of this chapter, NetApp recommends using the VSC as the primary method for provisioning datastores. I can see why; the VSC is very easy to use and reduces the number of configuration steps required in the environment. I think you might prefer to use it on a daily basis for provisioning and managing datastores.

In the context of SRM, the VSC may well speed up the process of initially allocating storage to your ESXi hosts in the Protected Site. Once the datastores are provisioned, it will merely be a case of setting up the appropriate SnapMirror relationship. Who knows; perhaps these storage vendor plug-ins may be extended to allow the configuration of SRM's requirements directly from within vSphere. In addition to provisioning new storage, NetApp VSC also has enhanced "storage views" and the ability to create virtual desktops using array-accelerated cloning technologies.

The NetApp VSC installs as a server-side plug-in, and can be installed along with vCenter or on a separate management server depending on your requirements. After installing the service, you will be required to open a Web page and "register" the VSC with your vCenter. This process enables the extensions to the vSphere client. Once you open the vSphere client, you should see that a NetApp icon is added to the Solutions and Applications section of the "home" location in vCenter, as shown in Figure 6.36.

This icon will allow you to carry out the post-configuration phase that involves updating the plug-in to be aware of the NetApp filers that cover the scope of your vCenter environment. The VSC is currently a collection of plug-ins that were, until recently, historically separate, and they have now been bundled together. As such, each component needs to be made aware of the NetApp filers in your environment. It's likely that in the next release there will be a single shared location from which all the plug-ins retrieve that configuration information. The following core plug-ins cover common administration tasks:

- Virtual Storage Console, which enhances the storage views within vSphere

- Provisioning and Cloning, which allows for the creation of new datastores and virtual machines automated for use as virtual desktop pools with systems such as VMware View and Citrix XenDesktop

- Backup and Recovery, which allows for a schedule of snapshots that can be mounted directly by the administrator and used in the event of the VM being corrupted or deleted

Under the Provisioning and Cloning tab, as shown in Figure 6.37, you can use the Add Storage Controller Wizard to configure the NetApp filer for use by vSphere.

The next page of the Add Storage Controller Wizard includes all the resources available to the NetApp filer. This window allows the administrator to control what resources are available to anyone creating new datastores or virtual desktops. In this rather simple way, it is possible to ensure that VMware administrators only can access the correct IP interface, volumes, and critical aggregates available, as shown in Figure 6.38. In my case, I made sure that my administrators did not have access to aggr0 which is the collection of disks used

Figure 6.36   Registering the NetApp VSC service causes a NetApp icon to be added to the Solutions and Applications section in vCenter.

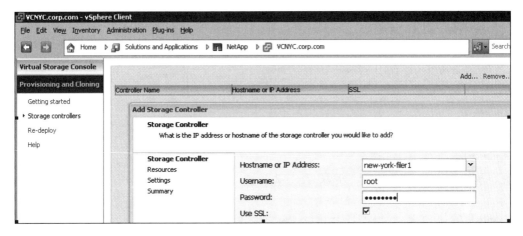

Figure 6.37 Each component of the VSC requires a configuration of the storage controller.

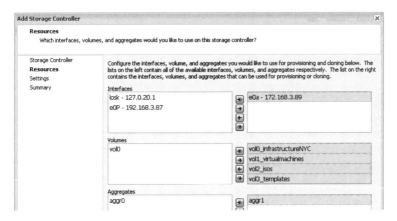

Figure 6.38 Using the field picker, the administrator can control which interfaces, volumes, and aggregates are visible to the VMware admin.

to hold the NetApp ONTAP system image, logs, and so forth, using the "Prevent further changes" option to stop other VMware admins from securing the right to make alterations.

The final part of the wizard allows you to configure advanced defaults, such as whether to allow the NetApp filer to reserve disk space for thinly provisioned volumes. Once this small configuration has been completed, the NetApp VSC will provide you with a sequence of buttons and menu options that let you configure new storage to your VMware clusters. This automates the creation of the volume and mounting of the volume to each ESXi host, as shown in Figure 6.39.

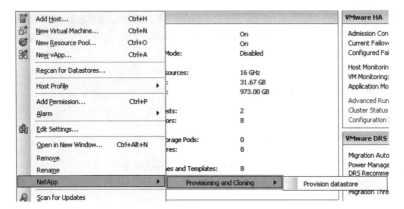

Figure 6.39   VSC provisioning is best targeted at a cluster, which automates volume creation and mounting to the ESX hosts.

If you would like to learn more about the NetApp VSC, I recently conducted a survey of
storage vendor plug-ins and wrote an extended article about the NetApp VSC on my blog:

www.rtfm-ed.co.uk/2011/03/02/using-netapp-vsc/

NOTE

In writing this chapter, I used the latest release of the VSC, Version 2.01. NetApp seems to
update or enhance the VSC with a rather frequent cadence, so you may want to check now,
and thereafter every six months or so, for updates/new releases.

Summary

In this chapter I briefly showed you how to set up NetApp SnapMirror, which is suitable
for use with VMware SRM. We configured two NetApp FAS arrays and then configured
them for replication or for use with SnapMirror. Lastly, we connected an ESXi host to
that storage. Additionally, I showed how the new plug-ins from NetApp allow you to
create volumes and mount them efficiently on the ESXi hosts.

From this point onward, I recommend that you create virtual machines on the NFS mount
point so that you have some test VMs to use with VMware SRM. SRM is designed to
only pick up on LUNs/volumes that are accessible to the ESXi host and contain virtual

machine files. In previous releases of SRM, if you had a volume that was blank it wouldn't be displayed in the SRM Array Manager Configuration Wizard. In the new release, it warns you if this is the case. This was apparently a popular error people had with SRM, but one that I rarely see, mainly because I always ensure that my replicated volumes have virtual machines contained on them. I don't see any point in replicating empty volumes! In my demonstrations, I mainly used virtual disks. VMware's RDM feature is now fully supported by SRM (it wasn't when Version 1.0 was first released). I will be covering RDMs later in this book because it is still an extremely popular VMware feature.

Since ESXi 3.5 and vCenter 2.5, you have been able to relocate the virtual machine swap file (.vswp file) onto different datastores, rather than locating it in the default location. A good tip is to relocate the virtual machine swap file onto shared but not replicated storage. This will reduce the amount of replication bandwidth needed. It does not reduce the amount of disk space used at the Recovery Site, as this will automatically be generated on the storage at the Recovery Site. I would also add that additional storage and replication bandwidth savings can be found by enabling data deduplication on the SAN or NAS datastores and compression in the SnapMirror settings.

Chapter 7

Installing VMware SRM

This chapter covers the installation of the VMware SRM. Before we install the VMware server, though, we'll review the architecture of the VMware SRM and discuss how to set up the VMware SRM database using Microsoft SQL Server 2008.

Architecture of the VMware SRM

Before you begin the process of setting up and configuring SRM for the first time, it's important to understand the structure of the product and its basic requirements. As you can see, there is quite a lot of interprocess communication, with the SRM server needing access to the vCenter at the site and to a database backend, as well as communication to the management layer of the storage array. Additionally, communication is required between the sites, and most likely across firewalls—for both the storage replication traffic as well as the communications from the SRM server at one site to the vCenter of another site. When I first started using SRM some years ago, I assumed these network challenges would be one of my customers' main pain points. It's a testament to how well managed most people's networks are that I discovered this is one of the minor challenges involved in deployment.

Network Communication and TCP Port Numbers

One major challenge of the architecture shown in Figure 7.1 is that the SRM server is likely to reside on one network, but the array management system will quite possibly be

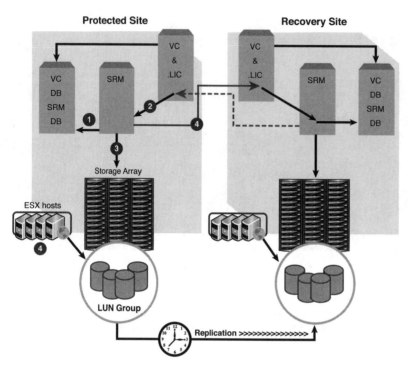

Figure 7.1 A high-level overview of relationships in the VMware Site
Recovery Manager

patched into a different network. In other words, the SRM server has four main communication paths coming to and from it.

- To/from the SRM database backend (SQL or Oracle).
- To/from the storage array via the VMware SRA written by your storage vendor.
- To/from the vCenter.
- To/from the vCenter server at the Recovery Site. This, in turn, communicates to
  the SRM server at the Recovery Site. If you like, vCenter acts as a "proxy" to its
  respective SRM server.

Of course, it is possible to host all these roles in one Windows instance (Database, vCenter,
and SRM). They are represented here as separate roles for clarity, and later to show the port
numbers used. Personally, I prefer to keep all these roles separate with dedicated vCenter,
SQL, and SRM servers in their own unique Windows instance. This means I can adjust the
allocation of virtual resources in the form of CPU and memory more easily.

In some arrays you have the option of presenting to the SRM server the "management" LUN/volume using VMware's SRM feature. This allows you to leverage your storage vendor's management tools natively in the SRM server. Personally, I prefer to use networking to facilitate this communication—although it is possible to do this, for example, with EMC Symmetrix arrays.

The following list explains the callouts in Figure 7.1. This information is also available in VMware Knowledge Base article 1012382, located at http://kb.vmware.com/kb/1012382. In total there are four main communication points to and from the SRM server.

1. The SRM server communicates to the backend database on the proprietary ports encoded for Microsoft SQL, Oracle, or IBM DB2.

2. Since the release of vSphere, there is no "license" server; licenses are merely text strings stored in the main vCenter database. You still need a license for vCenter and ESX hosts in the DR location. However, if you run vCenter in a "linked mode," licenses can be easily transferred between sites. In my case, both the New York and New Jersey sites are licensed. Remember, since September 2010, VMware SRM is now licensed on a per-VM basis with customers buying "bundles" of SRMs. Running SRM with vCenter in a linked mode makes licensing significantly easier; as you failover and failback, the license follows the VM.

    The SRM server is "paired" to the vCenter in its local site during the installation.

3. The SRM server, via its vendor-specific SRA, communicates on a range of ports dictated by the storage vendor. Please consult your vendor-specific documentation for more details.

4. SRM communicates to the vCenters at both the Recovery and Protected Sites on TCP port 443. It communicates to its own vCenter and the vCenter server at the Recovery Site. However, the communication at the Recovery Site is via the vCenter which acts as a proxy between the two SRM servers.

    The SRM service listens on SOAP-based TCP port 8095.

    Users of the vSphere client download the SRM plug-in from the SRM service on a custom HTTP port of 8096.

    If you choose to use the API, communication is on TCP ports 9007 and 9008 (SOAP and custom HTTP, respectively).

When you are configuring the SRM array manager, the SRM uses special SRA software, written by your storage vendor, to discover the LUNs/volumes being replicated. This will be network communication either to the management uplinks on the Fibre Channel array or directly to the management ports on an iSCSI or NFS target. In a production environment, you would need to configure routing or intra-VLAN communication to allow the SRM adapter to communicate with your array. With that said, some storage vendors use a gatekeeper LUN presented to the SRM hosts to allow direct communication to the array. It's well worth it to consult the release notes surrounding the SRA you are using, as well as any ReadMe files.

The other network challenge is to make sure firewalls allow for the vCenter-to-vCenter communication and the SRM-to-SRM communication that inherently exists. Finally, the last challenge is to actually get the two arrays to communicate to each other for the purposes of replication/snapshots. If you decide to deploy VMware replication, you will also need to consider the firewall changes required to allow the transfer of virtual disk changes to the Recovery Site.

Storage Replication Components

SRM assumes that you have two or more geographically dispersed locations. The first is your Protected Site. You might know this better as the primary site, the location where all your business-critical functions exist. If you lose this, the business cannot operate, so an investment is made in a Recovery Site which can be used in the event of such failures. You might know this better as your secondary location, or as your DR/BC location. Quite frequently, companies hire rack space at commercial rates to generate a Recovery Site location if they lack those resources internally in the business. It may also be possible to partner with another business and offer DR resources to each other—you should be aware that this incurs challenges of both security and trust, because to use SRM properly in Company A, the SRM administrator needs rights and privileges in Company B's vCenter.

In my case, I am going to begin by using very clear names for the primary and secondary sites. I'm going to assume that we have a dedicated location for recovery—perhaps we hire rack space for this—and that the failover is unidirectional. That is to say, the primary site always fails over to the secondary site. There is another distinct configuration, which is bidirectional. In this case, the secondary site's DR location is the primary site, and the primary site's DR location is the secondary site. A bidirectional approach would be used in a large business where New York's DR location might be the New Jersey office, and the New Jersey office's DR location would be New York. I will be looking at the configuration of SRM for a bidirectional DR in Chapter 13, Bidirectional Relationships and Shared Site Configurations. Another way to describe the difference between a unidirectional and bidirectional configuration is through more conventional active/standby or active/active terms, although these terms are probably more popular in our industry for describing the relationships we create for high availability. I will stick with the terms *unidirectional* and *bidirectional* because these are also the terms you will find in the official documentation from VMware. The bidirectional configuration does offer up the potential of reducing the impact of a disaster and decreasing the total time to run an SRM Recovery Plan. If you combine SRM with stretched clustered systems that allow for the applications and services to run in both locations, it could mean smaller RTOs and better RPOs than using SRM on its own. With that said, you should consider the complexity of deploying stretched clusters, and the challenges of getting your various application owners to agree on a common standard. In large corporations it's not unheard of for the same application—say, email—to be protected by totally different cluster vendors, although such a situation can hardly be regarded as ideal.

At one of these locations there are ESX hosts with virtual machines that need protection. The Protected Site VMs are being replicated to the protected location on a frequency that is a balance between your bandwidth and your tolerance of loss of data. Put very crudely, the more bandwidth there is between the Protected and Recovery Sites the more frequently you can replicate between the two locations. Most storage vendors do have tools that will assist you in calculating whether you have enough bandwidth in your links between sites to meet your RPO. The calculation is really a factor of three variables: the average rate of change, the link speed, and the percentage of available bandwidth. Once you know how long the replication process will take to complete, you can adjust your frequency to fit within those constraints. Failure to plan this correctly could result in a replication schedule which never completes properly. And I have come across situations where customers have to stop replication from occurring because it never completes because they have such poor bandwidth capabilities between the two locations. If you're looking for an analogy for this, just look at your backup strategy as an example. If your backup strategy is to have at least one day's worth of a complete backup, but the backup process takes more than 24 hours to complete, you have failed to meet your data recovery objective. Indeed, monitoring your backup jobs and measuring the volume of data that is incrementally backed up is a good starting point in measuring the amount of data change. Bear in mind that this might not reflect the data change occurring in smaller subsets of virtual machines that you may wish to protect with SRM. Another possibility to consider is to use your storage vendor's snapshot functionality. You could take a snapshot of a volume, and let it be active for a 24-hour period. At the end of the test, checking the size of the snapshot would give you a feel for the rate of change in the period of the test. If you repeat this snapshot process over the subsequent days and weeks, you could, over time, get a good feel for the volume of data needed to be replicated to the Recovery Site.

When all else fails, you could adopt what some have called "Rate of Change Rule of Thumb" (RCRT). This assumes that the average rate of change on any volume being replicated is 10%. Therefore, a 1TB volume will have a rate of change of 100GB. If you are looking for an example of a third-party vendor-neutral replication bandwidth calculator, the Virtualize-planet website (http://read.virtualizeplanet.com/?p=91) has an interesting application called

ReplicaCalc that you might find useful as a starting point. However, I recommend communicating with your storage vendor in the first instance, as not only will they assist you in finding the relevant statistics, but also they will help you configure your storage replication in the most efficient way relative to the bandwidth you have available.

Larger companies can and often do have a blend of replication technologies and cycles to facilitate shifting the data away from the Protected Site. Perhaps they have high-speed Fibre Channel links between site A and site B, but then use slower network pipes from site B to site C. In this configuration, the replication between site A and site B could be synchronous and with very low latency. So, as a write is being committed to a disk in site A, it is already being written to a disk in site B. Such frequency of replication allows for a very low chance of data loss. The replication from site B to site C will have a larger latency but is frequently selected as the best method of getting the data a significant distance away from the Protected Site while remaining economical. Currently, SRM is limited to a one-to-one pairing of sites, and it is possible to configure what is called a "shared site" setup. This is where one location—say, New Jersey—acts like a DR hub for a range of difficult locations in the vicinity.

VMware Components

Laying these storage considerations to one side, there are a number of VMware components that need to be configured. You may already have some of these components in place if you have been using VMware technologies for some time. At both the Protected and Recovery Sites you need the following.

- ESX 5.0.

- vCenter 5.0.

- A database for the SRM server at the Protected and Recovery Sites. Currently, VMware supports Microsoft SQL Server 2008 Standard or higher (SQL Server Express is supported as well), Oracle 11g Standard Release 1 or higher, and IBM DB2 Express C or higher.

- A protected SRM and recovery SRM instance which runs Windows 2003 SP1 or higher. SRM is certified to run on the 64-bit version of Windows 2003 and Windows 2008.

- An SRM adapter from your storage vendor installed on both SRMs.

- The SRM vSphere Client Management plug-in.

- LUN masking. With this capability, ESX hosts at the Protected Site see "live" LUNs, but the ESX hosts at the Recovery Site only see "replicated" LUNs or snapshots. This allows for tests without interrupting normal operations, and does not interrupt the normal cycle of replication between the two sites.

- DNS name resolution. As with vSphere 4, generally it is recommended that you thoroughly test all methods of name resolution: short hostnames, long FQDNs, and reverse lookups.

This is just a general list of requirements. For a more specific and comprehensive list, including specific patches, read the documents at the following Web page:

www.vmware.com/support/pubs/srm_pubs.html

In addition, a compatibility matrix guide is available that gives a comprehensive overview of what is supported and required for SRM to function. As this is likely to change, you are much better off consulting online guides rather than this book:

www.vmware.com/pdf/srm_compat_matrix_5_0.pdf

A common question people ask is if it is possible to replicate the vCenter database at the Protected Site to the Recovery Site. If you intended to use SRM, the answer is *no*. SRM assumes the two databases of vCenter are running independently of each other. In fact, one of the management tasks required during the configuration of SRM is "pairing" the protected SRM to the recovery SRM, and then "mapping" the vCenter objects (folders, resource pools, networks) in the Protected Site to the Recovery Site. Currently, the structure of the vCenter database does not allow for the use of SQL or Oracle replication to duplicate it at the Recovery Site. For the moment, if you are worried about the availability of the vCenter service you could run it in a VM on a DRS/HA and FT-enabled environment. Alternatively, if you are running vCenter on a physical machine (something which is no longer recommended) or a virtual machine you could use MSCS or the new vCenter Heartbeat Service.

For purposes of brevity I am going to assume you know how to set up ESX and vCenter so that I can more closely focus on the SRM part of the installation and configuration process. If this is something you are not familiar with, you may wish to read my other guides that cover this in some detail.

In my case, I used the following names for my components:

- The Protected Site:
    - dc01nyc.corp.com
    - vcnyc.corp.com
    - srmnyc.corp.com
    - sql2k8nyc.corp.com

- The Recovery Site:

  - dc01nj.corp.com

  - vcnj.corp.com

  - srmnj.corp.com

  - sql2k8nj.corp.com

Figure 7.2 shows the full configuration of my ESX hosts, VMware DRS/HA clusters, and other vCenter objects including folders and resource pools prior to starting the SRM installation (notice how the resource pool structure in NJ for recovered VMs is almost "mirroring" the resource pool structure of the Protected Site). If you're following this book you don't necessarily have to adopt my structures and naming conventions, but I will be using them throughout. Of course, none of these virtual machines are actually running on a live system in a production environment; this is merely a sandbox environment for playing with SRM and demonstrating the functionality of the product.

For obvious reasons I recommend this approach before rolling out SRM in a production environment. As you can see, I am running all components required to make SRM work in VMs. These VMs will not be replicated/snapshot to the Recovery Site; indeed, you could extend this concept to include "local" services that are not required or applicable at the Recovery Site, such as DNS, DHCP, WINS, and Print Services. They will remain in folders and resource pools separate from my "production" VMs. Generally, in my screen grabs you will find these nonreplicated VMs are in an "infrastructure" resource pool and an "infrastructure" VM folder. I could have hidden these VMs using permissions, but in an effort to be transparent I wanted you, the reader, to see exactly what my configuration is.

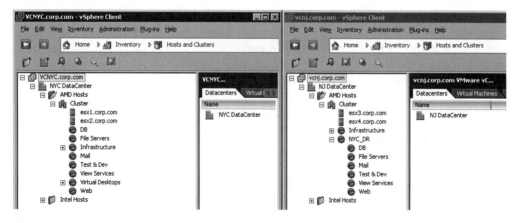

Figure 7.2   The Protected Site (NYC) and the Recovery Site (NJ)

As you can see in Figure 7.2, I've almost exactly mirrored the resource pool structure of the NYC datacenter, by creating similar subresource pools in the NYC_DR resource pool. This is to allow for a one-to-one inventory mapping (of resource pools, folders, and networks) within the SRM product from the Protected Site to the Recovery Site. I've carried a similar routine with the VM folders as well, as shown in Figure 7.3.

As I've said before, you can regard all the VMs in the Infrastructure folders/resource pools as "local" virtual machines that will not be replicated to the recovery location. Additionally, my Test & Dev resource pools/folders represent VMs that are not business-critical—and do not form a part of my Recovery Plan. As such, I have not created a Test & Dev resource pool or VM folder in the NYC_DR location of New Jersey. After all, why create objects in vCenter that you don't really need?

You might, in the first instance, dismiss this as just being overly fastidious. But please don't underestimate the importance of these structures and hierarchies. Get them wrong and you will find that the failback process has unexpected consequences. Without a good folder and resource pool structure, you will find yourself dumping all your VMs on a cluster or a folder, and potentially having to manually relocate thousands of VMs to the correct location.

More Detailed Information about Hardware and Software Requirements

As you know, software requirements and patch levels are endlessly changing; at the very least, you will want to know if your storage has been tested with SRM and is supported. It

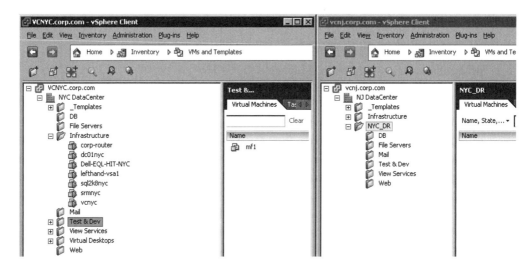

Figure 7.3   The folder structures in the Protected and Recovery Sites

seems very silly for me to list these requirements at length in a book, as this information will go very stale very quickly. So instead, visit this URL:

www.vmware.com/products/srm/

On this page, you will find all manner of useful information: PDFs, whitepapers, guides, webcasts, and so on. A little bit more direct than that is the information at this URL:

www.vmware.com/support/pubs/srm_pubs.html

This is where you will find the official administration guide (which, despite you having acquired this book, is always worth a read!) and some other guides, including the following:

- VMware vCenter Site Recovery Manager Release Notes
- Getting Started with VMware vCenter Site Recovery Manager
- VMware vCenter Site Recovery Manager Administration Guide
- Installing, Configuring, and Using Shared Recovery Site Support
- Adding a DNS Update Step to a Recovery Plan
- VMware Site Recovery Manager API

Additionally, VMware publishes compatibility matrix documents that tell you everything you need to know about what is and is not supported, including the following:

- What version of ESX and vCenter is supported and what patches are needed
- What Windows operating systems and service packs are required
- SRM database compatibility
- Guest operating systems protected by SRM
- Guest operating system customization (for example, Solaris is not currently on the list of supported guest OSes) that allows for the change of the IP address of the virtual machine
- Storage array compatibility

Treat the compatibility matrix like the now legendary VMware HCL for ESX servers; if it's not on the list, it's unsupported. Your configuration may well work, but if it breaks or is unreliable don't expect VMware Support to help. As for the "hardware" requirements (either physical or virtual) VMware currently recommends these minimums as a starting point for the SRM server:

- **Processor**   2.0GHz or higher Intel or AMD x86 processor

- **Memory**   2GB

- **Disk storage** 2GB

- **Networking**   Gigabit recommended

Scalability of VMware SRM

Another concern you will have about VMware SRM is whether it has any limits in terms of the number of ESX hosts and virtual machines it can protect, and how many Recovery Plans it can hold and run. A moment ago we talked about minimums, but it is worth mentioning SRM's current maximums. SRM 5.0 is tested up to a maximum of 1,000 protected virtual machines per site. You can create a maximum of 500 Protection Groups, which is almost three times as many as in the previous release. You can run up to ten Recovery Plans concurrently per site. The operative words here are *per site*. You could have thousands of virtual machines spread over many sites; in this case, you would be scaling out the SRM product to reflect that volume of virtual machines. I think it's fair to say that some of the scalability issues customers were concerned about in previous releases have been addressed by VMware. With that said, remember that, although you could theoretically run ten Recovery Plans simultaneously, the VMs that boot during these tests need compute resources from the Recovery Site. So the true limitations on scale may have little to do with the coding behind SRM, and everything to do with the quality and quantity of hardware in your recovery locale.

The official SRM guide has information about the scalability of this first release of SRM 5.0. It outlines the configuration maximums for both array-based and vSphere Replication–based implementations.

Array-Based Replication (ABR) scalability limits:

Protected VMs per Protection Group	500
Protected VMs	1,000
Protection Groups per Recovery Plan	150
Datastore groups	150
Concurrent recoveries	10

vSphere Replication (VR) scalability limits:

Protected VMs per single Protection Group	500
Protected VMs	500
Protection Groups per single Recovery Plan	250
Datastore groups	250
Concurrent recoveries	10

Designed for Both Failover and Failback?

As you can see, SRM was designed from day one to automate the failover from the Protected Site to the Recovery Site. It might surprise you to know that it was never part of the design strategy to automate failback to the Protected Site. You might regard that as a tremendously important, ahem, "oversite"—if you forgive the pun! In theory, invoking failback should be as simple as inverting the replication process to make sure we get the most recent set of virtual machine files, and taking your plan for DR/BC and reversing its direction. I'm pleased to say that with the new reprotect and automated failback support this is now infinitely easier than in previous releases. With that said, invoking failback and failover is still a huge decision—and one that you should not take lightly or try to achieve with or without virtualization software.

Here are some reasons why. In many respects, failback is more dangerous than failover. With failover there is really no choice but to hit the "Big Red Button" and start the process. After all, if a fire, flood, or terrorist attack has destroyed or partially destroyed your primary location, you will have no choice but to engage in DR. Now, let's says that DR is successful and you're at the Recovery Site. As long as you are operating successfully at the DR location and you can continue to do so for some time, what pressure or urgency is there to return? First, your salespeople are creating new orders and the accounts department is processing the invoices. They are generating income and revenue for the organization. Second, the application owners are happy because you managed to survive the disaster and get their services online. Due to these circumstances, you are more likely to want to gradually and carefully return to the primary location (if you can!). You certainly don't want failover to be a casual click-of-a-button affair. The very act of carrying out a failback in such a cavalier manner could actually undo all the good of a well-executed Recovery Plan. After all, you might take the argument that if your primary location was destroyed during a disaster, you may never want to return to that locale. In some respects failback is more complicated, because there are many reasons for the cause of the failover—which will result in different preparations. For example, you may need to procure new servers, networking, and storage—and critically, that new storage may have to replicate terabytes of data before beginning the failback process itself. That may well mean bringing a new array to the Recovery Site and carrying out a local sync of the data, and then "fork-lifting" that new array to the Protected Site, ready for the failback process. As you might expect, it's hardly likely or reasonable to expect VMware to be able to automate a business process that resides well outside its jurisdiction.

For many people in the world of corporate compliance, audit trails, and insurance, being able to push the "test" button is what they are really buying VMware SRM for. It means they can say to the business, their managers, and their auditors, "Look, we have a plan and it's been tested." However, to really, really test a Recovery Plan, many would say that the only true test is one that invokes DR for real. Some corporate environments hard-test their Recovery Plan biannually. For these organizations, the lack of an easy failback option in earlier releases of SRM was quite off-putting. What I hope you will see if you have used SRM before is that the failback process has been simplified, with fewer steps and stages than previously required, especially in the array of cleanup and cleanout which is currently needed, not least so that we can concentrate on what really matters: getting the business back up and running. Of course, this easier failback will be of particular interest to customers who need to carry out planned failovers caused by an event that is foreseeable, such as a power outage. Over time, the use cases for SRM will broaden as VMware makes it increasingly easier to failover and failback. So you could use SRM as part of a strategy for a planned datacenter move, or alternatively use the fact that you have an exact duplicate of your production site elsewhere as a way to test major changes to an environment without impacting your day-to-day operations. Looking to the future of cloud computing, I wouldn't be surprised to see SRM evolve into being an automation engine for moving significant numbers of VMs into an external provider or as tools automate to orchestrate so-called "long distance" vMotion events.

A Word about Resignaturing VMFS Volumes

This section is for people who have not attended the VMware vSphere authorized courses—or conversely, for those who have and promptly forgot most of what was said to them! Before I begin, it's important to emphasize that this does *not* apply to NFS volumes, it only applies to VMware's File System (VMFS) accessed by block-level storage such as Fibre Channel or iSCSI. It's not vitally important that you understand what the concept of resignaturing is and why SRM does this automatically. But I feel this will help you understand some of the "strangeness" that SRM sometimes displays. In fact, this strangeness is not strange at all. It's by design. It's the way it is. The main thing to be 100% clear about is that there is absolutely no need for you to change settings on ESX or go through any manual process for this to work. That's what you bought SRM for, after all.

Let's begin with a bit of revision about the properties of VMFS volumes. Before and after a format of a VMFS volume on a Fibre Channel or iSCSI volume, the storage can be addressed in many different ways:

- By its VMkernel "runtime" device name: vmhba1:0:15
- By is unique Network Address Authority (NAA) value: naa.6000...
- By its volume name which has to be unique to the ESX host: myvmfs
- By its datastore name which has to be unique to vCenter: myvmfs
- By its UUID: 47877284-77d8f66b-fc04-001560ace43f

It's important to know that, as with the NAA, the UUID value must be completely unique and an ESX host cannot have two UUIDs that are exactly the same presented to it at the same time. UUIDs are generated by using three core variables, including date, time, and LUN, in order to guarantee that the UUID value is absolutely unique. This can cause some interesting, or shall I say unpleasant, consequences if you are not consistent in your LUN numbering. That is to say, problems can occur if ESX1 believes the LUN/volume number is 15, and another ESX host in the same cluster believes the same block of storage is LUN/volume 20. It's also worth saying that currently, virtual machines do not find their VMDK and VSWP files using the friendly volume/datastore name. If you examine the contents of a .vmx file you will see references to the UUID value.

In Figure 7.4, you can see that the second virtual disk (srmnyc.vmdk) is being stored on a different volume (1558f9e9…) than the VM's VMkernel swap file (4d7dff7f…). If the virtual disk is stored in the same location as the VMX file, the /vmfs/volumes path is not displayed in the VMX file, but it is used.

As you can see, UUID numbers are very important. The requirement for unique UUIDs does present some interesting challenges to DR. By definition, any snapshot or replication process configured in the array is intended to create an exact duplicate of the VMFS volume that would, by definition, include the UUID value. In normal day-to-day operations an ESX host in the Protected Site should not get to see both the original LUN and

```
sched.swap.derivedName = "/vmfs/volumes/1558f9e9-af91d259/srmnyc/srmnyc-6880aad6.vswp"
replay.filename = ""
unity.wasCapable = "TRUE"
ide1:0.fileName = ""
scsi0:1.filters = ""
scsi0:1.fileName = "/vmfs/volumes/4d7dff7f-a8841ee2-2302-00110a57ed31/srmnyc/srmnyc.vmdk"
scsi0:1.mode = "persistent"
scsi0:1.ctkEnabled = "false"
scsi0:1.deviceType = "scsi-hardDisk"
scsi0:1.present = "true"
scsi0:1.redo = ""
/vmfs/volumes/1558f9e9-af91d259/srmnyc #
```

Figure 7.4   The UUID value from both the VM swap file and its second virtual disk on SCSI 0:1

replicated LUN/snapshot at the same time. If it did, ESX would suppress the second LUN/volume. If an ESX host was allowed to see both LUNs/volumes at the same time, the ESX host would be very confused—and not at all happy. It wouldn't know which LUN/volume to send its reads-writes to. In previous versions of ESX, the host would print a hard console error message suggesting that you may need to do a resignature of the VMFS volume. Since ESX 4.0, this hard console message has been deprecated and ESX no longer prints it which, I think, is a bit of a shame.

In previous versions, if this was a replicated/snapshot LUN or volume, the way to resolve this would be to modify the advanced settings in ESX to enable a resignature and issue a rescan of the HBA. In vSphere there are two ways to issue a resignature to a snapshot volume to make it visible to the ESX host: from the GUI or from the command line.

To demonstrate this manual approach of presenting the storage, which you would use if you were testing your DR plan and you didn't have SRM, I temporarily gave one of my ESX hosts a valid IP address to communicate to the vsa1.corp.com host. Then, in HP VSA, I added the ESX host as a server to the NJ_Group and assigned one of the snapshots to it. Then I ran the Add Storage Wizard on the ESX hosts.

As you can see in Figure 7.5, the volume is not blank, as it has a valid VMFS volume label. When the volume is selected, the ESX host's Add Storage Wizard realizes this is a replicated volume and offers me the chance to carry out a resignature manually.

As you can see in Figure 7.6, if you did proceed with this manual process, the resignature would change the UUID of the VMFS volume. That would mean the references in the .vmx file we saw earlier would be incorrect. That's why there is now a warning exclamation mark alerting you to the issue in ESX 5. The great thing about SRM is that it handles this resignature process automatically, and at the same time it fixes any references in the .vmx file so that when the recovered VM is powered on it successfully finds its virtual disks.

Alternatively, if you're a dab hand at the command line you should know that the new `esxcfg-volumes` command supports a `-l` switch to list all volumes/snapshots that have

Figure 7.5   Volumes waiting to be resignatured can be spotted easily from the Add Storage Wizard.

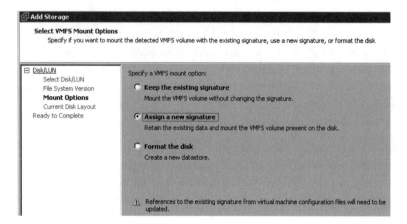

Figure 7.6   For some time, vSphere has supported the capacity to trigger a resignature of a VMFS volume from the Add Storage Wizard.

been detected as snapshots, and an -r switch to issue the instruction to resignature the volume. The following example is the command at the ESX console:

```
esxcfg-volumes -l
```

Here is the command with VMware's Remote vCLI:

```
vicfg-volume.pl --server esx3.corp.com --username root --password
  P@ssw0rd -l
```

These commands list the snapshots/replicated volumes the ESX host has discovered.

As you can see in Figure 7.7, the command shows that the VMFS is available to the resignature process. I could then follow that command with:

```
esxcfg-volumes -r hp-virtualmachines
```

Or with VMware's Remote vCLI:

```
vicfg-volume.pl --server esx3.corp.com --username root --password
  P@ssw0rd -r hp-virtualmachines
```

```
~ # esxcfg-volume -l
VMFS UUID/label: 4d82348d-ae6e8a8b-3078-0015600ea5bc/hplefthand-virtualmachines
Can mount: Yes
Can resignature: Yes
Extent name: naa.6000eb3948cde349000000000000019f:1      range: 0 - 1048319 (MB)
```

Figure 7.7   Those preferring command-line tools can see volumes waiting to be resignatured using the `vicfg-volume` command from the vCLI.

If the resignature wizard or the command were used to issue a resignature, the volume in the UUID would be changed, and it would be mounted to the ESX hosts. When this happens the volume is given a new volume name (snap-<*hexID*>originalvolumename) to allow you to identify it in the vSphere environment (see Figure 7.8). This behavior is the *same* for all storage vendors; I'm just using HP VSA as an example. In fact, I first saw this new way of managing resignaturing while working with EMC and its Replication Manager software.

This kind of behavior might have some very undesirable consequences if you are carrying out manual DR without the SRM product. The volume/datastore name would be changed and a new UUID value would be generated. If virtual machines were registered on that VMFS volume there would be a problem: All the VMX files for those virtual machines would be "pointing" at the old UUID rather than the new one. The VM would need to be removed from the vCenter inventory, and registered to pick up on this new UUID. So when you carry out manual DR the volume must be resignatured first, and then VMs are registered according to the new volume name and UUID. Much the same sequence of events happens when you test Recovery Plans.

Are you with me so far? Now, the good news is that SRM automatically resignatures volumes for you—but only in the Recovery Site—and it auto-magically fixes any issues with the VMX files. As the ESX hosts in the Recovery Site could have presented different snapshots taken at different times, SRM defaults to automatically resignaturing. It then corrects the VMX files of the recovery virtual machines to ensure that they power on without error. In the early beta release of SRM 1.0, VMware did an automatic rename of the VMFS volume to the original name. However, in the GA release of SRM 1.0 and 4.0, this renaming process was dropped. If you do want SRM to rename the snapshot of the VMFS to have the original volume name, you can do this by changing a setting in the Advanced Settings of SRM (see Figure 7.9). You can access the Advanced Settings dialog box by right-clicking the name of the site node in the vSphere client once SRM has been installed.

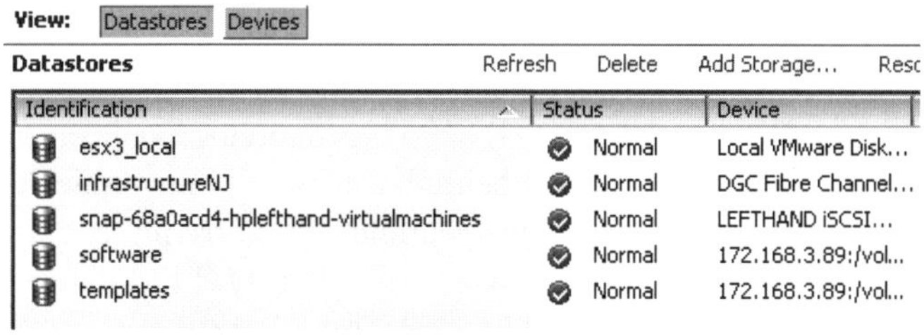

Figure 7.8 The snap-68a0acd4-hplefthand-virtualmachines volume has been resignatured.

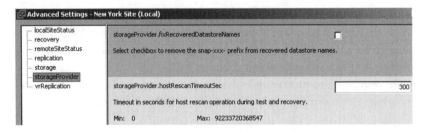

Figure 7.9   The option to retain the original volume name during the
resignature process

Some people may regard this mandatory resignature as somewhat "overly cautious,"
but it does guarantee fewer errors created by the ESX host having the potential of
being presented the same UUID more than once. If this automatic resignaturing did
not occur and the ESX host was presented two LUNs/volumes with the same VMFS
volume, datastore, and UUID values, the administrator would receive a hard error and
it would be up to the SRM administrator to resolve this problem. Some people might
take the position that these sorts of replication problems are best avoided altogether,
rather than taking unnecessary risks with data or adding a layer of unnecessary manual
configuration.

It's perhaps worth mentioning that there are products in the storage arena where an ESX
host might see both the original LUN and its snapshot at the same time. I'm thinking
of products such as HP's CrossLink/Continuous Access and EMC's TimeFinder. These
technologies are designed to protect your system from catastrophic failure of the storage
array. With these technologies the ESX host would have connectivity to two arrays that
would be constantly replicating to each other. The idea is that if an entire storage array
failed, it would still be able to access the LUN on another array. It's probably for this
reason that VMware SRM defaults to resignaturing LUNs to stop potential corruption.
After all, it's better to be safe than sorry.

VMware SRM Product Limitations and Gotchas

Do you read release notes? I didn't think so. Despite my "RTFM" credentials, I've been
caught not reading them for VMware products too. After being burnt twice, I now quickly
give them a run-through to spot potential problems before spending a week trying to
resolve what was mentioned in the release notes. In other words, if only I'd RTFM'd! See,
Mr. RTFM sometimes forgets to RTFM… I think we all know the moral of the story
here, don't we?

There are currently many known issues for the SRM 5.0 release, and these will in good time most likely be addressed by rerelease or a patch where necessary. The current URL for known issues is:

www.vmware.com/support/srm/srm_releasenotes_5_0_0.html#knownissues

Licensing VMware SRM

SRM is licensed by entering a valid license string. It's perhaps worth explaining at this point that VMware SRM has two different licensing models, because it can be configured in two separate ways: unidirectional (active/standby) and bidirectional (active/active). With unidirectional configuration, you only need an SRM license for the virtual machines protected by the SRM server at the site. We don't have to have a license at the Recovery Site for SRM. Now, this does not mean you can run vSphere 5 at the Recovery Site for free, gratis. Far from it!

As you are running ESX 5.0 and vCenter 5.0 at the Recovery Site you will need licenses to do that. SRM 5.0 is licensed on a per-VM basis; that means you buy SRM in bundles to license the number of VMs to be protected. In the per-VM model, licenses are assigned to the SRM servers (what is referred to in VMware licensing terminology as an "asset") either individually or as a group if using linked mode with vCenter. If you perform a planned failover where the original site survives, the per-VM keys essentially "follow" the protected VMs; if all keys are assigned to both SRM servers via linked mode you can reuse keys for failback. If your per-VM SRM licenses expire and you stop the service, when it is restarted no failover operations can be performed. Of course, it's entirely possible to protect more VMs than you have valid per-VM licenses. SRM will allow you to protect those VMs, *but* constant warnings will be generated because you have exceeded your quota of licenses.

The previous license model which used a "per-physical socket" approach did create problems in the past and a quick look at it will help explain why the per-VM licensing model was selected by VMware. Here is a good example. Let's say I have a 32-node DRS/HA cluster where each physical ESX host has four sockets, totaling 16 cores. That means I would have to purchase 128 socket licenses at the Protected Site. But what if I only had five virtual machines that needed protection? I think it's for reasons like this that VMware changed the licensing model around SRM. The per-VM model should be better for SRM, as customers only pay for what they protect.

I will admit it is rather unrealistic to suggest that an organization with this number of ESX hosts would have such a small number of virtual machines that would need protection—it's a quite unrealistic example. But I guess this problem does illustrate how dated counting CPU sockets or cycles has become as a way of licensing products, not least because the very act of virtualization has made licensing by CPUs seem increasingly arcane.

Anyway, these past couple of paragraphs on licensing might have left you feeling more confused than when we started; in a way, that is my point. Many vendors' licensing systems can be confusing and opaque; they are often like comparing one cell phone tariff to another. So here's a simple adage that, for the moment, works for VMware SRM:

Wherever you create a Protection Group (to protect virtual machines) you need a license—and you need a license that covers the total number of VMs at a site that will need protection.

Setting Up the VMware SRM Database with Microsoft SQL Server 2008

SRM requires two databases: one database in the Protected Site (in my case, New York) and the other on a separate database at the Recovery Site (in my case, New Jersey). Currently, SRM only supports SQL authentication if you intend to run the SQL Server database, as I do, separately from the SRM server. However, both SQL and SRM must be part of the same domain. In my lab environment I was successful in engineering a Windows authentication configuration where the SQL server was on a separate server from the SRM server.

In fact, I've been experimenting with this with a number of VMware products all the way back to vCenter 1.0, which didn't support Windows authentication on a separate SQL host. As with vCenter 1.0, if you try to use Windows authentication with SRM 4.0 the core SRM service will fail to start. It's a relatively trivial task to grant the SRM database user account the "right to log in as a service" on the SRM service from the Microsoft Services MMC. It's dead easy, and it works like a charm. But it's not supported, and using this configuration *will* cause issues during upgrades (which I have seen and worked around, and which are fine if you are prepared to live with them). But personally, until we get official support from VMware, I would give such a configuration a wide berth. In terms of what is supported for authentication, VMware outlined the following configurations.

- If you are using Windows authentication, the SRM server and database server must run on the same host.

- If the SRM server and database server run on different hosts, you must use mixed mode authentication.

- If SQL Server is installed locally, you might need to disable the Shared Memory network setting on the database server.

As for permissions and rights, for SQL Server the SRM database user merely needs to be made the "owner" of the database from the SQL Management Studio. In the next section,

I will be guiding you through the database configuration process. Of course, you may wish to consult with your database administration team to confirm that these steps conform to your database security policy.

Creating the Database and Setting Permissions

To create the database and set permissions, follow these steps.

1. Open Microsoft SQL Server Management Studio.

2. Right-click the Database node and then select New Database.

3. In the dialog box that opens, enter a friendly name for the database and set a location for the database files to be stored; then click the Add button. In my case, I store my databases away from the operating system C: drive, as shown in Figure 7.10.

4. Create a user account located internally to the SQL server. Expand the Security node, and right-click the Logins node and select New Login.

5. In the New Login dialog box, enter a friendly name for the user account, and select the SQL Server Authentication radio button as shown in Figure 7.11. Next, disable the password security options such as "Enforce password policy," "Enforce password expiration," and "User must change password at next login." Finally, at the bottom of the same dialog box, set the default database for the SRM database account user. Click OK.

6. The next step is to modify the ownership of the database, to grant the SRM database user account rights over it. To do this right-click the SRM database you created earlier, and select Properties in the context-sensitive menu.

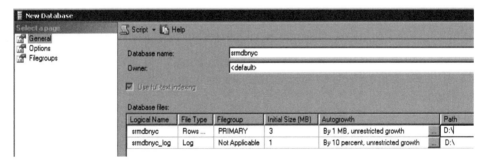

Figure 7.10　The creation of a database (srmdbnyc) on the root of the D: drive on Microsoft SQL Server

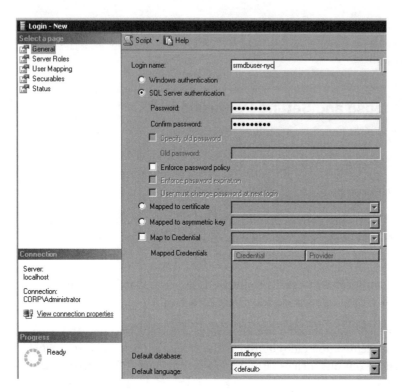

Figure 7.11   The Login – New dialog box in Microsoft SQL Server 2008

7. Select the Files node in the Database Properties dialog box. Figure 7.12 shows that currently the administrator is the owner of the database. This needs to be corrected to allow the SRM database user access to the srmdbnyc database.

8. Click the ellipsis (…) icon to open the Select Database Owner dialog box (shown in Figure 7.13) that allows the administrator to locate user accounts that either are in the Active Directory domain or are locally held within SQL itself.

9. Click the Browse button, and scroll down to locate the SRM database user account. Enable the checkbox next to the user account to indicate your selection (see Figure 7.14).

10. Once the account is selected, the default owner of corp\administrator is replaced with a new owner of the database, as shown in Figure 7.15.

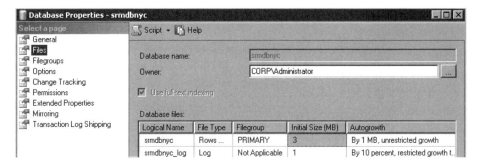

Figure 7.12   By default, the owner of a database created in SQL is the user who created the database in the first instance. This needs to be corrected.

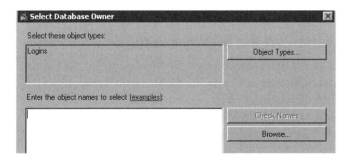

Figure 7.13   The Select Database Owner dialog box

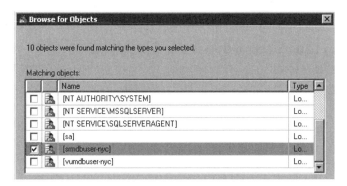

Figure 7.14   Selecting the srmdbuser-nyc account in the Browse for Objects dialog box

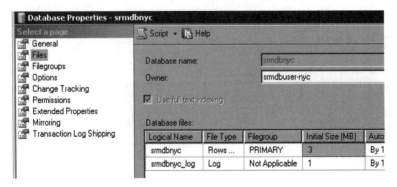

Figure 7.15   The default owner has now been replaced with our SRM database user account.

Configuring a DSN Connection on the SRM Server(s)

The next step in ensuring that the necessary prerequisites are in place prior to installation is to configure a data source name (DSN) connection on the SRM server(s). Before you create a connection to the database, you will most likely need to install the native SQL driver for the version of SQL you are using to the SRM server. This is a very simple installation and is not worth covering in this book. Additionally, you should know that, although the SRM software can be installed on a 64-bit operating system, it is in fact a 32-bit application, and as such you will need to use the older DSN manager. You can find it at C:\ Windows \SysWOW64 called odbcad32.exe.

1. Log in to the Protected Site SRM server. In my case, this is the srmnyc virtual machine with the Administrator account.

2. Open the ODBC Data Source Administrator from Administrative Tools at C:\ Windows \SysWOW64\odbcad32.exe.

3. In the ODBC Data Source Administrator choose the System DSN tab.

4. Click the Add button.

5. From the end of the list, choose SQL Native Client, and select Finish. Be careful not to select the older SQL Server driver from the list.

6. In the Name field of the Create a New Data Source to SQL Server dialog box, enter "VMware SRM".

7. From the drop-down list, select the SQL server used at your Protected Site and click Next.

8. Select "With SQL Server authentication…" and enter the username and password you set earlier when you created the database, as shown in Figure 7.16.

9. Enable the "Change the default database to:" radio button and select the protected SRM database you created earlier, as shown in Figure 7.17.

10. Click Next and then click Finish.

You should now be able to confirm all the dialog boxes associated with the ODBC setup—as well as test that you have connectivity to the database server. You can now repeat this DSN setup for the Recovery Site SRM server.

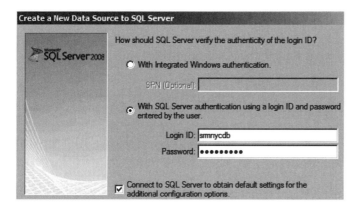

Figure 7.16   Entering the username and password used to access the database

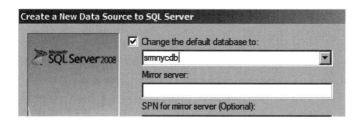

Figure 7.17   Allocation of the default database for the DSN

Installing the VMware SRM Server

You can install SRM into a single-site mode and a shared-site mode. In single-site mode there is a one-to-one "pairing" of a Protected Site with a Recovery Site. In shared-site mode the relationship is one in which the Recovery Site offers DR resources for many Protected Sites. If this is the configuration you intend, you might want to take a look at Chapter 13, on multisite configurations. Now, don't panic. You can take a single-site configuration and convert it to be a shared-site configuration at any time. It's just not a configuration that is terrifically popular at the moment, and I don't want to make the setup any more complex than it needs to be at this stage.

Installing the SRM Software

Installation of SRM is the same for both the Protected Site SRM server and the Recovery Site SRM server. During the install you will need to do the following.

- Supply the vCenter FQDN.

- Supply a username and password valid for authenticating to vCenter.

- Accept a default certificate or generate one of your own.

- Supply site identification values such as the name of the site and email contact details.

- Supply SQL/Oracle/DB DSN credentials for the correct database.

To install the SRM software, follow these steps.

1. Log in to the Protected Site SRM server. In my case, this is srmnyc.

2. Run the SRM installer.exe file. This extraction process does take some time, so be patient. I usually copy the SRM install file to the SRM server to speed up this extraction process.

3. Click Next to the usual suspects of the Welcome screen and accepting the EULA.

4. Select a disk location for the SRM software.

5. The first real question the installer will ask you is whether you wish to install the UI elements of vSphere Replication (VR), as shown in Figure 7.18. I recommend that you do include this component; this will allow you to easily deploy VR later, should you need it.

6. In the VMware vCenter Server dialog box, enter the name of your Protected Site vCenter and valid credentials to authenticate to vCenter, as shown in Figure 7.19.

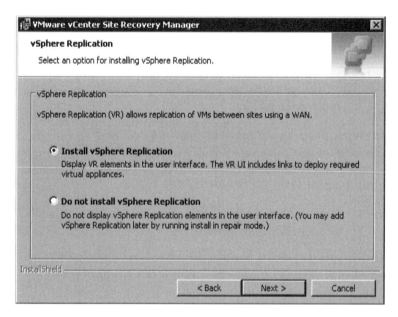

Figure 7.18 Option for enabling the GUI frontend of VR. I recommend always enabling this for possible future use.

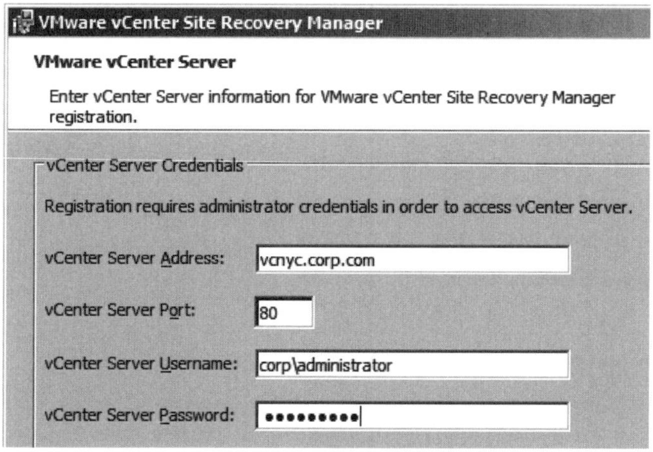

Figure 7.19 Pairing the SRM instance with vCenter

One anomaly with this dialog box is that, although the default port number used to communicate is TCP port 80, when you look at the details of a completed SRM install the system communicates with vCenter on port 443. You must have port 80 open for this dialog box to work, and if you try to alter the port in the dialog box to 443, you will receive an error. TCP port 80 is essentially a redirection port that redirects communication to port 443 anyway.

Additionally, I have cheated by using the built-in domain administrator account in Windows. It is recommended that you create a dedicated account for this purpose and exclude it from any "password reset" policies you have on your domain. In short, regard it as a service account.

7. After a short while, a certificate security warning dialog box will appear, as shown in Figure 7.20. Choose Yes to accept the thumbprint.

As mentioned a moment ago, despite the fact that the dialog box uses port 80 by default, there is an exchange of certificate details. This is used to confirm that the Protected Site SRM "trusts" the vCenter system. This warning is caused by the use of auto-generated certificates within the vCenter server, and the fact that

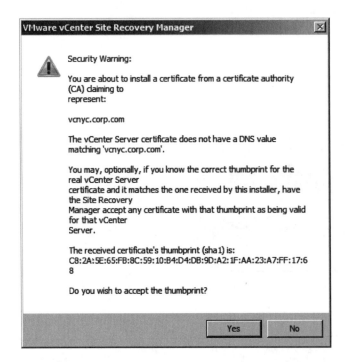

Figure 7.20 Auto-generated certificates are used to verify the identity of the servers used in SRM. Most customers use the built-in certificates.

the certificate does not match the FQDN of the vCenter system. To stop this message from appearing you would have to generate trusted certificates for both the Protected and Recovery Site vCenters.

Alternatively, you can choose to accept the default certificates by confirming that the certificates thumbprint presented in the dialog box (as shown in Figure 7.21) is the same as your vCenter servers by opening your Web browser on the vCenter server and viewing the certificate via your Web browser controls.

In Figure 7.21, you can see that the last three blocks of the thumbprint match the SRM installation dialog box (FF:17:68).

It's by no means a requirement to use trusted certificates either from an internal root certificate authority or even from a commercial certificate authority. I've found the built-in auto-generated certificates work fine for my purposes. However, if you do want to generate your own certificates and have them trusted and used by SRM, VMware has written a guide that explains exactly how to do that:

> http://communities.vmware.com/servlet/JiveServlet/down-load/2746-201687-1209882-20726/How_to_use_trusted_Certificates_with_VMware_vCenter_Site_Recovery_Manager_v1.0.2.pdf

The next dialog box also concerns security (see Figure 7.22). It is possible for the SRM install to generate a certificate to prove the identity of the SRM server itself. Alternatively, you can create certificates of your own.

8. Select "Automatically generate a certificate" and click Next.

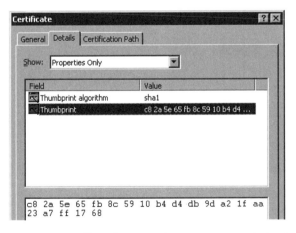

Figure 7.21 There is no requirement to generate trusted certificates for SRM. You can merely match the thumbprint values.

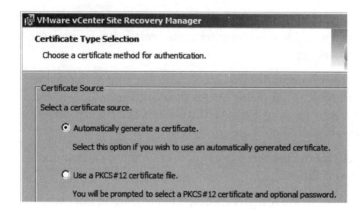

Figure 7.22   Most customers opt for the automatically generated certificate.

9. As part of the auto-generation of the SRM certificate you must supply your organization name and organization unit details, as shown in Figure 7.23. Letters, numbers, spaces, commas, and periods are all valid characters in this dialog box. Among the invalid characters are the dash and the underscore.

10. Set the site information details.

In the dialog box in Figure 7.24 I changed the default name of the site from "Site Recovery for vcnyc.corp.com" to the friendlier "New York Site," and then I added the email address details. I chose not to select the IP addresses that appeared in the Local Host pull-down box. I've never been a big fan of hardcoded IP addresses in any product, and I've always replaced them with an FQDN.

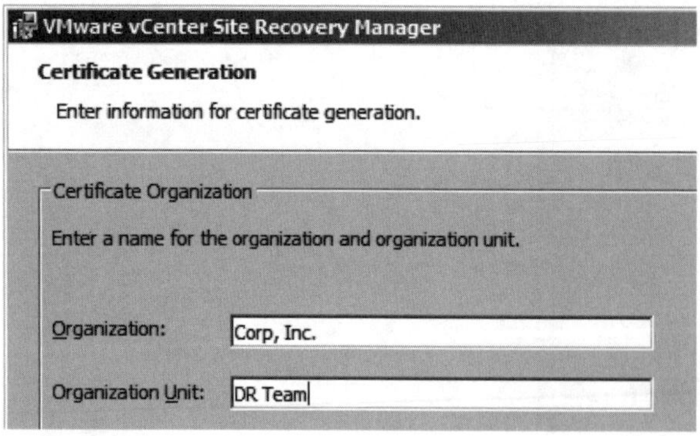

Figure 7.23   The organization name and organization unit information only appears in certificate data and isn't displayed in the SRM interface.

Two important processes are happening here. First, you are naming your site—the site name must be unique to the installation. Second, you are making vCenter aware that you're adding an extension to its management—it's this process that will allow you to download and install the SRM client plug-in to your management PC, extending the UI of vCenter with icons and menus particular to SRM.

SOAP/HTTP listener API ports (9007/9008) are only used if you choose to use the Software Development Kit (SDK) to create applications or scripts that further automate SRM. The SOAP listener port (8095) is used to send and receive requests/acknowledgments from the SRM service. The HTTP listener port (8096) is used in the process of downloading the SRM plug-in. The email settings can be found in the extension.xml file located on the SRM server after the installation.

The fields left for email are not currently used in the SRM product in any shape or form, except it does set the default recipient e-mail address with SRM alarms and alerts. Originally, VMware had envisioned a situation where these fields would be used at the main contact points in the event of a DR. In the end, this idea wasn't implemented, but the fields remain in the UI as a throwback to that original concept.

11. Complete the Database Configuration dialog box (see Figure 7.25). If you have forgotten to configure the ODBC DSN you can add it here; however, you will not be able to browse for it. You will have to manually type the DSN you have configured. This is a known issue with the way Microsoft Data Access Components (MDACs) refresh their status in Windows.

Figure 7.24   Site names can be changed after installation in the Advanced Settings dialog box under localSiteStatus.displayName.

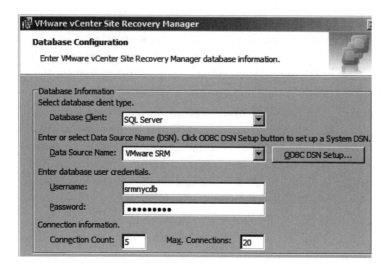

Figure 7.25   Completing the Database Configuration dialog box

Remember, these credentials have nothing to do with the username and password used to authenticate to vCenter. They are the credentials to authenticate to the SRM database.

The Database Client pull down allows you to select the type of database you are using (SQL, Oracle, IBM) and the Data Source Name pull down allows you to select the DSN created earlier. Although you can open the Microsoft ODBC DSN Setup Wizard from the installer, I prefer to have this configured and verified before I begin. It means less work during the installation phase. I've occasionally found that completing the ODBC configuration here does not update the pull-down list next to Data Source Name anyway. However, manually typing the DSN name does work.

The Connection Count option is used to set the initial pool size you want opened to connect to the database. The pool manages open connections to the database. It is a waste of resources to generate a new connection (and then tear it down) for each database operation; so existing connections are reused and they are referred to as a pool. The Connection Count option represents the initial size of the pool. If more connections are needed, the system will generate them (expanding the pool), up to the maximum specified by the Max Connections field. After that limit is reached, SRM database operations will pause until a connection is available.

It is possible that the database administrator may restrict how many open connections a database user may have at a given time. If that is the case, Max Connections should be set to not exceed that number. My default values have been reasonable for my testing, but they can certainly be increased as needed. In my experience, I have not come across any customer who has to modify these default values—yet.

12. After completing this dialog box you can proceed to the installation, where the main file copy process occurs. The final part of the installer where SRM creates the database tables can take some time. So I recommend you take a break for lunch or tea.

Installing a Storage Replication Adapter: Example HP SRA

IMPORTANT NOTE

Previous versions of SRM require a restart of the SRM service after installing an SRA. This is no longer the case. Instead, a new "refresh" or "reload" function allows the SRM administrator to force the service to check its directories for the SRA. This allows the administrator to add support for new storage arrays, without having to interrupt the core vmware-dr service.

In most cases, immediately after installing SRM you would follow through with an install of your vendor's SRA. An SRA is a third-party plug-in provided by your storage array vendor. Without the SRA installed you would find that options to control how SRM works with the replication engine would be unavailable. You can download your SRA from the SRA portion of VMware's website. In the first release of SRM there was some delay in the storage vendors' SRAs appearing on VMware's website. This is caused by the fact that VMware has its own "internal" QA process which runs independent of the vendors'—and the fact that some storage vendors were slow in getting their SRAs into the QA process. If you cannot find your storage vendor's SRA and you know it is supported, it's worth approaching the storage vendor directly. It still seems to be the case in SRM 5.0 that the storage vendor has an SRA which is newer than the one available on the VMware site. However, strictly from a support perspective your Support and Subscription agreement with SRM lies with VMware. So, if you bypass VMware and approach your storage vendor directly for an SRA, it would leave you in a difficult position from a support perspective. Direct links to a storage vendor are incredibly valuable, but it's best to not invalidate your support channel to VMware. VMware does significant QA work with SRAs once they are submitted by the storage vendor, so going directly to your storage vendor will not only break your support agreement with VMware, but it could also break your SRM installation. It is fair to say that this relationship is constantly under review at VMware, with the company always looking to improve the process by which customers gain access to the SRA in a way that is timely and ensures a quality experience.

Installing an SRA extends the functionality of the vSphere client to allow for the configuration of the array manager portion of SRM. Without an SRA installed you would not be able to complete the post-configuration part of the SRM setup. The dialog box shown in Figure 7.26 would have no options in the drop-down list.

Once the SRA has been installed, it allows VMware's SRM to discover LUNs/volumes on the Protected and Recovery Sites, and compute which LUNs/volumes are replicated. The real idea of this is to allow the Recovery Site administrator to run Recovery Plan tests without having to liaise with or manage the storage layer directly. The SRA will automate the process of presenting the right replicated LUNs or the latest snapshot to the ESX hosts at the Recovery Site when they are needed.

The SRA itself is often merely a collection of scripts, which carry out four main tasks.

- Communicate and authenticate to the array.

- Discover which LUNs are being replicated, and select/create a snapshot prior to a test or stop the normal pattern of replication and promote volumes to be read-writable at the point of running an SRM test or what you might call site failover.

- Work with SRM to initiate tests, clean up after tests, and trigger genuine failovers.

- Work with SRM to reverse the paths of replication when the administrator issues a "reprotect" as part of an automated failback process.

It's worth just pointing out that some SRAs have other software or licensing requirements.

- The EMC VMX SRA, and the EMC VNX Replicator Enabler for it, need to be installed. They are available from EMC's PowerLinks website.

- 3Par's SRA requires the Inform CLI for Windows to be installed before its SRA. Additionally, it requires .NET 2.0 which it will attempt to download from the Internet.

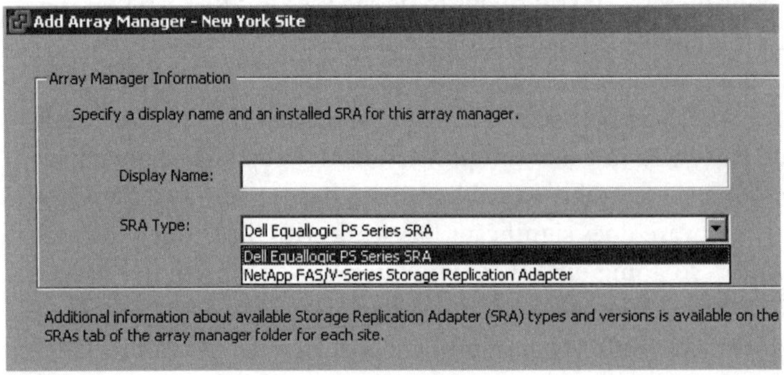

Figure 7.26 The drop-down list to select an SRA. This list only becomes available once an SRA has been installed.

- Compellent Storage Center's SRA requires .NET 2.0 and will attempt to download it from the Internet. After the install, you will be given the option to restart the SRM service.

- IBM's System Storage SAN Volume Controller SRA adds an "IBMSVCRAutil" to the SRM desktop, which is used to complete the configuration of the IBM SRA. This allows the administrator to set the variables for test, source, target, and space efficiency associated with the MDisk Group ID parameter.

- The FalconStore SRA requires a license string to be available during the installation, and requires that IPStor be the same version at the Protected and Recovery Sites. Also, it must be running on Version 6 or later. The user guide is copied to the main \Storage\sra\IPStor directory on the SRM server.

In my examples I am using an HP VSA virtual appliance, so I need to download and install the SRA from HP. The installation of SRA is very simple—in most cases it is a next-next-finish exercise. Most SRAs come with a variety of ReadMe files and these are well worth reading.

1. Download the HP SRA from Vmware.com.

2. Double-click at the exe.

3. After the extraction process, you will see a Welcome screen.

4. Click Next.

5. Accept the license agreement. The installer will then proceed to install the Java Runtime Environment (JRE) if it is not present, as shown in Figure 7.27.

In previous releases of SRM, after the install of the SRA you would have had to restart the core "vmware-dr" service for the installation to take effect. There is now a "refresh" link in the SRA area of the SRA tab in the SRM management UI, so this restart is no longer needed.

Once the installation to the Protected Site has completed, you can repeat this installation on the Recovery Site SRM server—in my case, this is the srmnj.corp.com server. After installing the HP SRA, you will find within the Start menu a Programs folder called HP, which holds a link to documentation in PDF format.

Installing the vSphere Client SRM Plug-in

As with the installation of the VMware Update Manager or VMware Converter, an installation of SRM "extends" the vSphere client with additional management functionality in the form of a plug-in. After the successful installation of SRM, you should find there is a

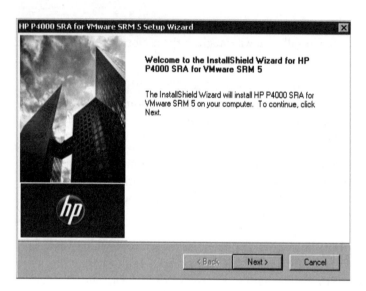

Figure 7.27   Installing the HP SRA

Site Recovery Manager plug-in available on the plug-ins menu. You will need to install this plug-in to carry out the first configuration or post-configuration of the SRM service.

1. Log in to the Protected Site vCenter with the vSphere client.

2. In the menu that opens, choose Plug-ins and Manage Plug-ins.

3. Under Available Plug-ins, click the Download and Install link, as shown in Figure 7.28.

    Installing a plug-in requires simply accepting the EULA and clicking the Next button. Although occasionally I find I have to close and reload the vSphere client once the plug-in has been installed for the SRM icon to appear in the Solutions and Applications tab in the Home location, as shown in Figure 7.29.

    When you click the Site Recovery button for the first time you will receive a security warning (shown in Figure 7.30) that is very similar to the warnings you receive when loading the vSphere client. This warning is caused by the use of the auto-generated certificate for SRM.

    If you do not want this message to appear again, enable the "Install this certificate and do not display any security warnings for 'srmnyc.corp.com' " option, and then click the Ignore button.

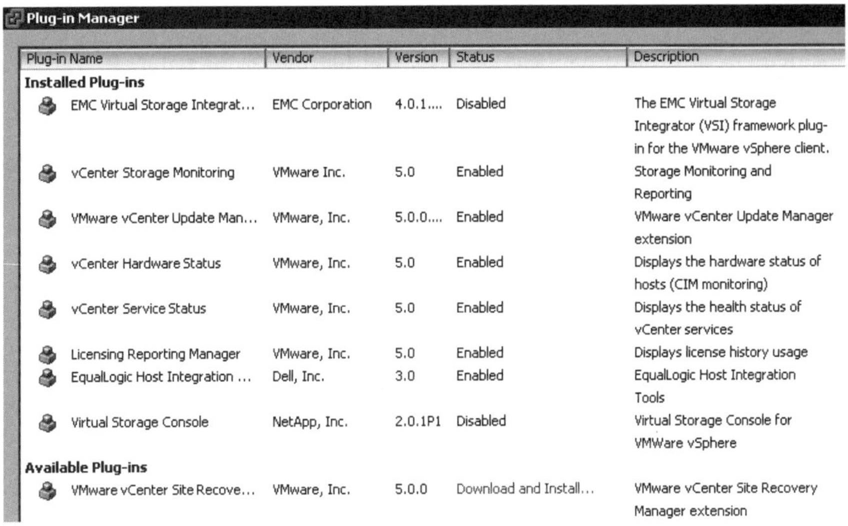

Plug-in Manager
Plug-in Name
Vendor
Version
Status
Description
Installed Plug-ins
EMC Virtual Storage Integrat... EMC Corporation 4.0.1.... Disabled The EMC Virtual Storage Integrator (VSI) framework plug-in for the VMware vSphere client.
vCenter Storage Monitoring VMware Inc. 5.0 Enabled Storage Monitoring and Reporting
VMware vCenter Update Man... VMware, Inc. 5.0.0.... Enabled VMware vCenter Update Manager extension
vCenter Hardware Status VMware, Inc. 5.0 Enabled Displays the hardware status of hosts (CIM monitoring)
vCenter Service Status VMware, Inc. 5.0 Enabled Displays the health status of vCenter services
Licensing Reporting Manager VMware, Inc. 5.0 Enabled Displays license history usage
EqualLogic Host Integration ... Dell, Inc. 3.0 Enabled EqualLogic Host Integration Tools
Virtual Storage Console NetApp, Inc. 2.0.1P1 Disabled Virtual Storage Console for VMWare vSphere
Available Plug-ins
VMware vCenter Site Recove... VMware, Inc. 5.0.0 Download and Install... VMware vCenter Site Recovery Manager extension

Figure 7.28 SRM registers its plug-in to the vCenter Plug-in Manager.

Solutions and Applications
Update Manager
Site Recovery

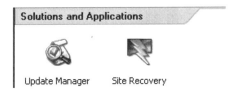

Figure 7.29 The main Site Recovery icon after the installation of the vCenter plug-in

Security Warning
Certificate Warnings
An untrusted SSL certificate is installed on "srmnyc.corp.com" and secure communication cannot be guaranteed. Depending on your security policy, this issue might not represent a security concern. You may need to install a trusted SSL certificate on your server to prevent this warning from appearing.
Click Ignore to continue using the current SSL certificate.
View Certificate
Ignore
Cancel
Install this certificate and do not display any security warnings for "srmnyc.corp.com".

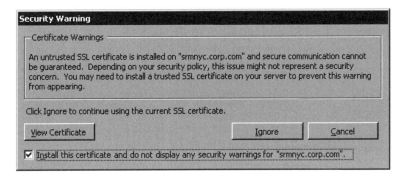

Figure 7.30 On the first connection to the SRM service a security warning dialog will appear.

Handling Failures to Connect to the SRM Server

If you lose connectivity to or restart the SRM service on either the Protected or Recovery Site and you have the vSphere client open, you will receive an Error dialog box, as shown in Figure 7.31. If a failure to connect to SRM occurs you will see this when you click the Site Recovery icon. If this happens, confirm that the SRM service has started; if the SRM service will not start, confirm connectivity to the SQL database, and other dependencies such as IP settings and DNS name resolution. Reconnections to the SRM service can be forced by clicking the Connect to Site Recovery Manager link (see Figure 7.32).

Additionally, if the Protected Site cannot connect to the Recovery Site's vCenter (perhaps you have lost connectivity to the Recovery Site) you will see in the Sites pane of the Site Recovery Manager window the error message shown in Figure 7.33. Note that the Protected Site and Recovery Site status can change to "Not Connected" and "Unknown," respectively, when a paired SRM server loses its connection. This status will also show while the SRM server is being authenticated for the first time to both sites.

If this happens to you, check the usual suspects, such as a failure of the vCenter service at the Recovery Site. Once you have resolved the communication problem, you should

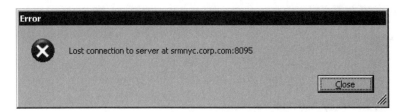

Figure 7.31   The Error dialog box that appears if the SRM service stops

Figure 7.32   Forcing a reconnection to the SRM service

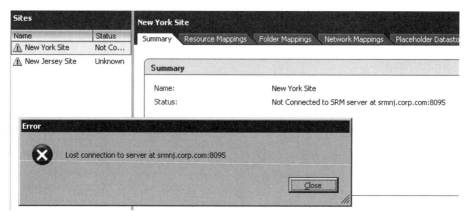

Figure 7.33 The error message that appears if the Protected Site cannot connect to the Recovery Site's vCenter

find that it automatically reconnects; if not, you may find yourself running through the Configure Connection Wizard again to force a reconnection of the sites. If this seems to take a long time, it is safe to click the Configure Connection button and resupply the credentials for the vCenter at the Recovery Site. If you do experience an outage of the Recovery Site's vCenter or SRM, you will find the Protection Setup pane will change the Connection Status to read "Not Connected."

Summary

In this chapter I've tried to jump-start you through the primary stages of getting the SRM service up and running. Essentially, if you can create a database and point Windows to that database you can install SRM—it's very similar in that respect to installing the VMware Update Manager. Remember, your biggest challenge with SRM is getting the network communications working between the Protected Site and the Recovery Site environments, and that's not just an IP and DNS issue. There are potential firewall considerations to take into account as well. That's where we're headed in the next chapter: the post-configuration stages of the SRM product that are initiated at the Protected Site vCenter. In the next chapter, we will be connecting the sites together and configuring both inventory mappings and Protection Groups. Once you have connected to the SRM service via the vSphere client a seven-stage post-configuration overview is displayed on the Getting Started tab. That is the configuration I will be guiding you through in the next couple of chapters. The only optional component is where you intend to use VMware's vSphere Replication.

Chapter 8

Configuring vSphere Replication (Optional)

In this release of SRM VMware added a feature called vSphere Replication (VR). Although it is branded with the name of "vSphere" it's actually a feature that is only available to customers who purchase the SRM product and is not a core feature of the vSphere platform. VR allows the replication of individual VMs on any datastore (local, FC, iSCSI, or NFS) to any other datastore at the Recovery Site. It's a technology that is attractive to customers on many levels. SMBs will be tempted by it because it removes the requirement for matching storage arrays at both sites. Enterprise organizations might be attracted to it because it is sometimes difficult to resolve array firmware compatibility requirements and satisfy the demands of a storage team. Finally, solution providers who offer DR as a service might like the fact that VR enables them to offer SRM to customers without them having to worry about the customers' storage array system. Essentially, VMware has done for replication what it achieved in the previous decade with the virtual machine: It has virtualized replication and in one stroke removed some of the hardware and firmware compatibility snags that have often dogged storage-array-based implementations of SRM. At the very least, VR offers folks who are new to SRM a chance to set up proofs of concept and home labs, without the heavy lifting that array-based replication sometimes requires.

How vSphere Replication Works

It's important to say that the setup and configuration of VR is not mandatory, which is why I added the word *Optional* to the chapter title. VR allows an organization to enable replication of VMs from one site to another without the need for native array-based replication. It's not a mandatory requirement to configure VR, but nonetheless you may find it very useful whether you're a large or small business. The main advantage of VR is that it is storage protocol neutral and storage vendor neutral, so as long as you're using storage that is supported by VMware's general HCL you will be fine. What VMware has done for virtual machines, it is doing for replication; if you like, call it *virtualized replication*. With VR it's possible, for instance, to replicate data held on a Fibre Channel protocol to NFS. This is because the core engine of VR sits above this layer in the architecture. All that VR "sees" are the files that make up a VM, and the fact that they reside on a datastore visible to the ESX host. VR is asynchronous replication of the VMs using ESXi as the main engine for moving data around. The VMs themselves need not be stored on replicated datastores; you could be using local storage, and the replication itself could be between two datastores that are not even from a common storage array vendor. VR should be attractive to the SMB/SME market which historically has balked at the cost of buying secondary storage merely for DR purposes. It may also be attractive to organizations that choose to partner with one another for DR purposes, but find they do not share a common storage array to get the replication going. Even large enterprises might be attracted to VR; it may allow VMware admins more control over the replication process, making them less dependent on the approval of their storage teams. It might provide a workaround in situations where a common storage platform is not in place, such as a recent acquisition of another business that needs either DR protection or the ability to move into a corporate datacenter for consolidation purposes. Use of VR could be to accelerate early proofs of concept of SRM, because the storage requirements are taken care of by VMware, without seeking approval or action from the storage team. Finally, a last use case is of providing an IT team with a DR offering for workloads that did not fit or warrant inclusion (possibly due to cost) in the existing replicated SAN DR architecture. For example, Tier 1/Tier 2 workloads could be on SAN replication with SRM and charged back appropriately, whereas Tier 3 and Tier 4 workloads are protected with VR integrated with SRM 5.0.

The feel of VR is quite different from that of array-based replication. VR is enabled on the properties of the VM or by multiple selections of VMs held in a VM folder. This allows you to be much more selective about which VMs are targeted for protection by SRM than with array-based replication, where currently the smallest unit is the LUN or volume, and every VM in that LUN or volume can be enrolled in a Recovery Plan. Personally, I like this form of very granular control, as it might help customers who have been less than circumspect on the storage placement of their VMs. This per-VM granularity empowers the administrator in a number of ways. It's possible for the administrator to opt to only replicate some and not all of the VMs' virtual disks, and select a per-VM recovery point objective (RPO). If the VMs you are replicating are large in size it's possible to supply an "initial copy" of the VM to save bandwidth, as VR only copies the deltas or the changes between the source and destination.

Now, to understand the core benefits of VR let's look at the structure of the technology (see Figure 8.1).

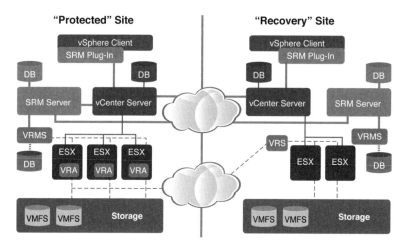

Figure 8.1   A management server (VRMS) is mandatory at both locations, but the VR appliance (VRS) that receives updates from ESXi is only required at the Recovery Site.

Source: Used by permission of VMware.

As you can see in Figure 8.1, there is a vSphere Replication Management Server (VRMS) at the Protected Site. This server has a database back end that is used to store your VRMS configuration, including such metadata as which VMs are protected by VR and their RPO configuration. Sitting inside the ESX host is a vSphere Replication Agent (VRA). This is used to intercept the changes that are taking place inside the VMs, and it is responsible for moving those deltas to the Recovery Site. Those changes taking place inside the VM are actually detected by an agent that is inside the ESXi host. At the destination side, the vSphere Replication server (VRS) is a virtual appliance that is used as the destination for shipping any deltas from the Protected Site. This virtual appliance then pushes those changes to the ESXi hosts in the Recovery Site, and updates the volumes where the VMs reside. A VRMS is required on both sides to handle the process; there is a pairing process that is very similar to the storage array manager's configuration that we will discuss in the next chapter.

vSphere Replication Limitations

This is the first implementation of VR, and it is important that you understand some of the limitations in this release. As always, you need to match your business needs and objectives against the functionality of the technology. There are a number of limitations, so let's begin with a checklist first and then delve a little deeper into the implications.

- Powered-off VMs are not replicated by VR (but can be protected).

- There is no automated failback of VMs protected by VR (manual failback is supported).

- ISOs and physical RDMs cannot be replicated.

- FT-protected VM templates and linked clones are not supported.

- The snapshot hierarchy is not replicated.

Once you understand the architecture of VR the first limitation becomes obvious: Powered-off VMs are not replicated. This is not so much a limitation, but a "feature" of the way the technology has been designed. Logically, then, if the VM is not powered on, the ESXi agent cannot detect any changes. The fact that a powered-off VM cannot make any changes in the file system perhaps makes this limitation less troublesome.

It is my understanding that currently, there is no automated failback of VMs protected by VR. I think this may be regarded by some as a limitation, especially given that one of the main new features of array-based protection is the automated failback and reprotect process. I think it's worthwhile remembering that this was the situation in both SRM 1.0 and SRM 4.0 for array-based replication, and it wasn't seen as a showstopper for those technologies. It does mean the failback process of VMs protected by VR will involve a few more manual steps, and these will be very similar to the process in previous releases of SRM. So, SRM has always been able to carry out failback; it's just an issue of understanding the process and working through it. Don't worry, my commitment to SRM is an ongoing one; I recently wrote a blogpost about this very process: www.rtfm-ed.co.uk/2011/10/05/failover-with-srm-and-vsphere-replication.

Finally, there are a range of vSphere components that cannot be protected with VR, such as ISOs, physical RDMs, FT-protected VMs, VM templates, linked clones, and snapshots. I think it's fair to say that some of these components would be unlikely to be protected by SRM even with array-based replication—for example, .iso images. Similarly, the lack of support for FT-protected VMs persists even with array-based replication. While SRM has always been able to offer recovery for the primary FT-protected VM, when it is recovered it becomes just another VM that is powered on in the plan. It's up to the SRM administrator to decide whether the environment in the Recovery Site meets the requirements for FT to be enabled. Remember, those requirements are quite stringent. So I wouldn't overstate these limitations too much, but you must be aware of them. It's my hope that in future releases of SRM automated failback will be ported to VR.

Installing vSphere Replication

The setup of VR involves a number of steps carried out in a specific order. As you complete each step at both the Protected and Recovery Sites, the Getting Started tab (as shown in Figure 8.2) for VR will update accordingly, and you should see a green checkmark appear next to each step.

Setting the vCenter Managed IP Address

Before you begin to deploy the VRMS, you will need to fulfill one prerequisite on both the Protected and Recovery Sites: ensuring that the vCenter Managed IP Address is correctly configured. By default, this value in vCenter is normally blank after a clean installation. Nonetheless, even if you have carried out an upgrade of vCenter from a previous release

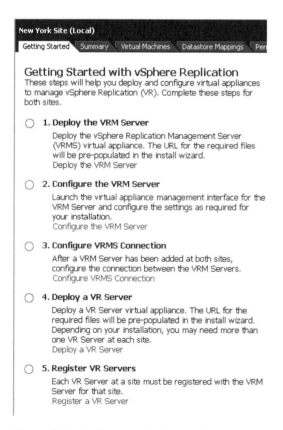

Figure 8.2 In this case, the Getting Started tab does a good job of outlining the steps required in the initial configuration of VR.

it is well worth confirming this address is correctly set. VR uses it to automate the registration process of the various appliances.

1. Log in to the vSphere client and the Protected Site vCenter.
2. In the menu that opens, select the Administration and vCenter Server settings.
3. In the vCenter Server Settings dialog box, select the Runtime Settings category.
4. In the Managed IP Address field, enter the IP address of your vCenter server (see Figure 8.3).

Configuring a Database for the VRMS

Before you begin the deployment process, you should set up a database for the VRMS. This database holds your configuration for the VMs protected by VR. Unlike the new vCenter virtual appliance, the VRMS does not support a database that is local to it. Instead, you will need to configure a database for the VRMS on an existing database server. Currently, the VRMS supports Microsoft SQL Server, Oracle, and IBM DB2. The following instructions assume you're configuring a database on Microsoft SQL Server 2008, which is the database platform I use throughout this book.

1. Log in to your Microsoft SQL Server and run the SQL Server Management Studio management console.
2. Right-click the +Database node and select the New Database option in the menu.
3. Enter a friendly database name and select the location to store the database files (see Figure 8.4). Click OK to create the database.
4. Create a user account to access the database. Expand the +Security node, and right-click +Logins and select New Login from the menu.

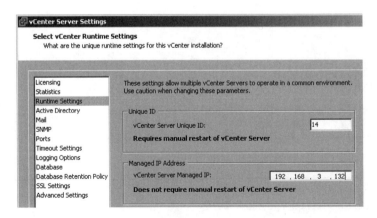

Figure 8.3   Make sure the Managed IP Address setting is correct.

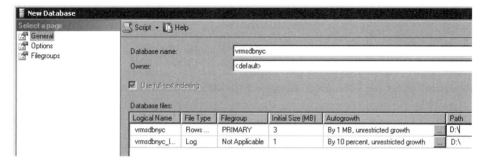

Figure 8.4 The VRMS requires a database to hold the VR's configuration, including which VMs are protected and what their RTO settings are.

5. Enter a login name for the database, such as "vrmsdbuser-nyc" (see Figure 8.5). Select "SQL server authentication" as the authentication type, and remove the tick next to "Enforce password policy." Finally, select the database you recently created as the default, and click OK.

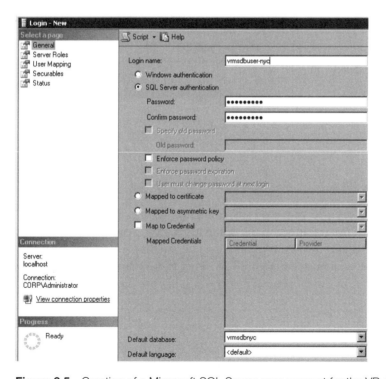

Figure 8.5 Creation of a Microsoft SQL Server user account for the VR database

We need to change the "ownership" of the database we recently created to give this new login account access rights. By default, the database will be owned by the account used to create it—in my case, the domain administrator account.

6. To change the ownership privileges, right-click the VRMS database and choose Properties. Select the Files page, and select the Browse button next to the current owner. This will allow you to change the owner to be the user account you recently created (see Figure 8.6).

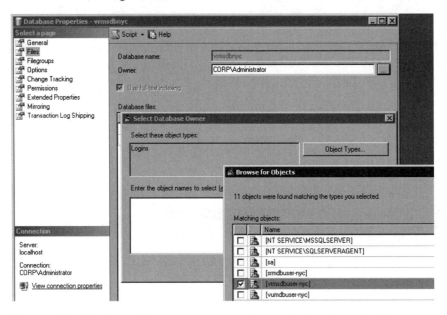

Figure 8.6   Selecting a SQL user account requires navigating through dialog boxes until you can select the account that should own the database.

Deploying the VRMS

The first step in configuring VR is to download and configure the management server. In the vSphere Replication tab, you should see in the Summary page a Deploy VRM Server link under the Commands pane. If this is not present, it is because the UI extensions were not installed during the main installation of SRM. That is something I would always recommend, even if you think in the short term that you will not use the VRS. To import the appliance manually you can use the Deploy OVF Template menu option under the File menu in the vSphere client. The appliance is located by default on the vCenter server at the following location:

C:\Program Files (x86)\VMware\VMware vCenter Site Recovery Manager \www\VRMS.ovf

Alternatively, if you did install the UI extensions, proceed as follows.

1. Log in to the Protected Site vCenter.

2. Select Home and connect to your SRM service.

3. Select the vSphere Replication tab and then click the Deploy VRM Server link in the Commands pane.

4. Acknowledge the welcome message by clicking OK.

5. Click Next to accept the default path for the location of the .ovf file.

6. Accept the default OVF Template Details information.

7. Enter a friendly name for your VRMS, and set a location in the inventory (see Figure 8.7).

8. Select a VMware cluster and resource pool location for the appliance (see Figure 8.8).

9. Select a datastore location to hold the appliance. Do not select one of your replicated datastores. This is an "infrastructure" component that is local to the site within which it is located. The VRMS is approximately 11GB in size and consists of two virtual disks: one 1GB thinly provisioned disk and one 10GB thick provisioned disk.

10. Select a network port group for the appliance; this should be the network you selected when creating the IP pool for the datacenter. In my case, this was the Virtual Storage Appliances port group. Whatever network port group you select, the appliance must be able to communicate with the vCenter server (see Figure 8.9).

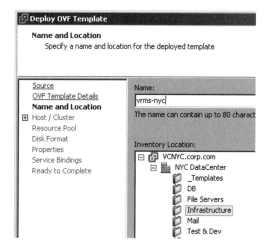

Figure 8.7 As with virtual machines, all virtual appliances need to be placed into an appropriate container in the vCenter inventory.

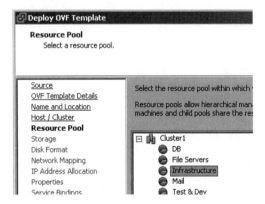

Figure 8.8   Resource pools are not mandatory. The virtual appliance could reside directly on a VMware cluster.

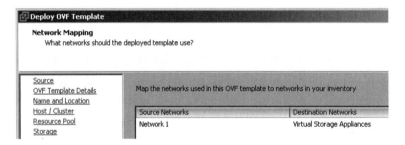

Figure 8.9   I placed my virtual appliances on my port group dedicated to this traffic.

11. Set a fixed IP address for the virtual appliance, and set a password for the root account (see Figure 8.10).

12. Accept the default for the service bindings; the .ovf file knows the correct path for this because of the configuration of the Managed IP Address value that was set previously in the Runtime Settings (see Figure 8.11).

13. While the appliance is downloading and then powering on, repeat this configuration at the Recovery Site.

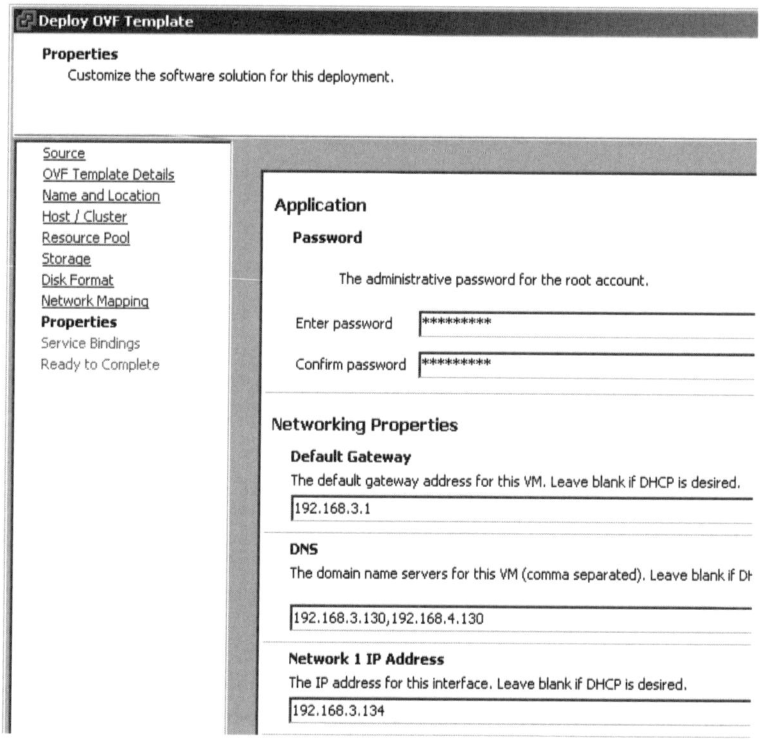

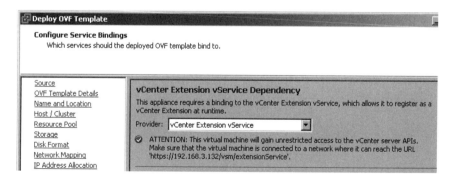

Figure 8.10 Setting static IP addresses and the password on the appliance

Figure 8.11 The VRMS registers itself with vCenter.

Configuring the VRMS

The next stage in the setup process is to configure the VRMS. The VRMS will need to be configured for its database, vCenter, and optionally, certificate settings. This is carried out via a Web page administration tool. If you haven't installed the GUI elements of the VRS during the setup of SRM you can log in to this configuration management page at:

https:/<IP address of VRMS host>:8080

Alternatively, if you did install the UI extensions, proceed as follows.

1. In the vSphere client, and in the SRM application, select the vSphere Replication tab and then click the Configure VRM Server link in the Commands pane. This should open a Web page to the virtual appliance. You may need to wait for the appliance to completely boot and VMware Tools to start successfully before clicking this link.

2. Log in to the appliance as root and with your password, and then select the Configuration page.

3. Configure the settings for the connection to the database (see Figure 8.12).

4. The VRMS host settings should show the IP address of the VRMS, together with a friendly default name of VRMS Site Name. I accepted the default settings here. It is possible to change this value after the setup of VRMS if you wish.

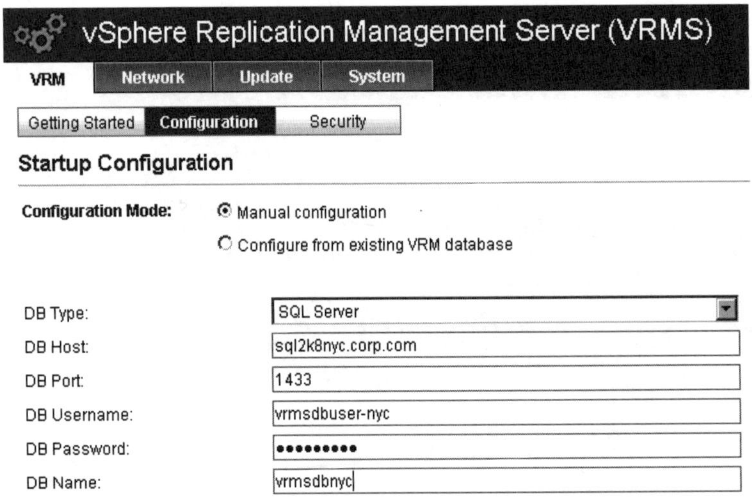

Figure 8.12 Provide the appropriate variables to complete a connection using Microsoft SQL Server.

5. Scroll down the Web page to locate your vCenter address settings and supply valid user account details to register the appliance with vCenter (see Figure 8.13). The email field is not mandatory.

6. Select the Save and Restart Service button. At this point, you should be prompted to accept or reject the built-in certificate from the vCenter server. This confirms that the appliance is connecting to a valid vCenter. Click the Accept button, and then wait for the "Successfully saved the start-up configuration" message in green to appear under the Startup Configuration heading.

Once the appliance is correctly configured, you may wish to confirm your time zone settings in the System tab, and configure them relative to the geographical locations of the VRMS.

If you have the vSphere client open, the VRMS will cause a certificate acceptance dialog box to open for you to confirm identity. Once this has been accepted, you will see that the icon for the VRMS appliance in the inventory has been modified (see Figure 8.14).

This process also extends the main vSphere client UI, adding a vSphere Replication icon to the end of the right-click menu option on the properties of an individual VM (see Figure 8.15).

7. Repeat this configuration at the Recovery Site.

Figure 8.13   In the same page, you will also need to provide credentials for the vCenter server.

Figure 8.14   Once the initial startup settings have been made, the icon for the VRMS virtual appliance changes.

Figure 8.15 The right-click context-sensitive menus are enabled for VR, and new tabs are available on the VMs' properties.

Configuring the VRMS Connection

The next step of the configuration is to "pair" the VRMS systems together. This is similar to the pairing processes we saw between the sites and the array managers.

1. Select the vSphere Replication tab, and then click the "Configure VRMS connection" link in the Commands pane.

2. In the dialog box that opens, click Yes to continue with the pairing process. If necessary, enter the username and password to connect to the Recovery Site vCenter.

3. Click OK to any certificate warnings.

4. The wizard should discover the other VRMS in the Recovery Site and pair the two management systems together (see Figure 8.16).

   In the VRMS status page you should see that the server has been successfully paired (see Figure 8.17). As with the pairing of sites in SRM there is a "Break VRMS connection" option in the Command pane should you need to change the relationship at a later stage.

Figure 8.16 Once the VRMS systems in the Protected Site and Recovery Site are configured it is possible to pair them together.

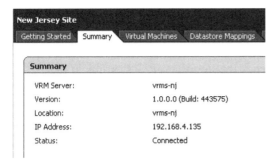

Figure 8.17 The VRMS should report that it is connected to the VRMS in the other site.

Deploying the VRS

The next stage is to deploy the VRS. If you remember, the VRS virtual appliance is a recipient of the changes taking place inside the VMs that have been protected by the VRMS. As a consequence, you need at least one at the Recovery Site for replication to work. It is possible to have more than one VRS to scale out the solution. For two-way replication to take place you would need at least one VRS at the Recovery Site and one at the Protected Site. Additionally, if you want to failback a VRS-protected VM, you would need a VRS at the Protected Site in order to synchronize any changes back to the Protected Site during the time you were running the VM at the Recovery Site; otherwise, data loss could occur. In my case, I decided to deploy a VRS appliance for both sites so that later on, when we come to carry out failover and failback tasks, everything will be in place for that to happen.

To import the appliance manually you can use the Deploy OVF Template menu option under the File menu in the vSphere client. The appliance is located by default on the vCenter server at the following location on the SRM server:

C:\Program Files (x86)\VMware\VMware vCenter Site Recovery Manager \www\VRS.ova

Alternatively, if you did install the UI extensions, select the vSphere Replication tab and then click the Deploy VRS Server link in the Commands pane.

The import process is almost exactly the same as the deployment of the VRMS that we covered earlier. The total disk size of the VRS is 9GB in the first instance constructed from two virtual disks (1GB thin and 8GB thick). The only difference with the VRS is that you are not prompted to set a password for the root account.

Registering the VRS

Once the VRS has been deployed and powered on you can register it with vCenter.

1. Select the vSphere Replication tab and click the Register VR Server link in the Commands pane.

2. In the Register VR Server dialog box (see Figure 8.18), navigate to the vCenter inventory and select the VRS that was imported in the previous steps.

3. After clicking OK, click Yes to confirm that you wish to register the VRS.

4. Click OK to confirm the certificate of the VRS.

5. Once the VRS has successfully registered, click OK to confirm the prompt.

At this point, you should have the VRS registered at both sites (see Figure 8.19).

Now that this deploy and configure process has been completed the Getting Started pages should indicate that all the setups have been successfully configured (see Figure 8.20).

Figure 8.18   The VRS must be located in a folder or datacenter, and cannot reside in a vApp for the registration process to work.

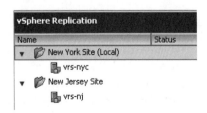

Figure 8.19   Once the VRMS and VRS are running, the vSphere client will update adding their site names to the list.

Getting Started with vSphere Replication

These steps will help you deploy and configure virtual appliances to manage vSphere Replication (VR). Complete these steps for both sites.

✓ **1. Deploy the VRM Server**

Deploy the vSphere Replication Management Server (VRMS) virtual appliance. The URL for the required files will be pre-populated in the install wizard.
Deploy the VRM Server

✓ **2. Configure the VRM Server**

Launch the virtual appliance management interface for the VRM Server and configure the settings as required for your installation.
Configure the VRM Server

✓ **3. Configure VRMS Connection**

After a VRM Server has been added at both sites, configure the connection between the VRM Servers.
Configure VRMS Connection

✓ **4. Deploy a VR Server**

Deploy a VR Server virtual appliance. The URL for the required files will be pre-populated in the install wizard. Depending on your installation, you may need more than one VR Server at each site.
Deploy a VR Server

✓ **5. Register VR Servers**

Each VR Server at a site must be registered with the VRM Server for that site.
Register a VR Server

Figure 8.20   The Getting Started Wizard steers you through the configuration process, acknowledging the completion of each stage.

Enabling and Monitoring vSphere Replication

Now that you have installed and configured the VR components it's time to enable replication for your virtual machines. To test the new VR functionality I created an NFS datastore at the Protected Site that was driven by one of my NetApp filers, and I created an iSCSI volume at the Recovery Site driven by one of my Dell EqualLogic arrays. This will be sufficient to demonstrate that VR works across two entirely different storage protocols and vendors. I decided to use local storage in my test to verify that no expensive storage was needed to replicate my VMs. Of course, without shared storage features, such as vMotion, HR, DRS, or DPM will not work. To enable VR on a VM, follow these steps.

1. Ensure that the selected VM is powered on; then right-click VM and select Site Recovery Manager vSphere Replication. If you want to protect multiple VMs, switch to the VMs and Templates view, select a folder, and then select the Virtual Machines

tab. Select multiple VMs using either Ctrl-Click or Shift-Click; once your selection is complete, right-click and select the option to enable VR.

2. In the Configure Replication dialog box in the Replication Settings page move the slider bar to your desired RPO.

3. Optionally, you can set the file system of the VM to be quiesced during the replication process. If your VM is Windows-based and supports Microsoft Volume Shadow Copy Service (VSS), this can improve the consistency of your VM when it's recovered in a DR event.

4. Using the Browse button select the datastore which will act as the destination or target for your replication. In this case, you are setting the location for the replication of the .vmx file. Notice how in the dialog box shown in Figure 8.21 the volume names indicate that the source is using NFS and the target is using iSCSI.

5. For each virtual disk that comprises the target VM, select a target location and, if you want, set what format the virtual disk should be in when it has been copied to

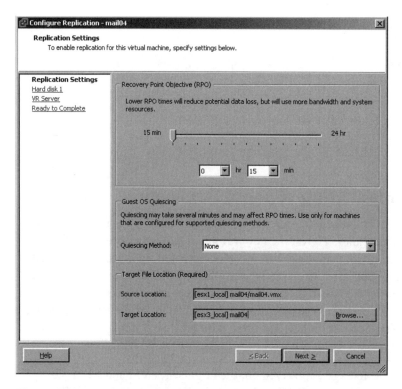

Figure 8.21   In the Replication Settings dialog box you can configure the replication schedule and destination for the replication event.

the target (see Figure 8.22). This allows you to have a virtual disk set as "thick" in the Protected Site, but stored in the "thin" format at the Recovery Site.

6. Assign a VRS as the target for updates. As I stated before, it's possible to have more than one VRS for scale-out capabilities; using auto-assign enables the system to pick the least loaded VRS hosts as the target (see Figure 8.23). Alternatively, you can manually assign the VRS for this VM. This would allow you to manually optimize your VR environment to make sure no single VRS is overloaded with updates.

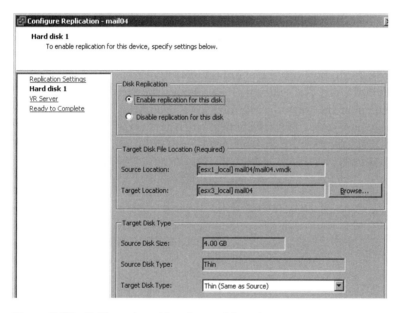

Figure 8.22   Setting a target location and format

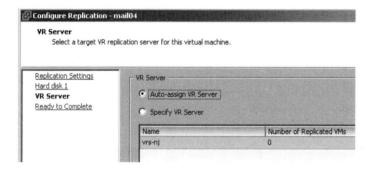

Figure 8.23   You can have the system choose the VRS, or you can choose one yourself.

Moving, Pausing, Resuming, Removing, and Forcing Synchronization

Once VR is in place, there are buttons to control the process. These options appear at the target or Recovery Site VRS (see Figure 8.24), and they are quite easy to understand. The "Move to" option allows you to move the VM from one VRS to another. You might start with a simple environment, but as your needs grow, so does your requirement for additional VRS. This option allows you to redistribute the load among your new VRS hosts. The Pause Replication and Resume Replication options allow you to temporarily stop and start replication between the two VRS at the Protected and Recovery Sites. You would do this if you were expecting some temporary network outage between the two sites, or if you were carrying out a major reconfiguration of your VR environment. The Remove Replication option removes and disables replication for a given VM, and removes it from the scope of the VRMS. You would carry out this task if a VM no longer needed protection, or at the end of the proof-of-concept phase. Finally, the Synchronize Now option is used to force an update between the two VRS hosts. You would use this if you had experienced an outage or a loss of network connectivity between the two VRS.

Figure 8.24   The controls for the replication process. Currently there are no controls to limit the bandwidth allocated to the replication process.

Enabling Replication for Physical Couriering

Sometimes, due to lack of bandwidth and a large virtual disk size, carrying out an initial synchronization becomes unfeasible. For this reason, it is possible to download the virtual disks that make up a VM to removable media, and then have the data securely couriered to the target Recovery Site. In this scenario, all that is required are the differences that have accrued during the physical shipping and uploading of the virtual disks. This is sometimes referred to as the sneakernet approach.

The process begins by taking a maintenance window on the VM, and powering it down. Then you can use vSphere's datastore browser to download the virtual disk to a location that facilitates transfer to some type of removable media (see Figure 8.25).

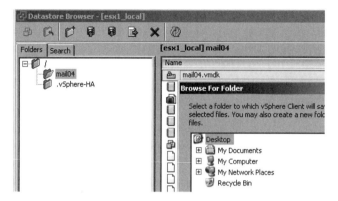

Figure 8.25   By using the vSphere client's download and upload buttons, it is possible to copy the VM to another location.

At the Recovery Site, you can browse the target datastore and create a folder with the same name as the VM—in my case, this is fs02. You can use the same datastore browser at the Recovery Site to upload the .vmdk file into this folder. When you run through the VR wizard the system will detect that there is already a .vmdk file there and will ask if you want to use it as the basis for an initial copy (see Figure 8.26).

Configuring Datastore Mappings

In my example, I only have one datastore at both locations utilized by the VRS. In more advanced configurations, you may have many datastores with many VMs on them protected by VR. Of course, it would be a chore for each VM, possibly with many disks, to have to specify the target location for every VM you protect. For this reason, VR has its own datastore mappings feature that allows you to configure the relationship between the

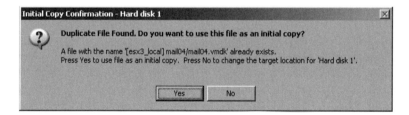

Figure 8.26   VR recognizes an existing image has been manually copied to the Recovery Site, and will use it as the source for the initial sync.

relevant datastores. This should reduce the number of steps required to configure a VM for VR. Those steps include the following.

1. Select the vSphere Replication tab, and then select the Protected Site inventory.

2. Select the Datastore Mappings tab, and select the datastore which holds your vSphere-protected VMs (see Figure 8.27). In my case, this is the VRS-NFS datastore.

3. Select the Configure Mapping link, and in the corresponding dialog box select the target datastore in the list. In my case, this is the esx3_local volume (see Figure 8.28).

Figure 8.27   It is possible, although not required, to map datastores in a Protected Site to datastores in a Recovery Site.

Figure 8.28   The mapping of one local store to another held at the Recovery Site

Summary

As you can see, the setup of VR is relatively straightforward, but it does require that you go through each step methodically and in the correct order. Once the actual virtual appliances are correctly configured, the features are relatively easy to set up and use. Remember, you only need one management system per vCenter install (the VRMS), but you may require more than one replication server (the VRS) depending on the number of changes you expect to see in the file systems of your virtual machines. The next stage in the process is to create a Protection Group for the vSphere-replicated VMs, and then to configure a Recovery Plan for them as well.

The process for creating Protection Groups for VMs that are being replicated by either the storage vendor or VR is the same. The only difference is that a radio button indicating which type of replication you are using is shown in the Protection Group dialog box, as you can see in Figure 8.29.

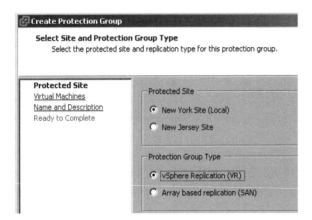

Figure 8.29 The configuration SRM differs only slightly once you are creating Protection Groups and Recovery Plans.

Chapter 9

Configuring the Protected Site

Now that the core SRM product is installed it's possible to progress through the post-configuration stages. Each of these stages depends highly on the previous configuration being completed correctly. It would be correct to assume that this then creates a dependency between each stage such that you must be careful about making changes once the components have been interlinked. Essentially, the post-configuration stages constitute a "workflow." The first step is to pair the two sites together, which creates a relationship between the Protected Site (NYC) and the Recovery Site (NJ). Then we can create inventory mappings that enable the administrator to build relationships between the folders, resource pools, or clusters and networks between the Protected Site and the Recovery Site. These inventory mappings ensure that VMs are recovered to the correct location in the vCenter environment. At that point, it is possible to configure the array managers. At this stage you make the sites aware of the identities of your storage systems at both locations; the SRM will interrogate the arrays and discover which datastores have been marked for replication. The last two main stages are to create Protection Groups and to create Recovery Plans. You cannot create Recovery Plans without first creating Protection Groups, as their name implies the point to the datastores that you have configured for replication. The Protection Groups use the inventory mappings to determine the location of what VMware calls "placeholder VMs." These placeholder VMs are used in Recovery Plans to indicate when and where they should be recovered and allows for advanced features such as VM Dependencies and scripting callouts. I will be going through each step in detail, walking you through the configuration all the way so that by the end of the chapter, you should really understand what each stage entails and why it must be completed.

Connecting the Protected and Recovery Site SRMs

One of the main tasks carried out in the first configuration of SRM is to connect the Protected Site SRM to the Recovery Site SRM. It's at this point that you configure a relationship between the two, and really this is the first time you indicate which is the Protected Site and which is the Recovery Site. It's a convention that you start this pairing process at the Protected Site. The reality is that the pairing creates a two-way relationship between the locations anyway, and it really doesn't matter from which site you do this. But for my own sanity, I've always started the process from the protected location.

When doing this first configuration, I prefer to have two vSphere client windows open: one on the protected vCenter and the other on the recovery vCenter. This way, I get to monitor both parts of the pairing process. I did this often in my early use of SRM so that I could see in real time the effect of changes in the Protected Site on the Recovery Site. Of course, you can simplify things greatly by using the linked mode feature in vSphere. Although with SRM new views show both the Recovery and Protected Sites at the same time, the benefits of linked mode are somewhat limited; however, I think linked mode can be useful for your general administration. For the moment, I'm keeping the two vCenters separate so that it's 100% clear that one is the Protected Site and the other is the Recovery Site (see Figure 9.1).

As you might suspect, this pairing process clearly means the Protected Site SRM and Recovery Site SRM will need to communicate to each other to share information. It is possible to have the same IP range used at two different geographical locations. This networking concept is called "stretched VLANs." Stretched VLANs can greatly simplify the pairing process, as well as greatly simplify the networking of virtual machines when you run tests or invoke your Recovery Plans. If you have never heard of stretched VLANs, it's well worth brushing up on them, and considering their usage to facilitate DR/BC. The stretched VLAN configuration, as we will see later, can actually ease the administrative

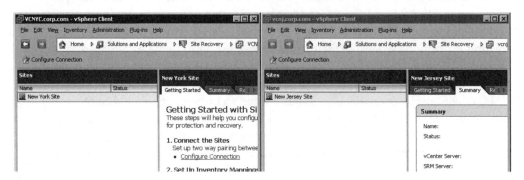

Figure 9.1   The Protected Site (New York) is on the left; the Recovery Site (New Jersey) is on the right.

burden when running test plans or invoking DR for real. Other methods of simplifying communications, especially when testing and running Recovery Plans, include the use of network address translation (NAT) systems or modifying the routing configuration between the two locations. This can stop the need to re-IP the virtual machines as they boot in the DR location. We will look at this in more detail in subsequent chapters.

This pairing process is sometimes referred to as "establishing reciprocity." In the first release of SRM the pairing process was one-to-one, and it was not possible to create hub-and-spoke configurations where one site is paired to many sites. The structure of SRM 1.0 prevented many-to-many SRM pairing relationships. Back in SRM 4.0, VMware introduced support for a shared-site configuration where one DR location can provide resources for many Protected Sites. However, in these early stages I want to keep with the two-site configuration.

Installing the SRM and vCenter software on the same instance of Windows can save you a Windows license. However, some people might consider this approach as increasing their dependence on the management system of vCenter. If you like, there is a worry or anxiety about creating an "all-eggs-in-one-basket" scenario. If you follow this rationale to its logical extreme, your management server will have many jobs to do, such as being the

- vCenter server

- Web access server

- Converter server

- Update Manager server

My main point, really, is that if the pairing process fails, it probably has more to do with IP communication, DNS name resolution, and firewalls than anything else. IP visibility from the Protected to the Recovery Site is required to set up SRM. Personally, I always recommend dedicated Windows instances for the SRM role, and in these days of Microsoft licensing allowing multiple instances of Enterprise and Datacenter Editions on the same hypervisor, the cost savings are not as great as they once were.

When connecting the sites together you always log in to the Protected Site and connect it to the Recovery Site. This starting order dictates the relationship between the two SRM servers.

1. Log in with the vSphere client to the vCenter server for the Protected Site SRM (New York).

2. In the Sites pane, click the Configure Connection button shown in Figure 9.2. Alternatively, if you still have the Getting Started tab available, click the Configure Connection link.

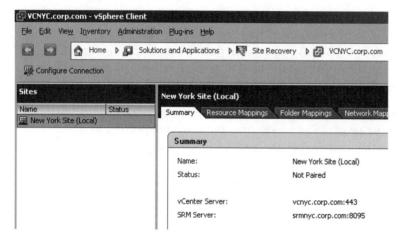

Figure 9.2   The status of the New York Site is "not paired" until the Configure Connection Wizard is run.

Notice how the site is marked as being "local," since we logged in to it directly as though we are physically located at the New York location. If I had logged in to the New Jersey site directly it would be earmarked as local instead.

3. In the Configure Connection dialog box enter the name of the vCenter for the Recovery Site, as shown in Figure 9.3.

When you enter the vCenter hostname use lowercase letters; the vCenter hostname must be entered exactly the same way during pairing as it was during installation (for example, either fully qualified in all cases or not fully qualified in all cases). Additionally, although you can use either a name or an IP address during the pairing process, be consistent. Don't use a mix of IP addresses and FQDNs together, as

---

Configure Connection

Remote Site Information
Connect to a remote vCenter Server that will recover virtual machines from this site in case of a disaster.

Remote Site Information	Enter the address and port for a remote vCenter Server.
Authentication	
Complete Connections	Address: vcnj.corp.com
	Example: vcserver.company.com
	Port: 80

Figure 9.3   Despite the use of port 80 in the dialog box, all communication is redirected to port 443.

this only confuses SRM. As we saw earlier during the installation, despite entering port 80 to connect to the vCenter system, it does appear to be the case that communication is on port 443.

Again, if you are using the untrusted auto-generated certificates that come with a default installation of vCenter you will receive a certificate security warning dialog box, as shown in Figure 9.4. The statement "Remote server certificate has error(s)" is largely an indication that the certificate is auto-generated and untrusted. It doesn't indicate fault in the certificate itself, but rather is more a reflection of its status.

4. Specify the username and password for the vCenter server at the Recovery Site.

Again, if you are using the untrusted auto-generated certificates that come with a default installation of SRM you will receive a certificate security warning dialog box. This second certificate warning is to validate the SRM certificate, and is very similar to the previous dialog box for validating the vCenter certificate of the Recovery Site. So, although these two dialog boxes look similar, they are issuing warnings regarding completely different servers: the vCenter server and the SRM server of the Recovery Site. Authentication between sites can be difficult if the Protected and Recovery Sites are different domains and there is no trust relationship between them. In my case, I opted for a single domain that spanned both the Protected and Recovery Sites.

5. At this point the SRM wizard will attempt to pair the sites, and the Complete Connections dialog box will show you the progress of this task, as shown in Figure 9.5, on the Recent Tasks of the Protected vCenter.

6. At the end of the process you will be prompted to authenticate the vSphere client against the remote (Recovery) site. If you have two vSphere clients open at the same

Figure 9.4 Dialog box indicating there is an error with the remote server certificate

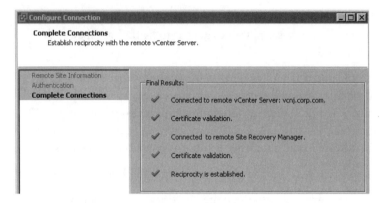

Figure 9.5 Pairing the sites (a.k.a. establishing reciprocity)

time on both the Protected and Recovery Sites you will receive two dialog login box prompts, one for each SRM server. Notice how in the dialog box shown in Figure 9.6 I'm using the full NT domain-style login of DOMAIN\Username. This dialog box appears each time you load the vSphere client and select the SRM icon.

At the end of this first stage you should check that the two sites are flagged as being connected for both the local site and the paired site, as shown in Figure 9.7.

Additionally, under the Commands pane on the right-hand side you will see that the Break Connection link is the reverse of the pairing process. It's hard to think of a use case for this option. But I guess you may at a later stage unpair two sites and create a different relationship. In an extreme case, if you had a real disaster the original Protected Site might be irretrievably lost. In this case, you would have no option but to seek a different site to maintain your DR planning. Also in the Commands pane you will find the option to export your system logs. These can be invaluable when it comes to troubleshooting, and you'll need them should you raise an SR with VMware Support. As you can see, SRM has a new interface, and even with vCenter linked mode available this new UI should reduce the amount of time you spend toggling between the Protected and Recovery Sites. Indeed, for

Figure 9.6 Entering login credentials for the Recovery Site vCenter

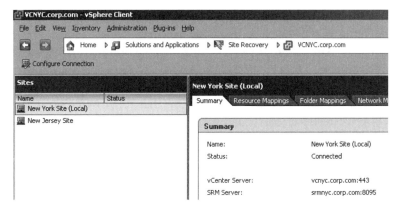

Figure 9.7   The sites are connected and paired together; notice how communication to the vCenter in the Recovery Site used port 443.

the most part I only keep my vCenters separated in this early stage when I am carrying out customer demonstrations; it helps to keep the customer clear on the two different locations.

From this point onward, whenever you load the vSphere client for the first time and click the Site Recovery Manager icon you will be prompted for a username and password for the remote vCenter. The same dialog box appears on the Recovery Site SRM. Although the vSphere client has the ability to pass through your user credentials from your domain logon, this currently is not supported for SRM, mainly because you could be using totally different credentials at the Recovery Site anyway. For most organizations this would be a standard practice—two different vCenters need two different administration stacks to prevent the breach of one vCenter leading to a breach of all others.

Configuring Inventory Mappings

The next stage in the configuration is to configure inventory mappings. This involves mapping the resources (clusters and resource pools), folders, and networks of the Protected Site to the Recovery Site. Ostensibly, this happens because we have two separate vCenter installations that are not linked by a common data source. This is true despite the use of linked mode in vSphere. The only things that are shared between two or more vCenters in linked mode are licensing, roles, and the search functionality. The remainder of the vCenter metadata (datacenters, clusters, folders, and resource pools) is still locked inside the vCenter database driven by Microsoft SQL, Oracle, or IBM DB2.

When your Recovery Plan is invoked for testing or for real, the SRM server at the Recovery Site needs to know your preferences for bringing your replicated VMs online. Although the recovery location has the virtual machine files by virtue of third-party replication software, the metadata that comprises the vCenter inventory is not replicated. It is up to the SRM administrator to decide how this "soft" vCenter data is handled. The SRM administrator needs to be able to indicate what resource pools, networks, and folders the replicated VMs will use. This means that when VMs are recovered they are brought online in the correct location and function correctly. Specifically, the important issue is network mappings. If you don't get this right, the VMs that are powered on at the Recovery Site might not be accessible across the network.

Although this "global default" mapping process is optional, the reality is that you will use it. If you wish, you can manually map each individual VM to the appropriate resource pool, folder, and network when you create Protection Groups. The Inventory Mappings Wizard merely speeds up this process and allows you to set your default preferences. It is possible to do this for each virtual machine individually, but that is very administratively intensive. To have to manually configure each virtual machine to the network, folder, and resource pool it should use in the Recovery Site would be very burdensome in a location with even a few hundred virtual machines. Later in this book we will look at these per-virtual-machine inventory mappings as a way to deal with virtual machines that have unique settings. In a nutshell, think of inventory mappings as a way to deal with virtual machine settings as though they are groups and the other methods as though you were managing them as individual users.

It is perfectly acceptable for certain objects in the inventory mappings to have no mapping at all. After all, there may be resource pools, folders, and networks that do not need to be included in your Recovery Plan. So, some things do not need to be mapped to the Recovery Site, just like not every LUN/volume in the Protected Site needs replicating to the Recovery Site. For example, test and development virtual machines might not be replicated at all, and therefore the inventory objects that are used to manage them are not configured. Similarly, you may have "local" virtual machines that do not need to be configured; a good example might be that your vCenter and its SQL instance may be virtualized. By definition, these "infrastructure" virtual machines are not replicated at the Recovery Site because you already have duplicates of them there; that's part of the architecture of SRM, after all. Other "local" or site-specific services may include such systems as anti-virus, DNS, DHCP, Proxy, Print, and, depending on your directory services structure, Active Directory domain controllers. Lastly, you may have virtual machines that provide deployment services—in my case, the UDA—that do not need to be replicated at the Recovery Site as they are not business-critical, although I think you would need to consider how dependent you are on these ancillary virtual machines for your day-to-day operations. In previous releases, such objects that were not included in the inventory mapping would have the label "None Selected" to indicate that no mapping had been configured. In this new release, VMware has dispensed with this label. Remember, at this stage we are not indicating which VMs will be included in our recovery procedure. This is done at a later stage when we create SRM Protection Groups. Let me remind you (again) of my folder, resource pool, and network structures (see Figure 9.8, Figure 9.9, and Figure 9.10).

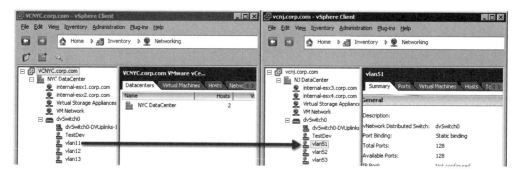

Figure 9.8 My vSwitch configuration at the Protected and Recovery Sites

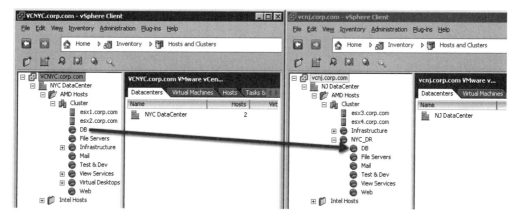

Figure 9.9 My resource pool configuration at the Protected and Recovery Sites

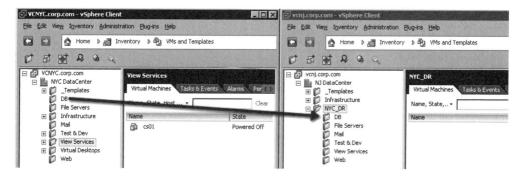

Figure 9.10 My VM folder configuration at the Protected and Recovery Sites

The arrows represent how I will be "mapping" these resources from the Protected Site to the Recovery Site. SRM uses the term *resource mapping* to refer to clusters of ESX hosts and the resource pools within.

Finally, it's worth mentioning that these inventory mappings are used during the reprotect and failback processes. After all, if VMs have been failed over to specific folders, resource pools, and networks, when a failback occurs, those VMs must be returned to their original locations at the Protected Site. No special configuration is required to achieve this—the same inventory mappings used to move VMs from the Protected to the Recovery Site are used when the direction is reversed.

Configuring Resource Mappings

To configure resource mappings, follow these steps.

1. Log on with the vSphere client to the Protected Site's vCenter.
2. Click the Site Recovery icon.
3. Select the Protected Site (in my case, this is New York), and then select the Resource Mapping tab.
4. Double-click your resource pool or the cluster you wish to map, or click the Configure Mapping link as shown in Figure 9.11.

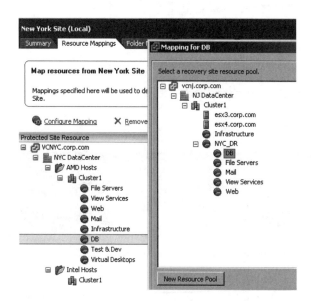

Figure 9.11   In the foreground is the Mapping for DB dialog box where the resource pool in New York is mapped to the NYC_DR\DB resource pool in New Jersey.

Notice how the "Mapping for…" dialog box also now includes the new option to create a new resource pool if it's needed. Remember that the use of resource pools is by no means mandatory. You can run all your VMs from the DRS-enabled cluster, if you prefer. Once you understand the principle of inventory mappings this becomes a somewhat tedious but important task of mapping the correct Protected Site vCenter objects to the Recovery Site vCenter objects.

Configuring Folder Mappings

In my early days of using SRM, I used to take all the VMs from the Protected Site and dump them into one folder called "Recovery VMs" on the Recovery Site's vCenter. I soon discovered how limiting this would be in a failback scenario. I recommend more or less duplicating the folder and resource pool structure at the Recovery Site, so it exactly matches the Protected Site. This offers more control and flexibility, especially when you begin the failback process. I would avoid the casual and cavalier attitude of dumping virtual machines into a flat-level folder.

As you can see in Figure 9.12, I have not bothered to map every folder in the Protected Site to every other folder in the Recovery Site. I've decided I will never be using SRM to failover and failback VMs in the Infrastructure or Test & Dev VM folder. There's little point in creating a mapping if I have no intention of using SRM with these particular VMs.

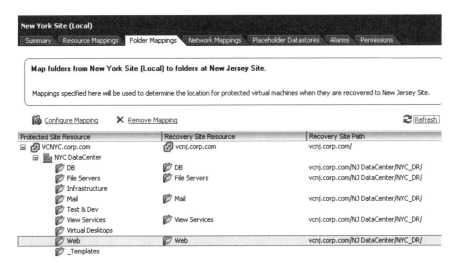

Figure 9.12   My folder inventory mappings. Only the folders and resource pools that SRM will need in order to protect the VMs must be mapped.

Configuring Network Mappings

By default, when you run a test Recovery Plan the Recovery Site SRM will auto-magically put the replicated VMs into a bubble network which isolates them from the wider network using an internal vSwitch. This prevents possible IP and NetBIOS in Windows conflicts. Try to think of this bubble network as a safety valve that allows you to test plans with a guarantee that you will generate no conflicts between the Protected Site and the Recovery Site. So, by default, these network settings are only used in the event of triggering your Recovery Plan for real. If I mapped this "production" network to the "internal" switch, no users would be able to connect to the recovered VMs. Notice in Figure 9.13 how I am not mapping the VM Network or Virtual Storage Appliance port group to the Recovery Site. This is because the VMs that reside on that network deliver local infrastructure resources that I do not intend to include in my Recovery Plan.

Networking and DR can be more involved than you first think, and much depends on how you have the network set up. When you start powering on VMs at the Recovery Site they may be on totally different networks requiring different IP addresses and DNS updates to allow for user connectivity. The good news is that SRM can control and automate this process. One very easy way to simplify this for SRM is to implement stretched VLANs where two geographically different locations appear to be on the same VLAN/subnet. However, you may not have the authority to implement this, and unless it is already in place it is a major change to your physical switch configuration, to say the least. It's worth making it clear that even if you do implement stretched VLANs you may still have to create inventory mappings because of port group differences. For example, there may be a VLAN

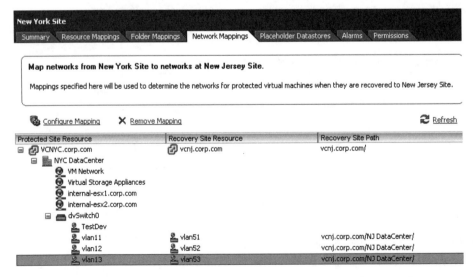

Figure 9.13 Map only the port groups that you plan to use in your Recovery Plan.

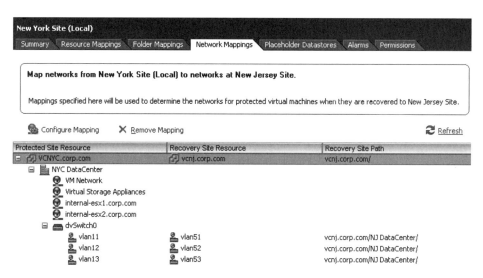

Figure 9.14   Network mappings can include different switch types if needed.

101 in New York and a VLAN 101 in New Jersey. But if the administrative team in New York calls their port groups on a virtual switch "NYC-101" and the guys in Chicago call theirs "NJ-101" you would still need a port group mapping in the Inventory Mappings tab.

Finally, in my experience it is possible to map between the two virtual switch types of Distributed and Standard vSwitches (see Figure 9.14). This does allow you to run a lower-level SKU of the vSphere 5 product in the DR location. So you could be using Enterprise Plus in the Protected Site and the Advanced version of vSphere 5 in the Recovery Site. People might be tempted to do this to save money on licensing. However, I think it is fraught with unexpected consequences, and I do not recommend it; it's a recipe for negative unforeseen outcomes. For example, an eight-way VM licensed for Enterprise Plus in the Protected Site would not start in the Recovery Site. A version of vSphere 5 that doesn't support DRS clustering and the initial placement feature would mean having to map specific VMs to specific ESX hosts. So you certainly can map DvSwitches to SvSwitches, and vice versa. To SRM, port groups are just labels and it just doesn't care. But remember, if VM is mapped from a DvSwitch to the SvSwitch it may lose functionality that only the DvSwitch can provide.

Assigning Placeholder Datastores

As we will see later in this chapter, an important part of the wizard for creating Protection Groups is selecting a destination for placeholders for the Recovery Site. This is a VMFS or NFS volume at the recovery location. When you create a Protection Group at the production site, SRM creates a VMX file and the other smaller files that make up the virtual machine from the Protected Site to the Recovery Site using the placeholder datastore selected in the wizard. It then preregisters these placeholder VMX files to the ESX host at the Recovery Site. This registration process also allocates the virtual machine to the default resource pool, network, and folder as set in the inventory mappings section. Remember, your real virtual machines are really being replicated to a LUN/volume on the storage array at the Recovery Site. You can treat these placeholders as an ancillary VM used just to complete the registration process required to get the virtual machine listed in the Recovery Site's vCenter inventory. Without the placeholder VMs, there would be no object to select when you create Recovery Plans.

If you think about it, although we are replicating our virtual machines from the Protected Site to the Recovery Site, the VMX file does contain site-specific information, especially in terms of networking. The VLAN and IP address used at the recovery location could differ markedly from the protected location. If we just used the VMX as it was in the replicated volume, some of its settings would be invalid (port group name and VLAN, for example), but others would not change (amount of memory and CPUs).

The main purpose of placeholder VMX files is that they help you see visually in the vCenter inventory where your virtual machines will reside prior to executing the Recovery Plan. This allows you to confirm up front whether your inventory mappings are correct. If a virtual machine does not appear at the Recovery Site, it's a clear indication that it is not protected. It would have been possible for VMware to create the virtual machine at the Recovery Site at the point of testing the Recovery Plan, but doing it this way gives the operator an opportunity to fix problems before even testing a Recovery Plan.

So, before you begin configuring the array manager of Protection Groups, you should create a small, 5–10GB volume on the storage array of your choice and present that to all the ESX hosts that will perform DR functions. For example, on my EMC NS-120 array I created a 5GB LUN visible to my Recovery Site ESX hosts (esx3/4), called using EMC's Virtual Storage Console formatted with VMFS, and giving it a friendly volume name of SRM_Placeholders. It's a good practice to keep the placeholder datastores relatively small, distinct, and well named to stop people from storing real VMs on them. If you wish, you could use datastore folders together with permissions to stop this from happening.

It's worth stating that if you ever want to run your Recovery Plan (failover) for real, either for planned migration or for disaster recovery, you would need a placeholder datastore at the Protected Site as well for returning to the production location as part of any reprotect and automated failback procedure. This has important consequences if you want to easily use the new automatic failback process or reprotect features. I'd go so far as to say that you might as well create a placeholder volume at both locations at the very beginning.

This placeholder datastore needs to be presented to every ESX host in the cluster that would act as a recovery host in the event of DR. The datastore could be used across clusters if you so wished, so long as it was presented to all the hosts that need to have access to it in the site. For me, each cluster represents an allocation of memory, CPU, network, *and* storage. In my case, I created placeholder datastores at New Jersey used in the process of protecting VMs in New York, and similarly I created placeholder datastores at New York used in the process of protecting VMs in New Jersey. In most cases you will really need only one placeholder datastore per cluster. As I knew at some stage I would need to do a failover and failback process in SRM it made sense to set these placeholder datastores at this stage, as shown in Figure 9.15.

Remember, the smallest VMFS volume you can create is 1.2GB. If the volume is any smaller than this you will not be able to format it. The placeholder files do not consume much space, so small volumes should be sufficient, although you may wish to leverage your storage vendor's thin-provisioning features so that you don't unnecessarily waste space—but hey, what's a couple of gigabytes in the grand scheme of things compared to the storage footprint of the VMs themselves? On NFS you may be able to have a smaller size for your placeholder datastore; much depends on the array—for example, the smallest volume size on my NetApp FAS2040 is 20GB.

It really doesn't matter what type of datastore you select for the placeholder VMX file. You can even use local storage; remember, only temporary files are used in the SRM

Figure 9.15   Placeholder datastores should be on nonreplicated datastores available to all hosts in the datacenter or clusters where SRM is in use.

process. However, local storage is perhaps not a very wise choice. If that ESX host goes down, is in maintenance mode, or is in a disconnected state, SRM would not be able to access the placeholder files while executing a Recovery Plan. It would be much better to use storage that is shared among the ESX hosts in the Recovery Site. If one of your ESX hosts was unable to access the shared storage location for placeholder files, it would merely be skipped, and no placeholder VMs would be registered on it. The size of the datastore does not have to be large; the placeholder files are the smaller files that make up a virtual machine, they do not contain virtual disks.

But you might find it useful to either remember where they are located, or set up a dedicated place to store them, rather than mixing them up with real virtual machine files. It is a good practice to use folder and resource pool names that reflect that these place-holder virtual machines are not "real." In my case, the parent folder and resource pool are called "NYC_DR" at the New Jersey Recovery Site. Once the placeholder datastore has been created, you can configure SRM at the Protected Site and use it to create the "shadow" VMs in the inventory.

1. In SRM, select the Protected Site; in my case, this is the New York site.

2. Select the Placeholder Datastores tab (see Figure 9.16).

3. Click the Configure Placeholder Datastore link.

4. In the subsequent dialog box, select the datastore(s) you created.

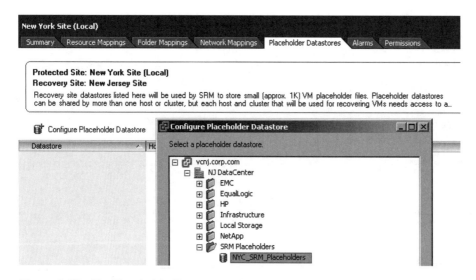

Figure 9.16 The Placeholder Datastores tab

The dialog box in Figure 9.16 does allow you to add multiple placeholder datastores for each cluster that you have. The choice is yours: one placeholder datastore for *all* your clusters, or one placeholder datastore for each cluster in vCenter. Your choice will very much depend on your storage layer and policies within your organization. For example, if you are using IP-based storage it will be very easy to present an iSCSI or NFS volume across many VMware clusters. If you're using Fibre Channel, this could involve some serious work with zoning and masking at the switch and storage management layer. It may be your storage team's policy that each ESX host in a VMware cluster represents a block of storage or a "pod" that cannot be presented to other hosts outside the cluster.

If you look closely at the screen grab you can see that from New York Site (Local), I am browsing the datastores in the New Jersey vCenter. From there I can locate the datastore I called "NYC_SRM_Placeholders" as the location for the placeholder files. I configured a similar setup at the New Jersey location to facilitate the new automatic failback and reprotect features in SRM.

Configuring Array Managers: An Introduction

The next essential part of SRM post-configuration involves enabling the array manager's piece of the product. The array manager is often just a graphical front end for supplying variables to the SRA. Of course I'm assuming you have a storage array which is supported for use with SRM. It may be that you don't, and you would prefer to use VMware's vSphere Replication (VR) instead.

If you do you have a storage array, it's in the Array Manager pane that you inform SRM what engine you are using to replicate your virtual machines from the Protected to the Recovery Site. In this process, SRA interrogates the array to discover which LUNs are being replicated, and enables the Recovery Site SRM to "mirror" your virtual machines to the recovery array. You must configure each array at the Protected Site that will take part in the replication of virtual machines. If a new array is added at a later stage it must be configured here. The array manager will not show every LUN/volume replicated on the storage array—just the ones used by your ESX hosts. The SRA works this out by looking at the files that make up the VM and only reporting LUNs/volumes which are in use by VMs on ESX hosts. This is why it's useful once you have set up the replication part of the puzzle to populate LUNs/volumes with VMs.

Clearly, the configuration of each array manager will vary from one vendor to the next. As much as I would like to be vendor-neutral at all times, it's not possible for me to validate every array manager configuration because that would be cost- and time-prohibitive.

However, if you look closely at the screen grabs for each SRA that I've included in this book you can see that they all share two main points. First, you must provide an IP address or URL to communicate with the storage array, and second, you must provide user credentials to authenticate with it. Most SRAs will have two fields for two IP addresses; this is usually for the first and second storage controllers which offer redundant connections into the array, whether it is based on Fibre Channel, iSCSI, or NFS. Sometimes you will be asked to provide a single IP address because your storage vendor has assumed that you have teamed your NIC interfaces together for load balancing and network redundancy. Different vendors label these storage controllers differently, so if you're familiar with NetApp perhaps the term *storage heads* is what you are used to, or if it's EMC CLARiiON you use the term *storage processor*. Clearly, for the SRA to work there must be a configured IP address for these storage controllers and it must be accessible to the SRM server.

As I stated in Chapter 7, Installing VMware SRM, there is no need now to restart the core SRM service (vmware-dr) when you install or upgrade an SRA. Of course, your environment can and will change over time, and there is room for mistakes. Perhaps, for instance, in your haste you installed the SRA into the Protected Site SRM server, but forgot to perform the same task at the Recovery Site. For this reason, VMware has added a Reload SRAs link, shown in Figure 9.17, under the SRAs tab in the Array Manager pane. If you do install or update an SRA it's worth clicking this button to make sure the system has the latest information.

Before beginning with the array manager configuration, it is worthwhile to check if there are any warnings or alerts in either the Summary tab or the SRAs tab, as this can prevent you from wasting time trying to configure the feature where it would never be successful. For example, if there is a mismatch between the SRAs installed at either the Protected or the Recovery Site you would receive a warning status on the affected SRA, as shown in Figure 9.18. This information displayed in the SRAs tab of the affected system can also tell you information about supported arrays and firmware.

Similarly, if your SRA has specific post-configuration requirements, and you subsequently fail to complete them, this can cause another status error message. For example, the message "The server fault 'DrStorageFaultCannotLoadAdapter'" was caused by my installation of the IMB SystemStorage SRA and not completing the configuration with the

Figure 9.17 With the Reload SRAs link, the SRM administrator doesn't have to restart the core vmware-dr service for changes to take effect.

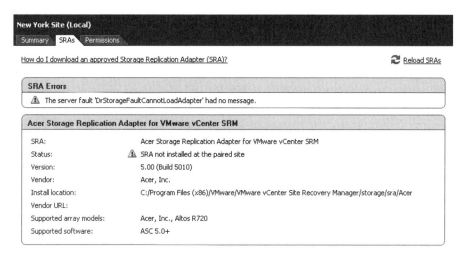

Figure 9.18 To avoid false alarms, ensure that the SRA is installed on all the SRM servers before reloading the SRAs.

IBMSVCRAutil.exe program. The moral of the story is to not unnecessarily install SRAs that you don't need. I did because I'm a curious fellow; however, that curiosity often leads to learning something new that I can pass on to my customers and colleagues.

Most SRAs work the same way: You supply IP information and user authentication details to the wizard. By supplying to the Protected and Recovery Sites details regarding both IP address and authentication, you allow SRM to automate processes that would normally require the interaction of the storage management team or interaction with the storage management system. This is used specifically in SRM when a Recovery Plan is tested as the ESX host's HBAs in the recovery location are rescanned, and the SRA from the storage vendor allows them access to the replicated LUNs/volumes to allow the test to proceed. However, this functionality does vary from one storage array vendor to another. For example, these privileges in some arrays would allow for the dynamic creation and destruction of temporary snapshots, as is the case with EMC Celerra or NetApp filers. With other vendors someone on the storage team would have to grant access to the LUN and snapshot for this to be successful, as is the case with the EMC CLARiiON.

You might think that allowing this level of access to the storage layer would be deeply political; indeed, it could well be. However, in my discussions with VMware and those people who were among the first to try out SRM, this hasn't always been the case. In fact, many storage teams are more than happy to give up this control if it means fewer requests for manual intervention from the server or virtualization teams. You see, many storage guys get understandably irritated if people like us are forever ringing them up to ask them to carry out mundane tasks such as creating a snapshot and then presenting it to a number of ESX hosts. The fact that we as SRM administrators can do that safely and automatically without their help takes this burden away from the storage team so that they can have time for other tasks. Unfortunately, for some companies this still might be a difficult pill for the storage team to swallow without fully explaining this to them before the remit of SRA. If there has been any annoyance for the storage team it has often been in the poor and hard-to-find documentation from the storage vendors. That has left some SRM administrators and storage teams struggling to work out the requirements to make the vendor's SRA function correctly.

Anyway, what follows is a blow-by-blow description of how to configure the array manager for the main storage vendors. If I were you, I would skip to the section heading that relates to the specific array vendor that you are configuring, because as I've said before, one array manager wizard is very similar to another. Array manager configuration starts with the same process, regardless of the array vendor.

1. Log on with the vSphere client to the Protected Site's vCenter—in my case, this is vcnyc.corp.com.

2. Click the Site Recovery icon.

3. Click the Array Managers icon.

4. Click the Add Array Manager button, as shown in Figure 9.19.

Once the array manager configuration has been completed and enabled, you will see in the Recent Tasks pane that it carries out four main tasks for each vCenter that is affected (see Figure 9.20).

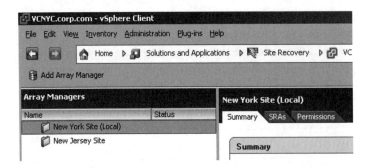

Figure 9.19 The Add Array Manager button that allows you to input your configuration specific to your SRA

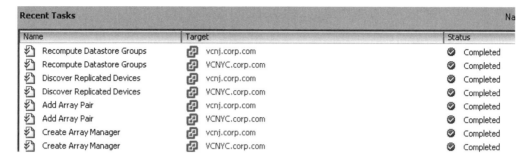

Figure 9.20   Updating the array manager configuration or refreshing it will trigger events at both the Protected and Recovery Sites.

Configuring Array Managers: Dell EqualLogic

To configure the array manager for the Dell EqualLogic, resume with these steps.

5. In the Add Array Manager dialog box, enter a friendly name for this manager, such as "Dell Array Manager for Protected Site".

6. Select Dell EqualLogic PS Series SRA as the SRA Type, as shown in Figure 9.21.

7. Enter the IP address of the group at the Protected Site in the IP Address field; in my case, this is my New York EqualLogic system with the IP address of 172.168.3.69.

8. Supply the username and password for the Dell EqualLogic Group Manager.

9. Complete this configuration for the Partner Group; in my case, this is 172.168.4.69, the IP address of the Group Manager in New Jersey, as shown in Figure 9.22.

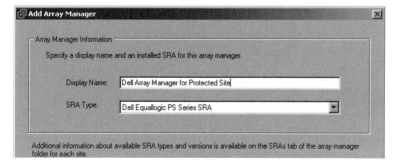

Figure 9.21   Dell uses the concept of groups as collections of array members. You may wish to use a naming convention reflecting these group names.

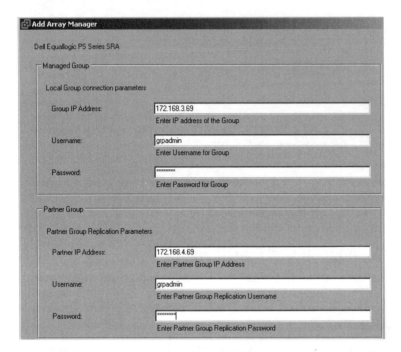

Figure 9.22   Configuration of the Protected Site (local group connection parameters) and Recovery Site (partner group replication parameters)

These dialog boxes occasionally require you to scroll down in order to see all the fields.

10. Click Next and then Finish. Once the array manager configuration for the Protected Site is added, it should also add the array manager configuration for the Recovery Site, as shown in Figure 9.23.

The next step is to enable the configuration. If you have used SRM before you will recognize this is a new step in the array manager configuration. It's designed to give the SRM administrator more control over the array pairs than was previously

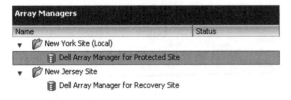

Figure 9.23   The array manager configuration for both sites. You may want to use a naming convention reflecting the Dell EqualLogic group names.

possible. If you do not enable the pairing you will be unable to successfully create Protection Groups.

11. To enable the configuration select the Array Pairs tab on the array configuration object and click the Enable link under the Actions column (see Figure 9.24).

Occasionally, I've had to click Enable twice. This appears to be an issue with the way SRM refreshes this page. Once the array manager configuration is in use by Protection Groups it cannot be disabled. Similarly, once a Protection Group is being used by a Recovery Plan it cannot be removed until it is not referenced in a Recovery Plan.

This will complete the Remote Array Manager column with the name of the array configuration for the Recovery Site. If you look under the Devices tab you should see the volumes you are replicating to the Recovery Site. Notice in Figure 9.25 how the device or volume is local to the New York Site. Also notice how the blue arrow indicates the volume is being replicated to the remote location of New Jersey. This arrow changes direction

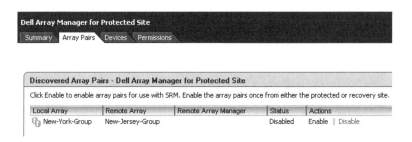

Figure 9.24   Enabling the configuration of the Dell EqualLogic

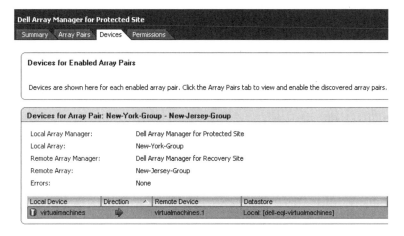

Figure 9.25   SRM's new interface shows the replication direction, and is useful when monitoring failover and failback procedures.

when you carry out an automated failback process, with the Reprotect button inverting the replication direction.

Configuring Array Managers: EMC Celerra

EMC has one SRA that covers both the Unisphere range of arrays and the newer VMX series of systems together with "enabler" software for particular types of replication. So, regardless of the generation you possess, you should be able to install and configure it. Installing the EMC SRA VNX Replicator is a relatively simple affair. In this section, I will walk you through the configuration of the EMC Celerra with VMware SRM.

With EMC Celerra systems the SRM server will communicate to the Celerra at the Protected Site (New York) to collect volume information. It's therefore necessary to configure a valid IP address for the SRM to allow this to occur *or* allow routing/intra-VLAN communication if your SRM and VSA reside on different networks. This is one of the challenges of installing your SRM and vCenter on the same instance of Windows. Another workaround is to give your SRM two network cards: one used for general communication and the other used specifically for communication to the Celerra. If you have no communication between the SRA and the Celerra you will receive an error message. Before you begin it's a good idea to confirm that you can ping both the Protected Site array and the Recovery Site array with the Celerra Control Station IP from the Protected Site (New York) SRM server.

To configure the array manager for the EMC Celerra, resume with these steps.

5. In the Add Array Manager dialog box, enter a friendly name for this manager, such as "EMC Celerra for Protected Site".

6. Select EmcSra as the SRA Type (see Figure 9.26).

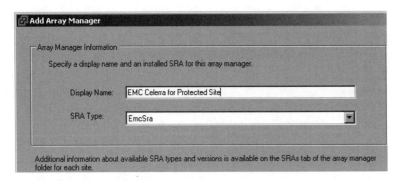

Figure 9.26   If you have many Celerra systems you may want to develop a naming convention that allows you to uniquely identify them.

7. Enter the IP address of the Control Station at the Protected Site in the IP Address field—in my case, this is my New York Celerra system with the IP address of 172.168.3.77.

If you are unsure of the IP address of the Control Station for your system, you can locate it in the Unisphere management pages under System Information, as shown in Figure 9.27.

8. Supply the username and password for the Control Station (see Figure 9.28).

These dialog boxes occasionally require you to scroll down in order to see all the fields.

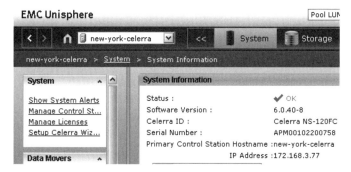

Figure 9.27 Selecting the Celerra from the pull-down list and clicking the System button will show you the Control Station IP address.

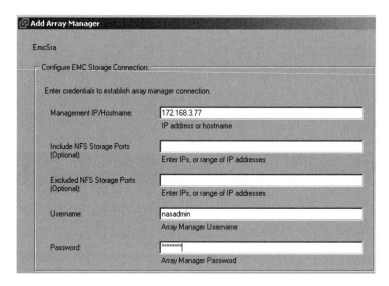

Figure 9.28 If you have NFS mount points as well as iSCSI these may be listening on different IP ports.

9. Click Next and then Finish. Once the array manager configuration for the Protected Site is added, you should also add the array manager configuration for the Recovery Site, as shown in Figure 9.29.

The next step is to enable the configuration, as shown in Figure 9.30. If you have used SRM before you will recognize this is a new step in the array manager configuration. It's designed to give the SRM administrator more control over the array pairs than was previously possible. If you do not enable the pairing you will be unable to successfully create Protection Groups.

10. To enable the configuration select the Array Pairs tab on the array configuration object and click the Enable link under the Actions column.

Occasionally, I've had to click Enable twice. This appears to be an issue with the way SRM refreshes this page. Once the array manager configuration is in use by Protection Groups it cannot be disabled.

This will complete the Remote Array Manager column with the name of the array configuration for the Recovery Site. If you look under the Devices tab you should see the volumes you are replicating to the Recovery Site. Notice how the device or volume is local to the New York Site. Also notice how the blue arrow indicates the volume is being replicated to the remote location of New Jersey. This arrow changes direction when you carry out an automated failback process, with the Reprotect button inverting the replication direction (see Figure 9.31).

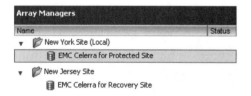

Figure 9.29   Although some array managers ask for the Recovery Site's IP and authentication details, you still must configure the Recovery Site SRA.

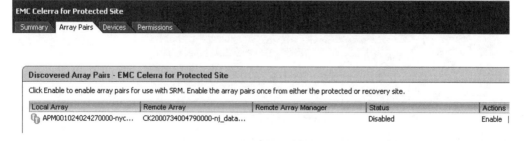

Figure 9.30   Enabling the configuration of the EMC Celerra

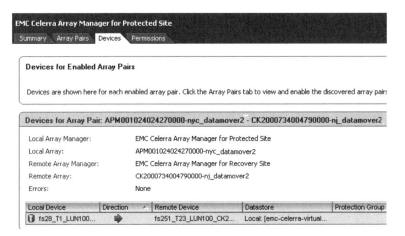

Figure 9.31   The SRM interface shows the replication direction, and is useful when monitoring failover and failback procedures.

Configuring Array Managers: EMC CLARiiON

EMC has one SRA that covers both the Unisphere range of arrays and the newer VMX series of systems together with "enabler" software for particular types of replication. So, regardless of the generation you possess, you should be able to install and configure it. Installing the EMC SRA VNX Replicator is a relatively simple affair. In this section, I will walk you through the configuration of the EMC CLARiiON with VMware SRM.

With EMC CLARiiON systems the SRM server will communicate to the CLARiiON at the Protected Site (New York) to collect volume information. It's therefore necessary to configure a valid IP address for the SRM to allow this to occur *or* allow routing/intra-VLAN communication if your SRM and VSA reside on different networks. This is one of the challenges of installing your SRM and vCenter on the same instance of Windows. Another workaround is to give your SRM two network cards: one used for general communication and the other used specifically for communication to the CLARiiON. If you have no communication between the SRA and the CLARiiON you will receive an error message. Before you begin, it's a good idea to confirm that you can ping both the Protected Site array and the Recovery Site array with the CLARiiON SP A and SP B ports' IP address from the Protected Site (New York) SRM server.

To configure the array manager for the EMC CLARiiON, resume with these steps.

5. In the Add Array Manager dialog box, enter a friendly name for this manager, such as "EMC Clariion for Protected Site".

6. Select EMC Unified SRA as the SRA Type, as shown in Figure 9.32.

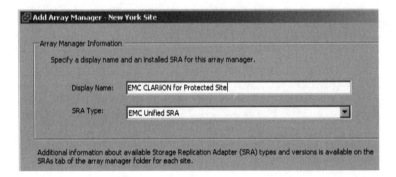

Figure 9.32   If you have many CLARiiON systems you might want to develop a naming convention that allows you to uniquely identify them.

7. Enter the IP address of the storage processors (SPA and SPB) at the Protected Site in the IP Address field—in my case, this is my New York CLARiiON system with the IP addresses 172.168.3.79 and 172.168.3.78.

    If you are unsure of the IP address of the storage processors for your system, you can locate it in the Unisphere management pages under System Information.

8. Supply the username and password for the CLARiiON together with the IP address for the SPA and SPB (see Figure 9.33).

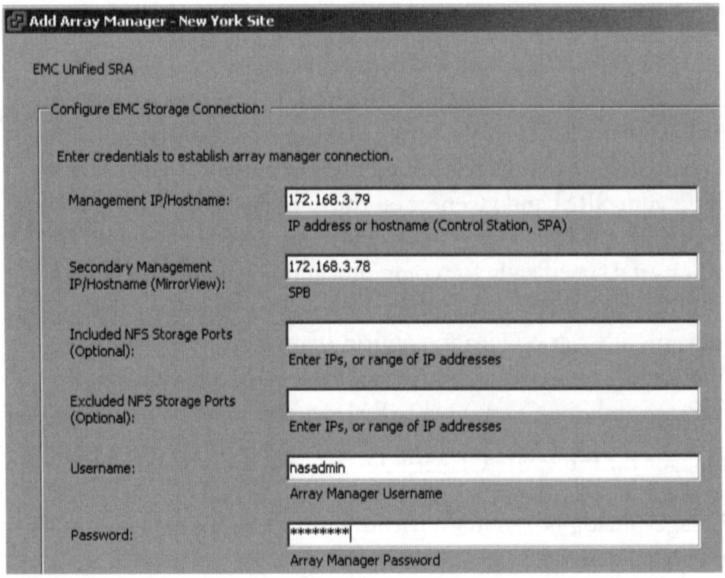

Figure 9.33   The IP address for SPA and SPB on the New York CLARiiON

These dialog boxes occasionally require you to scroll down in order to see all the fields.

9. Click Next and then Finish. Once the array manager configuration for the Protected Site is added, you should also add the array manager configuration for the Recovery Site, as shown in Figure 9.34.

   The next step is to enable the configuration, as shown in Figure 9.35. If you have used SRM before you will recognize this is a new step in the array manager configuration. It's designed to give the SRM administrator more control over the array pairs than was previously possible. If you do not enable the pairing you will be unable to successfully create Protection Groups.

10. To enable the configuration select the Array Pairs tab on the array configuration object and click the Enable link under the Actions column.

    Occasionally, I've had to click Enable twice. This appears to be an issue with the way SRM refreshes this page. Once the array manager configuration is in use by Protection Groups it cannot be disabled.

    This will complete the Remote Array Manager column with the name of the array configuration for the Recovery Site. If you look under the Devices tab you should see the volumes you are replicating to the Recovery Site. Notice how the device or volume is local to the New York Site. Also notice how the blue arrow indicates the volume is being replicated to the remote location of New Jersey. This arrow changes direction when you carry out an automated failback process, with the Reprotect button inverting the replication direction (see Figure 9.36).

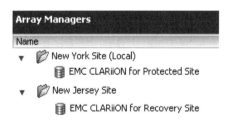

Figure 9.34 Although some array managers ask for the Recovery Site's IP and authentication details, you must configure the Recovery Site SRA.

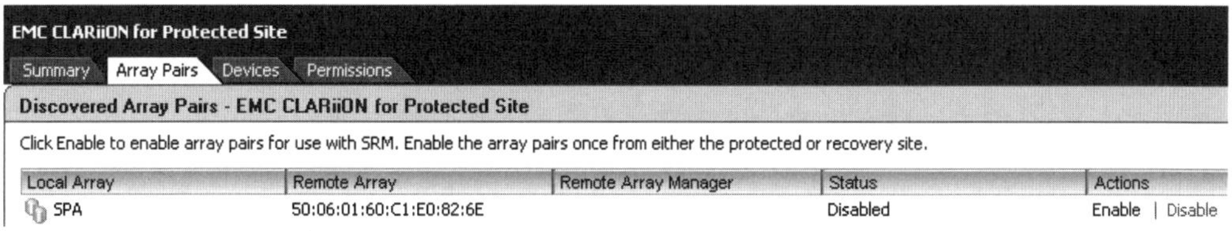

EMC CLARiiON for Protected Site				
Summary	Array Pairs	Devices	Permissions	
Discovered Array Pairs - EMC CLARiiON for Protected Site				
Click Enable to enable array pairs for use with SRM. Enable the array pairs once from either the protected or recovery site.				
Local Array	Remote Array	Remote Array Manager	Status	Actions
SPA	50:06:01:60:C1:E0:82:6E		Disabled	Enable | Disable

Figure 9.35 Enabling the configuration on the EMC CLARiiON

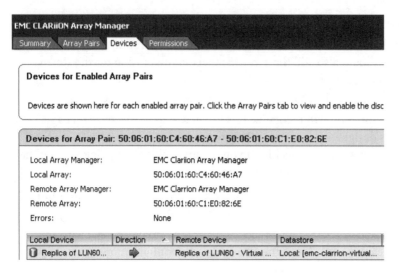

Figure 9.36 SRM can show the replication direction, and is useful when monitoring failover and failback procedures.

Configuring Array Managers: NetApp FSA

To configure the array manager for the NetApp FSA, resume with these steps.

5. In the Add Array Manager dialog box, enter a friendly name for this manager, such as "NetApp Array Manager for Protected Site".

6. Select NetApp Storage Replication Adapter as the SRA Type, as shown in Figure 9.37.

7. Enter the IP address of the group at the Protected Site in the IP Address field—in my case, this is my New York NetApp system with the IP address of 172.168.3.89

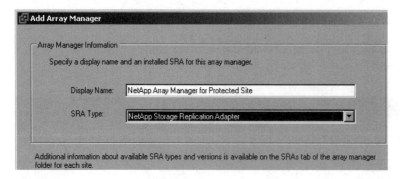

Figure 9.37 The NetApp SRA uses signal configuration for all its supported storage protocols.

(see Figure 9.38). I used the same IP address for the system as the NFS IP filter for NAS. This may not be the case in larger production systems where the management traffic is placed on separate network interfaces.

8. Supply the username and password for the NetApp filer.

These dialog boxes occasionally require you to scroll down in order to see all the fields.

Most customers like to have separate networks for management and data traffic. This is mainly for security reasons, but performance can also be a concern. Many storage admins will use the management network to copy their own data around, such as software packages, service packs, and firmware updates. When the SRA interrogates the NetApp system, it may find a bunch of interfaces using various address ranges. And when SRM interrogates vCenter, it may find a bunch of ESX VMkernel interfaces using various address ranges. So it's entirely possible that when SRM needs to mount an NFS datastore (either the SnapMirror destination volume in a real failover, or a FlexClone of that volume in a test failover), it may choose to use an IP address range such as, for example, the management network. NetApp added the NFS filter to ensure that the SRA only reports the desired addresses back to SRM, which would mean that SRM can only choose the IP network you specify. You can actually specify multiple IP addresses if you need to; just separate them with a comma—for example, 192.168.3.88,192.168.3.87. In my case, I have a much simpler configuration where my management network and my NFS network are the same set of team NICs in the filer.

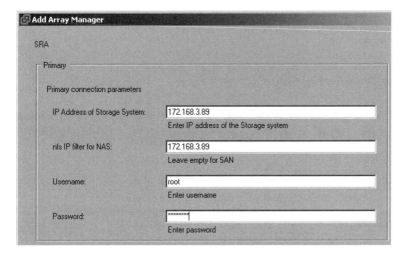

Figure 9.38 Entering the IP address of the group at the Protected Site

9. Click Next and then Finish. Once the array manager configuration for the Protected Site is added, you should also add the array manager configuration for the Recovery Site (see Figure 9.39).

The next step is to enable the configuration. If you have used SRM before you will recognize this is a new step in the array manager configuration. It's designed to give the SRM administrator more control over the array pairs than was previously possible. If you do not enable the pairing you will be unable to successfully create Protection Groups.

10. To enable the configuration select the Array Pairs tab on the array configuration object and click the Enable link under the Actions column (see Figure 9.40).

Occasionally, I've had to click Enable twice. This appears to be an issue with the way SRM refreshes this page. Once the array manager configuration is in use by Protection Groups it cannot be disabled.

This will complete the Remote Array Manager column with the name of the array configuration for the Recovery Site. If you look under the Devices tab you should see the volumes you are replicating to the Recovery Site. Notice how the device or volume is local to the New York Site. Also notice how the blue arrow indicates the volume is being replicated to the remote location of New Jersey. This arrow changes direction when you carry out an automated failback process, with the Reprotect button inverting the replication direction (see Figure 9.41).

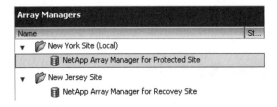

Figure 9.39   If you have multiple arrays, consider a naming convention that allows you to uniquely identify each system.

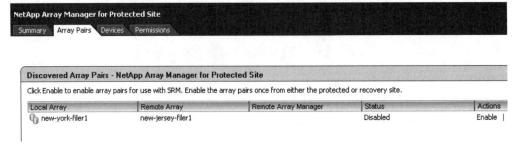

Figure 9.40   Enabling the configuration in NetApp FSA

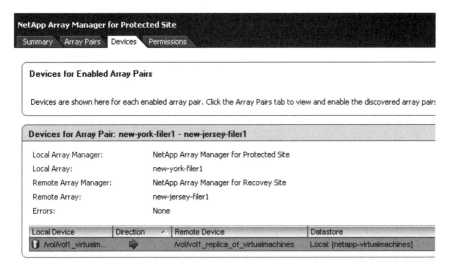

Figure 9.41 SRM can show the replication direction, and is useful when monitoring failover and failback procedures.

Creating Protection Groups

Once you are satisfied with your array manager configuration you're ready to carry on with the next major step: configuring Protection Groups. Protection Groups are used whenever you run a test of your Recovery Plan, or when DR is invoked for real. Protection Groups are pointers to the replicated vSphere datastores that contain collections of virtual machines that will be failed over from the Protected Site to the Recovery Site. The Protection Groups' relationships to ESX datastores can be one-to-one. That is to say, one Protection Group can contain or point to one ESX datastore. Alternatively, it is possible for one Protection Group to contain many datastores—this can happen when a virtual machine's files are spread across many datastores for disk performance optimization reasons or when a virtual machine has a mix of virtual disks and RDM mappings. In a loose way, the SRM Protection Group could be compared to the storage groups or consistency groups you may create in your storage array. However, what actually dictates the membership of a Protection Group is the way the virtual machines utilize the datastores.

> **TIP**
>
> When you create your first Protection Group you might like to have the vSphere client open on both the Protected Site vCenter and the Recovery Site vCenter. This will allow you to watch in real time the events that happen on both systems. Of course, if you are running in linked mode you will see this happening if you expand parts of the inventory.

To configure Protection Groups follow these steps.

1. Log on with the vSphere client to the Protected Site's vCenter (New York).

2. Click the Site Recovery icon.

3. Select the Protection Groups pane and click the Create Protection Group button, as shown in Figure 9.42.

   New to this release is the ability to create folders in the Protection Groups, to allow you to more easily lay out your Protection Groups if you have a significant number of them.

4. In the Create Protection Group dialog box (whether you are using VR or array-based replication), if you have more than one array manager select the one associated with this Protection Group, as shown in Figure 9.43. Then select the pairing of arrays contained within the array manager configuration.

5. Click Next. This should enumerate all the volumes discovered on the arrays in question. If you select the volume names, you should see the VMs contained within those ESX datastores (see Figure 9.44).

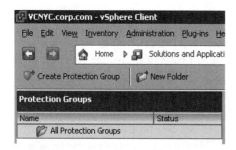

Figure 9.42   You can now create both Protection Groups and Protection Group folders.

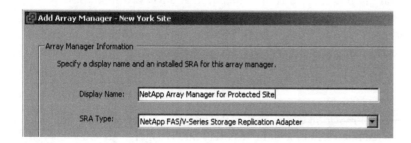

Figure 9.43   The EMC Celerra array manager configuration. You may have many array pairs, each hosting many datastores protected by replication.

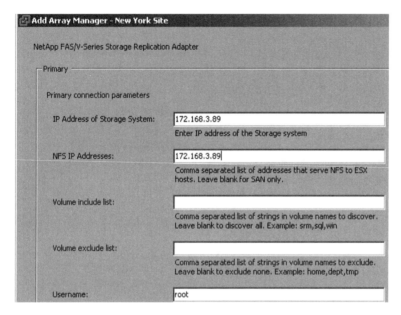

Figure 9.44 Dell EqualLogic datastore containing a number of virtual machines

6. In the Create Protection Group Name and Description dialog box, enter a friendly name and description for your Protection Group. In my case, I'm creating a Protection Group called "Virtual Machines Protection Group." Click Finish.

At this point, a number of events will take place. First, as the Protection Group is being created the icon of the Protection Group changes, and its status is marked as "Configuring Protection," as shown in Figure 9.45. Second, at the Recovery Site vCenter you will see the task bar indicate that the system is busy "protecting" *all* virtual machines that reside in the datastore included in the Protection Group (see Figure 9.46).

Meanwhile, the Recovery Site's vCenter will begin registering the placeholder VMX files in the correct location in the inventory, as shown in Figure 9.47. As you can see, each

Protection Groups

Name	Status
▾ All Protection Groups	
‖‖‖ Virtual Machines Protection...	Configuring Protec..

Figure 9.45 When Protection Groups are first created their status is modified to "Configuring Protection."

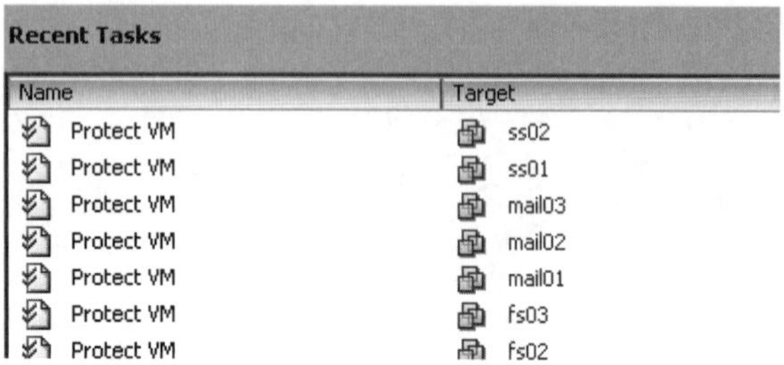

Figure 9.46   During the creation of Protection Groups each affected VM has a task associated with it.

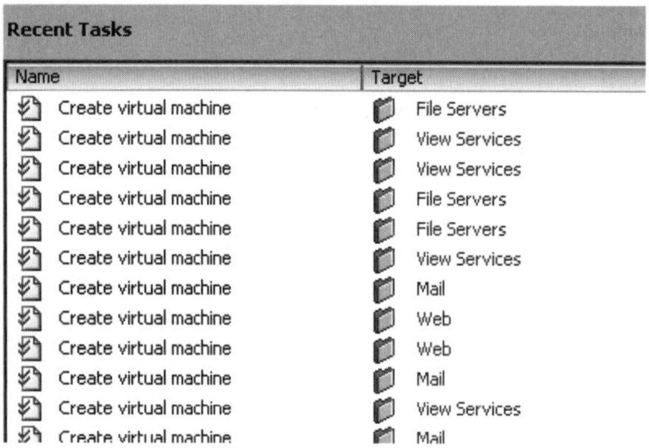

Figure 9.47   The Recovery Site's vCenter begins registering the placeholder VMX files in the correct location in the inventory.

Protect VM event has a "Create virtual machine" event. SRM isn't so much creating a new VM as it is registering placeholder VMs in the Recovery Site.

You will also have noticed these "new" VMs are being placed in the correct resource pool and folder. If you select one of the placeholder files you can see it only takes up a fraction of the storage of the original VM. You should also see that these placeholders have been given their own unique icon in the vCenter inventory at the Recovery Site. This is new to SRM. Previously, the placeholder VMs just had the standard "boxes in boxes" icon, and that made them difficult to identify. Even with the new-style icon, as shown in Figure 9.48, I still recommend a separate resource pool and/or folder structure so that you can keep these ancillary placeholders separate and distinct from the rest of your infrastructure.

If you browse the storage location for these placeholders you can see they are just "dummy" VMX files (see Figure 9.49). As I mentioned before, occasionally VMware SRM

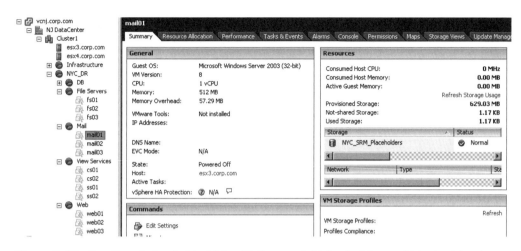

Figure 9.48 Creation of placeholder VMs with the new lightning bolt icon, which should make them easier to distinguish in the vCenter inventory

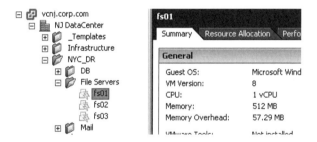

Figure 9.49 Placeholder VMs are created in the datastore specified in the Placeholder tab on the properties of each site.

refers to these placeholder VMs as "shadow" VMs. In the Virtual Machines and Template view, at the Recovery Site's vCenter the VMs have been allocated to the correct folder. SRM knows which network, folder, and resource pool to put the recovery VMs into, because of the default inventory mapping settings we specified earlier.

You should know that if you create a template and store it on a replicated datastore it will become protected as well. This means templates can be recovered and be part of Recovery Plans (covered in Chapter 10) just like ordinary VMs. Templates are not powered on when you run a Recovery Plan, because they can't be powered on without being converted back to being a virtual machine. As you can see, these placeholder VMs are very different from the VMs you normally see registered to vCenter. If you try to edit them like any VM you will be given a warning (shown in Figure 9.50) that this is not a recommended action.

Figure 9.50 The warning dialog box that appears if you try to edit the placeholder VMs listed in the Recovery Site

---

WARNING

Deleting Protection Groups at the Protected Site vCenter reverses this registration process. When you delete a protected group, it unregisters and destroys the placeholder files created at the Recovery Site. This does not affect the replication cycle of the virtual machines that are governed by your array's replication software. Be very cautious when deleting Protection Groups. The action can have unexpected and unwanted consequences if the Protection Groups are "in use" by a Recovery Plan. This potential problem is covered later in this book. To understand it at this point in the book would require additional details regarding Recovery Plans that we have not yet discussed. For now, it's enough to know that if you delete Protection Groups the placeholders get deleted too, and all references to those VMs in the Recovery Plan get removed as well!

Failure to Protect a Virtual Machine

Occasionally, you might find that when you create a Protection Group the process fails to register one or more virtual machines at the Recovery Site. It's important not to overreact to this situation as the causes are usually trivial ones caused by the configuration, and they are very easy to remedy. The most common cause is either bad inventory mappings, or a VM that falls outside the scope of your inventory mappings. In this section I will give you a checklist of settings to confirm, which will hopefully fix these problems for you. They amount to the kind of initial troubleshooting you may experience when you configure SRM for the first time.

Bad Inventory Mappings

This is normally caused by a user error in the previous inventory mapping process. A typical failure to protect a VM is shown in Figure 9.51. The error is flagged on the Protected Site with a yellow exclamation mark on the Protection Group, and the virtual machines that failed to be registered.

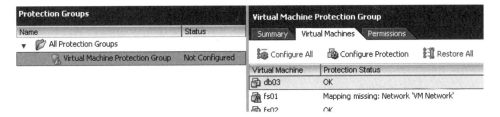

Figure 9.51   A VM failing to be protected because the VM Network port group was not included in the inventory mappings

As a consequence, you will also see errors in the Tasks & Events tab for the affected VMs. The classic clue that a VM has a bad inventory mapping is the "Unable to protect VM <VM name> due to unresolved devices" message shown in Figure 9.52.

This error is usually caused by the virtual machine settings being outside the scope of the inventory mapping settings defined previously, and therefore the Protection Group doesn't know how to map the virtual machine's current folder, resource pool, or network membership to the corresponding location at the Recovery Site. A good example is networking, which I just described above.

In the inventory mapping process, I did not provide any inventory mappings for the VM Network port group. I regarded this as a local network that contained local virtual machines that did not require protection. Accidentally, the virtual machine named "fs01" was patched into this network, and therefore did not get configured properly in the Recovery Plan. In the real world this could have been an oversight; perhaps I meant to set an inventory mapping for vlan10 but forgot to. In this case, the problem wasn't my virtual machine but my bad configuration of the inventory mapping.

Another scenario could be that the inventory mapping is intended to handle default settings where the rule is always X. A number of virtual machines could be held within the Protection Group and could have their own unique settings; after all, one size does

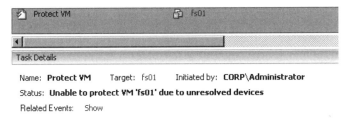

Figure 9.52   The unresolved devices error that usually indicates a problem with inventory mappings

not fit all. SRM can allow for exceptions to those rules when a virtual machine has its own particular configuration that falls outside the group, just like with users and groups.

If you have this type of inventory mapping mismatch it will be up to you to decide on the correct course of action to fix it. Only you can decide if the virtual machine or the inventory mapping is at fault. You can resolve this match in a few different ways.

- Update your inventory mappings to include objects that were originally overlooked.

- Correct the virtual machine settings to fall within the default inventory mapping settings.

- Customize the VM with its own unique inventory mapping. This does not mean you can have rules (inventory mappings) and exceptions to the rules (custom VM settings). A VM either is covered by the default inventory mapping or is not.

If you think the inventory mapping is good, and you just have an exception, it is possible to right-click the icon in the Protection Group, select Configure Protection in the menu that opens, and offer per-VM inventory settings. If you had a bigger problem—a large number of VMs have failed to be protected because of bad inventory mapping configurations—you can resolve that in the inventory mapping, and then use Configure All to try the protection process again.

I would say the most common reason for this error is that you have deployed a new VM from a template, and the template is configured for a network not covered by the inventory mapping. Another cause can concern the use of SvSwitches. It's possible to rename the port groups of an SvSwitch to be a different label. This can cause problems for both the inventory mapping and the affected VMs. As a consequence, when the Protection Groups are created for the first time the protection process fails because the inventory mapping was using the old name.

Placeholder VM Not Found

Another error that can occur is if someone foolishly deletes the placeholder that represents a VM in the Recovery Site, as shown in Figure 9.53. It is possible to manually delete a placeholder VM, although you do get the same warning message as you would if you tried to edit the placeholder settings. Nonetheless, these placeholder objects are not protected from deletion. If a rogue vCenter administrator deletes a placeholder you will see a yellow exclamation mark on the Protection Group, together with a "Placeholder VM Not Found" error message.

The quickest way to fix this problem is to choose either the Restore All link or the Restore Placeholder link in the Protection Group interface. The Restore All option rebuilds all

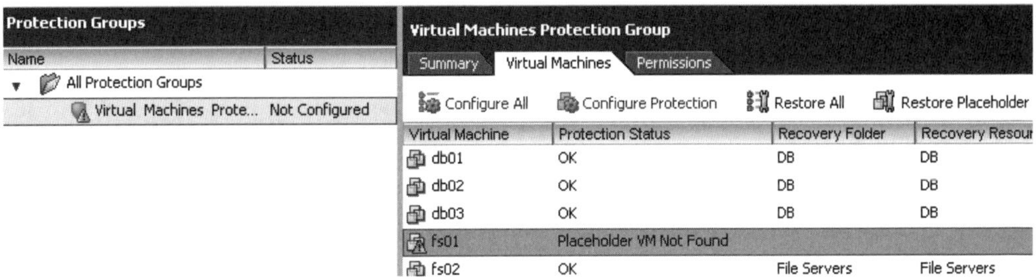

Figure 9.53 The "Placeholder VM Not Found" error message caused by accidental deletion of the placeholder in the inventory

the placeholders within the Protection Group, whereas Restore Placeholder fixes just one selected placeholder in the list.

VMware Tools Update Error—Device Not Found: CD/DVD Drive 1

Occasionally, the Protection Group can have a VM that displays an error on its own. For example, in Figure 9.54 the VM named "db01" has the error message "Device Not Found: CD-DVD drive1." This error is relatively benign and does not stop execution of the plan.

This issue was created by a faulty VMware Tools update using Update Manager. The CD-ROM mounted was to a Linux distribution where an automatic mounting and update of VMware Tools failed. The Update Manager was unsuccessful in unmounting the .iso file at /usr/lib/vmware/isoimages/linux.iso, but the auto-execution of VMware Tools does not work in the same way with Linux as it does with Windows. With Linux all that happens is that the .iso file is mounted as a CD-ROM device, but it is up to the administrator to extract the .tgz package and install VMware Tools to the guest system. This error was resolved by right-clicking the affected VM, and under the Guest menu

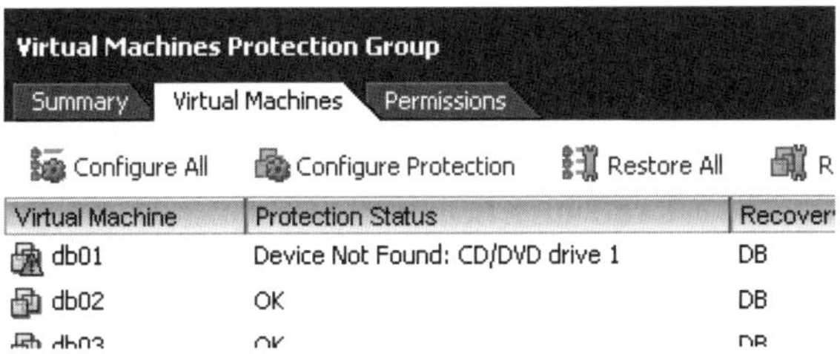

Figure 9.54 The old chestnut of connected CD/DVD drives can cause a benign error to appear on the Protection Group.

selecting "End VMware Tools install." This triggered an unmounting of the VMware Tools .iso image.

Delete VM Error

Occasionally, you will want to delete a VM that might also be a member of a Protection Group. The correct procedure for doing this is to unprotect the VM, which will then unregister its placeholder VMX file, and as a consequence remove it from any Recovery Plan. Of course, there's nothing to stop someone from ignoring this procedure and just deleting the VM from the inventory. This would result in an "orphaned" object in the Protection Group and Recovery Plan, as shown in Figure 9.55.

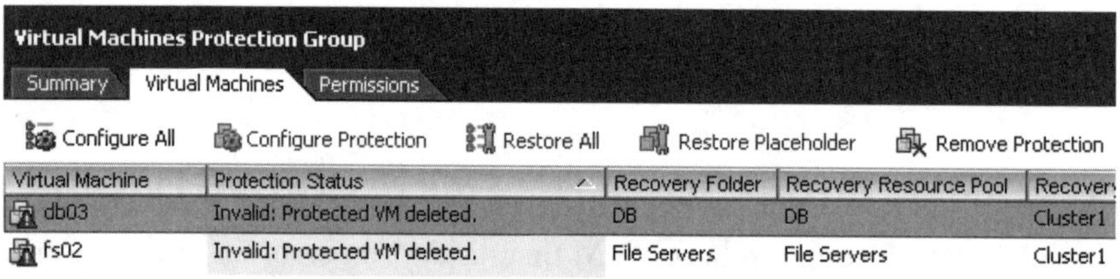

Figure 9.55 The error when a VMware administrator deletes a protected VM without first unprotecting it in SRM

To fix these VMs, select the affected VM and click the Remove Protection button.

It's Not an Error, It's a Naughty, Naughty Boy!

If you can forgive the reference to Monty Python's *The Meaning of Life*, the confusing yellow exclamation mark on a Protection Group can be benign. It can actually indicate that a new virtual machine has been created that is covered by the Protection Group. As I may have stated before, simply creating a new virtual machine on a replicated LUN/volume does not automatically mean it is protected and enrolled in your Recovery Plan. I will cover this in more detail in Chapter 11, Custom Recovery Plans, as I examine how SRM interacts with a production environment that is constantly changing and evolving.

Hopefully with these "errors" you can begin to see the huge benefit that inventory mapping offers. Remember, inventory mappings are optional, and if you chose not to configure them in SRM when you created a Protection Group every virtual machine would fail to be registered at the Recovery Site. This would create tens or hundreds of virtual machines with a yellow exclamation mark, and each one would have to be mapped by hand to the appropriate network, folder, and resource pool.

Summary

As you have seen, one of biggest challenges in SRM in the post-configuration stages is network communication. Not only must your vCenter/SRM servers be able to communicate with one another from the Protected Site to the Recovery Site, but the SRM server must be able to communicate with your array manager also. In the real world, this will be a challenge which may only be addressed by sophisticated routing, NATing, intra-VLAN communication, or by giving your SRM server two network cards to speak to both networks.

It's perhaps worth saying that the communication we allow between the SRM and the storage layer via the vendor's SRA could be very contentious with the storage team. Via the vSphere client you are effectively managing the storage array. Historically, this has been a manual task purely in the hands of the storage team (if you have one), and they may react negatively to the level of rights that the SRM/SRA needs to have to function under a default installation. To some degree we are cutting them out of the loop. This could also have a negative impact on the internal change management procedures used to handle storage replication demands in the business or organization within which you work. This shouldn't be something new to you.

In my research, I found a huge variance in companies' attitudes toward this issue, with some seeing it as a major stumbling block and others as a stumbling block that could be overcome as long as senior management fully backs the implementation of SRM—in other words, the storage team would be forced to accept this change. At the opposite extreme, those people who deal with the day-to-day administration of storage were quite grateful to have their workload reduced, and noted that the fewer people involved in the decision-making process the quicker their precious virtual machines will be online.

Virtualization is a very political technology. As "virtualizationists" we frequently make quite big demands on our network and storage teams that can be deemed as very political. I don't see automating your DR procedures as being any less political. We're talking about one of the most serious decisions a business can take with its IT: invoking its DR plan. The consequences of that plan failing are perhaps even more political than a virtualization project that goes wrong.

Of course, it is totally impossible for me to configure every single storage vendor's arrays and then show you how VMware SRM integrates with them, but hopefully I've given you at least a feel for what goes on at the storage level with these technologies together with insight into how SRM configuration varies depending on your storage vendor's technology. I hope you have enough knowledge now to both communicate your needs to the storage guys as well as understand what they are doing at the storage level to make all this work. In the real world, we tend to live in boxes—I'm a server guy, you're a storage guy, and he's a network guy. Quite frequently we live in ignorance of what each guy is doing. Ignorance and DR make for a very heady brew.

Lastly, I hope you can see how important inventory mappings and Protection Groups are going to be in the recovery process. Without them a Recovery Plan would not know where to put your virtual machines in vCenter (folder, resource pool, and network) and would not know on which LUN/volume to find those virtual machine files. In the next chapter we will look at creating and testing Recovery Plans. I'm going to take a two-pronged approach to this topic. Chapter 10 gets you up and running, and Chapter 11 takes Recovery Plans up to their fully functional level. Don't worry; you're getting closer and closer to hitting that button labeled "Test my Recovery Plan."

Recovery Site Configuration

We are very close to being able to run our first basic test plan. I'm sure you're just itching to press a button that tests failover. I want to get to that stage as quickly as possible so that you get a feel for the components that make up SRM. I want to give you the "bigger picture" view, if you like, before we get lost in the devil that is the detail.

So far all our attention has been on a configuration held at the Protected Site's vCenter. Now we are going to change tack to look at the Recovery Site's vCenter configuration. The critical piece is the creation of a Recovery Plan. It is likely you will have multiple Recovery Plans based on the possibility of different types of failures, which yield different responses. If you lost an entire site, the Recovery Plan would be very different from a Recovery Plan invoked due to loss of an individual storage array or, for that matter, a suite of applications.

Creating a Basic Full-Site Recovery Plan

Our first plan will include every VM within the scope of our Protection Group with little or no customization. We will return to creating a customized Recovery Plan in Chapter 11, Custom Recovery Plans. This is my attempt to get you to the testing part of the product as soon as possible without overwhelming you with too many customizations. The Recovery Plan contains many settings, and you have the ability to configure

- The Protection Group covered by the plan
- Network settings during the testing of plans

To create a plan follow these steps.

1. Log on with the vSphere client to the Recovery Site's vCenter.

2. Click the Site Recovery icon.

3. Select the Recovery Plans tab, and click the Create Recovery Plan button as shown in Figure 10.1.

   As with Protection Groups, Recovery Plans can now be organized into folders, should you require them. This is especially useful in bidirectional or shared-site configurations where you may want to use folders to separate the Recovery Plans of site A from those of site B.

4. Select the Recovery Site where the plan will be recovered, as shown in Figure 10.2. In my case, this will be the New Jersey site. The appearance of "(Local)" next to a site name is dictated by which vCenter you logged in to when opening the vCenter server. As a general rule, Protection Groups reside at the Protected Site and Recovery Plans at the Recovery Site.

5. Select the Protection Groups that will be included in the plan. In my case, I just have one demo Protection Group, shown in Figure 10.3. But later on I will develop

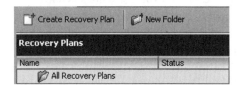

Figure 10.1   As with Protection Groups, Recovery Plans now support folders.

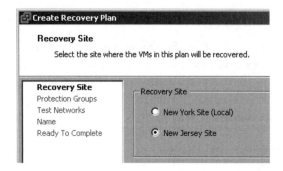

Figure 10.2   Selecting the Recovery Site where the plan will be recovered

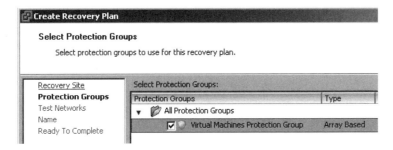

Figure 10.3 Protection Groups can contain many datastores. Here there is just one.

a model where each Protection Group represents an application or service I wish to protect, with datastores created for each application. This will allow for the failover and failback of a discrete application or business unit.

Creating a Recovery Plan for vSphere Replication (VR) is no different from creating one based on array-based replication, so long as you have re-created a Protection Group that covers your vSphere replicated VMs.

6. In the Test Networks dialog box you can control what happens to the networking of VMs (see Figure 10.4); specifically when you *test* a Recovery Plan. You may want for the networking to behave differently while you're *testing* the Recovery Plan compared to when you're *running* the Recovery Plan. Some customers like to set up a distinct network used just for testing purposes.

    The Auto option creates an "internal" Standard vSwitch (SvSwitch) called a "bubble." This ensures that no IP or NetBIOS conflicts can occur between the Protected Site VMs and the Recovery Site VMs. As Figure 10.4 shows, you can override this behavior and map the port group to a Recovery Site vSwitch that would allow communication between the VMs—but watch out for the possibility of creating conflicts with your production VMs.

    On the surface the Auto feature sounds like a good idea; it will stop conflicts based on IP or NetBIOS names. However, it can also stop two virtual machines that should communicate to each other from doing so. Here is an example. Say you have four ESX hosts in a DRS cluster; when the virtual machines are powered on you will have no control over where they will execute. They will *auto*matically be patched to an internal SvSwitch, which means, by definition, that although the virtual machines on that vSwitch will be able to communicate to each other, they will be unable to speak to any other virtual machine on any other ESX host in the cluster. This is what happens if you use the Auto option. The consequences for this are clear:

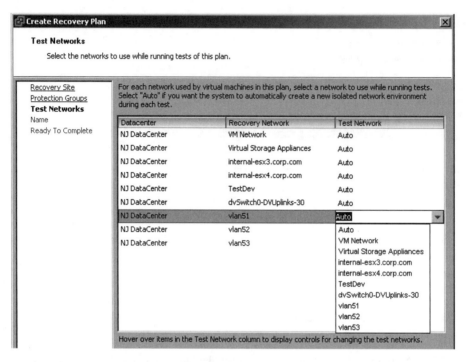

Figure 10.4 You can set up a dedicated VLAN if you don't want the system to automatically create a new isolated network environment.

Despite your ability to order the power on of virtual machines to meet whatever service dependency issues you have, those network services would fail to meet those dependencies, and therefore fail to start properly.

For the moment, the Auto feature in the Create Recovery Plan Wizard is best regarded as a "safety valve" that allows you to test a plan without fear of generating an IP or NetBIOS name conflict in Windows VMs. In my case, I'm going to leave Auto selected simply so that I can show you the effect of using this option. In the real world, I would actually choose a test VLAN configuration.

7. Set a friendly name for the Recovery Plan, as shown in Figure 10.5. As this Protection Group contains all my VMs, I called mine "Complete Loss of Site – Simple Test."

You should spend some time thinking of good names and descriptions for your Recovery Plans, as they will appear in any history reports you might export. You might want to develop your own versioning system which you can increment as you make major changes to the Recovery Plan. The Description field is very useful. It is

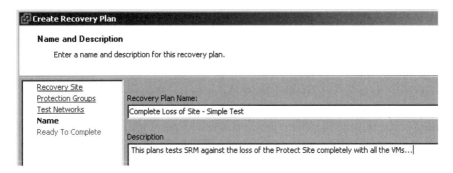

Figure 10.5   A Recovery Plan being created. Try to come up with more meaningful and descriptive names for your plans than I have.

your opportunity to express how the Recovery Plan is used, what is being recovered, and what the expected RTP/RPO values are. Try to view the Description field as your opportunity to embed documentation directly within the SRM product. As such, you could include information about the storage backend and network VLANs used.

8. Click Next and then click Finish to create the Recovery Plan.

As with Protection Groups, Recovery Plans can be much more sophisticated than the plan I just created. Once again, I will return to Recovery Plans in Chapter 11.

Testing Storage Configuration at the Recovery Site

By now you're probably itching to hit the big blue button in SRM, labeled "Test" (see Figure 10.6).

But before you do, if you want your test to complete correctly it is worth confirming that the ESX hosts in the Recovery Site will be able to access the storage array at the Recovery Site. Previously when we were setting this up we focused on making sure the ESX hosts in the Protected Site had access to the VMFS volume. You may have to take the same considerations into account at the Recovery Site as well.

It might be a good practice to make sure the ESX hosts in the Recovery Site have visibility to the storage, especially if you're using iSCSI where post-configuration of the ESX

Figure 10.6   The Test button

hosts is required to allow access to the storage array. In most cases, the hosts at both the Protected and Recovery Sites will already have been granted access to the array location where they reside, especially if you have set up and configured placeholder datastores on the very same arrays that hold the volumes you are replicating.

You may not even have to manually allow the ESX hosts in the Recovery Site when executing the Recovery Plan to a volume or LUN. For example, in the HP PS4000 SRA it will automatically allocate the ESX hosts access to the very latest snapshot if you have set these up as in the Scheduled Remote Copy format. The HP PS4000 VSA knows how to do this because that is one of its main jobs, and because we provided the IP address and user credentials during the array manager configuration at the Protected Site. This may not be the case in other storage vendors' management systems; you may well need to create management groups in the storage array, and allow your ESX hosts to access them for SRM to then present replicated LUNs/volumes to the ESX hosts. If you are unsure about this, refer back to Chapters 2 through 6 where I covered array-based replication for different storage vendors. The way to learn more about your vendor's SRA functions and capabilities is to locate the vendor's ReadMe files and release notes. Ask your storage representative to point you in the direction of implementation and deployment guides; remember, in life you don't get what you don't ask for.

This level of automation does vary from one storage array vendor to another. For example, with your type of storage array you may need to use your "LUN masking" feature to grant your Recovery Site ESX host access to the storage group (a.k.a. volume group, contingency group, consistency group, recovery group) that contains the replicated or snapshot LUN. It is worth double-checking the ReadMe file information that often ships with an SRA to confirm its functionality. Additionally, many storage vendors have such good I/O performance that they create a snapshot on-the-fly for the test and then present this snapshot to the ESX hosts in the Recovery Site. At the end of the test, they will normally delete this temporary snapshot—this is the case with NetApp's FlexClone technology. Figure 10.7 shows what happens at the storage layer during a Recovery Plan test, regardless of whether you use synchronous or asynchronous replication.

The only thing you need to configure on the array is for the ESX hosts in the Recovery Site to have access to the storage groups, which include the replicated LUNs. As long as you do this, when the test is executed the storage vendor's SRA will send an instruction to the storage array to create a snapshot on-the-fly, and it will then instruct the array to present the snapshot (not the R/O replicated LUN) to the ESX hosts (this is indicated by the dashed lines in the diagram). This means that when tests are executed, your production system is still replicating changes to the Recovery Site. In short, running tests is an unobtrusive process, and does not upset the usual pattern of replication that you have configured, because the ESX hosts in the Recovery Site are presented a snapshot of the replicated volume which is marked as read-write, whereas the replicated volume is marked

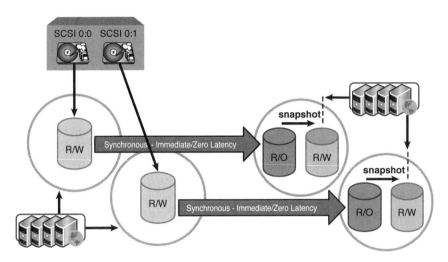

Figure 10.7   Array-based snapshots present a copy of the replicated volume without interrupting the normal cycle of replication.

as read-only—and is still receiving block updates from the Protected Site storage array. Storage vendors that do not create a snapshot on-the-fly will mount the latest snapshot in the replication cycle. This is the case with the HP PS4000 VSA.

Overview: First Recovery Plan Test

Well, we're finally here! If all goes to plan you should be able to run this basic Recovery Plan we have created and find that the VMs in the Recovery Site are powered on. A great many events take place at this point. If you have some software that records the screen, such as HyperCam or Camtasia, you might even want to record the events so that you can play them back. If you want to watch a video of the test, you can view one that I captured and uploaded to RTFM:

www.rtfm-ed.co.uk/srm.html

What Do We Mean by the Word *Test?*

Before we actually "test" our Recovery Plan, I think we should discuss what constitutes a proper test of your DR plan. In many ways the Test button in SRM is actually testing that the SRM software works and that your SRM Recovery Plan functions as expected. For many organizations, a real test would be a hard test of the Recovery Plan—literally hitting the red button, and actually failing over the Protected Site to the Recovery Site.

Think of it this way. If you have a UPS system or a diesel generator at your site, you could do all manner of software tests of the power management system, but you won't really know if the system behaves as hoped until you've lost power. With this attitude in mind, it's not unheard of for large companies to invoke and hard-test their DR plans twice a year. This allows them to identify flaws in the plan, to update their "run books" accordingly, and to keep the team in charge of controlling the DR plan up-to-date with those procedures and unexpected events that can and do happen. In short, clicking the Test button in SRM does not prove or guarantee that the business IT functions will still operate after a disaster. What it does allow is for nonintrusive tests to take place on a much more frequent basis than previously possible—this in itself is a huge advantage. It means you can validate your Recovery Plan on a daily or weekly basis, without ever having to interrupt normal business operations; and for many customers this is one of SRM's biggest advantages.

A common question customers ask is whether it is possible to trigger a plan automatically, perhaps with a script. Currently, the answer to that question is *yes*, but I urge you to use caution if you take this approach. No PowerCLI cmdlets exist that would allow you to test or run a Recovery Plan—although my sources at VMware say the company plans to develop cmdlets for SRM, as it has with other products in its lineup. There is, however, a SOAP-based API that allows for some automation of the tasks in SRM. For example, a method called `RecoveryPlanStart` can be invoked with the SRM API.

With that said, even if there were cmdlets for SRM, many people would worry about false positives—in other words, a DR plan could be acted on automatically, even if no disaster has actually occurred. Generally, people who ask this question are trying to make SRM an availability technology like VMware HA or FT. Nonetheless, some of the more enterprising members of the community have investigated use of the SRM API and .NET objects. So the message is this: Where there is a will, there is always a way, but the idea of automating the execution of a Recovery Plan without a human operator or senior management approval is an idea best avoided.

Another common question is whether it is possible to run two plans simultaneously. The answer is that it depends very much on your storage array vendor's architecture. For example, on my EMC NS-120 I can run two Recovery Plans almost at the same time. Remember that SRM 5.0 actually increases the number of plans you can run simultaneously from three in SRM 4.0 to 30 in SRM 5.0. However, you do need the resources at the Recovery Site in order for this to be successful. It stands to reason that the more Recovery Plans you run currently that depend on the number and configuration of those VMs, the more likely you are to run out of the necessary physical resources to make that viable use case. In the real world, customers often have to make compromises about what they recover based on the limited capabilities of their DR location.

What Happens during a Test of the Recovery Plan?

A significant number of changes take place at the Recovery Site location when a test is run. You can see these basic steps in the Recovery Steps tab shown in Figure 10.8. In previous releases the "test" phases of the plan would include a "cleanup phase" once the SRM administrator was satisfied that the test was successful. In this release, this cleanup phase has now been hived off into separate discrete steps. This will allow you to keep the Recovery Plan running in the "test" phase for as long as your storage at the Recovery Site has space for snapshots. One "guerrilla" use of this new functionality is being able to spin up an exact copy of your live environment for testing purposes, something some of my customers have been doing with SRM since its inception.

When you click the Test button, you can follow the progress of your plan. All errors are flagged in red and successes are marked in green; active processes are marked in red with a % value for how much has been completed. I would like to drill down through the plan and explain in detail what's happening under the covers when you click the Test button. Initially, SRM runs the Synchronize Storage process that allows the SRM administrator to say she wants to carry out an initial synchronization of data between the arrays covered by the Protection Group. This ensures that the data held at the Recovery Site exactly matches the data held at the Protected Site. This can take some time to complete, depending on the volume of data to be synchronized between the two locations and the bandwidth available between the two locations. When you test a Recovery Plan a dialog box appears explaining this process, as shown in Figure 10.9. This dialog box gives the administrator the opportunity to run the test without storage synchronization taking place.

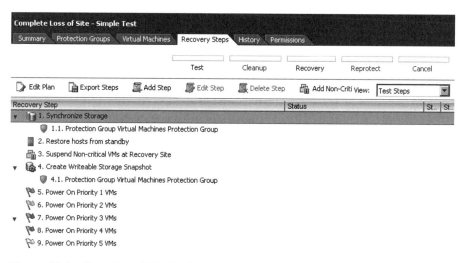

Figure 10.8   Steps 1 and 2 in the Recovery Plan are new to SRM 5.0.

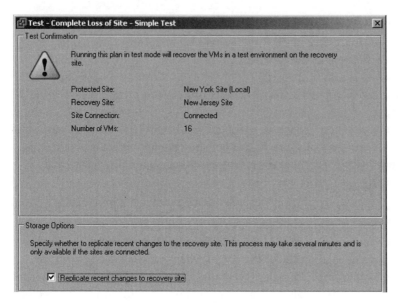

Figure 10.9   Tests now include the option to bring the Protected and Recovery Sites in sync with each other.

If you don't want the storage synchronization event to take place, merely uncheck the option that states "Replicate recent changes to recovery site." This replication of recent changes can take some time, and if you just want to crack on and test the plan you may wish to bypass it. After you click Next and the test is triggered, the SRA communicates to the storage array and requests that synchronization take place, and then a snapshot is taken of the volumes containing the replicated VMs. This takes place at the Create a Writable Storage Snapshot phase of the plan. Between these two stages, the plan takes the opportunity to unsuspend any ESX hosts that might be in a standby power state, and, if specified, suspend any unneeded VMs in the Recovery Site.

If you are working with either Fibre Channel or iSCSI-based storage, the ESX hosts' HBAs are rescanned. This causes ESX to discover the snapshot volumes that contain the VMs replicated from the Protected Site to the Recovery Site. In the case of NFS, these snapshots are then mounted, but with FC/iSCSI-based storage the ESX hosts refresh to see VMFS volumes. This replicated VMFS snapshot is resignatured and given a volume name of "snap-nnnnnnn-virtualmachines" where "virtualmachines" is, in my case, the original VMFS volume name. In the screen grab in Figure 10.10 you can see the Recovery Plan has been started, and the storage layer of the ESX hosts is in the process of being rescanned.

In the screen grab in Figure 10.11 you can see a VMFS volume has been mounted and resignatured. All resignatured values start with "snap-" so that they can be clearly

Figure 10.10   Several steps take place during a test. You may wish to watch one of my prerecorded videos to see this in real time.

Figure 10.11   A temporary snapshot created on a Dell EqualLogic system. SRM will clean these up once you are finished with your test.

identified. In this case, the Recovery Plan was executed using the Dell EqualLogic array I have in my test lab.

Once the snapshot of the replicated datastore has been presented to the ESX hosts at the Recovery Site, the next step is to unregister the placeholder VMs. Depending on the number of VMs covered by the Protection Groups and Recovery Plans, this can produce many "Delete file" entries in the Recent Tasks pane. This can be a little bit misleading. The placeholder files haven't been physically deleted from the placeholder datastore; rather, they have been "unregistered" from vCenter, as shown in Figure 10.12.

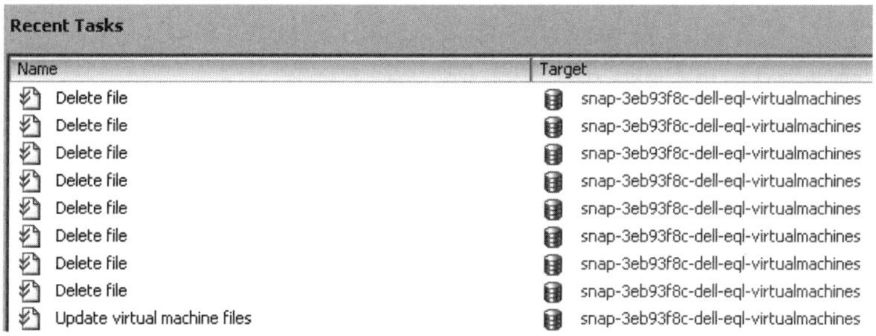

Recent Tasks	
Name	Target
Delete file	snap-3eb93f8c-dell-eql-virtualmachines
Delete file	snap-3eb93f8c-dell-eql-virtualmachines
Delete file	snap-3eb93f8c-dell-eql-virtualmachines
Delete file	snap-3eb93f8c-dell-eql-virtualmachines
Delete file	snap-3eb93f8c-dell-eql-virtualmachines
Delete file	snap-3eb93f8c-dell-eql-virtualmachines
Delete file	snap-3eb93f8c-dell-eql-virtualmachines
Delete file	snap-3eb93f8c-dell-eql-virtualmachines
Update virtual machine files	snap-3eb93f8c-dell-eql-virtualmachines

Figure 10.12   Placeholder VMs are unregistered, and replaced with the real VMs located on the mounted snapshot.

Next, the real VMX files located on the snapshot volume are loaded and then reconfigured, as shown in Figure 10.13. This reconfiguration is caused by changes to their port group settings. As you might recall, these VMX files would have an old and out-of-date port group label: the port group they were configured for at the Protected Site. These need to be remapped either to the internal switch that is created (if you used Auto when you defined your Recovery Plan; see Figure 10.14) or to the port group on the virtual switches at the Recovery Site.

At this stage, the VMs start to be powered on in the list, as controlled by their location in the priority groups. By default, all VMs from all Protection Groups backing the Recovery Plan are mapped to internal switches with the label "srmvs-recovery-plan-NNNNN" as shown in Figure 10.15. This SvSwitch also contains a port group called "srmpg-recovery-plan-NNNN." This naming convention is used to guarantee that both the SvSwitch and the port group are uniquely named.

Previous versions of SRM created a vSwitch called "testBubble-1 vSwitch" with a port group called "testBubble-1 group." For this reason, historically this vSwitch has been called the "bubble" vSwitch because its lack of a vmnic essentially means the VMs are locked in a network bubble on which they communicate to one another on the same

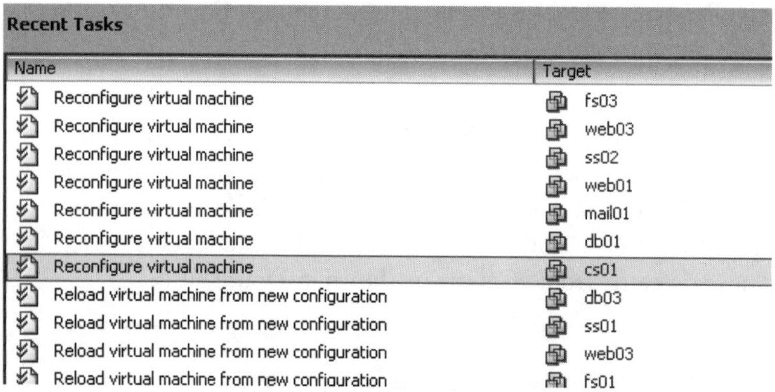

Figure 10.13   VMs are registered to the hosts during the Recovery Plan.

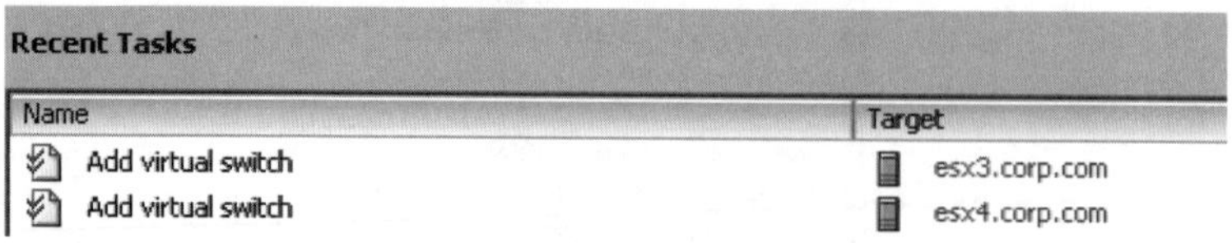

Figure 10.14   If Auto has been used as the switch type for the test, SRM adds a virtual standard switch on each host in the affected cluster.

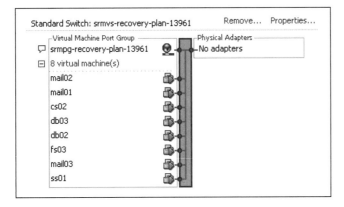

Figure 10.15 The Auto option generates a standard switch called "srmpg-recovery-plan."

vSwitch. So, if you come across colleagues who have used SRM before, it's this format of networking that they are referring to. Remember, this behavior only happens if you used the Auto feature when you first created the Recovery Plan.

> **IMPORTANT NOTE**
>
> Occasionally when the test hangs or goes seriously wrong, in previous versions of SRM I've seen the cleanup phase fail, and this error subsequently fails to remove the vSwitch/port group. It is safe to remove it manually once the test has completed. If your Recovery Plan fails halfway through the process, you can have components left over. For this reason, SRM 5.0 now includes a separate process to run a cleanup. If this cleanup fails for whatever reason, the cleanup plan can be run in a Forcible Cleanup mode. I have found this cleanup process to be very reliable, and the separation of the Recovery Plan from the cleanup process offers more flexibility over previous releases of SRM.

Practice Exercise: First Recovery Plan Test

To practice creating a Recovery Plan, follow these steps.

1. Log on with the vSphere client to the Recovery Site's vCenter.

2. Click the Site Recovery icon.

3. Open the Recovery Plans tab.

4. Select your plan. In my case, the plan was called "Complete Loss of Site – Simple Test."

5. Click the Test button.

6. In the dialog box that opens, select whether you want to replicate recent changes.

WARNING

Do not click the Recovery button. This actually invokes DR proper. Unless you are in a lab environment, you will need to seek higher approval from the senior management team in your organization to do this.

During the test phase, the icon of the Recovery Plan will change, and the status will change to Test In Progress, as shown in Figure 10.16.

Once all the VMs are in the process of being powered on, the process will progress to around 56% and SRM will wait for a successful response from the VMware Tools heartbeat service, indicating that the plan has been successful. At that point, the Recovery Plan will change to a Test Complete status indicated by a green arrow, as shown in Figure 10.17.

This icon will be accompanied by a "message" event in the Recovery Plan, as shown in Figure 10.18. Messages can be viewed in any of the tabs of a Recovery Plan. The administrator can add these messages to pause the plan to allow for some kind of manual intervention in the recovery steps, or to confirm that a recovery phase has completed successfully. (We will discuss custom messages in more detail in Chapter 11.) At this point, the test of your recovery has completed and the recovery VMs should be powered on. Of course, it is useful to examine any errors as a way to troubleshoot your configuration.

For example, I had two errors: The first appears to be benign, and the second is a configuration error. The first error indicated a timeout waiting for a heartbeat signal from the

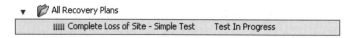

Figure 10.16 Pay close attention to plan status information; it can prompt you for the next step in the process, such as clean up or reprotect.

Figure 10.17 A successfully completed plan

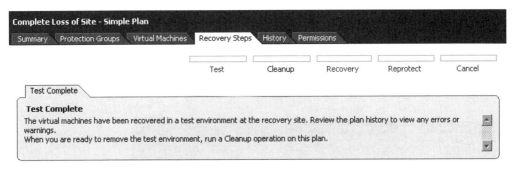

Figure 10.18   A "message" event in the Recovery Plan

VM called db02. I checked the VM at the Recovery Site, and found that VMware Tools was running but was not up-to-date. The second error was caused by a mistake in my inventory mappings for a template. I had not correctly allocated a valid port group for my template VM in the inventory. I had to let the Recovery Plan complete before I could review my inventory mappings.

Cleaning Up after a Recovery Plan Test

SRM 5.0 introduces a new and subtle change to the way Recovery Plans work. Previously, the Recovery Plan included a built-in cleanup phase. The Recovery Plan would be halted by a message step, leaving the administrator with a "continue" button. Once the button was clicked, the Recovery Plan would clean up after the test. In this release, VMware decided to separate these steps from each other, to give SRM administrators more control over when the cleanup phase begins. The other secondary use of the cleanup option is to force a cleanout if a Recovery Plan has gone wrong due to, for example, a failure of the vCenter or SRM service, or (more likely) an unexpected error at the storage layer, such as a failure to communicate to the array at the Recovery Site. In the past, if something went wrong during the plan it would be up to the SRM administrator to manually clean out any objects created during the Recovery Plan. A good example of this is manually deleting the temporary SvSwitch that was created when you used the Auto feature for handling the network during recovery.

If you're happy with the success of your test, you can trigger the cleanup process by clicking the Cleanup button or link (see Figure 10.19).

This will produce a pop-up dialog box asking you if you want to proceed with the cleanup process. Notice how the dialog box in Figure 10.20 has the option to Force Cleanup if something has gone wrong with the test of the plan.

Figure 10.19   The Cleanup button is used to power off and unregister VMs, as well as remove the temporary snapshot created during the test.

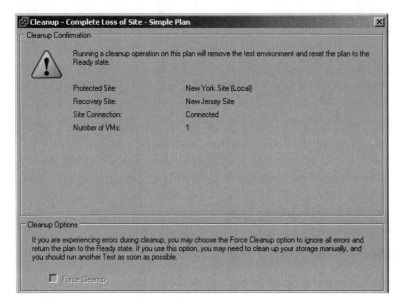

Figure 10.20   The Force Cleanup option is only available when the first attempt to clean up has failed.

This cleanup phase will carry out three main steps at the Recovery Site, as shown in Figure 10.21.

First, all the VMs recovered during the test will be powered off. Then, if VMs were suspended at the Recovery Site to save precious memory resources, for example, these VMs are resumed. Finally, the temporary writable snapshot of the replicated volume is un-mounted from the ESX hosts; this will normally trigger a rescan of the ESX host HBAs if you are using Fibre Channel or iSCSI-based storage. This reset of storage actually

Figure 10.21   The steps used in the cleanup phase of carrying out a test

Recent Tasks

Name	Target
Refresh host storage system	esx3.corp.com
Rescan all HBAs	esx4.corp.com
Rescan all HBAs	esx3.corp.com
XXX host.StorageSystem.deleteVmfsVolumeState....	esx4.corp.com
XXX host.StorageSystem.deleteVmfsVolumeState....	esx3.corp.com
XXX host.StorageSystem.deleteScsiLunState.label...	esx4.corp.com
XXX host.StorageSystem.deleteScsiLunState.label...	esx3.corp.com
Remove Internet SCSI static targets	esx4.corp.com
Remove Internet SCSI static targets	esx3.corp.com
Detach SCSI LUN	esx4.corp.com
Detach SCSI LUN	esx3.corp.com
Unmount VMFS volume	esx4.corp.com
Unmount VMFS volume	esx3.corp.com

Figure 10.22   The complete list of cleanup tasks for a Recovery Plan test

includes a number of steps. In the case of iSCSI-based VMFS volumes, you will first see SRM unmount the iSCSI volumes once the recovered VMs have been powered off and unregistered. Next, the iSCSI LUN will be detached and any static iSCSI targets will be removed from the ESX iSCSI initiator. Finally, SRM will rescan all the HBAs of the ESX hosts and carry out a general refresh of the storage system. Figure 10.22 shows the list of cleanup activities.

Controlling and Troubleshooting Recovery Plans

This section addresses management of your Recovery Plan.

Pause, Resume, and Cancel Plans

In previous releases of SRM, you were able to pause, resume, and stop a Recovery Plan. These features have been deprecated in this release. Manually canceling a test was not without consequences if you didn't allow the system to complete the test, as doing so could leave the SRM in a pending state where it would think a test was still running when it had been canceled. I think this is why VMware removed these options; either they created more problems than they solved, or other methods were deemed more efficient. With that said, there is still an option to cancel a plan if you need to—perhaps you have encountered a serious problem or tested a plan accidentally. If you do cancel a plan, you will most likely have to run a cleanup process, and that will likely require use of the new forcible cleanup capability in many cases. If possible, you should let the plan continue normally.

The resume option appears only if the SRM service has failed while testing a plan at the Recovery Site. Once the SRM service is restarted, you will be given the option to resume the plan.

Personally, if I want to pause or resume the progress of a Recovery Plan regularly, I always prefer to add a message to the plan at the appropriate point. For example, the SRM service can issue a "Test Interrupted" message if it detects a serious error, such as an inability to access a replicated LUN/snapshot, or if it believes another test is in progress or has hung. The screen capture in Figure 10.23 shows such a situation where the SRM service failed on my New Jersey SRM server.

The problem can be quickly remedied by restarting the SRM service using the Services MMC, or with the command net start vmware-dr. If the SRM service fails in the middle of testing a plan, once you reconnect to the service using the vSphere client you will be prompted with the error message shown in Figure 10.24.

Generally, rerunning the plan as indicated by the message is enough to fix the issue. However, sometimes this may be unsuccessful. For example, in one of my tests the recovery process worked but stopped midway through. Although the VMs had been registered with the temporary writable snapshot, they were still seen by the SRM host in the Recovery Site as though they were placeholder VMs complete with their special icon. As vCenter saw these VMs as only placeholders, vCenter could not power them on. Simply rerunning the plan didn't fix the problem; it just started another Recovery Plan that

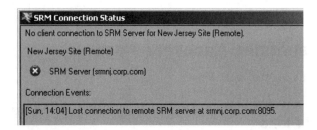

Figure 10.23   A failure of the SRM service while testing a Recovery Plan.
Once the SRM service has restarted, you can resume the test.

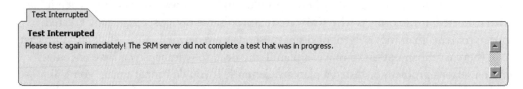

Figure 10.24   The message prompt generated if the test is interrupted for whatever reason

wouldn't complete. In the end I fixed the issue by manually unregistering each VM and then reregistering it. This allowed the plan to finish, and I was able to carry out a forcible cleanup of the plan. Once that process was completed, I was able to remove these VMs from the vCenter inventory and repair the placeholders that had not been restored by the Recovery Plans. Problems like this are rare, but it's important to know they are recoverable. The way to achieve this is to understand what is happening under the covers of SRM, so if it does fail you know how to handle the cleanup phase manually as well.

Error: Cleanup Phase of the Plan Does Not Always Happen with iSCSI

The cleanup and reset phase of the test plan does not always automatically stop access to the replicated iSCSI LUN/volumes. In my experience of using SRM, it's not unusual behavior to see that the replicated LUN/volume is still listed under datastores for the recovery ESX hosts after a test has completed. This was especially true in vSphere 4. In vSphere 5 and SRM 5 I have seen marked improvement in the process of unpresenting iSCSI volumes to the ESX host.

Of course, what can happen is that between one test and another a new snapshot could occur. Most SRAs default to using the most recent snapshots. However, some SRAs do not deny access to the snapshot after the test has completed. This can lead to a situation where the VMFS volume remains visible to the ESX host after the test is completed. Whatever happens, by default SRM will always prefer to use the most recent snapshot.

The actual cause of this is quite tricky to explain, as it depends on the time the test plan was run compared with the cycle of replication adopted at the storage array. The error is caused if SRM fails to manually resignature both volumes. There is an easy workaround to this issue: Rename your "older" snapshot VMFS volume to something else, such as "test1-virtualmachines." This should allow the additional snapshot to be presented without causing the rename annoyance.

You might be interested in knowing why this problem specifically afflicts iSCSI, and does not affect SAN and NFS systems. I've seen this a number of times back in the days of ESX 3.5 and ESX 4.0 with or without SRM; it does seem to be the case that even if you make big changes to the ESX host (changing its IQN, blocking the iSCSI port 3260, or denying access to an iSCSI volume) a mounting of iSCSI volumes persists. While I was at VMworld 2009, it was my very good fortune to finally meet VMware's Andy Banta. I'd known Andy for some time via the forums but hadn't met the guy face to face. Andy was part of the team involved in developing the ESX host's iSCSI stack. So, after the event, I made a point of asking Andy why this happens with iSCSI and ESX. It turns out that it all hinges on how your storage vendor implements iSCSI, and that ESX hosts will keep iSCSI sessions alive because it is too dangerous to simply tear them down when they could be in use by other targets. Here is Andy's explanation, albeit with a little tidying up by yours truly:

> First off, there's a distinction to be made: CLARiiONs serve LUNs, whereas HP PS4000 and EqualLogic systems present targets. The behavior on a CLARiiON should be the same for both FC and iSCSI: LUNs that go away don't show up after a rescan.
>
> What you're seeing are the paths to targets remaining after the target has been removed. In this case, there are not sessions to the targets and the system no longer has any access to the storage.
>
> However, ESX does hang on to the handle for a path to storage even after the storage has gone away. The reason for this is to prevent transient target outages from allowing one piece of storage to take over the target number for another piece of storage. NMP uses the HBA, target, and channel number to identify a path. If the paths change while I/O is going on, there's a chance the path won't go to the target that NMP expects it to. Because of this, we maintain a persistent mapping of target numbers to paths.
>
> We also never get rid of the last path to storage, so in this case, since SRM used the snapshot as storage, the ESX storage system won't get rid of it (at least for a while). In 3.5 we used an aging algorithm to let us know when we could reuse a target ID. What Dell EqualLogic finally ended up recommending to customers for 3.5 was to rescan after removal ten times (our length of aging before we gave up on the target).

Error: Loss of the Protection Group Settings

Occasionally, I've seen Recovery Plans lose their awareness of the storage setup. An SRM administrator deleting the Protection Group at the Protected Site usually causes this. If the administrator does this, all the placeholder VMs disappear. The Recovery Plan then becomes "orphaned" from the storage configuration at the other location—and doesn't know how to contact the storage array to request access to the replicated volumes/LUNs. Essentially it becomes a plan without any VMs to recover. If you delete a Protection Group or disable the last Protection Group within a plan, the plan's status will be updated to reflect this error state (see Figure 10.25).

You can fix this problem by reconfiguring the Recovery Plan and ensuring that it can see the Protection Group(s). If the Protection Group has been deleted, you will need to re-create it at the Protected Site.

1. Right-click each Recovery Plan.

2. Choose Edit.

3. Click Next to accept the existing plan site location.

4. Ensure that the checkboxes next to the affected Protection Groups are selected.

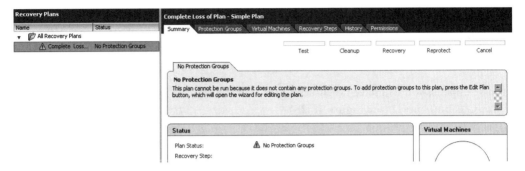

Figure 10.25 Recovery Plans can have their Protection Groups removed from them, resulting in this error message.

5. In the Edit Recovery Plan, set the options to handle networking when you run a test.

6. Click Finish.

As you can see, casually removing or deleting Protection Groups has a huge, huge impact on your configuration, essentially destroying the hard work you put into creating an effective Recovery Plan. For this reason you should, at all costs, avoid the Windows Administrator solution to all problems, which is "Let's just delete it and add it back in, and see if it works again." I highly doubt you will pay much heed to this warning—until you experience the problem firsthand. Like me, you probably learn as much from your mistakes as from your successes. In fairness you could say that the software should at least warn you about the impact of removing or deleting Protection Groups, and to some degree I think that's a fair comment.

Error: Cleanup Fails; Use Force Cleanup

When a Recovery Plan fails you might find that the test completes (with errors). When you run the cleanup part of the plan this can fail as well (see Figure 10.26).

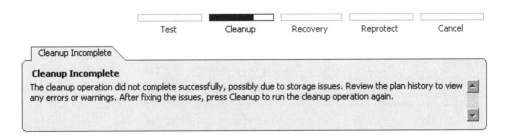

Figure 10.26 The error message if the cleanup failed

In my case, this was caused by a problem in presenting a writable snapshot to the recovery hosts. This was triggered by an error in the replication setup in one of my arrays. When the Recovery Plan was run no volume was presented to the host, and the cleanup failed as it attempted to destroy a volume that didn't exist (see Figure 10.27).

If this happens, you will have no choice but to run the cleanup process again, using the Force Cleanup option (see Figure 10.28).

Error: Repairing VMs

Occasionally, I've seen errors on both my Protection Groups and my Recovery Plans caused by the ESX host, in which the placeholder VMs for the affected VMs become "disconnected" or connectivity to the placeholder datastores is lost. Generally, I have to restart the management services on the ESX host, and then use the Restore All or Restore Placeholder option to fix the problem. It's important to resolve the cause of the problem before clicking the Repair All option; I've seen SRM wait a very long time before it gives up on the process.

Error: Disconnected Hosts at the Recovery Site

Before embarking on a test or a Recovery Plan, it's worth confirming that your ESX hosts in vCenter are active and are not displaying any errors or warnings. You might want to do this for a number of reasons. Any ESX host that is unavailable in a VMware cluster could become excluded by DRS and initial placement, and then will not be selected as the target

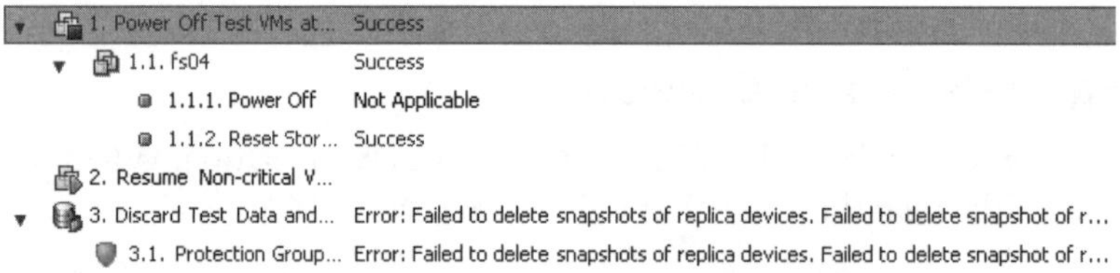

Figure 10.27   The system failing to remove the snapshot on one of my arrays

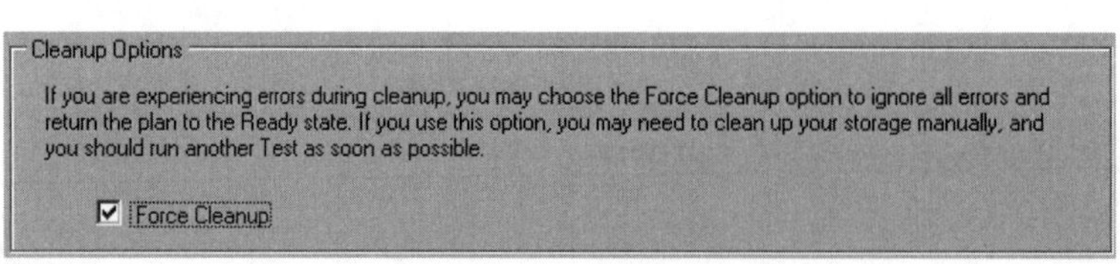

Figure 10.28   Failure to clean up successfully will result in a Force Cleanup.

Figure 10.29 Failure to suspend a VM called "test01" because the host it was on was disconnected from vCenter

for powering on VMs. That could significantly reduce the amount of compute resources at the Recovery Site, and as a consequence degrade the overall effectiveness of the Recovery Plan or degrade the quality of service provided by the Recovery Site. In some cases, a disconnected host can cause unwanted errors in a Recovery Plan. For example, in one of my Recovery Plans I asked for a VM in the Recovery Site to be suspended. Regrettably, at the time of running the plan an ESX host had become disconnected in the vCenter inventory—and that host was running the VM that was a target to be suspended. It caused the Recovery Plan error shown in Figure 10.29.

Recovery Plans and the Storage Array Vendors

In this section I will expose the changes taking place at the storage layer when a Recovery Plan is tested. A number of changes take place, and of course they vary significantly from one array vendor to another. On a day-to-day basis you shouldn't have to concern yourself with this functionality—after all, that's the point of SRM and SRA from your storage vendor. However, I feel it's useful to know more about these processes, for a couple of reasons. First, I think it's interesting to know what's actually going on under the covers. Second, the SRM administrator may need to explain to your storage team the changes that are taking place, and the more you understand the process the more confidence they should have in you. Third, if something does go wrong with the SRA's interaction with the storage array, you may have to manually clean up the array after a test or a run of a Recovery Plan if the plan fails or if the cleanup process with SRM is not successful.

Dell EqualLogic and Testing Plans

During the test of a Recovery Plan, you should see that the new VMFS volume is mounted and resignatured by the Dell EqualLogic SRA (see Figure 10.30).

The snapshot in Figure 10.30 relates to the snapshot in Figure 10.31 of the volume being replicated at the New Jersey group.

Remember, for Recovery Plans to work with iSCSI you will need to ensure that the ESX hosts in the Recovery Site are configured for iSCSI, and critically, that they have a target IP

Figure 10.30   As seen earlier, a snapshot of a Dell EqualLogic volume

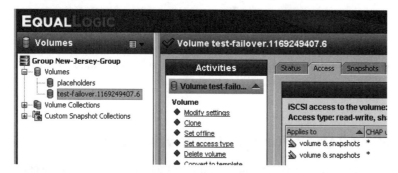

Figure 10.31   The temporary snapshot called "test-failover," created at the New Jersey Recovery Site

set so that they can communicate with the iSCSI array in the Recovery Site. If you don't do this, you will receive an error message in the Recovery Plan similar to the following.

> Error – Failed to create snapshots of replica devices. Failed to create snapshot of replica device iqn.2001-05.com.equallogic:0-8a0906-663bbfc03-0a34b38d90d4d838-virtualmachines.1. No initiators were found for hosts.

EMC Celerra and Testing Plans

During the test of a Recovery Plan, you should see that the new VMFS volume is mounted and resignatured by the Celerra SRA. In my case, this was a LUN with an ID of 128 at the ESX host (see Figure 10.32).

You can see this from the Unisphere management system, under the Recovery Site array and the sharing and iSCSI options (see Figure 10.33).

In the same windows, under the LUN Masks tab, you can see that LUN 128 has been presented to the ESX hosts in the Recovery Site (see Figure 10.34).

vcnj.corp.com
NJ DataCenter
EMC
EqualLogic
HP
Infrastructure
Local Storage
NetApp
SRM Placeholders
snap-76b3aa2d-emc-celerra-virtualmachines

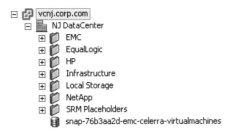

Figure 10.32 Snapshot of an EMC Celerra iSCSI volume

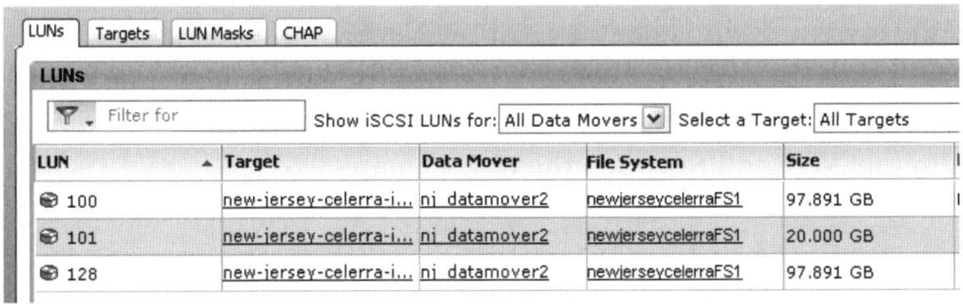
LUNs
Targets
LUN Masks
CHAP
LUNs
Filter for
Show iSCSI LUNs for: All Data Movers
Select a Target: All Targets
LUN
Target
Data Mover
File System
Size
100
new-jersey-celerra-i...
nj_datamover2
newjerseycelerraFS1
97.891 GB
101
new-jersey-celerra-i...
nj_datamover2
newjerseycelerraFS1
20.000 GB
128
new-jersey-celerra-i...
nj_datamover2
newjerseycelerraFS1
97.891 GB

Figure 10.33 The Unisphere management system and creation of a temporary snapshot with a LUN ID of 128

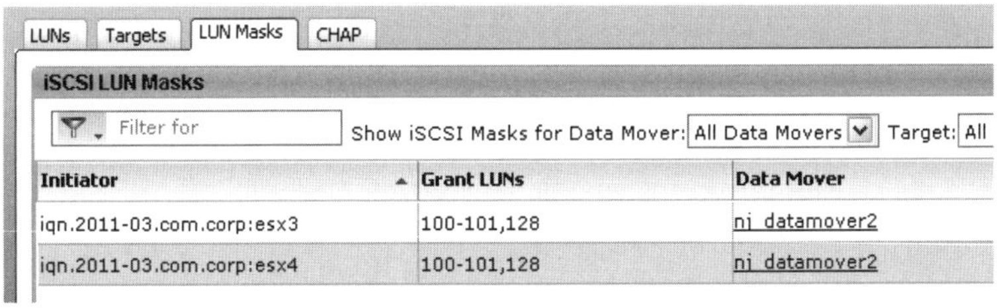
LUNs
Targets
LUN Masks
CHAP
iSCSI LUN Masks
Filter for
Show iSCSI Masks for Data Mover: All Data Movers
Target: All
Initiator
Grant LUNs
Data Mover
iqn.2011-03.com.corp:esx3
100-101,128
nj_datamover2
iqn.2011-03.com.corp:esx4
100-101,128
nj_datamover2

Figure 10.34 The LUN masks

Remember, for Recovery Plans to work with iSCSI you will need to ensure that the ESX hosts in the Recovery Site are configured for iSCSI, and critically, that they have a target IP set so that they can communicate with the iSCSI array in the Recovery Site. If you don't do this, you will receive an error message in the Recovery Plan similar to the following.

> Error – Failed to create snapshots of replica devices. Failed to create snapshot of replica device iqn.2001-05.com.celerra:0-8a0906-663bbfc03-0a34b38d90d4d838-virtualmachines.1. No initiators were found for hosts.

NetApp and Testing Plans

With a NetApp FSA you should see when you're testing plans that the ESX hosts in the Recovery Site mount the replicated NFS datastore automatically. With NFS there is no resignature process to be concerned with, as VMware's file system (VMFS) is not in use. In the screen grab in Figure 10.35 you can see esx3.corp.com and esx4.corp.com both mounted in an NAS datastore. The name of the datastore is exactly the same as the name in the Protected Site location.

The NetApp filer should also create a temporary FlexClone of the volume that contains the replicated VMs. This allows the existing schedule of SnapMirror to continue working during the period of the test. This means SRM tests can be carried out during operational hours without affecting the system. Using FilerView within NetApp FSA you should see in +Storage and +Volumes that a "testfailoverClone" is created for each volume you have set up for SnapMirror that is configured for a Recovery Plan in SRM. This temporary FlexClone is deleted from the NetApp FSA when the test is completed (see Figure 10.36).

vcnj.corp.com
NJ DataCenter
EMC
EqualLogic
HP
Infrastructure
Local Storage
NetApp
SRM Placeholders
netapp-virtualmachines

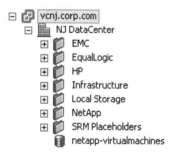

Figure 10.35 The mounting of an NFS-based snapshot from a NetApp system. The mount point name remains the same as in the Protected Site.

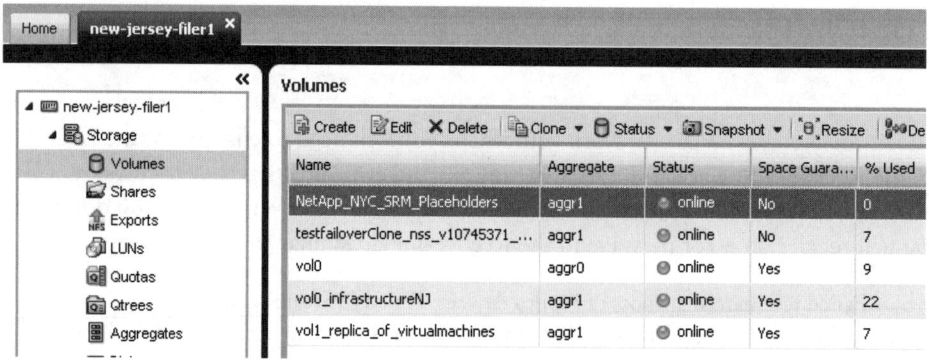

Home
new-jersey-filer1
new-jersey-filer1
Storage
Volumes
Shares
Exports
LUNs
Quotas
Qtrees
Aggregates
Volumes
Create
Edit
Delete
Clone
Status
Snapshot
Resize
Name
Aggregate
Status
Space Guara...
% Used
NetApp_NYC_SRM_Placeholders
aggr1
online
No
0
testfailoverClone_nss_v10745371_...
aggr1
online
No
7
vol0
aggr0
online
Yes
9
vol0_infrastructureNJ
aggr1
online
Yes
22
vol1_replica_of_virtualmachines
aggr1
online
Yes
7

Figure 10.36 A temporary snapshot called "testfailoverClone_nss_v" in NetApp System Manager

Summary

In this chapter I explained how to run a Recovery Plan. In fact, that's been my intention from the very beginning of this chapter, believe it or not, as I think that seeing a product "in action" is the quickest way to learn it.

As you saw, clicking the Test button generated a great deal of activity and changes. VMware's SRM is a very dynamic product in that respect. My hope is that you are following my configuration for real while you read. I know that is a big thing to ask, so if you were not in this fortunate position I highly recommend that you watch the video at www.rtfm-ed.co.uk/srm.html. No matter how much I screen-grab and document what happens in text, you won't really get the feel for running a Recovery Plan that you would if you worked your way through the process yourself or watched a video of the event.

I also tried to explain some of the "strangeness" you might see in the SRM product. In fact, it's not strangeness at all; it's by design. It's all about understanding how your storage layer's cycle of replication interacts with and intersects your activity in SRM. Critically, the quality of your vSphere build will have an impact on your SRM implementation. For example, suppose you incorrectly scaled your VMware cluster environment such that the cluster was so overloaded or misconfigured that you began to have "admission control." VMware uses the term *admission control* to describe a condition statement that is applied to resources. It essentially asks the system, "Are there enough resources in the cluster for both performance and failover to satisfy the VM's requirements?" By default, if the answer to this question is *no*, the VM will not be powered on and you will see something similar to the error shown in Figure 10.37.

Anyway, it's time to move away from this behind-the-scenes approach to Recovery Plans now that you are up to speed with the principle. In the next chapter you will spend most of your time creating custom plans which leverage all the features of SRM so that you can test your DR plans against one another, and for different scenarios. So far this book has been about getting the SRM product to work; the next chapter is really about why your organization bought the product in the first place.

Figure 10.37 The type of error you will see if the cluster lacks the performance and failover resources to satisfy the VM

Chapter 11

Custom Recovery Plans

So far we have simply accepted the default settings from the Recovery Plan. As you might expect and hope, it is possible to heavily customize the Recovery Plan. Customized Recovery Plans allow you to control the flow of the recovery process. Together with customized virtual machine mappings they allow you to completely automate the common tasks performed when invoking your DR plan. The creation of multiple Recovery Plans with different settings allows you to deal with different causes and scenarios that trigger the use of your Recovery Site—and additionally allows you to test those plans to measure their effectiveness. With custom Recovery Plans you can control and automate a number of settings. For example, you can

- Power on virtual machines at the Recovery Site by priority or order
- Create VM dependency groups that reflect the relationships between VMs
- Control VM start-up times and timeouts
- Suspend VMs at the Recovery Site that are not needed
- Add steps to a Recovery Plan to send a prompt or run a script
- Invoke scripts in the guest operating system
- Change the IP settings of the virtual machines
- Set custom per-VM inventory mappings

Additionally, in this chapter I will delve a little deeper into SRM to discuss managing changes at the Protected Site, and cover how changes in the operating environment impact your SRM configuration. I also will use this chapter to analyze the impact of changes to the storage on your SRM configuration. In short, I will be examining these types of issues:

- Creating/renaming/moving vCenter objects at the Protected/Recovery Site

- Using VMware's raw device mapping (RDM) feature

- More complicated storage scenarios where there are VMs with multiple virtual disks, held on multiple VMFS datastores with potential use of VMFS extents

- Adding new virtual machines, new storage, and new networks

- The impact of cold migration with file relocation and Storage vMotion

Before I begin, it's worth mentioning that some of the events that occur in the Recovery Plan will be executed depending on whether you are merely testing your Recovery Plan or actually running failover for real. For example, when you run a plan in Planned Migration mode, SRM will gracefully power down virtual machines at the Protected Site. This never happens in a Recovery Plan test, because it would impact your production operations.

Essentially, the next couple of pages of this book cover everything you can do with Recovery Plans. Once you know you can include scripts embedded in your plans the sky is really the limit. Your plan could include scripted components that affect a physical system or even modify the settings of the very VMs you are recovering. For now it's important to notice that the scope of our customization is limited to what happens when you run a test of a Recovery Plan. We do have other controls that allow us to control the cleanup process, recovery steps (when you execute the plan for real), and reprotect steps (carried out after a failover). I will be covering this aspect of Recovery Plans as we move on to look at real failover and failback.

SRM 5.0 has a new View component shown in Figure 11.1 that allows you to see the four main types of "steps" associated with the core features of SRM: test, cleanup, recovery, and reprotect. If you toggle between these views you can see a high-level value of what's involved in each process.

Figure 11.1   The new View pull-down list allows you to see the different steps that SRM is currently capable of carrying out.

Controlling How VMs Power On

It's this aspect of the Recovery Plan that many regard as being one of the most important configuration steps to complete. Our virtual machines in the Recovery Site must be brought online in the correct order for multitier applications to work. Core infrastructure systems such as domain controllers and DNS will need to be on-stream first. Most people have these services up and running in the Recovery Site before they even begin, and the services are not protected by SRM but use their own internal systems for availability, such as Microsoft Active Directory replication and integrated DNS transfers. Perhaps the earliest systems to be recovered are email and database systems. Those database system services will no doubt be using domain accounts during start-up, and without the directory service running, those services are likely to fail to start with the availability of the core Microsoft Active Directory and DNS services. Additionally, there's little point in bringing up front-end services such as Web servers if the back-end services with which they have dependencies are not yet functional. In fact, that's the shorthand we normally use for this concept: "service dependencies." It is often the case that for VM3 to function, VM1 and VM2 must be running, and for VM2 to work, VM1 must be started first, and so on.

Of course, determining the exact order you need for your plan to be successful is beyond the scope of this book, and is highly specific to your organization. SRM comes with a whole gamut of features to enable you to configure your VMs correctly, including the ability to configure such features as priorities, VM Dependencies, and start-up times. These features are all designed to ensure that VMs come up in a graceful and predictable manner. Therefore, one of the major tasks before you even think of deploying SRM is to appreciate how your applications and services work. In larger organizations this will often mean liaising with the application owner. Don't imagine for a moment that this will be an easy process, as regrettably, many application owners don't really understand the service dependencies surrounding the applications they support. Those that do may have already implemented their own "in-guest" availability solution that they will want to "stretch" across two sites if they have not done so already. You might find that these application owners are hostile or skeptical about protecting their applications with SRM. In an enterprise environment, expect to see as many different availability solutions in use as there are business units. VMware does have technologies you can use to assist in this process, such as Application Discovery Manager which can map out the dependency relationships that make an application work that are both physical and virtual.

Configuring Priorities for Recovered Virtual Machines

Priorities replace the use of the High, Low, and Normal settings which were available in the previous versions of SRM. Without this feature configured, as you might have seen, the virtual machines are more or less powered on randomly, though they are all contained under priority group 3. In this release, SRM introduces five priority levels, with 1 being the highest and 5 being the lowest, and with VMs being powered on relative to their location in the priority group. If it helps, you could regard each priority as representing different tiers of applications or services in your environment. If you can, try to map the VM priorities with the business priorities within the organization.

SRM, in conjunction with vCenter, attempts to start *all* the VMs within one priority group before starting the next batch of VMs within another priority group. By default, all the VMs are started in parallel unless ordered with the new VM Dependencies feature, which I will cover shortly. VM dependencies replace the old method of ordering the start-up of VMs that involved the use of up and down arrows to move the VM around in the plan. So, regardless of which priority order you use (1, 2, 3, 4, or 5) the VMs are started up in parallel, not serially, unless VM dependencies are configured.

For me this makes perfect sense. After all, if every virtual machine was started up serially rather than in parallel, people with very large numbers of virtual machines would have to wait a very long time to get their virtual machines up and running. Some VMs can be powered on at the same time because there is no dependency between them; others will have to start first in order to meet our precious service dependencies. Of course, the use of parallel start-up by SRM does not mean that all VMs within a priority group are powered on simultaneously. The number of VMs you can power on at any one time is governed by the amount of available compute resources in the Recovery Site. SRM does not power on all the VMs simultaneously, as this runs the risk of overloading your VMware clusters with an excessive burst or demand for resources. SRM will work together with DRS to ensure the efficient placement of VMs. With this said, SRM cannot defy the laws of VMware clusters, and your admission control settings on the cluster and resource pools will take precedence. If you do try to power on more VMs than you have resources available—for example, if a number of ESX hosts are down and unavailable—expect to see admission control error messages within the Recovery Plan, as shown in Figure 11.2.

Whatever you do, remember that you cannot fit *War and Peace* on a postage stamp. By this I mean you cannot power on your entire estate of VMs from a 32-node cluster on a two-node ESX cluster at the Recovery Site. The buck will have to stop somewhere, and in

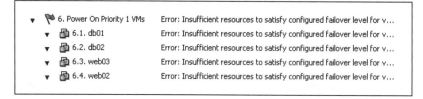

Figure 11.2 A poorly implemented vSphere deployment will result in problems within Recovery Plans such as an inconsistent Standard vSwitch configuration.

the world of virtualization, that usually means memory. You'd be shocked at the number of customers who don't think along these lines.

To change the priority level of a VM, follow these steps.

1. Click your Recovery Plan, and select the Recovery Steps tab.

2. Expand the priority that contains your VM.

3. Right-click the VM and select the Priority menu option, as shown in Figure 11.3.

4. Select the priority level appropriate for this VM.

Additionally, you can modify priority orders by using the Configure option of each VM, as shown in Figure 11.4.

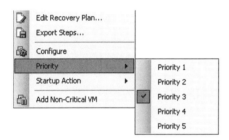

Figure 11.3 You might find that priority levels meet your service dependency needs, without having to use VM dependencies.

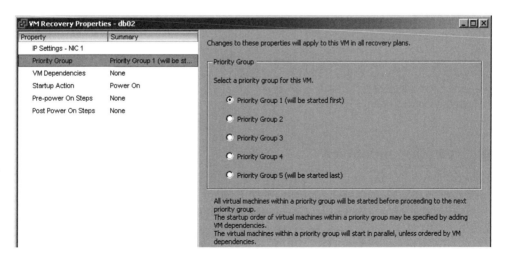

Figure 11.4 Priority orders can be set on the properties of the VM listed in the Recovery Plan.

When the Recovery Plan is tested, *all* VMs, regardless of their priority status, will be taken through the primary step of storage configuration. They will then pause and wait for the power-on instruction.

Although these per-VM methods may be helpful for just one or two VMs that may need to be moved, if you have many VMs that need to be relocated to the correct priority level you can use the Virtual Machines tab on the properties of the Recovery Plan, as shown in Figure 11.5. In the list that appears, you can use the Ctrl or Shift key to select the VMs you wish to locate to a new priority.

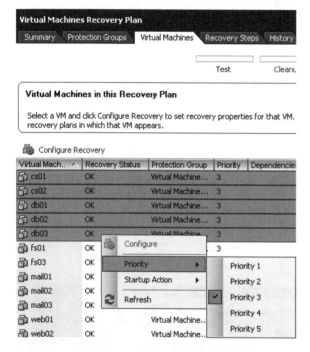

Figure 11.5   The bulk method of setting priority orders is a welcome enhancement in SRM 5.0.

Adding VM Dependencies

It's unlikely that priorities alone will deliver the Recovery Plan you need. Critically, you will also want to control the start-up order to meet your service and application dependencies. Within a priority order, it's possible to configure a power-on order on the property of a VM. The important point to know is that these new VM dependencies are *ignored* if you include a VM that is not in the *same* priority group. As an example, my priority 1 category has four VMs (db01, db02, web01, and web02); I want to configure them so that they power on in the correct order. You apply the VM dependency settings by selecting a VM, and on the properties of that VM, indicating which VMs will be started *before* it. So, if the databases (db01 and db02) must start before the Web servers (web01 and web02) I would select the Web servers in the UI first, and then use their configuration options to set the dependency. The way to look at it is the Web servers have a dependency on the database, so it's the Web servers that need to be selected to express that relationship. To configure VM dependencies, follow these steps.

1. Click your Recovery Plan and select the Recovery Steps tab.

2. Expand the priority that contains your VM.

3. Right-click the VM and select the Configure menu option.

4. In the dialog box that opens select VM Dependencies from the list, as shown in Figure 11.6.

5. Use the Add button to add a VM to the list to indicate that it must be started first, before the currently selected VM.

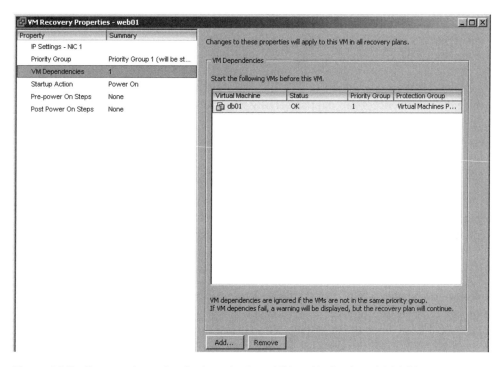

Figure 11.6 Express dependencies by selecting a VM and indicating which VMs must start before it. VMs must reside within the same priority group.

In my case, I indicated that db01 must be powered on before web01. Notice that if the power on of db01 failed, this would not stop the power on of web01. Although a failure to start db01 would create a warning in the Recovery Plan, it would not halt the recovery process. If I added to this list the VM called db02, both db01 and db02 would have to power on before SRM would power on web01. In that case, I would be stating that web01 had dependencies on two database systems (db01 and db02).

This process does reorder the VMs in the Recovery Plan. In my case, I repeated this VM dependency configuration for both db02 and web02; as a result, you can see in Figure 11.7 that the VMs are ordered in the priority list accordingly.

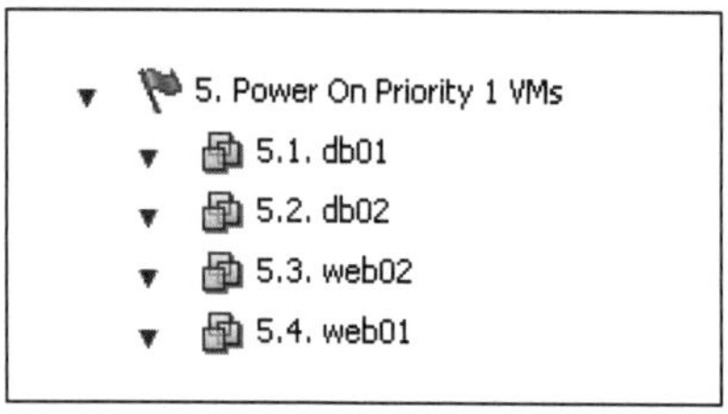

Figure 11.7   In this case, db01 and db02 will start simultaneously. Web01 and web02 will not start until the "parent" VM has started first.

Sadly, in the Recovery Steps tab the UI's 2D representation can give a false impression that this power-on process will happen serially, especially because the numbering system suggests that db01 will start first, followed by db02. In fact, in this case db01 and db02 will be started in parallel. Then, depending on which database completes its power on first (db01 or db02), the VM dependency will trigger the power on of either web01 or web02.

For example, Figure 11.8 shows that when I ran this test for the first time, both web01 and web02 completed their storage configuration process before db01 and db02. They then waited for db01 and db02 (at steps 5.3.2 and 5.4.2) to complete their power-on process. The VM db02 was actually the first VM to complete the power-on process (at step 5.2.2), and as such, this triggered the power-on event for web02.

I think it would be nice if the UI of the recovery steps could be improved to show the VM dependency relationship, and for the VMs that will be started in parallel to be marked in some way; it is my hope that VMware will improve the UI in the future to make this more intuitive. If you want to see a list of your VM dependencies you can view them in the Virtual Machines tab of the Recovery Plan, as shown in Figure 11.9.

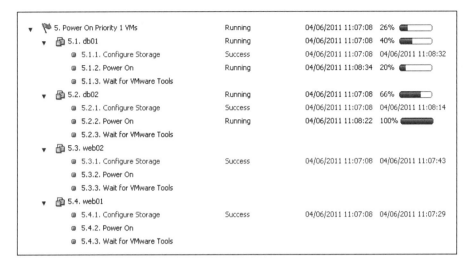

Figure 11.8   Sadly, the rather 2D representation of VM dependencies makes it difficult to "visualize" the relationship between VMs.

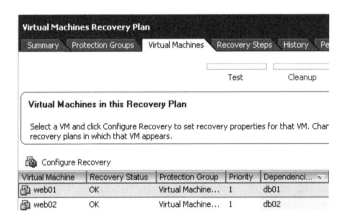

Figure 11.9   The Virtual Machines tab allows the SRM administrator to see the VM dependencies that have been configured.

Configuring Start-Up and Shutdown Options

Our third and last method of controlling the boot process of a VM in a Recovery Plan is via the VM's start-up and shutdown options. By default, all VMs that are configured in a Protection Group and enrolled in a Recovery Plan are powered on. It's possible to turn off this behavior and allow a VM to be recovered but not powered on automatically. This would allow you to make a manual choice about whether a VM is powered on and available.

A good example of this is where you have an application that can be scaled out for performance and availability. Let's say you have ten VMs, and in your capacity planning you assume you will only need seven up and running for production-level quality of service. You could protect all ten, but only power on seven. This would give you a "Plan B" on a number of levels. First, if one of the seven malfunctions in the recovery process for whatever reason, you would have two spare VMs ready to take their place. Second, if your capacity planning was incorrect, you would still have three additional VMs to power on to add capacity, assuming your vSphere environment has enough resources. If, however, the seven come up correctly without error, you have saved resources by not powering on an unnecessary number of VMs. So, by default, any VM that is protected is added to the Recovery Plan by virtue of being included in a Protection Group. If you do disable this automatic power on of a VM, it disables it for all Recovery Plans where it is present.

In addition to controlling whether a VM is recovered or recovered and powered on, there are also controls for how long the Recovery Plan waits until powering on the next VM. These are quite closely tied to the VM Dependencies feature we saw just a moment ago. After all, it's one thing to say that db01 must be booted up before web02, but certain conditions control whether that is regarded as a successful boot process—not to mention the time it takes for the operating system to boot up and for the services it hosts to be available too. By default, the next VM powers on in the sequence based on the interplay of two values in the start-up options: time and the VMware Tools heartbeat service. The default behavior is that a VM will wait five minutes before proceeding with the next step in the plan, unless SRM receives a response from the VMware Tools heartbeat service sooner. In many cases, when you run a Recovery Plan the VMs will start in parallel so long as there are enough compute resources to allow this. But where a relationship has been made between VMs, as is the case with VM dependencies, the start-up conditions will come into play. It's at this point that the start-up delay times become significant, as you may have a service that takes longer to start than normal, and longer to start than VMware Tools. In this case, you may need to adjust the gap between one power-on event and another. A classic example of this is when you have a two-node Microsoft cluster pair that has been virtualized—one of the nodes in the MSCS cluster must come up and be started fully, before the second partner joins the cluster. If the power-on process is not staged correctly, the cluster service will not start properly, and in some extreme cases could cause the corruption of data.

Finally, start-up actions in SRM also control the shutdown process. As I hope you saw when you ran a test of a Recovery Plan, the VMs that were recovered by the test were shut down gracefully by vSphere using a Guest Shutdown option. These shutdown options only apply when you clean up the plan. Some VMs do not respond well to this command, so you may wish to carry out a hard power-off for certain VMs that react in this way. As with start-up actions, shutdown actions also have a timeout configuration that allows the next VM to be shut down, based on a condition controlled by time, or when a VM has been powered off completely. By selecting a VM in the plan and clicking the Configure option in the menu, you can control these start-up and shutdown parameters, as shown in Figure 11.10.

Beware of removing the tick next to "VMware Tools are ready" as this can add a significant wait time before the next VM is powered on. Also, by removing the tick you could significantly increase the time it takes for a VM to be classed as completed, to the default value of five minutes.

If you want to change the start-up action in terms of whether a VM is powered on or off, you can use the standard multiple select options in the Virtual Machines tab of a Recovery Plan, as shown in Figure 11.11.

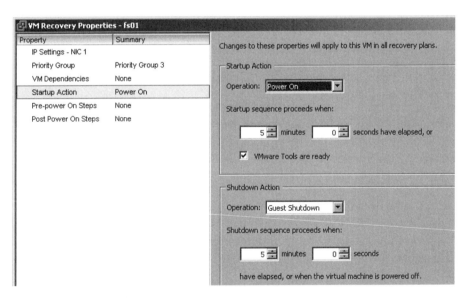

Figure 11.10   SRM has a sophisticated set of power-on and guest shutdown options.

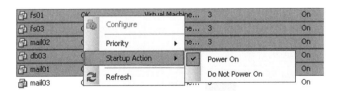

Figure 11.11   The Virtual Machines tab on a Recovery Plan allows for bulk changes of the power-on state of VMs.

Suspending VMs at the Recovery Site

As I mentioned earlier in the book, it is possible to suspend VMs at the Recovery Site. If you include this as part of your Recovery Plan, the selected VMs are suspended. By configuring this option, you are freeing up valuable compute resources, which should mean you can recover more VMs. Of course, suspending a VM is not free from a resource perspective; during the suspend process the selected VM's memory contents are flushed to a suspend file. This process is similar to using the "hibernate" option that is available on most Windows-based PCs. So, critically, suspending VMs generates disk IOPS as the suspend file is created—and you need the spare disk space to accommodate the suspend file. I think the final point to make about this feature is that although a VM might seem trivial to you, bear in mind that it might be in use when you run a test! To configure VMs to be suspended, follow these steps:

1. Select the Recovery Plan in the SRM inventory.

2. Right-click the Suspend Non-critical VMs at the Recovery Site option. By default, this should be step 3, but adding additional steps above it can alter this number.

3. In the context menu, select the Add Non-Critical VM option to suspend VMs at the Recovery Site (see Figure 11.12).

4. In the Add Local VMs to Suspend window select the VMs you consider noncritical. In my case, I have just one, the Test & Dev VM, that will be suspended whenever the Recovery Plan is tested or run, as shown in Figure 11.13, but this dialog does allow for multiple selections.

When the plan is run you should see this as a successful event. You should also see that select VMs have the "paused" icon next to their names (see Figure 11.14). These VMs are "resumed" as part of the standard cleanup process when you have finished with your test. During this time, it is possible to manually resume the VMs that have been suspended (see Figure 11.15).

Figure 11.12 Selecting the Add Non-Critical VM option frees up spare CPU and memory resources for recovered VMs.

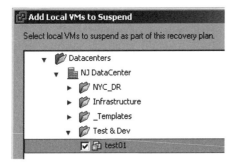

Figure 11.13 You can suspend test or ancillary VMs during a test or run of a Recovery Plan. These VMs are "resumed" during cleanup.

Figure 11.14 The "pause" icon on a VM that has been suspended by SRM

Figure 11.15 VMs that have been suspended by SRM can be manually resumed if needed.

Adding Additional Steps to a Recovery Plan

Within SRM you are not limited to the predefined steps within the Recovery Plan. It's possible to add additional steps where you deem it appropriate. You can add additional steps to a Recovery Plan to prompt the operator running the plan, as well as to execute scripts to further automate the recovery process.

Adding Prompt Steps

It is possible to interrupt the flow of a Recovery Plan to send a prompt to the operator. If you have been following this book as a tutorial you will have seen this already. It is a default that when all Recovery Plans are created and tested there is a built-in message at the end of the test informing you that the test has completed, and prompting you to carry out the cleanup phase of the test once you are satisfied with the results. In this case, the message is intended to give the operator an opportunity to review the results of the test and confirm/diagnose the success (or otherwise) of the Recovery Plan.

It's possible to add your own messages to your custom Recovery Plan. In my case, I would like a message to occur after all my priority 1 virtual machines have been powered on. I want a message to appear before the priority 2 VMs are started, asking me to confirm that the primary VMs are up and functioning before allowing the other VMs to be powered on.

1. In the Recovery Plan select Power on Priority 2 VMs; by default, this would be step 6.

2. Click the Add Step icon, as shown in Figure 11.16. Alternatively, you can right-click and choose Add Step.

3. In the Add Step dialog box, select the radio button labeled "Prompt (requires a user to dismiss before the plan will continue)." Enter a friendly name in the Name field for the additional step in the plan, and then enter helpful text in the Content field, as shown in Figure 11.17. Remember that a real execution of the plan might not be carried out by the administrator who configures SRM, so these prompts must be meaningful to all concerned. With that said, you want to avoid anything overly specific that is open to change in the longer term, such as "Call John Doe on 123-456-7891," as without proper maintenance this type of content can quickly become stale and meaningless.

Timeout settings do not apply to prompts; only to scripts, which we will configure shortly. Selecting the "Before selected step" setting will make my prompt occur before the priority 2 VMs are run. This will cause a global renumbering of all the steps that come after the prompt as well (see Figure 11.18).

When the plan is tested or run, it will halt at the prompt statement. You should see the icon for the Recovery Plan change (see Figure 11.19), as well as the status value being adjusted to Waiting for User Input.

Finally, it is possible to insert messages and commands on the properties of each virtual machine. In the Virtual Machines tab of the Recovery Plan, each virtual machine can be edited and per-virtual machine messages can be added. These are referred to as Pre-Power On Steps and Post Power On Steps, as shown in Figure 11.20. In fact, you can have as many

Figure 11.16   The Add Step button can be used to add a message or command steps to a Recovery Plan.

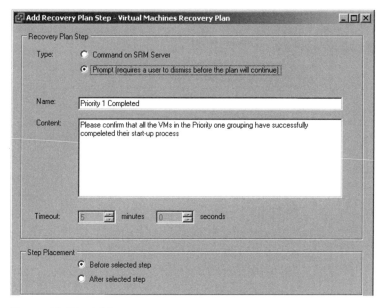

Figure 11.17   Adding a message prompt

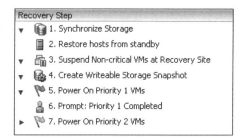

Figure 11.18   Adding prompt steps or command steps causes a renumbering within the Recovery Plan.

steps as you need before a VM powers on or off. These run in the order they are listed, and there are small up and down arrows that allow you to reorder these steps on the VM.

Configuration of these VM steps is almost the same as the Recovery Plans steps. The only difference is that they are the property of the VM, as you can have more than one step backing a VM in the interface, allowing you to control their running order. I will be using these pre-power-on steps when we cover scripting later in this section. Figure 11.21 shows that the properties of a VM in the Recovery Plan change as you add message or command steps.

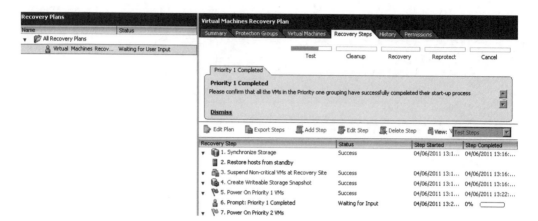

Figure 11.19   The Recovery Plan's status has changed, indicating that the plan is waiting for a human operator to accept the message.

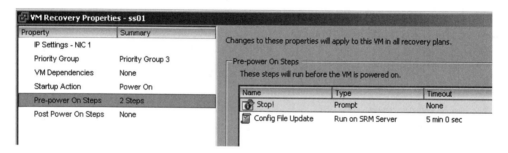

Figure 11.20   SRM demonstrates its granularity by allowing as many pre-power-on and post-power-on steps as you need.

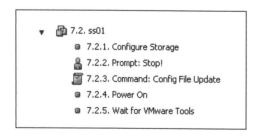

Figure 11.21   A prompt step is indicated by an icon of a human, and a command step is indicated by an icon of a scroll or script with a checkmark.

Adding Command Steps

As with messages, it's possible to add commands to the Recovery Plan. These commands could call scripts in a .bat, .cmd, .vbs, .wmi, PowerShell, or Perl file to automate other tasks. In fact, you're not limited to these scripting languages; as long as the guest operating system supports the command-line engine you want to run, it should work. As I hope you can tell, SRM is all about providing a friendly environment within which you can test Recovery Plans or carry out datacenter moves. It's unlikely that you will be able to get the plan to do what you want it to do without some level of scripting. So try not to see SRM as being a killer to scripts. Instead, try to see it as removing most of the heavy lifting required to get virtual recovery working—and empowering you to spend more time handling the unique requirements of your organization. SRM it is not a silver bullet.

When you call these scripts you must provide the full path to the script engine and the script file in question. For example, to run a Microsoft .bat or .cmd script you would supply the following path:

```
c:\windows\system32\cmd.exe /C c:\alarmscript.cmd
```

The path in this sample is relative to the SRM server. So, in this case, the script would be located on the C: drive of the Recovery Site SRM server. Of course, there's no need to store your scripts on the disk of the SRM host. They could be located on a network share instead.

> **IMPORTANT NOTE**
> Although I've used an uppercase /C at the command line that is just a convention. The command will work with a lowercase /c. Also, remember that in the world of Windows, if you have filenames or directory names which contain spaces you will need to use "speech marks" around these paths.

These scripts are executed at the Recovery Site SRM server, and as a consequence you should know they are executed under the security context of the SRM's "local system" services account. As a test, I used the msg command in Windows to send a message to another Windows system. In case you don't know, the msg command replaced the older net send command and the older Messenger service. So, in the alarmscript.cmd file, I set up the msg script and stored it on the C: drive of the Recovery Site host:

```
@echo off
msg /server:mf1 administrator "The Process has completed. Please come back
    to SRM and examine the Plan."
```

1. In the Recovery Plan select where you would like the step to be located. In my case, I chose "+ 6. Prompt: Priority 1 Completed."

2. Click the Add Step icon.

3. Select the Command on SRM Server radio button, as shown in Figure 11.22. Enter a friendly name for the step, the path to the script command interpreter, and the script you would like to run.

4. Configure a timeout value that befits the duration that the script needs to execute successfully.

5. Select whether your step is triggered before or after your selection in the plan.

I sometimes add a pop-up message to my management PC at the end of the Recovery Plan (see Figure 11.23). This means I can start a Recovery Plan and go off and perform other tasks, such as checking my email, browsing Facebook, and tweeting my every thought in a stream-of-consciousness manner that James Joyce would be proud of. My pathetic attempts at social media will be conveniently interrupted by the pop-up message that reminds me I'm supposed to be doing real work.

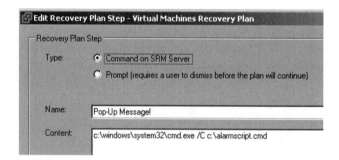

Figure 11.22   A simple script that will use cmd.exe to run a basic Microsoft "batch" file

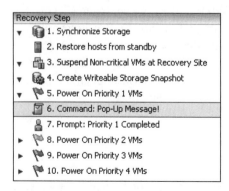

Figure 11.23   A command prompt has been added to the Recovery Plan.

Adding Command Steps with VMware PowerCLI

Although using classic-style "batch" files to carry out tasks is nice, it's not an especially powerful API for manipulating and modifying the vSphere platform. If you want to make subtler scripts, you really need a more robust scripting engine. Fortunately, VMware has for some time embraced the Microsoft PowerShell environment, supplementing it with cmdlets that are specific to managing VMware vSphere and other technologies such as VMware View. If you are new to PowerCLI and PowerShell I heartily recommend following Alan Renouf's "Back to Basics" series of tutorials that will get you quickly up to speed. Alan helped me with this chapter immensely, and some of his scripts are reproduced here with his kind permission:

> http://blogs.vmware.com/vipowershell/2011/06/back-to-basics-part-1-installing-powercli.html

PowerShell offers the SRM administrator a plethora of scripting opportunities. PowerShell could be used to send commands to services running in the Windows operating system, or VMware PowerCLI could be used to actually modify the properties of the Recovery Site or the VMs being recovered. Start by downloading and installing VMware PowerCLI to the SRM server in the Recovery Site. I think it is very likely that you will want to use these scripts in your failback process as well, so install PowerCLI to the Protected Site SRM as well:

> www.vmware.com/support/developer/PowerCLI/index.html

After the installation, confirm that the PowerCLI execution policy is correctly set, and that you can successfully communicate to the vCenter to which the SRM server is configured. In order to allow PowerCLI scripts to execute silently I set the policy to be `remote-signed`. You may need to consult your datacenter policies regarding this configuration, as you might find you need a higher level of trusted certificate signing for your scripts. Remember, your PowerCLI scripts may run a combination of both 32-bit and 64-bit cmdlets. These are controlled by separate execution policies, so make sure the policy is correctly configured for both types of cmdlets.

```
set-executionpolicy remotesigned
```

Next, I confirm that I can connect successfully to the vCenter server with the `connect-viserver` cmdlets, like so:

```
connect-viserver vcnj.corp.com -username corp\administrator -password
  vmware
```

If you fail to configure the execution policy correctly you will get this error message:

```
Warning - The command 'c:\windows\system32\cmd.exe' has returned a non-zero
   value: 1
```

This error is normally caused by a typo in the string in the Edit step or an error in your script—for example, typing "redirect.bat" instead of "redirect.cmd" or giving a script file a bad name, such as "web-half-ram.ps1.ps1". Test your scripts manually from an inter-active login prompt at the SRM server, and invoke them with the same redirect.cmd file that the Recovery Plan will use. I also recommend running each line of a PowerCLI script to confirm that it works. Another good tip is to create a Recovery Plan with just a couple of VMs. This will allow you to test your Recovery Plan and associated scripts quickly. There's nothing more annoying than discovering you have a typo in a script—where the Recovery Plan takes 30 minutes to test each time, and ten minutes to clean up. I speak from bitter experience. Nine times out of ten any problems you have will arise from typos and you will kick yourself when you find out it's your fault and not the system's fault!

One of the most common questions asked on the SRM Forums is how to reduce the amount of RAM used by the VMs during the recovery process. This is because people sometimes have less powerful ESX hosts in the Recovery Site. For example, an organi-zation could have ESX hosts in the Recovery Site that are configured with less physical memory than the production ESX hosts in the Protected Site. Using PowerCLI we can automate the process of reducing the VMs' RAM allocation by running .ps scripts before the power-on event. There are a couple of ways to do this with PowerCLI.

Example 1

You could have a .ps1 script for every VM and reduce its memory. The scripts that modify the configuration of the VMs themselves would need to execute before the VM powers on for them to take effect.

Following is a sample .ps script that will do just that for my web01 VM. This script uses the set-vm cmdlet to reduce the recovery VM's memory allocation to 1,024MB. The -confirm:$false command prevents the script from waiting for a human operator to confirm the change. The disconnect statement at the end of the script is important. Without the disconnect statement, a session could remain open at the vCenter, resulting in wasted resources at the vCenter.

```
connect-viserver vcnj.corp.com -user corp\administrator -password vmware
Set-VM web01 -MemoryMB "1024" -Confirm:$FALSE
Disconnect-VIServer -Server vcnyc.corp.com -Confirm:$FALSE
```

Example 2

Of course, a .ps script for every VM would be very administrator-intensive, but it may be necessary, as VMs can be quite varied in their requirements. So you might prefer to search for VMs based on their name, and make changes that affect many VMs simultaneously. For example, in the following .ps script, the get-vm cmdlet is used to find every VM which starts with the text "web01" and then "pipelines" this to the set-vm command. This will modify the memory of VMs web01, web02, and so on.

```
connect-viserver vcnj.corp.com --user corp\administrator --password vmware
start-sleep -s 300
get-vm web* | Set-VM -MemoryMB "1024" -Confirm:$FALSE
Disconnect-VIServer -Server vcnj.corp.com -Confirm:$FALSE
```

The line that pauses the script for 300 seconds (five minutes) needs a little explanation. Clearly, we can't use PowerCLI to decrease the amount of memory after the VM is powered on. Additionally, we cannot start modifying the VMs' settings until we are sure the Configure Storage stage on each affected VM has completed; you know when this process has properly completed when all the "Reconfigure virtual machine" events have been completed. If we carried out this task too quickly in the Recovery Plan we might find the script changes the memory settings on the placeholder, not on the recovered VM. As you might recall from Chapter 10, Recovery Site Configuration, it's during the Configure Storage step in a Recovery Plan that a placeholder VM is removed and replaced with the real .vmx file from the replicated storage. How long it takes for all your VMs to be converted from placeholders to VMs will vary based on the number of VMs in the Recovery Plan. If the script were attached directly to the VM (as would be the case with Example 1) as part of its pre-power-on step this sleep stage would not be required. If the script only modifies VMs in the lower-priority lists such as level 2, 3, 4, or 5 it's likely that these VMs will already be in the right format for the PowerCLI script to modify them. So you can regard this sleep stage as being somewhat overcautious on my behalf, but I would rather have a script that works perfectly all the time than a script that only works intermittently.

Example 3

One of the difficulties with using the VM's name as the scope for applying a change like this is the fact that you cannot always rely on a robust naming convention being used within an organization from the very first day of deploying virtualization. Additionally, VMs are easily open to being renamed by an operator with even very limited rights. So you might prefer to perform your scripts against a resource pool or folder where these objects can be protected with permissions. This would allow for bulk changes to take place in all VMs that were in that resource pool or folder location.

```
connect-viserver vcnj.corp.com -user corp\administrator -password vmware
start-sleep -s 300
get-folder web | get-vm * | Set-VM -MemoryMB "1024" -Confirm:$FALSE
Disconnect-VIServer -Server vcnj.corp.com -Confirm:$FALSE
```

Example 4

Perhaps a more sophisticated script would not set a flat amount of memory, but instead would check the amount of memory assigned to the VM and then reduce it by a certain factor. For example, perhaps I want to reduce the amount of memory assigned to all the recovered VMs by 50%. The following script finds the current amount of memory assigned to the VM, and then reduces it by 50%. For each VM found with the web* string in its name, it finds the amount of memory assigned and then uses the set-vm cmdlet to set it correctly by dividing the VM.MemoryMB amount by 2.

```
connect-viserver vcnj.corp.com -user corp\administrator -password vmware
start-sleep -s 300
Foreach ($VM in Get-VM web*)
{
    $NewMemAmount = $VM.MemoryMB / 2
    Set-VM $VM -MemoryMB $NewMemAmount -Confirm:$FALSE
}
Disconnect-VIServer -Server vcnj.corp.com -Confirm:$FALSE
```

In my case, I decided to use this final method to control the amount of memory assigned to the Web VMs. I would like to thank Al Renouf from the UK, as he helped write this last example. In case you don't know, Al is very handy with PowerShell, and his Virtu-Al blog (www.virtu-al.net) is well worth a read. He has also coauthored a recent book on VMware PowerCLI, and in 2011 became a VMware employee.

Step 1: Create a redirect.cmd File

The next phase involves getting these .ps files to be called by SRM. One method is not to call the .ps script directly, but instead to create a .cmd file that will call the script at the appropriate time. This helps to reduce the amount of text held within the Add Step dialog box. By using variables in the .cmd/.bat file, we can reuse it time and time again to call any number of .ps files held on the SRM server. I first came across the redirect.cmd file while reading Carter Shaklin's PowerCLI blog which discussed using .ps scripts with vCenter alarms:

http://blogs.vmware.com/vipowershell/2009/09/how-to-run-powercli-scripts-from-vcenter-alarms.html

And with help from Virtu-Al's website, I was able to come up with a .cmd file that would call my .ps1 PowerShell files. The script loads the Microsoft PowerShell environment together with the PowerShell Console file (.psc1) that allows VMware's PowerCLI to function. The variable at the end (%1) allows for any .ps1 file to be called with a single redirect.cmd file. The only real change in recent times is my move to using Windows 2008 R2 64-bit, as this changed the default paths for the location of the vim.psc1 file. The contents of the file are then saved as "redirect.cmd":

```
@echo off
C:\WINDOWS\system32\windowspowershell\v1.0\powershell.exe -psc "C:\Program
   Files (x86)\VMware\Infrastructure\vSphere PowerCLI\vim.psc1" "& '%1'"
```

Step 2: Copy the redirect.cmd and PowerCLI Scripts to the Recovery SRM Server

Now you need to copy your redirect.cmd and .ps file(s) to a location on the recovery SRM server if they are not there already, or to some shared location that is used to hold your scripts. It doesn't really matter where you place them, so long as you correctly type the path to the script when you add a command to the Recovery Plan. In this case, web01-ram. ps1, web-bulk-ram.ps1, and web-ram-half.ps1 represent some of the different examples discussed previously (see Figure 11.24).

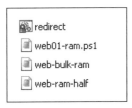

Figure 11.24 Arrangement of different PowerShell script files together with my redirect.cmd file

Step 3: Add a Command to the Recovery Plan

At this point, you need to add a command step to the Recovery Plan. In this example, I'm using the script I created to reduce all the Web-based VMs' memory allocation by half. I am adding the step high in the plan, before any of the VMs have powered on, to make sure that wherever my Web VMs are located—be they in priority 1 or priority 5—they are properly reconfigured.

1. In the Recovery Plan, select Priority 1.

2. Click the Add Step button.

3. Enter the full path to the command interpreter (cmd.exe) and include the redirect. cmd file and the .ps file you would like to execute (see Figure 11.25). In my case, this was the script:

```
c:\windows\system32\cmd.exe /C c:\redirect.cmd c:\web-ram-half.ps1
```

This will appear in the plan as shown in Figure 11.26.

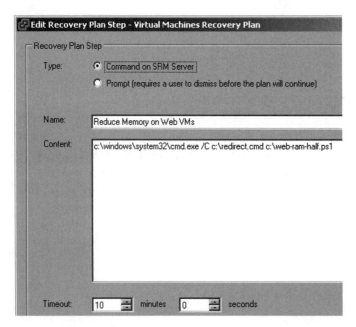

Figure 11.25   A command step being added to run the script that reduces the RAM allocation by 50%

Figure 11.26   The command step appears before the first priority level, enabling the reconfiguration to complete before power-on events begin.

Step 4: Add a Command to the Individual VM

My script assumes that *all* VMs that are Web servers need to have their RAM increased. But what if I have exceptions to this? What if I have a VM for which I want to increase the allocation of memory, or have some unique per-VM setting? This is where VM-based pre-power-on and post-power-on scripts come in handy. They work in much the same way as scripts added as major steps to the Recovery Plan.

1. In the Recovery Plan, select the VM. In my case, I chose the web01 VM that I had created a specific script for earlier.

2. Right-click and select Configure in the context menu.

3. In the property list select the Pre-power On Step option, and in the dialog box click Add.

4. Enter the full path to the command interpreter (cmd.exe) and include the redirect. cmd file and the .ps file you would like to execute (see Figure 11.27). In my case, this was:

```
c:\windows\system32\cmd.exe /C c:\redirect.cmd c:\web01-ram.ps1
```

So long as any pre-power-on script executes after any other PowerCLI script, you can be pretty sure that it will take effect over any other scripts you run.

Managing PowerCLI Authentication and Variables

So far I've focused on using PowerCLI with the -username and -password fields to handle authentication settings that are hardcoded to the PowerShell script file. It strikes me that most system administrators would prefer to use these scripts in a more secure manner. This would also allow the SRM administrator more flexibility to be able to "pipe" variables to the PowerCLI scripts. For example, say you want to use the ability to reduce

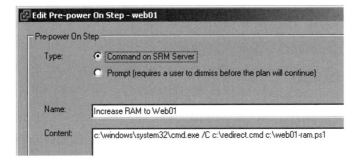

Figure 11.27 Pre-power-on scripts allow for "exceptions to the rule" situations where every VM is configured the same way, except web01.

memory on a VM by specifying the vCenter, VM, memory allocation, and a log file location to confirm that the script has executed.

It's a little-known fact that PowerCLI supports Active Directory authentication natively, and as such there is no need to specify the username and password credentials so long as the user account you log in as is the domain account with the correct privileges in vCenter to carry out the required task. For this to work in SRM an account must be created in Active Directory and granted privileges at the Recovery Site vCenter. As you will undoubtedly need the same rights at the Protected Site vCenter, this account could be used as part of any failback procedure you undergo, which would reverse or undo the changes made while you were in a failover situation. As you may recall, by default the SRM service account is the "local system," and as such, for this "pass-through authentication" to be successful this will need to change, as shown in Figure 11.28. You can do this by locating the VMware vCenter Site Recovery Manager services in the Services MMC, and using the This Account option to reset the default account used; by default, the process grants the selected user the right to log on as a service.

Of course, this service account under which the SRM scripts will execute needs to be granted privileges in vCenter in order for the scripts to run successfully. In my case, I allowed user srmnj the rights to run scripts only in the scope of the resource pool where the recovered VM would be located (see Figure 11.29). There are many ways to handle

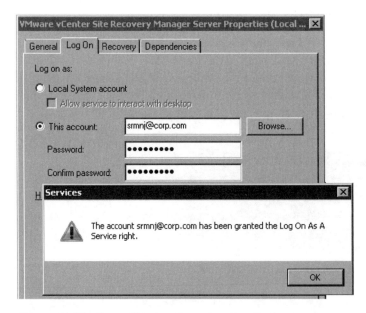

Figure 11.28 PowerCLI pass-through authentication requires a domain account, and permissions and rights in vCenter.

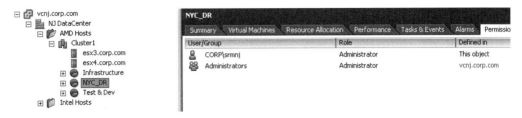

Figure 11.29 The srmnj account being given administrator privileges to the NYC_DR resource pool where New York's VMs will be recovered

this delegation of privileges, such as using an existing group, or granting the service account privileges over more objects in the Recovery Site vCenter. The important point here is to ensure that the rights do cover the scope of your scripting activities, and that they are the least permissive available.

Example 5

In terms of the PowerCLI script that offers more flexibility, an example follows. The `Param` value allows the author of the script to define parameters that can be passed along the command line to PowerCLI. In this case, four parameters have been defined: the name or IP address of the vCenter, the VM to be modified, the amount of memory to allocate, and log file location for the script itself. This log file allows the administrator to check a text file to confirm the result of the script.

```
Param (
$vCenter,
$VM,
$Memory,
$LogFile
)

If ($LogFile) {
      Start-Transcript $LogFile
}

if (!(get-pssnapin -name VMware.VimAutomation.Core -erroraction
  silentlycontinue)) {
    add-pssnapin VMware.VimAutomation.Core
}
```

```
Connect-VIServer $vCenter

Set-VM -VM $VM -MemoryMB $Memory -Confirm:$false

Disconnect-ViServer * -Confirm:$false

If ($LogFile) {
    Stop-Transcript
}
```

This script can be added to the Pre-power On Step for a VM. Remember, the full path to the PowerShell.exe must be specified in the dialog box together with the path to the script and log file location, as shown in Figure 11.30. I can invoke the script on a per-VM basis using the following syntax. Notice in this case the PowerShell environment is being called directly, with the .ps1 file containing the necessary lines to load the VMware PowerCLI extensions.

```
C:\Windows\System32\WindowsPowerShell\v1.0\PowerShell.exe -File
   C:\SetMemory.ps1 -vCenter vcnj.corp.com -VM web01 -Memory 512 -Logfile
   C:\SetMemoryLog.txt
```

Another good way to handle scripts is to hold the variables in a .csv file. This could prove quite useful if you want to reconfigure the memory settings of many VMs, and at the same time hold the original memory allocations of your VMs before the failover occurred (say, for use in a failback process). This would also allow you to use a spreadsheet application like Microsoft Excel to change the variables you needed. In my case, I created a .csv file in Excel, using columns for the VM name, failover memory, and failback memory. Column B is used whenever failover occurs between New York and New Jersey, and column C is used to reset the memory allocation in the event of a failback to the New York site (see Figure 11.31).

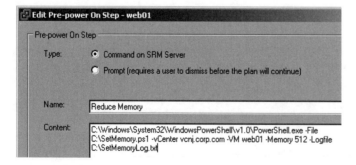

Figure 11.30   Passing parameters to the command line is a much more flexible approach to adjusting memory allocations.

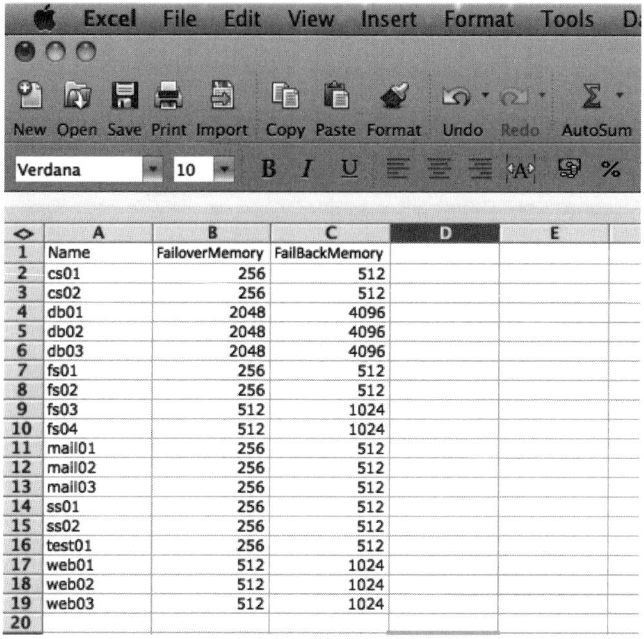

	A	B	C	D	E
1	Name	FailoverMemory	FailBackMemory		
2	cs01	256	512		
3	cs02	256	512		
4	db01	2048	4096		
5	db02	2048	4096		
6	db03	2048	4096		
7	fs01	256	512		
8	fs02	256	512		
9	fs03	512	1024		
10	fs04	512	1024		
11	mail01	256	512		
12	mail02	256	512		
13	mail03	256	512		
14	ss01	256	512		
15	ss02	256	512		
16	test01	256	512		
17	web01	512	1024		
18	web02	512	1024		
19	web03	512	1024		
20					

Figure 11.31 Sadly, I've found the Mac version of Excel incorrectly formats .csv files.

Example 6

This .csv file can be called at the beginning of the Recovery Plan, resetting the memory allocation by a similar PowerCLI script that we saw earlier in this section. In this case, three new extra variables are added that allow the SRM administrator to specify the location of the .csv file and which memory variable is being used in the script—either `FailOverMemory` or `FailBackMemory`. In this case, because the script is being run just before the VMs are powered on, I've included a `sleep` statement to ensure that the VM is correctly recovered by SRM before changing its configuration.

```
Param (
        $vCenter,
        $CSV,
        $Failover,
        $Failback,
        $LogFile
)
```

```
If ($LogFile) {
        Start-Transcript $LogFile
}

if (!(get-pssnapin -name VMware.VimAutomation.Core -erroraction
  silentlycontinue)) {
    add-pssnapin VMware.VimAutomation.Core
}

Connect-VIServer $vCenter
start-sleep -s 300

Import-Csv $CSV | Foreach {
        If ($Failover) {
                Set-VM -VM $_.VM -MemoryMB $_.FailOverMemory -Confirm:$false
        }

        If ($Failback) {
                Set-VM -VM $_.VM -MemoryMB $_.FailBackMemory -Confirm:$false
        }
}

Disconnect-ViServer * -Confirm:$false

If ($LogFile) {
        Stop-Transcript
}
```

The SRM administrator can invoke this script with this syntax in the Add Script dialog box
(see Figure 11.32):

```
C:\Windows\System32\WindowsPowerShell\v1.0\PowerShell.exe -File C:\
  SetMemoryAdvanced.ps1 -vCenter vcnj.corp.com -CSV C:\MemorySizes.csv
  -Failover True -Logfile C:\SetMemoryCSVLog.txt
```

If you wanted to reverse the process, the script would be edited before running the
Recovery Plan in failback mode. The big difference here is that I'm connecting to the
location where the VMs are being recovered. In a failback process, this would be the
vCenter at the Protected Site (in my case, the vcnyc vCenter at New York). Notice also
that the variable -Failback True is being used in this case:

```
C:\Windows\System32\WindowsPowerShell\v1.0\PowerShell.exe -File C:\
  SetMemoryAdvanced.ps1 -vCenter vcnyc.corp.com -CSV C:\MemorySizes.csv
  -Failback True -Logfile C:\SetMemoryCSVLog.txt
```

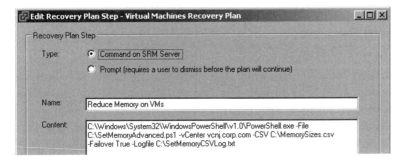

Figure 11.32 In a failback scenario, you need to replace `-Failover` with `-Failback` to reset the VMs' memory to their original settings.

Finally, you might feel uncomfortable with SRM running these scripts automatically. Remember, you can just put message steps in the Recovery Plan and run these commands manually if you wish. You may want to think about the consequences of using PowerCLI to modify VMs for failback. These changes could be replicated back to the Protected Site should you decide to failback to the Protected Site. Remember, you are making changes to the VMX file in the case of the memory allocation VMs. When you failback upon triggering a "reprotect" process, you're reversing the replication direction—to make changes accrued in the Recovery Site replicate back to the Protected Site. As a consequence, in my example when I failback to the Protected Site the VMs will not have correct production memory allocations. To stop this I will need a PS script that undoes the changes made by the Recovery Plan. If you want to know a funny story about this, I once used my "halve memory" script over and over again in a failover and failback manner, without increasing the memory allocation during the failback process. After doing this a couple of times I found Windows VMs would no longer reboot because their memory allocation was just 4MB. I have described this to customers by quoting Sir Isaac Newton's Third Law of Motion: "To every action there is always an equal and opposite reaction." The moral of the story is that if you use PowerCLI to massively modify your VMs when they are recovered, make sure you have corresponding scripts that undo that process during failback. As with all scripting, there's an element of monitoring and maintenance that is beyond the scope of SRM to control. If a new VM is created that needs specialist scripting in order for it to work, you will need to tie a management process around enrolling into the Recovery Plan, and either attach scripts to it or update repositories which hold script data and information. For example, in the case of the .csv method of reducing the allocation of memory, you would need to add and remove VMs from the memorysize.csv file and keep it up-to-date with your environment.

Adding Command Steps to Call Scripts within the Guest Operating System

In PowerCLI 4.0 Update 1, a new cmdlet was introduced to allow you to call scripts within the guest operating system. The new cmdlet is called `Invoke-VMscript`. For `Invoke-VMscript` to work Microsoft PowerShell must already be installed in the VM. Additionally, VMware Tools needs to be up-to-date with the ESX host to prevent a warning message from occurring when the script executes; although this warning will not stop the script from executing and completing, it could cause unexpected problems. The `Invoke-VMscript` cmdlet works natively with cmd, bin, and bash shell scripts in Linux. By default, in Windows it assumes you will want to run a PowerShell script inside the VM; it is possible using the `ScriptType` parameter to specify the type of script you want to run.

Below is a syntax example where I used `Invoke-VMscript` to list a VM's IP address settings directly from the Windows guest operating system running inside the VM. There are two important points here. First, despite authenticating PowerCLI against vCenter, the `Invoke-VMscript` *requires* root credentials on the ESX host itself to function, and this could inhibit its use where no consistent password is used for the root password, or it is company policy not to disclose it. Second, you clearly need to authenticate against the guest operating system running inside the VM for the script to work. Put bluntly, the bar set to authenticate with the `Invoke-VMscript` cmdlet is a high one.

```
Invoke-VMscript -VM db02 -ScriptText "ipconfig" -HostUser root
  -HostPassword password -GuestUser corp\administrator -GuestPassword vmware
```

Without the correct credentials, an authentication failure will occur. In the case of an authentication failure to the ESX host, PowerCLI will state the following:

```
"Insufficient permissions in host operating system"
```

This message is a little confusing, as we all know ESX is not an operating system but a virtualization hypervisor! In the case of an authentication failure to the guest operating system, PowerCLI will state the following:

```
"Authentication failure or insufficient permissions in guest operating
  system"
```

This invoke-script example above would cause the guest operating system to "echo" the results of a Windows `ipconfig` command back to the PowerCLI window (see Figure 11.33).

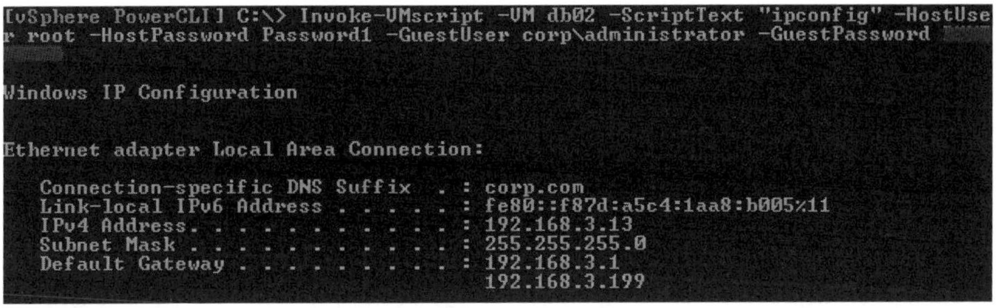

```
[vSphere PowerCLI] C:\> Invoke-VMscript -VM db02 -ScriptText "ipconfig" -HostUse
r root -HostPassword Password1 -GuestUser corp\administrator -GuestPassword

Windows IP Configuration

Ethernet adapter Local Area Connection:

   Connection-specific DNS Suffix  . : corp.com
   Link-local IPv6 Address . . . . . : fe80::f87d:a5c4:1aa8:b005%11
   IPv4 Address. . . . . . . . . . . : 192.168.3.13
   Subnet Mask . . . . . . . . . . . : 255.255.255.0
   Default Gateway . . . . . . . . . : 192.168.3.1
                                       192.168.3.199
```

Figure 11.33   Using the `Invoke-VMscript` cmdlet to determine the IP address of a VM

Used in this simple way, the `Invoke-VMscript` cmdlet could be used to restart a service within one of the recovery VMs. Start by creating some kind of script within the VM:

```
@echo off
echo Stopping the Netlogon Service…
net stop netlogon
ipconfig /registerdns
echo Starting the Netlogon Service
net start netlogon
echo Success!!!
```

Then call this script with the `Invoke-VMscript` cmdlet:

```
Invoke-VMScript -VM db02 -ScriptText "c:\restartnetlogon.cmd" -HostUser
   root -HostPassword Password1 -GuestUser corp\administrator -GuestPassword
   vmware
```

Configuring IP Address Changes for Recovery Virtual Machines

One task you may wish to automate is changing an IP address within the virtual machine. Previously, VMware achieved this by calling Microsoft Sysprep from the Guest Customization Settings part of vCenter. With SRM 5.0, a new engine has been developed for changing the IP address of a VM. This new engine is significantly quicker than the previous Sysprep approach. In addition, there is a new graphical method of setting both the Protected and Recovery Site IP addresses. If you have many virtual machines you can also use a command-line utility that imports the IP configuration from a .csv file. This .csv file would need management and maintenance as the VM's IP address could occasionally change, and the .csv file would need updating for any new VM that was added to a Protection Group and Recovery Plan in SRM.

The downside of this approach is that it is very administrator-intensive even with a .csv file. Additionally, you might find that although changing the IP address at the OS level works, applications continue to use the old IP address because it has been stored in some other configuration file. So it's well worth considering other approaches which do not require a change in each and every virtual machine's IP configuration. These approaches could include

- Retaining the existing IP address and redirecting clients by some type of NAT appliance which hides the IP address of the VM

- Using stretched VLANs so that virtual machines remain on the same network regardless of the physical location on which they are based

- Allocating the IP address by DHCP and Client Reservations

Creating a Manual IP Guest Customization

SRM 5.0 introduces a new graphical method of setting the Protected and Recovery Site IP addresses for the VM, as shown in Figure 11.34. This "update" feature can actually retrieve the IP address from a protected VM, and complete some (but not all) of the VM's IP configuration. For this feature to work the VM needs to be powered on and VMware Tools must be running in the guest operating system. Then you need to follow these steps.

1. Locate a VM within your Recovery Plan, right-click, and choose the Configure option in the menu.

2. Select the virtual NIC in the Property column, and enable the option to "Customize IP Settings during recovery."

3. Click the Configure Protection button, and click the Update button to retrieve the VM's IP configuration (see Figure 11.34).

   Review the IP data that is retrieved and add any additional parameters you feel need changing. Occasionally, I've seen the Update button not retrieve every single parameter; often this is caused by the VM not being properly configured.

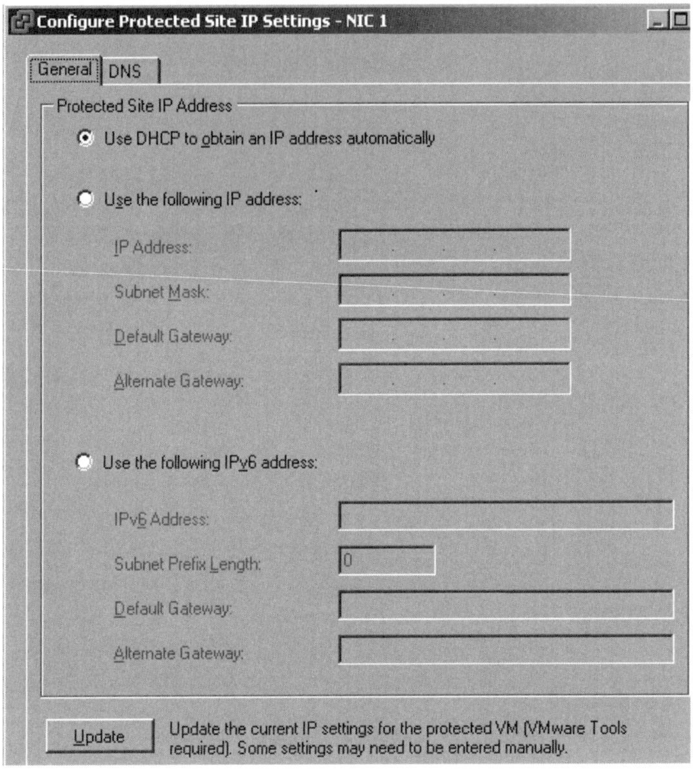

Figure 11.34   The GUI for IP configuration can discover the VM's IP settings.

4. Once the Protected Site is configured, click the Configure Recovery button and repeat this process for the Recovery Site IP settings. Once completed, the dialog box will show the IP settings used for both failovers and failbacks, so a VM's IP settings are returned to their original state if a VM is returned to the Protected Site. The new IP configuration dialog box shown in Figure 11.35 can also deal with situations where the VM has multiple virtual NIC adapters.

Once you click OK, the VM will have an additional step called "Customize IP" (see Figure 11.36).

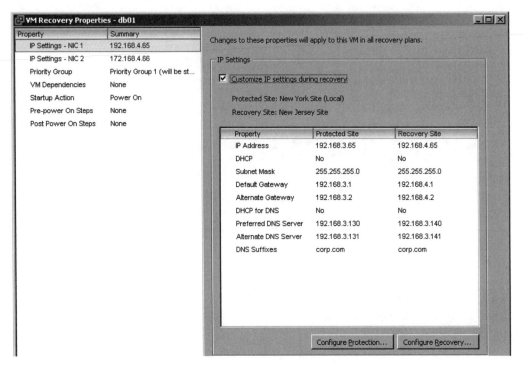

Figure 11.35   The new GUI allows the administrator to easily see the VM's IP configuration.

Figure 11.36   The "Customize IP" step on the db01 virtual machine

Configuring Bulk IP Address Changes for the Recovery Virtual Machine (dr-ip-exporter)

For some, VMware SRM has had a command utility called dr-customizer.exe, which allows users to bulk-generate guest customization settings from the .csv file. This is better than having to manually run through the IP configuration for each and every VM, because manually typing an IP address for each VM can be time-consuming. Using .csv together with a spreadsheet tool like Microsoft Excel can allow you to manage the system in a much more efficient way.

1. Open a command prompt on the Recovery Site SRM server.

2. Change the directory to the SRM Bin file location held at C:\Program Files (x86)\ VMware\VMware vCenter Site Recovery Manager\bin.

3. Run this command:

```
dr-ip-customizer --cfg ..\config\vmware-dr.xml --out c:\nyc.csv --cmd
    generate --vc vcnj.corp.com –i
```

4. After the first connection, if necessary, choose [Y] to trust the SRM server.

5. Provide the login details for the Recovery Site vCenter server.

When opened in Microsoft Excel the .csv file will look similar to the screen grab shown in Figure 11.37.

The command creates a .csv file using the --out and --cmd switches. The --vc switch indicates which initial vCenter to connect to when building the .csv file. As you can see, this process does not retrieve the IP details of the VM at the Protected Site, but instead creates a .csv file that contains the VM ID. This VM

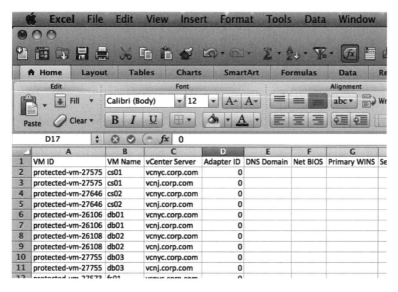

Figure 11.37   A VM is uniquely identified by its VM ID. Unprotecting and reprotecting a VM generates a new VM ID and placeholder object, and this can invalidate the settings in the .csv file.

ID value is referred to as a managed object reference (MOREF) number, which uniquely identifies the VM in the SRM inventory. You will see the VM appears twice: once for its reference in the Protected Site (managed by the vCenter vcnyc) and once again for the Recovery Site (managed by the vCenter vcnj). These object numbers are unique to the vCenter that you connected to when you first ran the dr-ip-exporter utility. So, when the administrator goes to "import" the modified .csv file it must be to the *same* vCenter that was used to generate the .csv file; otherwise, you will receive an error. If you create a .csv file from one vCenter, and subsequently try to apply it to another vCenter, you will receive a generic error message that states:

```
ERROR: The Protected VM 'protected-vm-27575' does not exist. Please
   check your CSV file to make sure that it is up to date. Also, please
   connect to the same VC server for which you generated the CSV file.
   The VM Ids are different in each site.
```

As you can see, the .csv is a simple file that maps the name of the virtual machine as it is known in SRM, with the VM ID. The VM Name column is merely there to assist you in mapping these "shadow" VMs to the actual VMs contained in the Recovery Plan.

The Adapter ID column is used to control how settings are applied. If the Adapter ID column is set to 0, this acts as a global setting that is applied to *all* LANs within the VM. This setting cannot be used to change the IP address of a LAN; however, it can be used to globally set values that would be the same for all network interfaces such as the DNS configuration. If a VM has multiple NICs it's possible to specify each NIC by its number (1, 2, 3) and apply different settings to it. For example, suppose you wished to give two different NIC interfaces two different IP settings—together with more than one default gateway and DNS setting; you would simply add another row for each VM. If all your VMs have a single NIC and you just need to re-IP them you could use a much simpler configuration. In this case, I set the Adapter ID column to be 1 for every VM. I then used the Complete Series feature of Microsoft Excel to generate a unique IP address for each VM, and so on, as shown in Figure 11.38. (Note that in the figure, columns have been hidden in Excel for space considerations.)

This .csv approach can become quite complex if you are dealing with VMs with multiple NICs with multiple default gateway and DNS settings (see Figure 11.39). Such a configuration could apply to a pair of VMs that were being used in a Microsoft Cluster Service (MSCS) configuration. For example, my VM db01 has two NICs that required eight entries in the spreadsheet to complete its configuration (again, note that in the figure, rows have been hidden in Excel for space considerations).

	A	B	C	D	I	J	K	O	P
1	VM ID	VM Name	vCenter Server	Adapter ID	IP Address	Subnet Mask	Gateway(s)	DNS Server(s)	DNS Suffix(es)
2	protected-vm-25444	ss02	vcnyc.corp.com	1	192.168.3.60	255.255.255.0	192.168.3.1	192.168.3.130	
3	protected-vm-25444	ss02	vcnj.corp.com	1	192.168.4.60	255.255.255.0	192.168.4.1	192.168.4.130	
4	protected-vm-26106	db01	vcnyc.corp.com	1	192.168.3.61	255.255.255.0	192.168.3.1	192.168.3.130	
5	protected-vm-26106	db01	vcnj.corp.com	1	192.168.4.61	255.255.255.0	192.168.4.1	192.168.4.130	
6	protected-vm-26108	db02	vcnyc.corp.com	1	192.168.3.62	255.255.255.0	192.168.3.1	192.168.3.130	
7	protected-vm-26108	db02	vcnj.corp.com	1	192.168.4.62	255.255.255.0	192.168.4.1	192.168.4.130	
8	protected-vm-26110	web03	vcnyc.corp.com	1	192.168.3.63	255.255.255.0	192.168.3.1	192.168.3.130	
9	protected-vm-26110	web03	vcnj.corp.com	1	192.168.4.63	255.255.255.0	192.168.4.1	192.168.4.130	
10	protected-vm-27237	ss01	vcnyc.corp.com	1	192.168.3.64	255.255.255.0	192.168.3.1	192.168.3.130	
11	protected-vm-27237	ss01	vcnj.corp.com	1	192.168.4.64	255.255.255.0	192.168.4.1	192.168.4.130	

Figure 11.38 A simple .csv file where every VM has just one NIC

	A	B	C	D	I	J	K	O	P
1	VM ID	VM Name	vCenter Server	Adapter ID	IP Address	Subnet Mask	Gateway(s)	DNS Server(s)	DNS Suffix(es)
2	protected-vm-25444	ss02	vcnyc.corp.com	1	192.168.3.60	255.255.255.0	192.168.3.1	192.168.3.130	corp.com
3	protected-vm-25444		vcnyc.corp.com	1			192.168.3.2	192.168.3.131	
4	protected-vm-25444	ss02	vcnj.corp.com	1	192.168.4.60	255.255.255.0	192.168.4.1	192.168.4.130	corp.com
5	protected-vm-25444		vcnj.corp.com	1			192.168.3.2	192.168.4.131	
6	protected-vm-26106	db01	vcnyc.corp.com	1	192.168.3.61	255.255.255.0	192.168.3.1	192.168.3.130	corp.com
7	protected-vm-26106		vcnyc.corp.com	1			192.168.3.2	192.168.3.131	
8	protected-vm-26106	db01	vcnj.corp.com	1	192.168.4.61	255.255.255.0	192.168.4.1	192.168.4.130	corp.com
9	protected-vm-26106		vcnj.corp.com	1			192.168.3.2	192.168.4.131	
10	protected-vm-26108	db02	vcnyc.corp.com	1	192.168.3.62	255.255.255.0	192.168.3.1	192.168.3.130	corp.com
11	protected-vm-26108		vcnyc.corp.com	1			192.168.3.2	192.168.3.131	
12	protected-vm-26108	db02	vcnyc.corp.com	2	172.168.3.62	255.255.255.0	172.168.3.1	172.168.3.130	corp.com
13	protected-vm-26108		vcnyc.corp.com	2			172.168.3.2	172.168.3.131	
14	protected-vm-26108	db02	vcnj.corp.com	1	192.168.4.62	255.255.255.0	192.168.4.1	192.168.4.130	corp.com
15	protected-vm-26108		vcnj.corp.com	1			192.168.4.2	192.168.4.131	
16	protected-vm-26108	db02	vcnj.corp.com	2	172.168.4.62	255.255.255.0	172.168.4.1	172.168.4.130	corp.com
17	protected-vm-26108		vcnj.corp.com	2			172.168.4.2	172.168.4.131	

Figure 11.39 A configuration where every VM has one NIC but is configured for multiple gateways (or routers) and multiple DNS servers

6. To process the .csv file you would use the following command:

```
dr-ip-customizer -cfg ..\config\vmware-dr.xml --csv c:\nyc.csv --cmd
   create
```

7. Provide the username and password to the vCenter, and accept the certificate of both the vCenter and SRM hosts if necessary. The create command generates the IP customizations for you based on the parameters of the .csv file. The dr-ip-customizer command supports a --cmd drop parameter which removes IP customizations from vCenter, and a --cmd recreate parameter which applies any changes to the .csv file after the use of create and can be used to reconfigure existing settings.

You can edit these settings to double-check that output is as you expect, but you should not make any changes. I did this a few times while I was writing this to confirm that my .csv file was formatted correctly.

Creating Customized VM Mappings

As you might remember, inventory mappings are not mandatory, but they are incredibly useful because without them you would have to do mappings of the network, resource pool, and folder on a per-virtual-machine basis. Occasionally, a virtual machine will fail to be added to the Recovery Site because SRM cannot map the virtual machine to a valid network, folder, or resource pool. Alternatively, because you haven't configured an inventory map, you will have to decide which customized virtual machine mappings are for you. VMs like this are flagged with the status message of "Mapping Missing." This is a very common error and it's usually caused by the VM's network settings being changed, but not being included in the inventory mapping error. You should really resolve these errors from the Inventory Mappings location first, unless you have a VM like the one in Figure 11.40 which is unique and needs an individual per-VM mapping configured for it.

1. In SRM, select the Protection Group and click the Virtual Machines tab (see Figure 11.40).

2. Select the affected virtual machine and click the Configure Protection button.

As you can see, this VM was not automatically protected alongside the other VMs because the inventory mapping was missing a definition for the built-in "VM Network." If you are carrying out a manual mapping like this the dialog box that appears when you configure the VM's protection will indicate which components are missing the required parameter. This dialog box, shown in Figure 11.41, offers you the chance to modify the default mapping to another location if you wish.

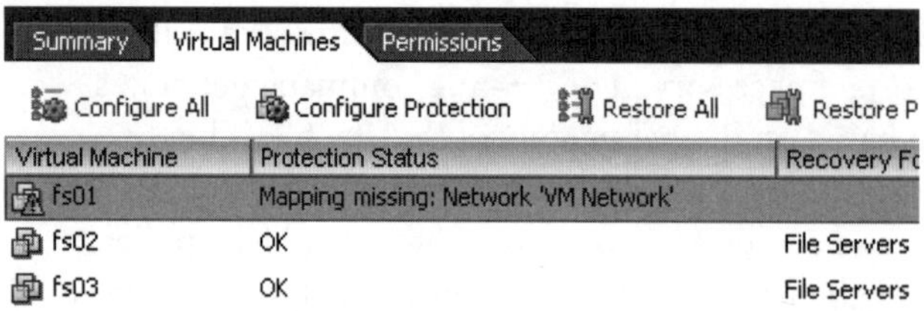

Summary	Virtual Machines	Permissions	
🖳 Configure All	🖳 Configure Protection	🖳 Restore All	🖳 Restore P
Virtual Machine	Protection Status		Recovery Fc
🖳 fs01	Mapping missing: Network 'VM Network'		
🖳 fs02	OK		File Servers
🖳 fs03	OK		File Servers

Figure 11.40   The fs01 VM lacks a mapping for the VM Network port group. You can override the default inventory mapping with a custom per-VM mapping.

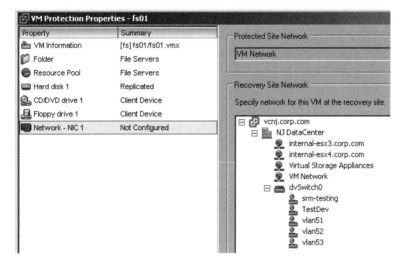

Figure 11.41 NIC 1 is not configured because "VM Network" was not included in the inventory mapping.

Managing Changes at the Protected Site

As you might now realize, SRM will need management and maintenance. As your Protected (production) Site is changing on a daily basis, maintenance is required to keep the Protected and Recovery Sites properly configured. One of the primary maintenance tasks is making sure newly created virtual machines that require protection are properly covered by one or more of your Recovery Plans. Simply creating a virtual machine and storing it on a replicated datastore does not automatically enroll it in your Recovery Plan. After all, not all VMs may need protection. If you follow this fact to its logical conclusion you could ask why you should create a new virtual machine on a replicated datastore if you don't require it. Prior to vSphere 4 it was impossible to guide or restrict a user to only being able to select a certain datastore when he created a new virtual machine. There was a risk that a user could unintentionally place a VM on a replicated datastore when he shouldn't have. In addition, there is a distinct possibility that he could store his new VM on an unprotected volume. Since vSphere 4, it is now possible to set permissions on datastores within folders, so it is possible to guide the user to creating VMs in the right locations.

Creating and Protecting New Virtual Machines

You might wrongly assume that as you create a new virtual machine—so long as it is created on the right replicated storage, in the right resource pool, in the right folder, and in the right network—it will automatically be "picked" up by SRM and protected by default. However, this is not the case. While creating a new virtual machine on a replicated datastore should ensure that the files of the virtual machine are at least duplicated at the Recovery Site, a new virtual machine is not automatically enrolled in the virtual machine Protection Group defined on the Protected Site. To enroll a new virtual machine, follow these steps.

1. At the Protected Site, select the Virtual Machine Protection Group, and select the virtual machine that is currently not protected.

2. Click the Configure All button, as shown in Figure 11.42.

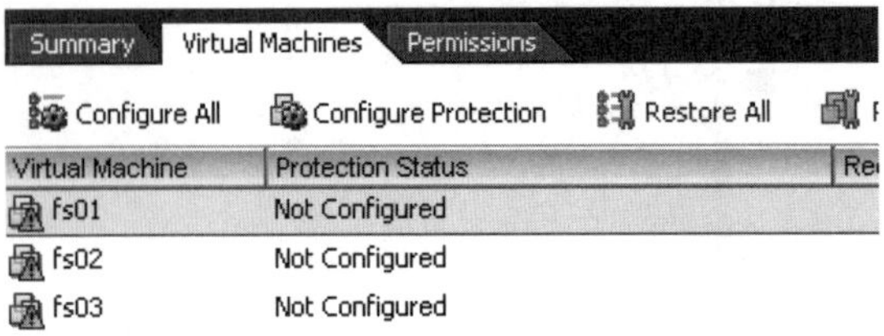

Figure 11.42   Remember, new VMs are not automatically enrolled into the Protection Group and added to a Recovery Plan.

So long as the VM's settings are covered by the inventory mappings, the protection should complete automatically without further interaction. If, however, the VM's settings fall outside the inventory mapping, you will be presented with a number of dialog boxes to manually set the location of the VM from a cluster, folder, or resource pool perspective.

The Configure All button allows you to protect multiple new VMs—and both methods will add the virtual machine to the Recovery Site's inventory. The VM will be enrolled to every Recovery Plan that is configured for the Protection Group where the VM resides.

Remember, simply "protecting" new VMs is not the end of the task; the next stage is to ensure that the VMs were correctly ordered in the Recovery Plan, and any additional settings such as command scripts and messages are set correctly.

Renaming and Moving vCenter Inventory Objects

Despite the use of the linked mode feature, you can see that SRM depends highly on the operator correctly pairing and then mapping two separate vCenter inventories. These two vCenters do not share a common data source or database. So you might be legitimately concerned about what happens if vCenter inventory objects in either the Protected or Recovery Site are renamed or relocated. This has been a problem in some other management add-ons from VMware in the past; a notable example is VMware View:

www.rtfm-ed.co.uk/?p=1463

There are some rules and regulations regarding renaming various objects in vCenter. In the main, renaming or creating new objects will not necessarily "break" the inventory mappings configured earlier; this is because the mappings actually point to Managed Object Reference Numbers. Every object in the vCenter inventory is stamped with a MOREF value. You can consider these like SIDs in Active Directory—renaming an object in vCenter does not change the object's MOREF value. The only exception to this is port groups which are not allocated a vCenter MOREF; in fact, their configuration and identifiers are not held by vCenter, but by the ESX host. If we examine the scenarios below we can see the effect of renaming objects in vCenter.

Managing Changes at the Protected Site

A number of changes can occur as part of day-to-day operational adjustments in your production environment. It's important to know which of these can impact the SRM configuration.

Renaming Virtual Machines

This is not a problem. Protection Groups are updated to the new VM name, as are Recovery Plans. The same is true of the placeholder VMs in the Recovery Site. Previous versions of SRM required the administrator to unprotect and then reprotect a VM for the placeholder name to be updated. This is no longer the case.

Renaming Datacenters, Clusters, and Folders in the Protected Site

This is not a problem. The Inventory Mappings window automatically refreshes.

Renaming Resource Pools in the Protected Site

This is not a problem. The Inventory Mappings window automatically refreshes.

Renaming Virtual Switch Port Groups in the Protected Site

This depends on whether you are an Enterprise Plus customer with access to Distributed vSwitches (DvSwitches). If you are, there are no problems to report. All the VMs are automatically updated for the new port group name, and the inventory mappings remain in place.

It's a very different story if you're using SvSwitches. This will cause all the affected VMs to lose the inventory mapping. The VMs do remain protected, and no warning message will appear that is obvious to see in SRM. This is a bad outcome because someone could rename port groups on ESX hosts without understanding the consequences for the SRM implementation. Without a correct inventory mapping, the Recovery Plans would execute but they would fail with every VM that lacked a network mapping. This would create an error message when the Recovery Plan was tested or run. The nature of these error messages varies if it is the port group at the Protected Site that has been renamed or if it's the port group at the Recovery Site that has been modified. If the port group is renamed at the Recovery Site, by default SRM will use the Auto function and create a bubble network if a real VLAN and port group are not available. The VMs will power on but they will only be able to communicate with other VMs on the same ESX host on the same bubble network. The Recovery Plan will display the following warning:

> "Warning – Network or port group needed for recovered virtual machine couldn't be found at recovery or test time."

It's often difficult to spot that this situation has occurred, but you can generally see traces of it behind Recovery Plans and their network settings (see Figure 11.43).

So, put very simply, renaming port groups on an SvSwitch should be avoided at all costs! If you have renamed port groups after configuring the inventory mapping, two main corrective actions need to take place to resolve the problem. First, a refresh of inventory mappings is required. This is a relatively simple task of revisiting the inventory mapping at the Protected Site, looking for the renamed port group(s), and establishing a new relationship. In Figure 11.44, the renamed port group (vlan14 had been renamed to vlan14-test) has no association with a port group in the Recovery Site.

Edit Recovery Plan

Test Networks

Select the networks to use while running tests of this plan.

	For each network used by virtual machines in this plan, select a network to use while running tes Select "Auto" if you want the system to automatically create a new isolated network environmer during each test.
Recovery Site Protection Groups **Test Networks** Name Ready To Complete	

Datacenter	Recovery Network	Test Network
NJ DataCenter	VM Network	Not found: network-646
NJ DataCenter	Virtual Storage Appliances	Not found: network-646
NJ DataCenter	internal-esx3.corp.com	Not found: network-646
NJ DataCenter	internal-esx4.corp.com	Not found: network-646
NJ DataCenter	TestDev	Not found: network-646
NJ DataCenter	dvSwitch0-DVUplinks-30	Not found: network-641
NJ DataCenter	srm-testing	Not found: network-641
NJ DataCenter	vlan51	Not found: network-641
NJ DataCenter	vlan52	Not found: network-641
NJ DataCenter	vlan53	Not found: network-641
Not found	Not found: network-641	Not found: network-641
Not found	Not found: network-646	Not found: network-646

Figure 11.43   The effect that deleting port groups can have on inventory mappings

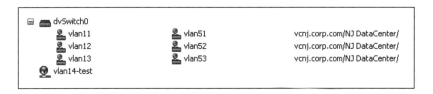

Figure 11.44 A rename of a port group can cause the loss of your inventory mappings.

Second, as you might know already, if you rename port groups on SvSwitches, the virtual machines configured at the Protected Site become "orphaned" from the port group, as shown in Figure 11.45. To create this example, I simply renamed the vlan14 port group to "vlan14-test." You can see that if port groups are renamed while they are in use by VMs, the port group label is dimmed and italicized in the vSphere client.

This orphaning of the virtual machine from the virtual switch port group has been a "feature" of VMware for some time, and is not specifically an SRM issue. However, it does have a significant effect on SRM. It can cause the Protection Group process, which creates the placeholder/shadow virtual machines on the Recovery Site, to fail. Correcting this for each and every virtual machine using the vSphere client is very laborious. You can automate this process with a little bit of scripting, with the PowerCLI from VMware:

```
get-vm | get-networkadapter | sort-object -property "NetworkName" | where
   {'vlan14' -contains $_.NetworkName} | Set-NetworkAdapter -NetworkName
   'vlan14-test'
```

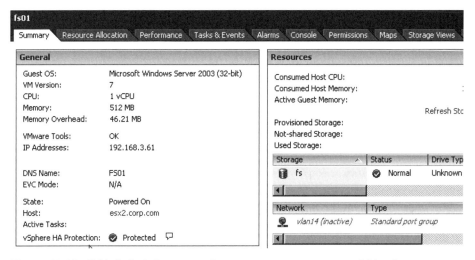

Figure 11.45 With SvSwitches, renaming a port group can cause a VM to become orphaned from the network when it is next powered on.

Managing Changes at the Recovery Site

So far we have examined changes at the Protected Site, and how they impact SRM. Now it's time to turn the tables and look at the effect on an SRM configuration as changes take place there. Generally, the impact of changes in the Recovery Site is less significant, but there are some noteworthy situations to be forewarned about.

Renaming Datacenters, Clusters, and Folders

This is not a problem. The Inventory Mappings window automatically refreshes.

Renaming Resource Pools in the Protected Recovery Site

This is not a problem. The Inventory Mappings window automatically refreshes.

Renaming Virtual Switch Port Groups in the Recovery Site

Once again, I found there were no issues with renaming port groups at the Recovery Site if you are using DvSwitches. Any rename of a DvSwitch port group at the Recovery Site results in the inventory mapping at the Protected Site. However, the same situation presents itself with SvSwitches in the Recovery Site as it did in the Protected Site. I renamed my port groups from vlan50-54 to vlan60-64. However, no manner of refreshes or restarts updated the Inventory Mappings window at the Protected Site. The window switched to "None Selected." The only resolution was to manually remap the port groups.

Other Objects and Changes in the vSphere and SRM Environment

In my experience, other changes can take place in vSphere and SRM which cause the relationships we configure in SRM to break. For example, I've found that renaming datastores at the Protected Site that are covered by replication cycles can potentially cause issues. It's possible that when you rename a datastore at the Protected Site before it has been covered by the next replication cycle, a test is run. The test fails because the test expects to see the old name, not the new name, and it is still being presented with the old name at the Recovery Site. Symptoms include "File not found" error messages when the test plan is executed; rather worryingly you can find your replicated datastore is empty! My solution was to simply enable the option to "Replicate recent changes to the recovery site"; this should force an update caused by the renaming of a datastore.

Setting the renaming of datastores to one side, it's worth stating that the SRM configuration stages do occur in a specific order for a reason, and each stage has a dependency on the preceding stage. You should configure SRM in the following order.

1. Pair the sites.

2. Configure the array manager.

3. Configure the inventory mappings.

4. Create the Protection Groups.

5. Create Recovery Plan.

Say, for example, that you remove your Protection Group. In that case, the Recovery Plan has references to Protection Groups that don't exist. If you create a new Protection Group, you have to manually go to the Recovery Plan and configure it to use the correct Protection Group. As deleting and re-creating configurations is a very popular (if unsophisticated) way to "fix" problems in IT generally, you must be very careful. You must understand the implications of deleting and re-creating components. For example, say you delete and re-create a Protection Group, and then tell your Recovery Plan to use it. You will discover that all priority/order settings in the plan are lost, and have been reset to the default. You will find all the virtual machines are rehoused into the priority 3 category for both the power down and power on of virtual machines. Additionally, other customizations to your Recovery Plan could be lost, such as any per-VM scripting or re-IP settings. This is deeply annoying if you have spent some time getting all your virtual machines to power on at the right time in the right order. As you can tell by the tone of my writing, I've found this out through my own bitter experience!

Lastly, a word of caution: As we have seen, SRM can accommodate most changes that take place. However, this is currently a significant attribute of a protected/production virtual machine that is not propagated to the Recovery Site. If you increase or decrease the amount of memory allocated to a virtual machine after it has been covered by a Protection Group, the only way (currently) to fix this issue is to remove the protection of the affected virtual machine, and reprotect it; this causes the destruction of the virtual machine placeholder VMX at the Recovery Site, and its re-creation. The mismatch between the real .vmx file and the placeholder is not technically significant, and is largely a cosmetic irritation. When the plan is tested the amount of memory allocated to the VM from the Protected Site will be used. As we saw earlier, if you do want the Recovery Site VMs to have different settings, you are better off using PowerCLI to make those modifications at the point of recovery. So the moral of the story is this: View the casual removal of inventory mappings and Protection Groups with extreme caution.

Storage vMotion and Protection Groups

WARNING

Storage vMotion does not impact vSphere Replication configurations. Replication jobs in VR are automatically updated if the source VM is moved from one datastore to another. Officially, VMware does not support Storage DRS with SRM. You should plan your Storage vMotion to replicated datastores as this could have significant impact to your network, and as consequence, your RPOs and RTOs.

In 2006, VMware Virtual Infrastructure 3.5 (VI3) offered a new feature called Storage vMotion. This allowed you to relocate the files of a virtual machine from one datastore to another, while the virtual machine was running, regardless of storage type (NFS, iSCSI, SAN) and vendor. At that time, Storage vMotion was carried out by using a script in the Remote CLI tools which are downloadable from VMware's website. With vSphere 4 you can simply drag and drop and work your way through a wizard to complete the process. Storage vMotion still has implications for VMware Site Recovery Manager. Additionally, I found I had to use the Rescan Arrays option from within the Array Manager Wizard to force an update.

Basically, there are four scenarios.

Scenario 1

The virtual machine is moved from nonreplicated storage to replicated storage, effectively joining a Protection Group. In this case, the outcome is very straightforward; it's as if a brand-new virtual machine has just been created. The Protection Group will have a yellow exclamation mark next to it, indicating the virtual machine has not been configured for protection.

Scenario 2

The virtual machine is moved from replicated storage to nonreplicated storage, effectively leaving a Protection Group, and as such is no longer covered by SRM. With this scenario the outcome is less than neat. Removing a virtual machine from a replicated LUN/volume to nonreplicated storage can result in an error message in the Tasks & Events tab and the virtual machine being listed in the Protection Group as "invalid," as shown in Figure 11.46. In my case, I moved the fs01 VM from a replicated datastore to local storage. The full message read:

```
"Invalid: Cannot protect virtual machine 'FS01' because its config
    file '[esx2_local] fs01/fs01.vmx is located on a non-replicated or
    non-protected datastore"
```

Figure 11.46   To avoid this scenario, unprotect the VM in the Protection Group and then move it to its new location with Storage vMotion.

The "solution" to this issue is to select the VM and choose the Remove Protection option. If you wish to relocate a VM in this way, perhaps the best method is to remove the protection from it and then carry out the Storage vMotion. Once the Storage vMotion has completed, a refresh of the Protection Group would cause any reference to the VM to be removed.

Scenario 3

The virtual machine is moved from one replicated storage location to another replicated storage location; essentially, the virtual machine is moved out of the scope of one Protection Group and into the scope of another Protection Group. In this case, when the virtual machine moves from one Protection Group to another, it should be "cleaned out" from the old Protection Group. In my case, I moved the ss02 VM with Storage vMotion from one Protection Group to another. This generates a yellow exclamation mark on both Protection Groups because ss02 is still listed in two locations. If you try to protect the VM at the "destination" Protection Group it will fail, and the Tasks & Events tab will show an error (see Figure 11.47).

At the "source" Protection Group there will be an error similar to the one observed in scenario 2 (see Figure 11.48).

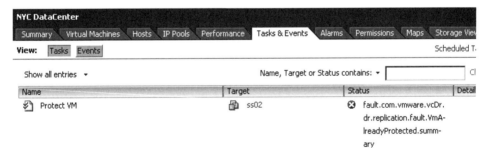

Figure 11.47   In previous releases a more visible pop-up box appeared with a friendly description. VMware may reinstate this functionality with SRM.

Figure 11.48   SRM believes the administrator is trying to protect the VM twice in two different Protection Groups.

Generally, selecting an "invalid" virtual machine and clicking the Remove Protection option will fix the problem, and will allow you to protect the VM in the destination Protection Group.

Scenario 4

The virtual machine is moved from one replicated storage location to another replicated storage location, but the SRM administrator has created one Protection Group containing many datastores. In this scenario, the Protection Group does not generate an error and everything works in SRM without a problem. For this reason, it might be tempting to decide that creating one "jumbo" Protection Group that contains all of your datastores would be the best way to stop any of these Storage vMotion woes. However, I think this will limit the flexibility that SRM is trying to deliver. Most of my customers prefer one Protection Group to contain one datastore, as this allows them to run Recovery Plans that failover and failback a certain subset of VMs. As soon as all the VMs are lumped together unceremoniously in one Protection Group you at one stroke diminish and remove a great deal of flexibility in the SRM product.

Virtual Machines Stored on Multiple Datastores

Of course, it is entirely possible to store virtual machine files on more than one datastore. In fact, this is a VMware recommendation. By storing our boot VMDK, log VMDK, and data VDMK files on different datastores, we can improve disk I/O substantially by reducing the disk contention that could take place. Even the most disk-intensive virtual machine could be stored on a LUN of its own, and as such it would not face any competition for I/O at the spindle level. You will be pleased to know that SRM does support a multiple disk configuration, so long as all the datastores, which the virtual machine is using, are replicated to the Recovery Site and exist on the same storage array. What SRM cannot currently handle is if a VM has two virtual disks stored on two different storage arrays.

The datastore location of a virtual disk is controlled when it is added into the virtual machine using the Add Hardware Wizard on the virtual machine. These virtual disks appear seamlessly to the guest operating system, so from Windows or another support guest operating system it is impossible to see where these virtual disks are located physically; they are presented seamlessly to the guest operating system.

In the situation shown in Figure 11.49, I added another datastore, called "db-files," to my environment, and then added a virtual disk to each of my DB virtual machines, placing them on the new datastore. All I did after that was to make sure the db-files datastore was scheduled to replicate at exactly the same interval as my volume called "virtual machines." If you have existing Protection Groups, these will have yellow exclamation marks next to them to reflect the fact that the virtual machines are utilizing multiple datastores, and that they need updating to reflect this change (see Figure 11.50).

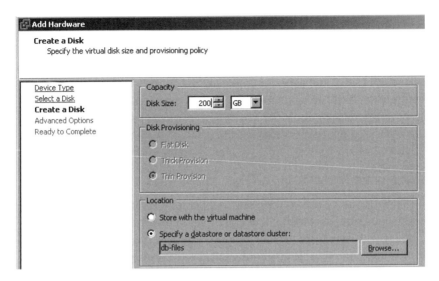

Figure 11.49 A 200GB virtual disk being placed on a different datastore from the boot OS virtual disk. This is a common practice to improve performance.

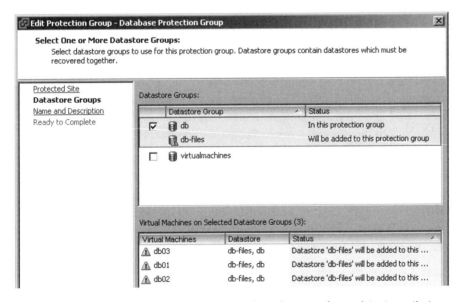

Figure 11.50 Protection Groups alert you to the existence of new datastores that are being replicated and used by VMs.

Notice how Figure 11.50 shows the DB datastore and db-files datastore as being "grouped" together; this is because the db01–db03 VMs have virtual disks on both datastores.

If your storage array vendor supports the concept of consistency groups, this configuration will look very similar to the situation where multiple LUNs/volumes have been placed into the same consistency group. In this respect, the Protection Group configuration can come to be almost a mirror image of the groups you create at the storage layer to ensure that LUNs/volumes are replicated on a consistent schedule.

Virtual Machines with Raw Device/Disk Mappings

In this chapter I began with one VMFS volume and LUN in the Protected Site. Clearly this is a very simplistic configuration which I deliberately chose to keep our focus on the SRM product. Here, I will go into more detail with more advanced configurations such as VMware's RDM features and multiple disk configurations that more closely reflect the real-world usage of a range of VMware technologies. It's perhaps worth reminding you that RDMs offer no real tangible improvement in performance. The fact that many VMware admins erroneously believe they do probably makes RDMs the most misunderstood feature in vSphere. RDMs are useful and, in fact, in some cases are mandatory for some clustering software that runs inside a VM. They are also necessary if your storage array has management capabilities that require the VM to have "direct" access to the storage array.

When I started writing this section, I faced a little bit of a dilemma: Should I repeat the storage section all over again to show you the process of creating a LUN/volume in the storage array, and then configuring replication and how to present that to ESX hosts? Following on from this, should I also document the process of adding an RDM to a virtual machine? In the end, I figured that if you, the reader, got this far in the book, you should be able to double back to the relevant storage chapter and do that on your own.

Assuming you've done that if necessary, I'll now describe my RDM configuration process. I added to my Dell EqualLogic array an RDM that was then added to the db01 virtual machine. The thing to notice in the screen grab in the Path ID column on the virtual machine shown in Figure 11.51 is the vmhba syntax of the RDM on the protected VM; it says the path is vmhba34:C0:T6:L0. SRM cleverly updates this mapping at the point of recovery so that it points to the correct target and LUN/volume.

For the moment, I want to concentrate on the specific issues of how SRM would handle this addition of new storage to the system, and how it handles the RDM feature. After creating the new volume/LUN, configuring replication, and adding the RDM to the virtual machine, the next stage is to make sure the array manager has correctly discovered the new RDM.

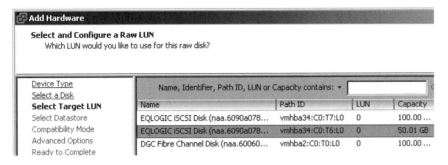

Figure 11.51   FC systems stick to the (L)UN value, but most iSCSI systems will use the (T)arget value as a way to present each LUN presented.

It is worth saying two critical facts about RDMs and SRM. First, the RDM mapping file itself must be stored on a VMFS volume covered by a replicated LUN. If you don't do this, there simply won't be an RDM mapping file available in the Recovery Site for the recovery VM to use. Second, SRM resolves hardware issues with RDM. RDM's mapping files have three main hardware values: a channel ID (only used by iSCSI arrays), a target ID, and a LUN ID. These values held within the mapping file itself are likely to be totally different at the Recovery Site array. SRM fixes these references so that the virtual machine is still bootable, and you can still get your data. If you were not using SRM and carrying out your Recovery Plan manually, you would have to remove the RDM mapping file and add it to the recovery virtual machine. If you don't, when the replicated virtual machine is powered on, it will point to the wrong vmhba path.

You might want to know what happens if you create a new virtual machine which contains an RDM mapping to a LUN which is not replicated or a VMDK that is not a replicated volume. If you try to protect that virtual machine, SRM will realize that you're trying to protect a virtual machine which has access to a LUN/volume which is inaccessible at the Recovery Site. When you try to add such a virtual machine to the Protection Group the VM will display a message stating "Device Not Found: Hard Disk *N*". If you try to configure protection to that VM the corresponding dialog box will show that the VM's RDM mapping is pointing to a LUN or volume that is not being replicated (see Figure 11.52).

When you try to protect the VM a wizard will run to allow you to deal with this portion of the VM that cannot be protected. Ideally, you should resolve the reason the RDM or VMDK is not replicated, but the wizard does allow you to work around the problem by detaching the VMDK during execution of the Recovery Plan.

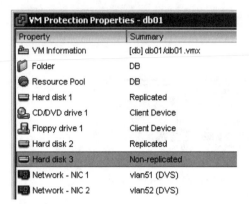

Figure 11.52 There is a problem. An RDM has been added to a VM but it is not being replicated to the Recovery Site.

Multiple Protection Groups and Multiple Recovery Plans

This section is quite short, but it may be the most important one to you. Now that you have a very good idea of all the components of SRM, it's time for me to show you what a popular configuration might look like in the real world. It is perfectly possible—in fact, I would say highly desirable—to have many Protection Groups and Recovery Plans. If you recall, a Protection Group is intimately related to the LUNs/volumes you are replicating. One model for this, suggested earlier in the book, is grouping your LUNs/volumes by application usage so that they can, in turn, easily be selected by an SRM Protection Group. I've set up such a situation in my lab environment to give you insight into how such a configuration would look and feel. I don't expect you to reproduce this configuration if you have been following this book in a step-by-step manner. It's just here to give you a feel for how a "production" SRM configuration might look and feel.

Multiple Datastores

In the real world, you are likely to put your virtual machines in different datastores to reflect that those LUNs/volumes represent different numbers of disk spindles and RAID levels. To reflect this type of configuration I simply created five volumes called DB, FS, MAIL, VIEW, and VB. In Figure 11.53 I used the NetApp FAS2040 System Manager as an example.

So you could create volumes based on business units or applications—or indeed the applications used by each business unit. This would allow you to failover a particular application of a particular business unit while the other business units remain totally unaffected.

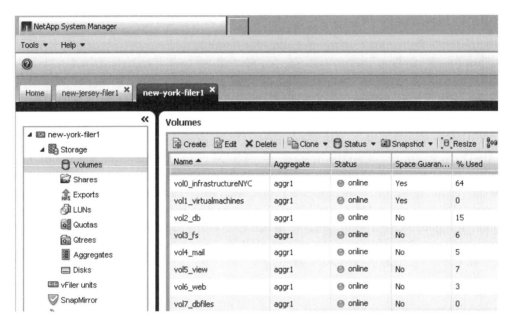

Figure 11.53 Here NetApp volumes are being created reflecting different VMs. It's all about separation—separation allows for control.

Multiple Protection Groups

The storage changes outlined in this section were then reflected in the Protection Groups I created. I now had six Protection Groups reflecting the six types of virtual machines. When I created the Database Protection Group, I selected the datastore I created for that application. If we follow this to its logical conclusion, I end up creating another five Protection Groups for each of my replicated datastores (see Figure 11.54).

Figure 11.54 Over time, your Protection Groups will come to mirror your storage configuration.

Multiple Recovery Plans

These multiple Protection Groups now allow for multiple Recovery Plans; one Recovery Plan just for my mail environment, and so on. Also, in the case of complete site loss, I could create a Recovery Plan that included all my Protection Groups. At the end of this process, I would have a series of Recovery Plans that I could use to test each application set, as well as to test a complete Recovery Plan (see Figure 11.55).

It's worth mentioning a limitation surrounding this configuration and scalability in SRM: The marketing around the new release of SRM claims to allow you to run up to 30 plans simultaneously. While this is technically true, it's not without limitations, as you can see in Figure 11.56. Although a Protection Group can be a member of many Recovery Plans, it can only be used by one Recovery Plan at any one time. In my configuration in Figure 11.55, I would be able to run each of my "application" based Recovery Plans simultaneously. However, if I ran the "DR Recovery Plan – All VMs" that references *all* of my Protection Groups, I would find that my "application" based Recovery

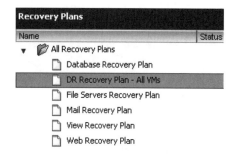

Figure 11.55   A good storage layout at the array level leads to a good Protection Group layout. This pays dividends when creating Recovery Plans.

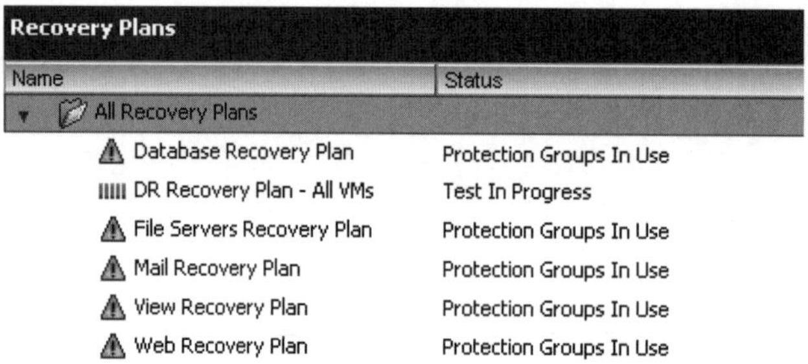

Figure 11.56   Once a datastore is in use, no other Protection Group, and therefore, no other Recovery Plan, can use it.

Plans would be unusable until the plan had completed. Their status would change to indicate "Protection Groups In Use."

The SRAs in SRM currently only allow one snapshot to be created per datastore. As a consequence, the datastore becomes locked exclusively for the duration of the plan. This would stop two separate SRM administrators from running the Mail Recovery Plan at the same time.

If you selected one of these Recovery Plans and looked at its Summary tab you would get a more detailed explanation (see Figure 11.57).

This occurs because currently the SRA does not allow for *multiple* snapshots to be taken of the same datastore. Many storage vendors support this functionality, but for the moment, the SRA does not leverage this capability. So, once a Recovery Plan is tested and the LUN/volume snapshot is presented, the Protection Group that backs this datastore does not itself become available until the plan has been cleaned up.

As you can see, the most powerful and sensible way to use SRM is to make sure various virtual machines that reflect big infrastructure components in the business are separated out at the storage level. From an SRM perspective, it means we can separate them into logically distinct Protection Groups, and then use those Protection Groups in our Recovery Plans. This is infinitely more functional than one flat VMFS volume and just one or two Recovery Plans, and trying to use such options in the Recovery Plan as "Recover No Power On Virtual Machines" to control what is powered on or not during a test of a Recovery Plan. The goal of this section was not to try to change my configuration, but just to illustrate what a real-world SRM configuration might look and feel like. I was able to

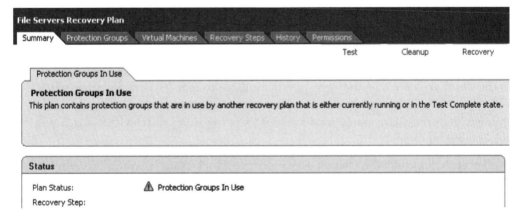

Figure 11.57   The Recovery Plan is unavailable because the Protection Group that backs it is in use elsewhere.

make all of these changes without resorting to powering off the virtual machines, by using Storage vMotion to relocate my virtual machines on the new LUNs/volumes.

The Lost Repair Array Managers Button

If you have used SRM in previous releases you might wonder what has become of the Repair Array Managers button. This button didn't repair the storage array so much as it allowed you to repair your configuration of the Recovery Site's communication to that array. It allowed the SRM administrator to deal with array configuration settings even in disaster mode. For example, it could be used in the following scenarios.

- The first IP used to communicate to the array is good, but the first controller is unavailable. When the SRA tries to use the second controller it fails because the SRM administrator typed in the wrong IP address, or indeed failed to specify it.

- An individual at the Recovery Site changed the IP address used to communicate to the Recovery Site storage array without informing the SRM administrator.

- An individual at the Recovery Site changed either the username or the password used to authenticate to the array.

In SRM 5.0 the Repair Array Managers button has been deprecated. It is no longer required because SRM 5.0 has departed significantly from the original design we saw in previous releases. This redesign is such that the feature became redundant and no longer needed in the product.

Summary

For me, this is one of my biggest chapters in the book because it really shows what SRM is capable of and perhaps where its limitations lie. One thing I found a little annoying is the way there's no drag-and-drop option available to reorder virtual machines in a priority list; clicking those up and down arrows for each and every virtual machine is going to get pretty darn annoying. I found it irritating with just ten virtual machines, never mind hundreds.

Nonetheless, hopefully this chapter gave you a good background on the long-term management of SRM. After all, virtual machines do not automatically become protected simply by virtue of being stored on replicated VMFS volumes. Additionally, you saw how other changes in the Protected Site impact the SRM server, such as renaming datacenters, clusters, folders, networks, and datastores—and how, for the most part, SRM does a good job of keeping that metadata linked to the Recovery Site. It's perhaps worth highlighting the dependencies within the SRM product, especially between Protection Groups and Recovery Plans.

I find the fact that we cannot yet back up our Recovery Plans to a file does introduce a worry: that major changes at the Protected Site, such as unprotecting a VM or even deleting a Protection Group, can lead to a damaged Recovery Plan with no quick and easy way to restore it. As you might have seen, deleting Protection Groups is a somewhat dangerous thing to do, despite the relative ease with which they can be re-created. It unprotects all the virtual machines affected by that Protection Group and removes them from your Recovery Plans. Re-creating all those Protection Groups does not put the virtual machines back in their original location, thus forcing you to re-create all the settings associated with your Recovery Plans. What we could really use is a way to export and import Recovery Plans so that those settings are not lost. Indeed, it would be nice to have a "copy Recovery Plan feature" so that we can create any number of plans from a base, to work out all the possible approaches to building a DR plan.

Finally, I think it's a shame that events such as cold migration and Storage vMotion still do not fully integrate seamlessly into SRM. Hopefully, you saw that a range of different events can occur, which SRM reacts to with various degrees of automation. However, as you will see in the next chapter, it's possible to configure alarms to tell you if a new virtual machine is in need of protection.

Chapter 12

Alarms, Exporting History, and Access Control

You will be very pleased to learn that SRM has a large number of configurable alarms and a useful reporting feature. Alarms are especially well defined, with lots of conditions that we can check on. SRM 5.0 introduces a whole series of new alarms, including ones that cover the vSphere Replication (VR) process. The action we can take in the event of an alarm being triggered includes sending an email, sending an SMNP trap, or executing a script. It's perhaps worth stating something very obvious here: SMTP and SNMP are both networked services. These services may not be available during a real disaster; as such, you may not wish to rely on them too heavily.

Additionally, you will find that SRM does not have its own specific "events" tab. Instead, SRM events are included alongside your day-to-day events. I think that as long as you have allocated used roles and permissions for SRM you should be able to filter by these accounts, which should improve your traceability. After I have covered the topic of access control, I will include some filtering/searching screen grabs to illustrate what I mean.

vCenter Linked Mode and Site Recovery Manager

Before I jump into looking at alarms, I want to take a moment to discuss the importance of vCenter linked mode to this chapter. The usefulness of linked mode to the SRM administrator is somewhat diminished what with the improvements to the SRM interface that allow for almost seamless switching from one site to another using the core UI. Previously, without linked mode, an SRM administrator would require two vSphere client windows to be open: one on the Protected Site vCenter and one on the Recovery Site vCenter.

With that said, I still think it is useful to have linked mode available in the day-to-day management of environments comprising multiple vCenters.

When I started to write this edition of the book I was tempted to introduce this feature in Chapter 7, Installing VMware SRM, but I was worried that the distinction between a Protected Site and a Recovery Site might be obscured by the use of this feature. At this point in the book, I think that if you are new to VMware SRM this distinction is more than clear. I would like to introduce linked mode into the picture for one main reason. When you have your vCenter set up with linked mode among the licensing data, the vCenter also shares the "roles" created in vCenter; this will have a direct impact on our coverage of access control in this chapter. I feel that if you use linked mode it will dramatically cut down the number of logins and windows you will need open on your desktop, and significantly ease the burden of setting permissions and rights with the Site Recovery Manager product itself.

My only worry about linked mode in the context of SRM is that you are creating a relationship or dependency between the Protected and Recovery Sites. SRM doesn't require the linked mode feature to function. However, when balanced against the advantages of linked mode I think this anxiety is unfounded. Anything that eases administration and reduces the complexity of permissions and rights has to be embraced.

Normally, you enable linked mode when installing vCenter. If you haven't done this, a wizard exists on the vCenter Start menu that lets you rerun that portion of the vCenter installation. When you run the Linked Mode Wizard you must use a domain account that has administrative rights on both the Protection Site and the Recovery Site vCenters. To run the wizard, follow these steps.

1. Log in to the Recovery Site vCenter.

2. Select Start | Programs | VMware and then click the vCenter Linked Mode Configuration Properties option. Click Next.

3. Select the radio button to "Modify linked mode configuration."

4. Ensure that in the "Linked Mode configuration" dialog box the option to "Join vCenter server instance to an existing linked mode group or instance" is selected. Click Next.

5. In the Connect to a vCenter Instance dialog box, enter the FQDN of the Protected Site vCenter. After the installation is complete, you will see something similar to Figure 12.1.

Figure 12.1   Two vCenter instances in one window, aggregating the vCenter inventory into a single view

When you click the Site Recovery Manager icon after the first login, you will still be asked for a username and password to communicate to the Site Recovery Manager server. Switching between the Protected and Recovery Sites is simply a matter of selecting them from the navigation bar (see Figure 12.2).

When you first do this you will be asked for the credentials of the SRM host. Although linked mode cuts down on the number of vCenter logins, you still must authenticate to the SRM host. This is an additional layer of security, and it is worth noting that your vCenter credentials might not be the same as your SRM credentials. When you are asked for authentication via SRM be sure to use the DOMAIN\username format to complete the login process.

Figure 12.2   Select the site from the navigation bar.

Alarms Overview

Alarms cover a huge array of possible events including, but not limited to, such conditions as the following:

- License status
- Permission status
- Storage connectivity
- Low available resources, including
    - Disk
    - CPU
    - Memory
- Status of the Recovery Site, including
    - Recovery Site SRM is up/down
    - Not pingable
    - Created/deleted
- Creation of
    - Protection Groups
    - "Shadow" placeholder virtual machines
- Status of Recovery Plans, including
    - Created
    - Destroyed
    - Modified

The thresholds for disk, CPU, and memory alarms are set within the GUI from the Advanced Settings dialog box within the vSphere client. You will see the Advanced Settings option when you right-click the Site Recovery node (see Figure 12.3).

Once the Advanced Settings dialog box has opened, it's the localSiteStatus node that contains the default values for these alarms (see Figure 12.4).

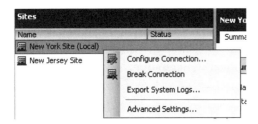

Figure 12.3   The Advanced Settings option is available when you right-click each site in the SRM inventory.

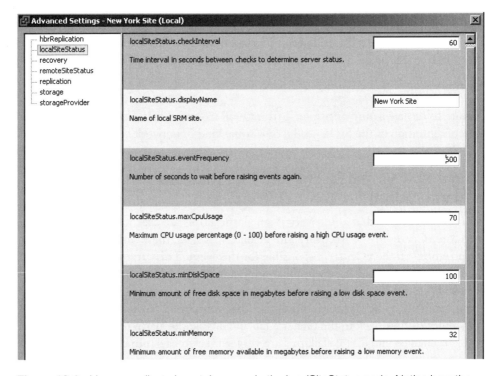

Figure 12.4   You can adjust alarm tolerances in the localSiteStatus node. Notice how the friendly name of the site can be modified here also.

As you would expect, some alarms are more useful than others, and in some respects they can facilitate the correct utilization or configuration of the SRM product. Additionally, you will notice that both the Recovery and Protected Sites hold the same alarms. Configuring both sites would be appropriate in a bidirectional configuration.

Here are some examples.

- Example 1

  You may want an alarm to be raised whenever there is a failure to protect a VM within a Protection Group.

- Example 2

  Although Recovery Plans have a notification or message feature, you will only see the message if you have the vSphere client open with the Site Recovery Manager plug-in. It might be desirable to send an email to the appropriate person as well.

- Example 3

  Failure to receive a ping or response from the Recovery Site could indicate misconfiguration of the SRM product, or some kind of network outage.

Creating a New Virtual Machine to Be Protected by an Alarm (Script)

Unlike the scripts executed in a Recovery Plan, alarm scripts are executed by either the Protected Site vCenter or the Recovery Site vCenter. As such, these scripts must be created and stored on the vCenter responsible for the event. This can be identified by the use of the word *Protected* or *Recovery* in the event name. One of the most common administrator mistakes is simply forgetting to enable the alarm. Administrators seem to be so focused on configuring the alarm condition that they forget that once it is defined they must remember to click back to the General tab and enable the alarm in the first instance. The icons for enabled and disabled alarms are very similar to each other and have the same color, so you may struggle to spot the difference. An alarm that has yet to be enabled has a red cross next to its name; an enabled alarm does not have this cross (see Figure 12.5).

Figure 12.5   Alarms that are not configured are marked with a red cross (bottom), whereas configured alarms are clear (top).

To set an alarm, follow these steps.

1. Select the Protected Site.

2. Select the Alarm tab and double-click the VM Not Protected alarm (see Figure 12.6).

3. In the Edit Alarm dialog box, select the Actions tab.

4. Click the Add button.

5. From the pull-down list, select Run a Script, and enter the following, as shown in Figure 12.7:

   C:\Windows\System32\cmd.exe /c c:\newvmscript.cmd

   One alarm can have multiple actions, so it's possible to create a condition that will send an email and SNMP trap, as well as run a script.

6. On the Protected Site SRM, create a script called newvmscript.bat with this content:

   ```
   @echo off
   msg /server:mf1 administrator "A new VM has been created and is
       waiting to be configured for protection"
   ```

This script is only intended as an example. I do not recommend use of the Messenger Service in production.

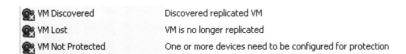

Figure 12.6 A range of alarms covering virtual machines, and their relationship with SRM

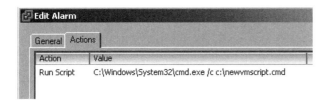

Figure 12.7 Alarms can contain scripts just like Recovery Plans.

Creating a Message Alarm (SNMP)

To create a message alarm, follow these steps.

1. At the Recovery Site, click the SRM button.

2. Select the Alarm tab and double-click the Recovery Profile Prompt Display alarm.

   The Recovery Profile Prompt Display alarm means the Recovery Plan has paused with a message step and is waiting for an operator to respond to it.

3. In the Edit Alarm dialog box, select the Actions tab.

4. Click the Add button.

5. From the pull-down list, select "Send a notification trap."

Unlike with the "Send a notification email" option, the destination/recipient is not defined here; instead, it is defined in vCenter by selecting Administration | vCenter Server Settings | SMNP. By default, if you run an SNMP management tool on vCenter in the "public" community you will receive notifications. To test this functionality I used the free utility called Trap Receiver (www.trapreceiver.com/); VMware also uses this in its training courses to test/demonstrate SMNP functionality without the need for something like HP Overview. I installed Trap Receiver to the Recovery Site vCenter server to test the SNMP functionality.

In my case, I added a message at the end of my Database Recovery Plan that simply states "Plan Completed!" (see Figure 12.8).

Creating an SRM Service Alarm (SMTP)

To create an SRM service alarm, follow these steps.

1. At the Recovery Site, click the SRM button.

2. Select the Alarm tab and double-click the Remote Site Down and Remote Site Ping Failed alarm.

3. In the Edit Alarm dialog box, select the Actions tab.

4. Click the Add button.

5. From the pull-down list, select "Send a notification email" and enter the destination/recipient email address (see Figure 12.9).

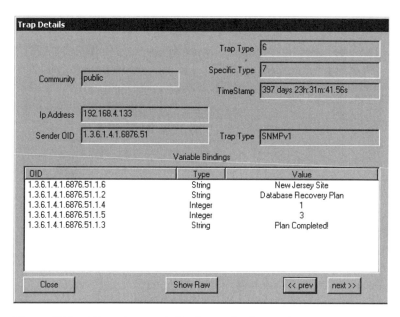

Figure 12.8 Although not suitable for production environments, Trap Receiver is useful for basic configuration tests.

Figure 12.9 The Send Email action defaults to the email address specified in the SRM installation; you can change it to any email address required.

In the Edit box, enter an email address of an individual or a group that should receive the email. Again, configuration of the SMTP service is set in vCenter by selecting Administration I vCenter Management Server Configuration I SMNP. By default, SRM will use the email address provided during installation of SRM for the administrator's email. Emails will be trigged when the "Disconnected" message appears in the SRM Summary page. The actual emails produced with alarms can sometimes be cryptic, but I think they do the job required.

Exporting and History

It is possible to export a Recovery Plan out of Site Recovery Manager as well as to export the results of a Recovery Plan out of Site Recovery Manager. The export process can include the following formats:

- Word
- Excel
- Web page
- CSV
- XML

Although Recovery Plans can be exported out of SRM, they cannot be imported into SRM. The intention of the export process is to give you a hard copy of the Recovery Plan, which you can share and distribute without necessarily needing access to SRM. Currently, SRM defaults to open the exported file at the location where your vSphere client is running. If the system on which you are running the vSphere client does not have Microsoft Word/Excel, this will fail. The plan is still exported, but your system will fail to open the file. In my experiments, Microsoft Word Viewer 2007 worked but Microsoft Excel Viewer 2007 did not. Additionally, Excel Viewer could not open the CSV format. I found I needed the full version of Excel to open these files successfully. The XLS file comes with formatting, but as you would expect the CSV file comes with no formats whatsoever.

Exporting Recovery Plans

To export a Recovery Plan, follow these steps.

1. In SRM, select your Recovery Plan.
2. Click the Export Steps icon (see Figure 12.10).
3. From the Save As dialog box, select the format type. The output of the plan looks like Figure 12.11, which was taken from Word Viewer.

Figure 12.10   Recovery Plans and the history of Recovery Plans are exportable in many different formats.

Recovery Plan Steps Report
VMware Site Recovery Manager 5.0

Recovery Step
1. Synchronize Storage
1.1. Protection Group Database Protection Group
1.2. Protection Group File Servers Protection Group
1.3. Protection Group View Protection Group
1.4. Protection Group Mail Protection Group
1.5. Protection Group Web Protection Group
2. Restore hosts from standby
3. Suspend Non-critical VMs at Recovery Site
3.1. test01

Figure 12.11   A sample export of a Recovery Plan

Recovery Plan History

SRM has a History tab which will show success, failure, and error summaries, and allows you to view previous runs of the Recovery Plan in HTML format or export them in other formats as indicated earlier. For many people this is one of the top features of SRM; it means they can test their Recovery Plan throughout the year and demonstrate to external auditors that correct provisions have been made for potential disasters. To see the Recovery Plan history you simply do the following.

1. At the Recovery Site SRM, select a Recovery Plan.
2. Click the History tab, select a previously run Recovery Plan, and click View or Export (see Figure 12.12).

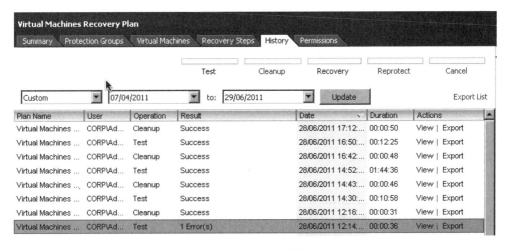

Figure 12.12   Recovery Plan history is viewable in HTML and exportable to many other formats.

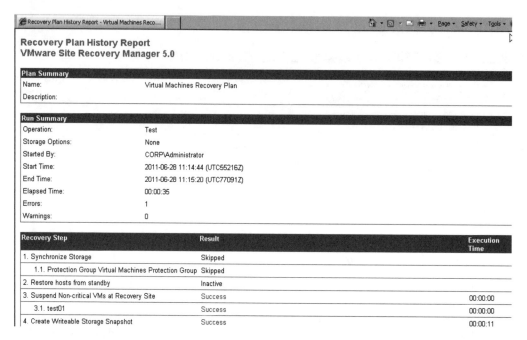

Figure 12.13   The results of a successful Recovery Plan

Clicking View automatically outputs the report of the Recovery Plan in HMTL format, whereas clicking Export enables output in the other formats discussed previously. Figure 12.13 shows the results of a successful Recovery Plan.

Although the report shows a successful test, these reports truly become useful in trouble-shooting scenarios. When errors do occur in a Recovery Plan it is sometimes tricky to see the long "status" messages when the plan is executing. The easiest way to grab these error messages is to generate an output of the report, and then use copy and paste to grab the message that way. The message can then be pasted into service requests, forums, and blog posts.

Access Control

Call it what you will, but permissions, access control, and change management are part and parcel of most corporate environments. So far we have been managing SRM using a default "administrator" account for every task. This is not only unrealistic, but also very dangerous—especially in the realm of DR. DR is such a dangerous undertaking that it should not be triggered lightly or accidentally. Correctly setting permissions should allow

SRM to be configured and tested separately from the process of invoking DR for real. Although this is a high-level "C-Class" executive decision, management of the process should be in the hands of highly competent, trained, and ideally well-paid IT staff. Alarms can be very useful if you have an environment that is changing rapidly or if you don't have tight change control management in place. At least with alarms the SRM administrator can be alerted to changes in the environment caused by others. In an ideal world, the left hand knows what the right hand is doing. But we don't always live in an ideal world, so if alarms are configured, your attention is at least drawn to changes in the environment that could impact SRM and a successful recovery process.

SRM introduces a whole raft of roles to vCenter, and as with day-to-day vCenter rights and privileges, the SRM product displays the same "hierarchical" nature as vCenter. An additional layer of complexity is added by having two vCenter systems (Protected and Recovery Site vCenters) that are delegated separately. It's worth saying that in a bidirectional configuration these permissions would have to be mutually reciprocal to allow for the right people to carry out their designated tasks properly.

As with the alert actions, access control is driven by authentication services. For many people, this will mean Microsoft Active Directory and Microsoft DNS. If these services fail or are unavailable you may not even be able to log in to vCenter to trigger your Recovery Plan. Proper planning and preparation are required to prevent this from happening; also, you may wish to develop a Plan B where a Recovery Plan could be triggered without the need for Active Directory. Depending on your corporate policies, this could include the use of physical domain controllers, or even the use of local user accounts on your vCenter and SRM system. From a security perspective, local user accounts are frowned upon, to say the least, in most corporate environments. So the first step is to review the default vCenter permissions which allow full access to vCenter using the local administrator account on the vCenter server itself. You should also notice that with the release of VR new roles have been added to vCenter.

The Site Recovery Manager roles include

- SRM Administrator

- SRM Protection Groups Administrator

- SRM Recovery Administrator

- SRM Recovery Plans Administrator

- SRM Recovery Test Administrator

- VR Replication Viewer

- VR Recovery Manager

- VR Virtual Machine Replication User

- VR Administrator

- VR Diagnostics

- VR Target Datastore User

You can see these roles in the vSphere client by selecting Home I Administration I Roles. If you copy these roles to create new ones, it can take time if you are in linked mode for them to be replicated to other vCenters in the environment. At the bottom of the roles list in the vSphere client you will see the warning shown in Figure 12.14.

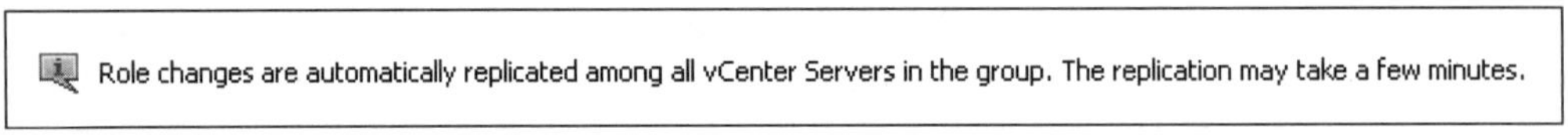

 Role changes are automatically replicated among all vCenter Servers in the group. The replication may take a few minutes.

Figure 12.14   New roles in vCenter require some time to be duplicated to other vCenters in a linked mode configuration.

Creating an SRM Administrator

It might be seen as interesting to define each of these roles, but I think transposing the definitions of them into this book would be quite tedious. Instead, I think it's more helpful to think about the kinds of tasks an SRM administrator might need to perform during the course of maintaining and managing an environment. For example, if a new datastore were created, potentially a new Protection Group would be needed. Similarly, as new virtual machines are created, they must be correctly configured for protection. We would also want to allow someone to create, modify, and test Recovery Plans as our needs change. In the following scenario, I'm going to create some users—Michael, Lee, Alex, and Luke— and allocate them to a group in Active Directory called SRM Administrators. I will then log in as each of these users to test the configuration and validate that they can carry out the day-to-day tasks they need to perform. The plan is to allow these guys to *only* carry out SRM tasks, with the minimum rights needed for day-to-day maintenance of the SRM environment. The configuration will allow these four individuals to manage a unidirectional or active/passive SRM configuration. In other words, they will be limited to merely creating and executing Recovery Plans at the Recovery Site.

For me, one of the first stages in taking control of any system is to make sure I do not need or use the built-in administrator(s) delegation, and that there is a dedicated account that has access to the environment. This will allow me to consider removing the default allocation of privileges to the system. As usual, Windows defaults to allow the first administrator to log in. To create an SRM administrators delegation you need to create the group in Active Directory, before assigning it to the inventory in SRM. Then, from SRM, you can start your delegation. It doesn't really matter which vCenter you connect to as your rights and privileges will be assigned to whichever site you select. However, in keeping with the style of the book, I connected to the Protected Site vCenter, because the two sites are paired together.

1. Select the Protected Site (Local) and click the Permissions tab.

2. Right-click underneath Administrators for the local site, and select Add Permission (see Figure 12.15).

3. Use the Add button in the Assign Permissions dialog box to locate your SRM Administrators group. From the Assigned Role pull-down list select the role of SRM Administrator, and ensure that the option to Propagate to Child Objects is selected (see Figure 12.16).

You can repeat this process for the Recovery Site location as well. This should give the SRM Administrator group complete control over the SRM system, and it means you no longer need the built-in administrator delegation.

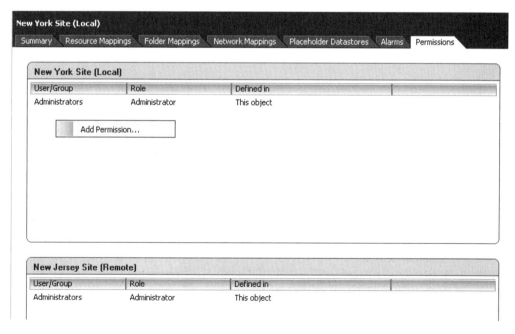

Figure 12.15   SRM has its own permission tab, as with elsewhere in the vCenter inventory a right-click is used to add permissions.

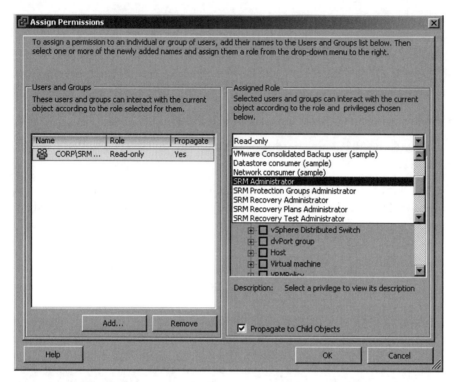

Figure 12.16   From the pull-down list you can select the built-in SRM roles.

Summary

As you can see, SRM significantly extends and adds to vCenter's alarm, report, and access control features. And while alarms may not have the configurable options you might see in the main vCenter product, such as triggers and reporting tabs, the sheer number of alarms or conditions we can trap on is a very welcome addition to what was once an underdeveloped aspect of the core vCenter product until vSphere 4 was released. Again, the ability to run reports in SRM is a great addition, as once again it's a feature we don't usually see in the core vCenter product. In one respect, VMware's investment in vCenter is paying dividends in allowing its developers to extend the product's functionality with plug-ins. Personally, I feel other additions to the VMware stable of applications, such as VMware View, need to join in the party too. In this respect, I think VMware SRM engineers have lit a torch for others to follow.

This more or less concludes this particular configuration type. So far this book has adopted a scenario where your organization has a dedicated site purely for recovery purposes, and I now want to change this scenario to one in which two datacenters have spare CPU, memory, and disk capacity from which they can reciprocate recovery—for example, a situation where New Jersey is the Recovery Site for New York and New York is the Recovery Site for New Jersey, or where Reading is the Recovery Site for London and London is the Recovery Site for Reading. For large corporations, this offers the chance to save money, especially on those important and precious VMware licenses. In the next chapter we will also look at the multisite features which allow for so-called "spoke-and-hub" configurations in which one Recovery Site offers protection to many Protected Sites.

Chapter 13

Bidirectional Relationships and Shared Site Configurations

So far this book has focused on a situation where the Recovery Site is dedicated to the purpose of recovery. This Recovery Site could be hired rack space provisioned by a third-party company; this is very popular in smaller organizations that perhaps only have one datacenter or have a datacenter that is small and does not have the resources to be both a Protected Site and a Recovery Site at the same time. As with conventional redundancy, this "dedicated" Recovery Site model is not especially efficient as you are wasting valuable financial resources to protect yourself from an event that might never happen. Like home insurance and car insurance, this is a waste of money—until, that is, someone breaks into your house, or steals your car, drives around like a lunatic, and sets on it fire for kicks.

Due to licensing and other associated costs, it is much more efficient for two or more datacenters to be paired together to offer DR resources to each other. Such a configuration is referred to as a bidirectional configuration in the official VMware SRM documentation. I've left this type of configuration for the end of the book—not because I thought most people wouldn't be interested, but because of the following three main reasons. First, I wanted to make it 100% crystal-clear which tasks are carried out at the Protected Site (site pairing, the array manager configuration, and inventory mappings) and which tasks are carried out at the Recovery Site (Recovery Plans). Second, permissions are simpler to explain and test in a conventional Protected Site and dedicated Recovery Site configuration. And third, at this stage my hope is that you should now have a very good understanding of how SRM works, so it shouldn't be too difficult to add a bidirectional configuration to an existing unidirectional configuration.

I want to say something about the process of setting up bidirectional configurations in general. Simply put, it is *much* easier than it has been in any previous release of SRM. It's a difficult fact to explain or prove if you haven't used the product before. Configuring this kind of active/active relationship used to require several steps, especially around the array manager configuration. I think the new UI has a lot to do with this. Now that the SRM sites are more visible to one another, rather than being locked to their specific vCenter instances, the whole operation is much more seamless. At this stage, I did make some major storage changes. Previously, the Recovery Site (New Jersey) just had access to replicated volumes from the Protected Site (New York). For a bidirectional configuration to work you clearly need replication in the opposite direction. When this happens the clear distinction between the Protected and Recovery Sites breaks down, as they are both Recovery and Protected Sites for each other. If it helps, what I'm changing from is an active/passive DR model to an active/active DR model, where both sites reciprocate to each other—both running a production load, while at the same time using their spare capacity to offer DR resources to each other.

Configuring Inventory Mappings

I created a new resource pool and folder structure on both the New Jersey and New York sites. This was to allow for inventory mappings created for the first time between New Jersey and New York. Personally, I feel that for simplicity the various sites should almost be a complete "mirror" of each other. In other words, the resource pools and folder structures are identical wherever possible. In reality, this mirroring may not be practical or realistic, as no two sites are always identical in terms of their infrastructure or operational capabilities. To reflect this, and to make this section more interesting, I decided that the New Jersey location would take a totally different approach to how it allocated resources. The New Jersey location uses LUNs/volumes to reflect different line-of-business applications such as Finance, Help Desk, Sales, and Collaboration, and it also uses vSphere vApps in its configuration (see Figure 13.1).

SRM now supports the mapping of vApps at the Protected Site to vApps in the Recovery Site. So I created a resource pool called DR_NJ and mapped all the vApps in New Jersey

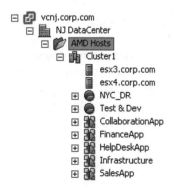

Figure 13.1   The New Jersey site with a collection of applications in the format of vApps

to vApps created manually in New York (see Figure 13.2). The important fact to note here is that there is no fancy option; just right-click a vApp and click the Protect button. vApps are themselves just collections of VMs. What's new here is SRM's ability to map a vApp in the Protected Site to a vApp in the Recovery Site.

IMPORTANT NOTE

SRM does not link vApps together, so the settings in the vApps in the Protected Site are not duplicated over at the Recovery Site. SRM does not use the start-up orders present in the vApp, but by default leverages the priority orders and VM dependencies created in the Recovery Plan.

Of course, this process didn't stop with just the resource mappings. I also needed to create mappings for folders and networks as well. Additionally, I confirmed that there was a placeholder datastore. So I mapped a single folder that contained New Jersey's vApps to a single folder on the New Jersey location called NJ_DR_vApps (see Figure 13.3).

I also mapped the port groups representing the VLANs at New Jersey to the port groups in New York (see Figure 13.4).

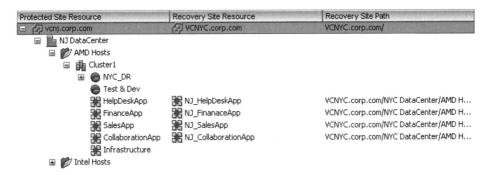

Figure 13.2   vApps in New Jersey (vcnj.corp.com) mapped to vApps in New York. The recovery vApps are labeled NJ_**ApplicationName**.

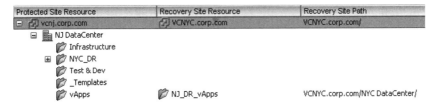

Figure 13.3   vApps exist as a container in the VMs and Templates view, so there is no need to create a folder for each vApp.

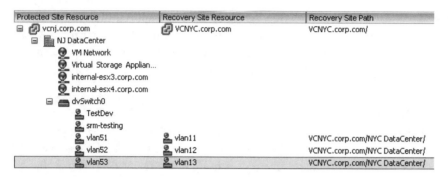

Protected Site Resource	Recovery Site Resource	Recovery Site Path
⊟ vcnj.corp.com	VCNYC.corp.com	VCNYC.corp.com/
⊟ NJ DataCenter		
VM Network		
Virtual Storage Applian...		
internal-esx3.corp.com		
internal-esx4.corp.com		
⊟ dvSwitch0		
TestDev		
srm-testing		
vlan51	vlan11	VCNYC.corp.com/NYC DataCenter/
vlan52	vlan12	VCNYC.corp.com/NYC DataCenter/
vlan53	vlan13	VCNYC.corp.com/NYC DataCenter/

Figure 13.4   In this case, vlan51 is mapped to vlan11 and vlan52 is mapped to vlan12, and so on.

Refreshing the Array Manager

Unlike the first time we set up SRM, the two locations are paired already; there is no need to pair the two sites together again. We must refresh the array manager so that the SRM and SRA at New Jersey are aware of which volumes are available and which are replicated. I updated my datastore folder structures to take into account the fact that I was building out a bidirectional configuration (see Figure 13.5). This was largely a cosmetic decision, but I thought it would make it clear to me, and hopefully to you. For me, this aptly shows how flexible and dynamic a vSphere 5.0 and SRM 5.0 environment can be. It takes a matter of minutes to totally restructure your environment based on your business needs and organizational changes.

To refresh the array manager, follow these steps.

1. In SRM, select the Array Manager pane.

2. Select the Devices tab.

3. Locate the Refresh button (see Figure 13.6) on the far right, and click it.

Once the refresh has completed, you should see that the device list is updated and includes arrows pointing in both directions (see Figure 13.7). In my case, this represents the replication from New Jersey to (→) New York and from New York to (←) New Jersey. In this case, I had the New Jersey site selected as "local." If I'd logged in to the New York vCenter first, the arrows would be in opposite directions. This view is useful before, during, and after the failover and failback process to validate your configuration.

You can see that my new datastores at the New Jersey site have yet to be allocated to Protection Groups.

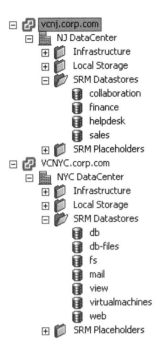

```
□ 🔲 vcnj.corp.com
   □ 🏢 NJ DataCenter
      ⊞ 📁  Infrastructure
      ⊞ 📁  Local Storage
      □ 📂 SRM Datastores
            🗄 collaboration
            🗄 finance
            🗄 helpdesk
            🗄 sales
      ⊞ 📁  SRM Placeholders
□ 🔲 VCNYC.corp.com
   □ 🏢 NYC DataCenter
      ⊞ 📁  Infrastructure
      ⊞ 📁  Local Storage
      □ 📂 SRM Datastores
            🗄 db
            🗄 db-files
            🗄 fs
            🗄 mail
            🗄 view
            🗄 virtualmachines
            🗄 web
      ⊞ 📁  SRM Placeholders
```

Figure 13.5   VMware vSphere folders are an effective way to organize datastores. Remember, these folders can have permissions set on them.

Figure 13.6   If new datastores are created it's good to refresh the array manager to confirm that SRM is aware of the new storage.

Local Device	Direction ⌃	Remote Device	Datastore	Protection Group
🔘 /vol/replica_of_vol..	⬅	/vol/vol3_fs	Remote: [fs]	File Servers Protection Group
🔘 /vol/replica_of_vol..	⬅	/vol/vol4_mail	Remote: [mail]	Mail Protection Group
🔘 /vol/replica_of_vol..	⬅	/vol/vol7_dbfiles	Remote: [db-files]	Database Protection Group
🔘 /vol/replica_of_vol..	⬅	/vol/vol5_view	Remote: [view]	View Protection Group
🔘 /vol/replica_of_vol..	⬅	/vol/vol6_web	Remote: [web]	Web Protection Group
🔘 /vol/replica_of_vol..	⬅	/vol/vol2_db	Remote: [db]	Database Protection Group
🔘 /vol/vol1_replica_...	⬅	/vol/vol1_virtualmachines	Remote: [virtualmachines]	
🔘 /vol/vol5_helpdesk	➡	/vol/replica_of_vol5_helpd...	Local: [helpdesk]	
🔘 /vol/vol4_finance	➡	/vol/replica_of_vol4_finance	Local: [finance]	
🔘 /vol/vol3_collabor...	➡	/vol/replica_of_vol3_collab...	Local: [collaboration]	
🔘 /vol/vol2_sales	➡	/vol/replica_of_vol2_sales	Local: [sales]	

Figure 13.7   This view, taken from New Jersey, shows that the "application" datastores are being replicated to New Jersey.

Creating the Protection Group

Again, creating a Protection Group does not differ substantially in a bidirectional configuration. But you might now begin to see the value of Protection Group folders. When Protection Groups are created they are visible to both the Protected and Recovery Sites. This is because they are needed for failover as well as failback. By default, they are presented in a flat window, so unless you have a good naming convention and you know your environment well, determining which Protection Groups belong where could become tricky (see Figure 13.8). Simply using Protection Group folders remedies this potential confusion quickly and easily. In my case, there is almost a one-to-one relationship between datastores and Protection Groups, except in the case of the Database Protection Group that contains two datastores.

Figure 13.8   Protection Group folders will help you quickly and easily separate Protection Groups available from one site to another.

Creating the Recovery Plan

Again, Recovery Plans do not differ substantially in a bidirectional configuration, and you will see that using Recovery Plan folders makes more sense once you have two locations offering DR resources to each other (see Figure 13.9).

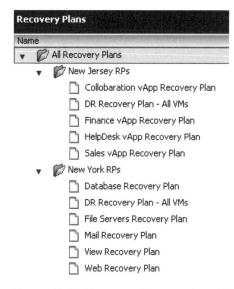

Figure 13.9   Recovery Plans are placed into Recovery Plan folders to make it easy to see that they are associated with particular sites.

Using vApps to Control Start-Up Orders

As you might know, vApps do have their own start-up orders that are configured on the properties of the vApp itself (see Figure 13.10).

It is possible to "turn off" SRM's method of powering on VMs and expressing VM dependencies. I don't recommend this approach as it largely defeats the point of using SRM as a tool for automating DR, and it has not been tested by VMware as a supported configuration. Nonetheless, I thought you might be interested in how it is done, and what the advantages and disadvantages are. You can turn off SRM's power-on function using the Virtual Machines tab on the Recovery Plan; select all the VMs, and change their Startup Action to be Do Not Power On (see Figure 13.11). A legitimate use of this feature is to recover VMs and then manually decide if they are needed in the DR event. This could be used as a way to preserve key resources such as memory.

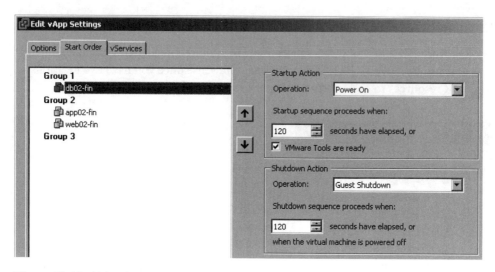

Figure 13.10   Using the up and down arrows, it is possible to set the start-up orders on VMs.

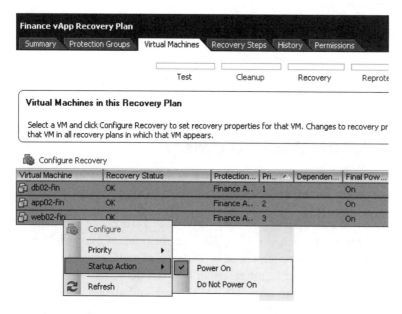

Figure 13.11   Through the standard multiple-select options present in Windows it is possible to select groups of VMs to not be powered on.

Then you need to add a custom script that will use PowerCLI to power on the vApp that will force the system to power on using the order defined in the vApp itself. This script will leverage the redirect.cmd batch file I created in Chapter 11, Custom Recovery Plans, and the pass-through authentication of PowerCLI when the service account in SRM has been changed to one that has rights in the vCenter environment.

```
c:\windows\system32\cmd.exe /C c:\redirect.cmd c:\start-finance.ps1
```

The start-finance.ps1 file has a PowerCLI command in it that uses the `Start-vApp` cmdlet together with the name of the vApp in the Recovery Site. The `start-sleep` command is used to ensure that the script runs after the VM storage recovery process has completed, and the VMs contained in the vApp are in a fit state to be powered on.

```
start-sleep -s 300
start-vapp NJ_FinanceApp
```

Finally, all you need to do now is add a command step to the Recovery Plan using redirect.cmd to in turn call the PowerCLI script. That command step is step 5 in Figure 13.12.

For me, the biggest downside of this approach is evident if the VM is referenced in more than one Recovery Plan. Disabling the power-on function of a VM in one Recovery Plan disables it for *all* Recovery Plans if it is referenced elsewhere (see Figure 13.13).

Figure 13.12 A 300-second wait is added to the script to ensure that the VM storage is correctly configured before initiating a power on.

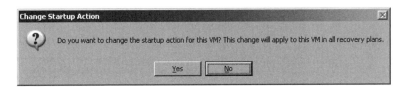

Figure 13.13 Removing a VM's power-on function in the Virtual Machines tab disables it from being started in SRM in all Recovery Plans.

In short, this approach means abandoning SRM's built-in power-on and VM dependencies functionality, and resorting to manual power on of *all* affected VMs. I hope that by seeing what's involved in this process you realize this approach is not viable. Sometimes you can learn a lot by knowing the wrong way to do something, as well as the right way. Personally, I think the power-on process could be more easily managed using the priority orders in the Recovery Plan. If my finance application has three roles—a back-end database, an application server, and a Web front end—nothing would be stopping me from putting db01, db02, and db03 in priority order 1, and app01, app02, and app03 in priority order 2.

This completes our discussion of configuring a bidirectional relationship, and hopefully you can see the heavy lifting is mainly taken care of by the initial configuration of the Protected Site when SRM was first deployed. There are some unique one-off settings that can be reused when building out a bidirectional model, such as the fact that the sites are already paired together, and that the array configuration is already in place.

Shared Site Configurations

> **WARNING**
>
> The term *shared site* should not be uttered by someone who has poorly fitting false teeth or who has consumed large amounts of alcohol.

A shared site configuration exists in SRM when more than one production location is set to receive its DR resources from SRM's Recovery Site services. It allows for a so-called "spoke and hub" configuration to be created where one Recovery Site offers DR resources for many production sites or Protected Sites. Such a configuration would be used by a large company or by a service provider that offers SRM as an outsourced solution to companies that do not have the resources to manage their own DR location. Clearly, in this commercial scenario permissions must be correctly assigned so that the customer does not start managing the Recovery Plans of a totally different business! It's also necessary to prevent duplicate name errors, which could happen if two different companies had VMs with the same VM name. Although this separation sounds complete—even with the correct permissions—one customer can see the events and tasks of a different customer.

At the moment, running the SRM installer with command-line switches triggers the shared site configuration. In time this may become integrated into the Install Wizard or, better still, as part of the wizard used to pair sites together. The command-line switches allow you to generate what VMware calls an SRM "extension" ID. In terms of the product, the configuration of SRM remains the same (array manager, Protection Groups, inventory mappings, and Recovery Plans) and this allows for each SRM instance to be uniquely created. The requirements for the shared site configuration are quite simple. The new site—say, Washington DC—would need its own ESX hosts, vCenter, VMs, and SRM server. The New Jersey site, for example, would act as its DR location and would have a second SRM host added to it. In this scenario, New Jersey's site would have two SRM hosts configured to one vCenter—one facilitating failovers from New York and another facilitating failovers from Washington DC. Also, the New Jersey site would become a DR "hub" for New York and Washington DC.

From a DR provider's perspective, this means customers have their own dedicated SRM host, but they can share the compute resources of the entire DR location. Some customers might not be happy with this, and may want their own dedicated ESX hosts that are used to bring VMs online. Of course, they will pay a premium for this level and quality of service. It's perhaps worth stating that some service providers I have spoken to are not yet satisfied that this level of separation is sufficient for their needs. Admittedly, these providers are looking toward DR delivered via the cloud model that is still in early development.

When you log in to the SRM you log in to a particular extension which relates to the Recovery Site that you are managing. Rather than running the installation normally, you would run the SRM installer with this switch:

```
/V"CUSTOM_SETUP=1"
```

This adds two more steps to the installation wizard. First, a mandatory step enables the custom plug-in identifier, followed by the settings for the custom SRM extension. The extension has three parameters.

- The SRM ID

  A piece of text of no more than 29 characters, although you can use characters such as underscores, hyphens, and periods. I recommend you stick to purely alphanumeric characters, as underscores, hyphens, and periods can cause problems if they are used at the beginning or end of the SRM ID. The SRM ID should be the same on both SRM hosts in the Protected and Recovery Sites. Essentially, this makes SRM pair the sites on the shared SRM Site ID value. The SRM ID creates a variable by which multiple SRM instances can be uniquely identified—and must be the same on both the Protected and Recovery Site SRM hosts for them to be successfully paired together. In my case, there will be an SRM server in Washington DC and an SRM server in New Jersey. The SRM ID for both installs will be the string WashingtonDCsite.

- Organization

  A friendly 50-character name. No restrictions apply to this field with respect to special characters.

- Description

  A friendly 50-character description. No restrictions apply to this field with respect to special characters.

Once the install has been completed, you continue to pair up the sites as you would normally. When the pairing process has completed, during the logon process you will be able to see *all* the custom extension IDs together with their descriptions. While this information is not commercially sensitive, it is not possible to hide these references; they need to be visible so that folks can select which site contains their recovery configuration.

In my current configuration, my Protected Site and Recovery Site are already paired together. This configuration cannot be changed without uninstalling the SRM product. So it's perhaps worth thinking about how important the shared site feature is to you, before you embark on a rollout. That might sound like bad news, but it is not the end of the world. There is nothing stopping me from creating a new site representing, say, Washington DC, and then adding a new SRM server in the Recovery Site to be paired with the new site that needs protection. As you can see, I created a new vCenter instance for the Washington DC datacenter (vcwdc.corp.com) together with the SRM server for that location (srmwdc.corp.com). To allow for the shared site configuration I created another SRM server at the Recovery Site, called srmwdc-rs. Also, I created a resource pool in the New Jersey datacenter to hold the placeholders for Washington DC, called WDC_DR. Of course, for this to work a SQL database was created for Washington's vCenter and SRM instances (see Figure 13.14).

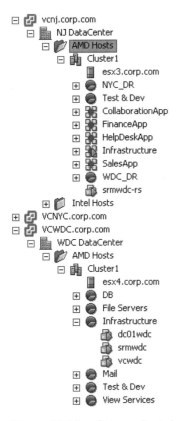

Figure 13.14 vSphere client view, now with three datacenters
and multiple instances of SRM servers

Installing VMware SRM with Custom Options to the New Site (Washington DC)

The first task will be to install the SRM server at the new location—in my case, Washington DC. We will run the SRM installer with a special custom option that will show new steps in the graphical wizard that assists in the installation process. This will allow us to set the SRM ID for the site which will be used at both the Protected and Recovery Sites to enable the pairing process.

1. Log in to the new Protected Site SRM server. In my case, this is srmwdc.

2. Open a command prompt and run the SRM installer with the following switch:

```
/V"CUSTOM_SETUP=1"
```

The complete string will look something like this, with *N* representing the version and build number of SRM:

```
VMware-srm-5.N.N-NNNNNN.exe /V"CUSTOM_SETUP=1"
```

3. Complete the setup routine as normal. At the Protected Site, I used the name "Washington DC" (see Figure 13.15).

4. In the plug-in identifier window, select the Custom SRM Plug-in Identifier option (see Figure 13.16).

5. Enter the SRM ID, organization name, and a description (see Figure 13.17).

Once the installation is complete, you will be able to log in to the site's vCenter and connect to the SRM service. The only noticeable difference at this stage is that there is an additional field in the Summary tab of the site that shows the SRM ID field (see Figure 13.18).

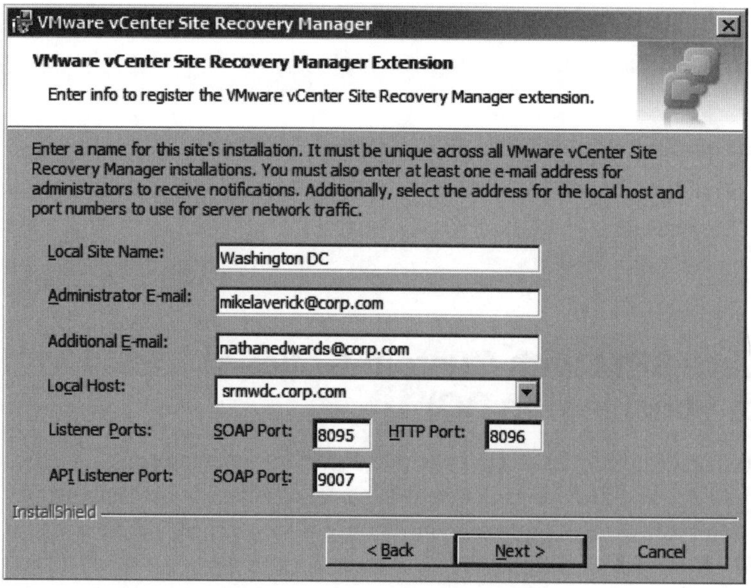

Figure 13.15 The local site name of "Washington DC" will make it easy to identify in the user interface.

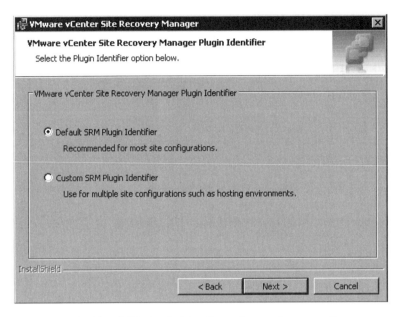

Figure 13.16   The SRM plug-in identifier options only appear if you use the custom setup option.

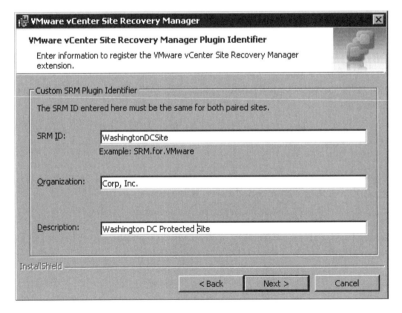

Figure 13.17   SRM will use the SRM ID in the pairing process, and will expect the Washington DC SRM server in the Recovery Site to have the same ID.

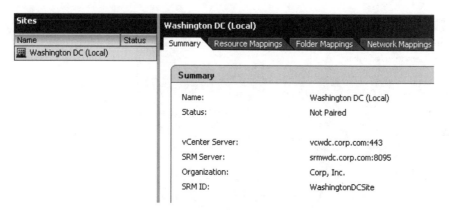

Figure 13.18   A shared site configuration differs visually only by the reference to the SRM ID value in the Summary tab of the site.

Installing VMware SRM Server with Custom Options to the Recovery Site

Now that the Protected Site is installed, it's time to run the same routine at the new SRM server at the Recovery Site; this is the VM I called srmwdc-rs. During the install, it's important to remember that when prompted for the vCenter details you need to specify the vCenter at the Recovery Site (in my case, this is srmnj.corp.com). The site name must be unique, as you cannot pair two sites together that have identical locations; however, the two sites will be paired together and identified uniquely by the Site ID parameter specified during the custom installation. Again, run the installation as before with the additional /V switch:

```
VMware-srm-5.N.N-NNNNNN.exe /V"CUSTOM_SETUP=1"
```

At the Recovery Site I used "Washington DC Recovery Site" as the friendly name (see Figure 13.19). Washington DC doesn't have a dedicated Recovery Site. Instead, it shares the DR resources of New Jersey with its sister location of New York.

During the configuration of the Custom SRM plug-in you *must* enter the same SRM ID as you did during the install of the Protected Site SRM (see Figure 13.20).

Figure 13.19   In this case, I labeled the site differently by adding the word Recovery to its friendly name.

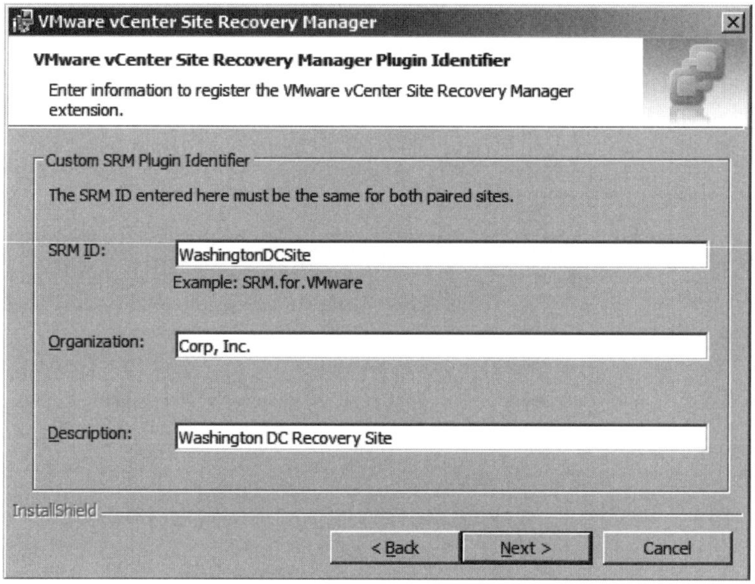

Figure 13.20   The SRM ID is the same for both the Protected Site SRM host in Washington DC and its dedicated SRM host in New Jersey.

Pairing the Sites Together

After this process, you use the Configure Connection Wizard to pair the two sites together. Previous versions of SRM required a special plug-in to be installed to extend the vSphere client functionality; this is no longer required, although the installer still references this with the term *plug-in identifier*. All that is required now is the install of SRM with the SRM ID specified. During the pairing process, the Site ID is matched at the Protected Site with the SRM host with the same SRM ID at the Recovery Site. So, at the heart of any shared site configuration is the unique SRM ID value that must be the same at the Protected and Recovery Sites for the pairing to work. If you like, the pairing is being made not just between one SRM server and another, but to the specific SRM ID value which is the same at the Protected and Recovery Sites (see Figure 13.21).

In Figure 13.21, it looks as though Washington DC has its own Recovery Site. In reality, there is still only one vCenter in New Jersey, which is now the DR location for both New York and Washington DC. When the pairing process takes place the administrator for Washington DC would still require login details to the New Jersey vCenter and as the inventory mappings were configured the administrator would see all the resources in New Jersey allowed by user rights and privileges.

Once this pairing is complete, the rest of the configuration proceeds in exactly the same manner as the standard installation, and you can begin to configure the array manager, Protection Groups, and Recovery Plans. Figure 13.22 shows my Washington DC Site and Washington DC Recovery Site paired together. Although they have different site names, they are linked by virtue of the SRM ID.

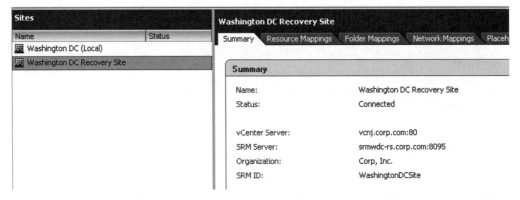

Figure 13.21   The Protected Site (Washington DC) and Recovery Site (Washington DC Recovery Site). The shared SRM ID pairs them together.

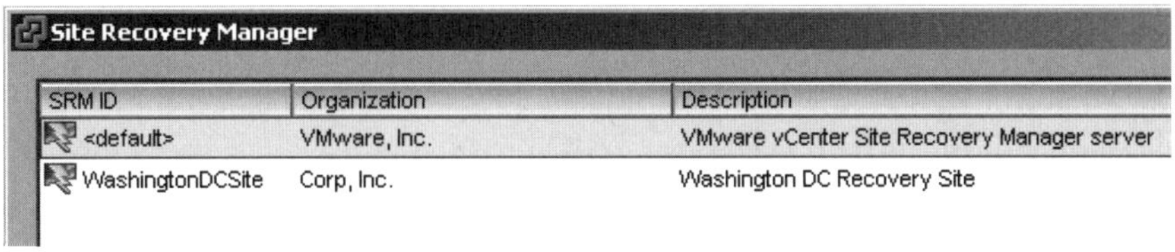

SRM ID	Organization	Description
<default>	VMware, Inc.	VMware vCenter Site Recovery Manager server
WashingtonDCSite	Corp, Inc.	Washington DC Recovery Site

Figure 13.22   This dialog box appears whenever the administrator at Washington DC switches from the local site to the Recovery Site.

When you come to switch from the Protected Site (New York or Washington DC) to the Recovery Site (New Jersey), you will be presented with a dialog box from which to select your SRM ID and add friendly descriptions (see Figure 13.22). The reference to <default> is the initial site pairing between my New York and New Jersey sites, which I created in Chapter 7, Installing VMware SRM.

Finally, if I was connected to the Recovery Site (New Jersey) and wanted to switch from one SRM ID to another—say, I wanted to switch to the New York site—I could click the Log Out option at the Recovery Site and then reconnect to the SRM Service (see Figure 13.23). This option is available from the Commands option on the far right-hand side of the Sites view in SRM.

Figure 13.23   The Log Out option lets you log out of the current instance of SRM.

Decommissioning a Site

Let's assume, for whatever reason, that the Washington DC site was to be decommissioned. A good example of this is if you were using SRM to facilitate a datacenter move from Washington DC to New Jersey. The removal process from an SRM perspective would be a reversal of the normal work. Once the virtual machines in the old site (Washington DC) were up and running, the old site could be removed. In this case you would do the following.

1. Remove the Recovery Plans used for the planned migration.

2. Remove the Protection Group used for the planned migration. This should unregister and delete the placeholder VMs and their corresponding .vmx files.

3. Remove the array manager configuration from the old Protected Site (Washington DC in my case).

4. "Break" the pairing of the Protected Site to the Recovery Site.

   Strictly speaking, there is no requirement to "break" the site relationship. I just like to do it. The real reason for this is to undo the pairing process in cases where the administrator makes an error, such as pairing two sites together accidentally.

5. Rerun the vCenter Linked Mode Wizard, to remove the old site's vCenter instance and isolate it to being a stand-alone vCenter.

6. Uninstall the SRM product from the Protected Site SRM and from its previously paired Recovery Site SRM server.

7. Revisit your licensing and remove any stale sites that may be listed. On the right-click of a stale site there is a Remove Asset option that is used to complete this process.

This process must be carried out in this particular order; otherwise, error messages will appear. For example, removal of the array manager configuration while it is in use with Protection Groups will create a pop-up message preventing you from making that change.

Summary

Once you understand the principles and concepts behind SRM, a bidirectional or shared site configuration is really an extension of the same principles we covered in earlier chapters. The only complexity is getting your mind around the relationships. Perhaps occasionally you stopped in the chapter to clarify to yourself what the relationships were between the two locations, both in SRM and in the storage array. You are not alone; I did the same thing. I got so wrapped up in the Protected Site/Recovery Site view of the world that it took me some time to adjust my thinking to accept that each location can have a dual functionality. Of course, I always knew it could, but adjusting to that switch once you have the concept that Site A is the Protected Site and Site B is the Recovery Site just takes a little time. In a bidirectional configuration, if your Protected Site (New York) and Recovery Site (New Jersey) are configured similarly it's sometimes tricky to keep the relationships clear in your head—and that's with just two sites!

You will find this becomes more so when we deal with failover and failback—especially with failback. I really had to concentrate when I was doing my first failback and writing it up. Anyway, I digress, as that is the subject of the next chapter: failover and failback, and running our Recovery Plans for real—what some folks call "Hitting the Big Red Button."

Chapter 14

Failover and Failback

When I started writing this chapter I really struggled to explain how much SRM has improved, given that it now has an automated method of failing back after a DR event. When I finished writing the chapter it became very clear to me. In my previous books this chapter ran to about 50 pages and 10,000 words; with the improvements that VMware has made to SRM this chapter will probably run to about 25 pages and 5,000 words. Those small stats will hopefully give you some idea of how much has improved since SRM 4.0. By simplifying the process significantly, VMware has given me less work to do, and you can't say that isn't a good deal for everyone concerned.

The one thing we have yet to discuss or cover is what SRM is all about. A disaster occurs and you must trigger your Recovery Plan for real. This is sometimes referred to as "Hitting the Big Red Button." I left this discussion for this chapter because it's a major decision that permanently changes the configuration of your SRM environment and your virtual machines, and so it is not to be undertaken lightly. It's perhaps worth considering how long it takes to get senior management approval to run the Recovery Plan. The time it takes for decisions to be made can be added to your hoped-for recovery time objective. An actual DR event responds well to prompt and decisive leadership.

My second reason for covering this issue now is that before I started this chapter I wanted to change the viewpoint of the book completely, to cover bidirectional configuration. The previous chapter was a precursor to preparing a failover and failback situation. I didn't want to trigger a real run of the DR plan before making sure a bidirectional configuration was in place and understood. A real execution of your Recovery Plan is just like a test, except the Recovery Step mode of the plan is actually executed. You can view the recovery steps by selecting a Recovery Plan and changing the View options (see Figure 14.1).

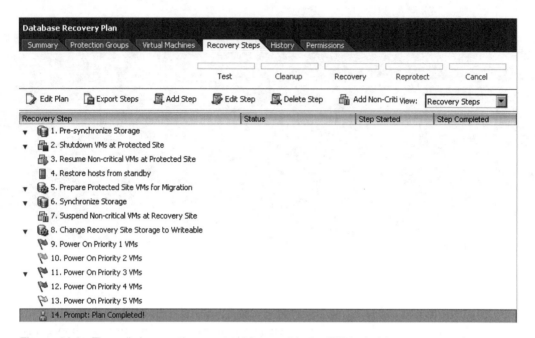

Figure 14.1   The pull-down options next to View enable the SRM administrator to see the steps taken during recovery.

The Recovery Steps mode differs from a test step in a few ways. First, it includes a step to presynchronize storage. This attempts to ensure that during the process of planned migration the VMs in the Recovery Site are in the same consistent state as the Protected Site. It occurs twice: once when the VMs are powered on (step 1), and then after the VMs are powered off (step 6). Of course, this will only be successful during a planned migration when both the Protected and Recovery Sites are available at the same time. In a real disaster this step would be ignored because it's unlikely that there would be any communication paths available between the sites—what happens when the Recovery Plan is run very much depends on the nature of the disaster itself. Second, during a planned migration SRM attempts to gracefully shut down the VMs in the Protected Site that are covered by the plan. In other words, if possible, SRM will power off VMs at the Protected Site (New York) if it's available. Unlike the test of the plan, no attempt is made to "clean up" after the plan, which resets all the recovery VMs. It leaves them up and running. Essentially, the VMs that once lived in the Protected Site—in my case, New York—will live in the Recovery Site of New Jersey.

In the real world, clicking the big red button requires senior management approval, usually at the C-Class level (CEO, CTO, CIO), unless these guys are in the building that was demolished by the disaster itself, and someone farther down the management chain is delegated to make the decision. You could regard this issue as part and parcel of the DR/BC plan. If we have lost senior decision makers either temporarily or permanently, someone else will have to take on their roles and responsibilities. Additionally, there will be subtle and important changes at the storage array. The storage vendors' SRA will automatically stop the normal cycle of replication between the Protected Site and the Recovery Site, and will usually change the status of the LUNs/volumes from being secondary/slave/remote/replica (or whatever terminology the storage vendor uses) to primary or master. All this is done without you having to bug those guys on the storage team. For example, if you were using an HP P4000 VSA you would see the volumes that are normally marked as being "Remote" switched to being "Primary."

Triggering the plan from SRM is very easy to do—some might say too easy. You click the Recovery button, read a warning, click the radio button to confirm that you understand the consequences, and click OK. Then you watch the sparks fly depending on the plan's success and whether you sought higher approval! Actually running the recovery is very easy and I think is a good use case for deploying a correct permissions and rights model so that recoveries are not run accidentally. Of course, a run of your disaster Recovery Plan need not be executed merely for an out-and-out loss of a site. If you have planned both the datastore and Protection Groups properly, there should be no reason why you can't failover and failback on an application level. This becomes very important when you consider that, by default, VMs at the Protected Site are powered down. If you have not planned your LUN/volume layout correctly, and you have different applications and business units mixed together on the same datastores, it will be very difficult to run a Recovery Plan without it powering off and moving over a VM that you actually were not ready to failover to the new location. If this is the case, I would consider a root and branch review of your datastore layout, and seriously consider an amount of Storage vMotion to relocate VMs into more discrete datastores. SRM does not react well to folks who just sort datastores based on their amount of free space, and use that as the criterion for where they store their VMs. You have been warned!

There are some larger issues to consider before hitting the big red button. Indeed, we could and should argue that these issues need addressing before we even think about implementing SRM. First, depending on how you have licensed SRM, you *may* need to arrange the transfer of the SRM license between the Protected and Recovery Sites to remain covered by the EULA with VMware. VMware issues SRM licenses on the basis of trust. You need a license assigned to the site that has protected VMs located in the vCenter. As a failback is essentially a reversal of the day-to-day configuration, the Recovery Site will need licensing, albeit temporarily, to facilitate the failback process. Of course, if you have bidirectional configuration, this license concern does not apply, as both sites are licensed since they both possess Protection Groups. The process is significantly simplified by the use of linked mode as the license follows the VM as it is moved from one site to another. SRM 5 will never prevent a failover from happening due to license issues. It will (if a license has expired or doesn't exist) prevent you from creating new Protection Groups but it won't stop Recovery Plans running to completion. If you are using the Enterprise SRM Edition it will still let you protect VMs; you'll just get warnings about your violation of the EULA.

Second, if you are changing the IP addresses of the virtual machines, your DNS systems will need to have the correct corresponding IP address and hostnames in DNS. Ideally, this will be achieved in the main by using your DNS Server Dynamic DNS Name Registrations feature, but watch out for any static records in DNS and the caching of those DNS records on other systems.

Planned Failover: Protected Site Is Available

The main obvious difference when running the Recovery Plan when the Protected Site is available is that the virtual machines in the Protected Site get powered off based on the order specified in the plan. However, a subtler change is effected as well: the suspension of the replication or snapshot between the Protected Site and the Recovery Site. The diagram in Figure 14.2 illustrates the suspension of the normal replication cycle. This must happen to prevent replication conflicts and data loss; after all, it's the virtual

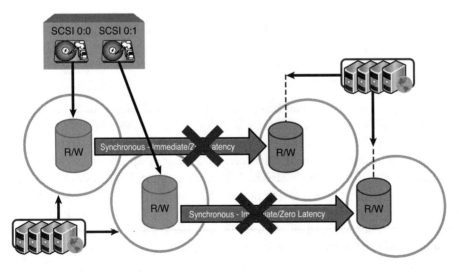

Figure 14.2   Here the X represents the suspension of the normal pattern of replication.

machines at the Recovery Site which users will be connecting to and making data changes to. For all intents and purposes they are the primary virtual machines after a failover has occurred. In the figure, the volumes in the Recovery Site are marked as primary/master and are set as being read-write by the SRA from your storage vendor.

As you can see, the X indicates replication of data has been suspended, and the LUNs that were once marked as R/O in our tests are being marked as R/W in our execution of the Recovery Plan. In manual DR without SRM, this is normally a task triggered at the storage array by a human operator using the vendor's failover/failback options, but as the SRA has administrative rights to the storage array this can be automated by SRM. Once the plan has successfully completed, you should be able to see this change in the status pages of your given storage system. For example, in a NetApp system you will see that the SnapMirror relationship will be broken off and the destination volume held in New Jersey is no longer in a SnapMirror relationship (see Figure 14.3).

Additionally, for each and every volume affected by the planned recovery, the array manager's configuration, when viewed from the Recovery Site, will display that replication has been stopped between the two sites with a broken gray line (see Figure 14.4).

In this example I'm going to assume that the New York site will be unavailable for some hours or days. This could be caused by an incoming hurricane that local weather has given us reliable information about, or a warning from the power company that there will be a major outage of the mains supply for some time as part of a power grid upgrade and maintenance plan.

SnapMirror

🛅 Create	📝 Edit	✖ Delete	🔍 Operations ▾	📇 Remote Access	🔄 Refresh

Source	Destination	SnapMir...	State	Status	Transfer Status	Lag Time (Days ...
new-jersey-filer1:vol5_...	new-york-filer1:replica_of_vol5...	volume	source	idle	● ok	00 00:02:45
new-york-filer1:vol1_vir...	new-jersey-filer1:vol1_replica_...	volume	snapmirrored	idle	● ok	01 23:59:01
new-york-filer1:vol2_db	new-jersey-filer1:replica_of_vol...	volume	snapmirrored	idle	● ok	01 23:59:01
new-york-filer1:vol3_fs	new-jersey-filer1:replica_of_vol...	volume	snapmirrored	idle	● ok	01 23:59:01
new-york-filer1:vol4_mail	new-jersey-filer1:replica_of_vol...	volume	snapmirrored	idle	● ok	01 23:59:01
new-york-filer1:vol5_view	new-jersey-filer1:replica_of_vol...	volume	snapmirrored	idle	● ok	01 23:59:01
new-york-filer1:vol7_db...	new-jersey-filer1:replica_of_vol...	volume	snapmirrored	idle	● ok	01 23:59:01
new-york-filer1:vol6_web	new-jersey-filer1:replica_of_vol...	volume	broken-off	idle	◐ destination is not in snapmirro...	02 00:03:16

	SnapMirror Relationship's State	
is not in snapmirrored state	Destination state (new-jersey-filer1):	broken-off
every 5 minutes	Source state (new-york-filer1):	source

Figure 14.3 The vol6_web volume is marked as no longer being in a snapmirrored state, and the relationship state is marked as "broken-off."

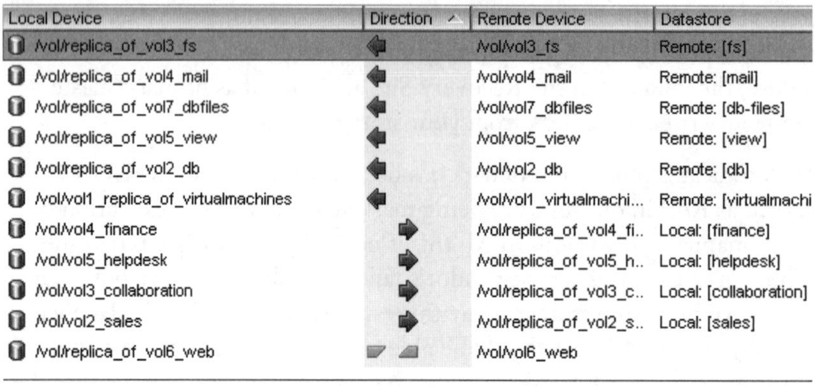

Local Device	Direction	Remote Device	Datastore
/vol/replica_of_vol3_fs	⬅	/vol/vol3_fs	Remote: [fs]
/vol/replica_of_vol4_mail	⬅	/vol/vol4_mail	Remote: [mail]
/vol/replica_of_vol7_dbfiles	⬅	/vol/vol7_dbfiles	Remote: [db-files]
/vol/replica_of_vol5_view	⬅	/vol/vol5_view	Remote: [view]
/vol/replica_of_vol2_db	⬅	/vol/vol2_db	Remote: [db]
/vol/vol1_replica_of_virtualmachines	⬅	/vol/vol1_virtualmachi...	Remote: [virtualmachi
/vol/vol4_finance	➡	/vol/replica_of_vol4_fi..	Local: [finance]
/vol/vol5_helpdesk	➡	/vol/replica_of_vol5_h..	Local: [helpdesk]
/vol/vol3_collaboration	➡	/vol/replica_of_vol3_c..	Local: [collaboration]
/vol/vol2_sales	➡	/vol/replica_of_vol2_s..	Local: [sales]
/vol/replica_of_vol6_web	◹ ◿	/vol/vol6_web	

Figure 14.4   SRM indicates a broken replication relationship with a broken gray line rather than the blue arrow that shows the direction of replication.

STOP!

Before running the plan, you might want to carry out a test first to make sure all VMs recover properly. VMs that display errors will be left merely as placeholders in the Recovery Site.

To run the plan, follow these steps.

1. Select the Recovery Plan and click the Recovery button. In my case, I picked the Web Recovery Plan within the New York Recovery Plan folder.

2. Read the Confirmation text, enable the checkbox that indicates you understand the results of running the plan, and select the Planned Migration radio button (see Figure 14.5). Note that the Recovery dialog box shows both the Planned Migration and Disaster Recovery options only if the SRM plug-in is able to connect to both the Protected and Recovery Sites at the same time. In a truly unexpected DR event you most likely would find the Planned Migration option is, by definition, unavailable.

   If everything goes to plan (forgive the pun) you won't see much difference between a true run of the plan and a test of the plan. What you will see are power-off events at the Protected Site. I have a live recording of me running this very plan on the RTFM website. If you want to see what happened when this plan was executed you can watch it at www.rtfm-ed.co.uk/srm.html.

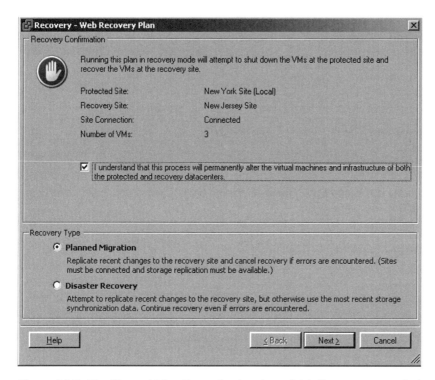

Figure 14.5   The Planned Migration option is only available if you are connected to both the Protected and Recovery Sites at the same time.

3. Once the Recovery Plan has been successful it will be marked with a status of "Recovery Complete" and the SRM administrator will be left with a default message indicating the next stages (see Figure 14.6).

   Alongside this message you should see that any of the Protection Groups that were leveraged during the running of the Recovery Plan will have had their status changed, and be marked as "recovered" (see Figure 14.7).

Before we look at the reprotect and failback process, I want to look at each storage vendor array that I'm using, and reveal the changes made by the SRA to the storage systems themselves. This is pulling back the covers to reveal what goes on at the storage layer when you carry out a planned failover.

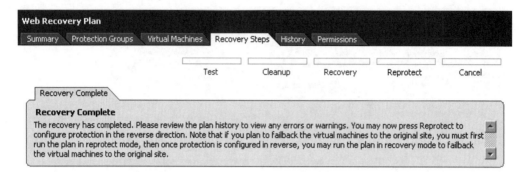

Figure 14.6   The option to Reprotect inverts the replication process to facilitate the running of the Recovery Plan for failback purposes.

Figure 14.7   In this case, just the Web Recovery Plan was run, and therefore only the Web Protection Group is so marked.

Dell EqualLogic and Planned Recovery

When you run a Recovery Plan for planned migration a number of changes take place at the Dell EqualLogic array, as the plan stops the replication between the Protected Site and the Recovery Site. Assuming you have access to the storage array at the Protected Site you would see that volumes affected by the scope of the Protection Groups utilized by the Recovery Plan would be taken "offline" (see Figure 14.8).

At the Recovery Site, the replication object under Inbound Replicas would be removed for the affected volumes, and new volumes created with the hosts in the Recovery Site would automatically be added to the access control list (see Figure 14.9).

At the time of this writing, the Dell EqualLogic SRA does not establish a schedule for replication. EqualLogic arrays hold their schedules at the source of the replication, not the destination. Currently, this means whenever you failover or failback with SRM, you will need to remember to create a new schedule for replication to the volumes where they reside.

Figure 14.8 At the Protected Site, volumes are marked as "offline" after a Recovery Plan is executed.

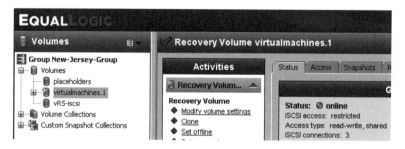

Figure 14.9 At the Recovery Site, the volumes touched by the Recovery Plan are brought online and marked as being read-writable.

NetApp and Planned Recovery

When you run a Recovery Plan with NetApp-based storage a number of changes take place to your existing configuration. At the Protected Site location you will see that because the SnapMirror relationship has been "broken off," no management can be done there (see Figure 14.10). All you can do is view the SnapMirror. As with all relationships, if the break was not done in a timely manner there isn't much you can do about it. I don't think the current state of my NetApp filers says much about the relationship that New Jersey enjoys with New York. That's another one of my jokes, by the way—laughing is not mandatory.

Additionally, if you were viewing the volumes in FilerView rather than System Manager you would see the affected volumes are no longer marked as being "read-only." In my case, I ran a Recovery Plan just against the VMs held in the Web volume. As you can see in Figure 14.11, unlike the other volumes, the replica_of_vol6_web volume does not show the "read-only" or "snapmirrorcd" option, indicating it is available as a writable volume to the ESX hosts in the Recovery Site.

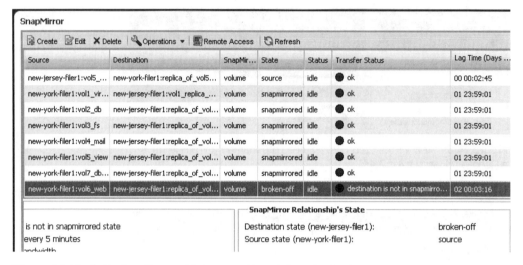

Figure 14.10   In NetApp System Manager, vol6_web is no longer in a snapmirrored state, and the relationship state is marked as "broken-off."

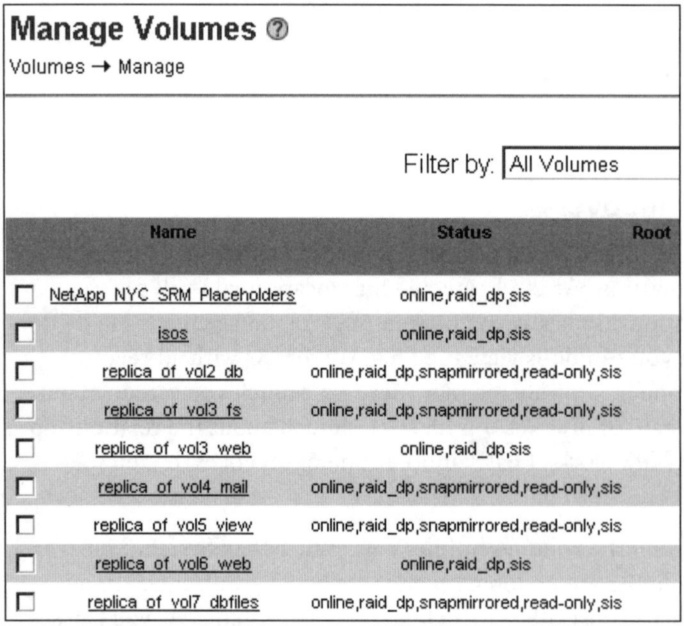

Manage Volumes ⓘ

Volumes → Manage

Filter by: All Volumes

Name	Status	Root
☐ NetApp_NYC_SRM_Placeholders	online,raid_dp,sis	
☐ isos	online,raid_dp,sis	
☐ replica_of_vol2_db	online,raid_dp,snapmirrored,read-only,sis	
☐ replica_of_vol3_fs	online,raid_dp,snapmirrored,read-only,sis	
☐ replica_of_vol3_web	online,raid_dp,sis	
☐ replica_of_vol4_mail	online,raid_dp,snapmirrored,read-only,sis	
☐ replica_of_vol5_view	online,raid_dp,snapmirrored,read-only,sis	
☐ replica_of_vol6_web	online,raid_dp,sis	
☐ replica_of_vol7_dbfiles	online,raid_dp,snapmirrored,read-only,sis	

Figure 14.11   The replica_of_vol6_web volume is not marked as being "snapmirrored" or "read-only."

Automated Failback from Planned Migration

As you probably know, this release of SRM marks a significant milestone in terms of improving the process of failback to the Protected Site. It's worth remembering that previous versions of SRM supported a failback process. SRM 5.0 makes that process much easier. From a storage perspective, failback means inverting your normal path of replication from the Protected Site to the Recovery Site. Previously this was a manual task carried out with great care following the storage array vendor's documentation on how to complete the reconfiguration. SRM 5.0 introduces a reprotect feature that now handles this process for you by using an enhanced and improved SRA that handles the communication to the array for this process. As well as handling the array relationships, this reprotect feature also removes much of the manual cleanup that was required in previous releases. The automatic failback is really the combination of three discrete stages: the reprotect, the test of the Recovery Plan, and assuming that was successful, a planned migration back to the original site. VMware introduced reprotect and failback as a result of direct consultation with customers; VMware found existing customers of SRM were doing many planned migrations and failbacks, and it was these events that will really benefit from reprotect. Remember, a true physical site loss event will always require some kind of manual intervention.

If the array at the Protected Site has not been destroyed in the disaster, the data held on it will be out of sync with the Recovery Site. How much out of sync depends on how long you were at the Recovery Site, and the rate of data change that has taken place. If the data change rate is small, it is possible to merely replicate the differences (the deltas) that have accrued over this time. Alternatively, if it is massively out of sync, you might find yourself actually bringing the new array to the Recovery Site and doing the replication locally or even resorting to using a courier service to move large quantities of data around. Much depends on how long your VMs were active at the Recovery Site, and the quantity of data change that has taken place.

After the use of planned migration, you will find the Recovery Plan will have finished, indicating that you should now carry out the reprotect process. For this to be successful you need a placeholder datastore for both the Protected Site and the Recovery Site; if you don't do this, the reprotect process will fail. You can see if this is the case in a few areas. First, there should be a placeholder datastore assigned for both sites. This can be viewed on the properties of the sites affected in the Placeholder Datastores tab (see Figure 14.12).

Additionally, you should be able to see that in the old Protected Site (New York), the VMs there have a different label next to their name. Each VM affected by the planned migration should have an underscore character appended to the beginning of the name, as shown in Figure 14.13.

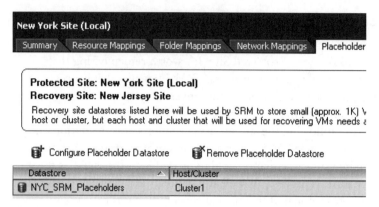

Figure 14.12   NYC_SRM_Placeholders, allocated to the New York site, resides at the Recovery Site and holds the Recovery Plan placeholder files.

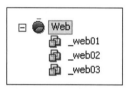

Figure 14.13   These VMs are ready to be made into full-fledged placeholder files during the reprotect phase.

These are not real VMs, as those are now residing over at the Recovery Site (in my case, New Jersey). Instead, they are "shadow" VMs waiting to be converted into fully protected VMs; when you carry out the reprotect procedure these shadow VMs' icons will change to be the default for protected VMs—the so-called "boxes-in-boxes" logo with a lightning bolt appended to them. You should see that these shadow VMs are being held on the placeholder datastore configured for the site (see Figure 14.14).

Once you are satisfied that the old Protected Site is ready for the reprotect phase, you can proceed to run this from your system. Just as there are test and recovery steps there are reprotect steps; you can view them by selecting the Recovery Plan you wish to use, and switching from View mode to Reprotect mode (see Figure 14.15).

As you can see, the reprotect process reverses the direction of replication and reverses the use of Protection Groups for the failback process. In previous releases of SRM there would have been a convoluted "cleanup" phase that is now handled by SRM. It's hard to appreciate the level of automation that has been added here by VMware engineers. Previously

Figure 14.14 NJ_SRM_Placeholders is used as part of the reprotect process, and holds VMs protected by the SRM administrator at the Recovery Site.

Figure 14.15 Switching to Reprotect reveals the reprotect steps, including those instructing the array to reverse the direction of replication.

the step required for failback would have comprised 20 to 30 individual processes, and would require very detailed knowledge of the storage array system. In my previous books, this chapter was exceedingly long as I detailed those steps.

You can trigger the reprotect steps by selecting the Recovery Plan and then clicking the Reprotect button or link. When this is done you will receive a warning box that will summarize the changes being made by SRM and the SRA. You can view this process as a reversal of personality in your SRM configuration. At the end of the reprotect process your Recovery Site will be regarded as the Protected Site, and the Protected Site will be the Recovery Site. The path of replication will be inverted so that, in my case, New York receives updates from New Jersey (see Figure 14.16). The synchronization process should not take too long; how long depends on the volume of the changes since the failover process. As both the source and destination have been initialized before (albeit in the opposite direction), all that needs to be synchronized are the changes to the volume since the failover event.

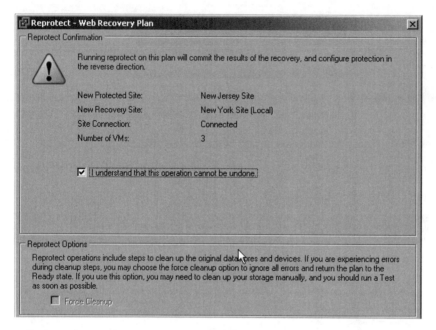

Figure 14.16   It's important to confirm that after the replication path is inverted, both sites are in sync and the normal replication pattern is reestablished.

If the reprotect is successful you should see that the shadow VMs are now full-fledged SRM placeholders (see Figure 14.17).

Additionally, you should notice that the cycle of replication has now been inverted so that volumes that were being replicated from the Protected Site to the Recovery Site (New York → New Jersey) are now being replicated back in the other direction (New York ← New Jersey). You can see this by viewing the array manager configuration. In my case, you can see in Figure 14.18 that /vol/replica_of_vol6_web is now being replicated back to the original source /vol/vol6_web. In other words, the source is now the destination and the destination is now the source. Essentially, the Recovery Site now "owns" this datastore. The replica_of_vol6_web datastore is read-writable, whereas vol/vol6_web is read-only and merely receiving updates.

This situation can have some interesting and unexpected consequences. Suppose, for example, that you had a Recovery Plan that contained Protection Groups that contained datastores replicating five datastores from New York to New Jersey. However, a separate Recovery Plan is executed to failover just one of those five datastores, followed by the reprotect process. It is possible for a Recovery Plan to contain a mix of Protection Groups that are replicating in opposite directions; if this happens a Recovery Plan is marked

Figure 14.17 The _vmname placeholders are registered as full-fledged placeholder VMs replete with their special SRM protected icon.

Local Device	Direction	Remote Device	Datastore
/vol/replica_of_vol3_fs	←	/vol/vol3_fs	Remote: [fs]
/vol/replica_of_vol4_mail	←	/vol/vol4_mail	Remote: [mail]
/vol/replica_of_vol7_dbfiles	←	/vol/vol7_dbfiles	Remote: [db-files]
/vol/replica_of_vol5_view	←	/vol/vol5_view	Remote: [view]
/vol/replica_of_vol2_db	←	/vol/vol2_db	Remote: [db]
/vol/vol1_replica_of_virtualmachines	←	/vol/vol1_virtualmachines	Remote: [virtualmach..
/vol/vol4_finance	→	/vol/replica_of_vol4_finance	Local: [finance]
/vol/vol5_helpdesk	→	/vol/replica_of_vol5_helpdesk	Local: [helpdesk]
/vol/vol3_collaboration	→	/vol/replica_of_vol3_collabo...	Local: [collaboration]
/vol/vol2_sales	→	/vol/replica_of_vol2_sales	Local: [sales]
/vol/replica_of_vol6_web	→	/vol/vol6_web	Local: [web]

Figure 14.18 The replica_of_vol6_web datastore is now being replicated from New Jersey to New York.

as having a "direction error" (see Figure 14.19). Therefore, some Protection Groups containing datastores were replicating from Site A to Site B, and other Protection Groups were replicating from Site B to Site A.

This is a direction error, and it's precisely the configuration I have at the moment in my environment. Some datastores are being replicated from Site A to Site B, whereas others referenced in the same Recovery Plan are being replicated from Site B to Site A.

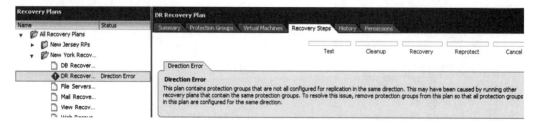

Figure 14.19   In the DR Recovery Plan there are multiple recovery Protection Groups that have opposing replication directions.

You might not find the help contained in the SRM message useful. It may be easier to complete the process of reprotect and failback such that all the datastores referenced in the Protection Groups point in the right direction. If you like, the message is generated by the process that has yet to be fully completed by the SRM administrator.

So, it is important to consider how you want to run your Recovery Plans. For a planned failover, I would prefer to take applications from the Protected Site to the Recovery Site in a staged manner—perhaps taking each application over to the new location step by step, or perhaps carrying out the planned migration on a business unit by business unit basis. As each application or business unit was recovered I would validate that those VMs were functioning before embarking on my next block of moves. Admittedly, this would depend highly on how much time I had for the planned migration—the less advance notification there is the less time there is for time-consuming validation. I'd be more tempted to run my DR Recovery Plan in the event of a real disaster where time was of the essence.

To be honest, I wasn't expecting to see this happen. I've found 99% of what I've learned in life has been from mistakes or unexpected errors; this doesn't mean, however, that I make mistakes or errors 99% of the time. Thought about logically, this message makes perfect sense. Normally, a Protection Group contains datastores that are being replicated in one direction. It's understandable that SRM would be irritated by a Protection Group that contains multiple datastores that are being replicated in different directions. In the situation above, so long as I failback my Web VMs relatively quickly, the DR Recovery Plan will return to a normal state with all the Protection Groups pointing in the same direction.

Once we are satisfied that the reprotect process had been successful, the next stage is to test the Recovery Plan, in which we would test the recovery of the VMs to the original location. Before you run the Recovery Plan to failback the VMs, I think it would be a best practice to confirm that the LUNs/volumes on the arrays at the Protected and Recovery Sites are in sync with each other. Another best practice is to test the Recovery Plan. In my case, this means checking that when I run the Web Recovery Plan the VMs power on correctly at the New York location. Once that test is successful, we run the Recovery Plan as part of a planned migration, this time from New Jersey back to New York. Of course, once that is complete, we would need to carry out yet another reprotect process to reestablish the normal pattern of New York being protected by the New Jersey Recovery Site. If you want a high-level view of this, I think it could be easily summarized once you understand the concept of failover, reprotect, and failback. So, for a planned failover, the workflow would be as follows.

1. Test the Recovery Plan from the Protected Site (New York) to the Recovery Site (New Jersey).

2. Run the Recovery Plan using the Planned Migration option.

3. Run the reprotect steps.

   At this point you could stop if you wanted the VM's failover to the Recovery Site to remain there for the foreseeable future—say, as part of a longer-term datacenter move. Once you were ready you could decommission the old datacenter using the approach I outlined in Chapter 13, Bidirectional Relationships and Shared Site Configurations. Alternatively, if this was just a temporary move to cover the business—say, from a planned power outage—you would continue at a later stage.

4. Test the Recovery Plan from the Protected Site (New Jersey) to the Recovery Site (New York).

5. Run the Recovery Plan using the Planned Migration option.

6. Run the reprotect steps.

7. Test the Recovery Plan as part of your normal round of testing of your preparedness for disaster.

It is certainly possible to observe this reprotect process at the storage management layer if you wish, and some of these systems do a good job of showing you in real time what is happening. For example, Dell EqualLogic Group Manager does a good job of showing you the reversal of the replication process during the reprotect stages in the Failback tab on volumes contained in the Outbound Replicas folder (see Figure 14.20).

The status bar in the Dell EqualLogic Group Manager shows active tasks. In Figure 14.20 it is demoting the primary volume to be secondary, and then creating a replica that sends updates from New Jersey to New York. Not all SRAs reinstate the schedule for replication during this reprotect phase. It is worth validating with storage management software that the LUNs/volumes are in sync, and that replication has returned to the normal, expected cycle.

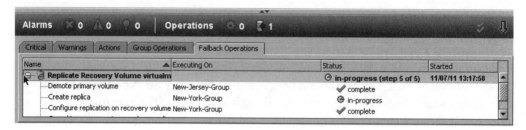

Figure 14.20   Many storage vendors' management tools show SRA tasks in real time. There is educational value in watching this process.

Finally, it's worth stating that after a failover, reprotect, and failback, you may have some nominal cleanup work to do of your own. First, if you use datastore folders, as I do, to organize your datastores logically you will probably find yourself having to relocate datastores into the correct location. By default, when a datastore is remounted it is placed in the default datacenter container rather than its original folder. This is because SRM sees this datastore as brand new to the system. In Figure 14.21 you can see my Web datastore has been dropped into the NYC datacenter rather than in its normal location of SRM Datastores.

Additionally, if you are dealing with block-based storage and a VMware VMFS file system, you will probably need to reinstate the original VMFS volume name. As you might recall, when either a test or a recovery takes place VMFS volumes are resignatured (see Figure 14.22).

Of course, when you carry out a reprotect process the VMFS volume, including its metadata, is replicated to the original Protected Site—this includes the VMFS resignatured volume name. For neatness you might wish to rename this VMFS volume back to its proper name, and if you are using datastore folders you would want to drag and drop the volume to its intended location. Renaming is very easy to do—just click the VMFS volume once, and edit out the reference to "snap-*NNNNNNNN*" in the datastore label.

Figure 14.21   SRM does not know to place your recovered datastores into the correct datastore folder if you use them.

Figure 14.22   Because it's often tricky to know if volumes are snapshots created by tests or recovered volumes, I would recommend you rename them to their original names after running a Recovery Plan.

Unplanned Failover

Since my planned test, I've put my configuration back in place, and I even went so far as to test my Recovery Plan for my protected virtual machines in New York to make sure they work properly. Now I want to document the same process of failover, reprotect, and failback based on a total loss of the Protected Site (New York).

Protected Site Is Dead

To emulate this I did a hard power off of all my ESX hosts in the Protected Site using my ILO cards. I also stopped communications between New York and New Jersey by disabling my routers—the effect of this is to stop all forms of IP-based replication between the two locations. To achieve the same scenario at the Fibre Channel level, I modified my zone configuration on the FC switches to stop replication from occurring between the two locations. This emulates a total catastrophic failure—nothing is running at the Protected Site (New York) anymore. I did a hard power off to emulate a totally unexpected and dirty loss of the system. My main reason for doing this is so that I can document how it feels to manage SRM when this situation happens. You might never get to try this until the fateful day arrives.

The first thing you'll notice when you arrive at the Recovery Site—apart from a lot of worried faces, that is—is that your storage management tools will not be able to communicate to the Protected Site. The main difference when the Protected Site (New York) is unavailable is that as you log in to the Recovery Site (New Jersey) the vSphere client will ask you to log in to the vCenter in the Protected Site (New York)—and this will fail, because remember, the vCenter at the Protected Site is dead. You will be presented with a dialog box stating that there are problems communicating with the vCenter at the Protected site, and if you are in linked mode you'll find that the vCenter for the Protected Site will not appear in the inventory. If you have the vSphere client open at the time of the site outage you will see that the vCenter server and the SRM server will be unavailable. Additionally, you will see in the bottom right-hand corner of the vSphere client that connectivity to the Protected Site vCenter has been lost (see Figure 14.23).

Of course, in this scenario you would want to run your Recovery Plan. It may be possible in this state to run a test of the Recovery Plan, if you wish. Whether you can test a Recovery Plan depends highly on the storage array vendor as some do not allow tests in this DR state. When you do switch to the SRM view you will be asked for the username and password of the vCenter at the Protected Site. There is little point in trying to complete the authentication dialog box as the Protected Site is down and unavailable. So you may as well just click Cancel. Once you have bypassed the authentication dialog box, you will find that both the Protected and Recovery Sites will be marked "Not Connected" and "Unknown" (see Figure 14.24).

In my case, this is because the Recovery Site of New Jersey cannot connect to its Protected Site SRM server in New York. The status of the New York site is unknown because we are unable to communicate or authenticate to it.

Even in this state it may be possible to test the Recovery Plan prior to running the recovery test. When you do this you will find that the option to "Replicate recent changes to recovery site" will be dimmed in the dialog box (see Figure 14.25), because in this disconnected state the SRM and SRA cannot work together to sync up the storage on the Protected and Recovery Sites.

Figure 14.23   There are many reasons you cannot connect to a vCenter. Here, the New York location was made unavailable deliberately.

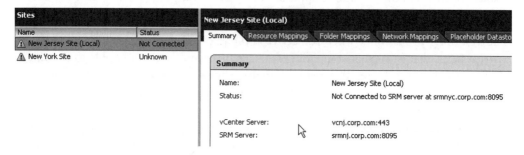

Figure 14.24   The status of the New York site is Unknown. The New Jersey site cannot connect to New York as it is down and unavailable.

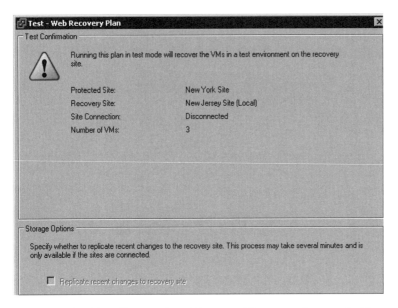

Figure 14.25   If the Protected and Recovery Sites are not connected the ability to replicate recent changes becomes unavailable.

Similarly, when you attempt to run the Recovery Plan you should find the option to carry out a planned migration will be disabled, as this is only available when both the Protected and Recovery Sites are connected (see Figure 14.26).

When you run the Recovery Plan you will see a number of errors in the early stages. The SRM service will attempt to trigger a replication event at step 1, "Pre-synchronize storage," in an attempt to capture recent changes, but clearly there is no guarantee that this will be possible. If the storage arrays are unable to communicate, SRM will bypass the synchronization process. It will also attempt to power off VMs in the Protected Site, despite the fact that the Protected Site is unavailable. After all, SRM cannot power off VMs at the Protected Site if it's a smoking crater—there would be nothing to power off. Additionally, you will see errors as SRM at the Recovery Site attempts to "Prepare Protected Site VMs for Migration" and "Synchronize Storage" a second time. You should regard these errors as benign and to be expected, given that they are all tasks in the Recovery Plan that require a connection from the Recovery Site to the Protected Site. As you can see in Figure 14.27 at step 8, "Change Recovery Site Storage to Writeable," the storage has been successfully presented and VMs are in the process of being powered on.

At the end of the plan you should see that the plan is marked as "Disaster Recovery Complete" and other plans that contain the same Protection Groups will be marked with the same status (see Figure 14.28).

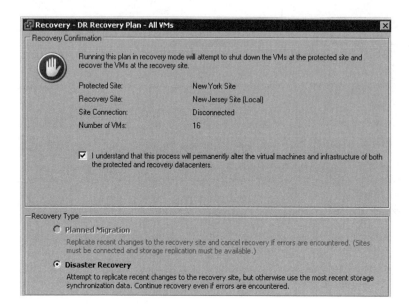

Figure 14.26   Planned migrations are only available when both the Protected and Recovery Sites are connected together.

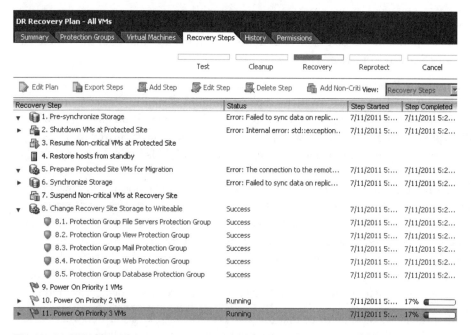

Figure 14.27   Certain errors are expected as SRM tries to execute all the recovery stages but cannot because the Protected Site is unavailable.

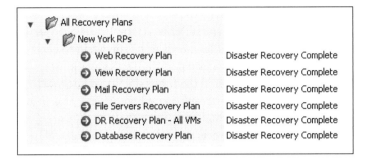

Figure 14.28   Green arrows on Protection Groups, together with a Disaster Recovery Complete status, indicate a successful outcome from a DR plan.

Planned Failback after a Disaster

Of course, the reprotect and failback process can only proceed by definition if the Protected Site (New York) is available again. In this respect, it shouldn't be that different from the failback process covered earlier in this chapter. Nonetheless, for completeness I wanted to cover this. Now, I don't intend to cut and paste the entire previous section. For brevity I only want to cover what made this failback look and feel different. The extent of your work to failback will depend highly on the nature of your disaster. Let's say, for example, you invoked DR and ran your Recovery Plan because a hurricane was on its way. At the time of running the Recovery Plan you have no idea of the extent of damage you might incur. You might be lucky and find that although many structures have been destroyed, your facility has more or less remained intact. In this scenario, you would confirm the underlying integrity of your physical infrastructure (power, servers, storage, and network) was in a fit state, as well as your virtual infrastructure in the shape of vSphere and SRM was in a good state, and carry out quite a graceful and seamless failback. If, on the other hand, you experienced extensive damage you would be faced with a rebuild of your vSphere environment (and indeed, major repair work to your building!). This could well entail a brand-new installation of vSphere and SRM, and necessitate re-pairing the sites, configuring inventory mappings, and creating Protection Groups—in short, everything we covered in the early chapters of this book.

To emulate this I powered back on my ESX—I allowed the system to come up in any order to generate a whole series of errors and failures. I wanted to make this as difficult as possible, and so made sure my storage array, SQL, vCenter, and SRM server were all back online again, but starting up in the wrong order. I thought I would repeat this process again to see if there were any unexpected gotchas I could warn you about.

Once you have logged in to both the Protected and Recovery Sites, the first thing you will see is that the Recovery Plans will have a status warning on them stating that "Original

Protected VMs are not shutdown," and you will be asked to run the recovery process again (see Figure 14.29). This does not affect the recovered VMs. As the Protected Site was not contactable during the disaster the Recovery Plan needs to be run again to clean up the environment. As far as the Protected Site is concerned, it thinks the relationship is still one where it is the Protected Site (New York), and the other site was the recovery location (New Jersey). The failover to the Recovery Site was carried out when it was in an unavailable state. If you like, it's as if both New York and New Jersey believe they are the Protected Site. Running the Recovery Plan again corrects this relationship to make New York the Recovery Site and New Jersey the Protected Site.

In this scenario, the VMs will still be registered on the Protected Site, rather than being replaced with the shadow VMs that have the underscore as their prefix. Once this mandatory recovery has been completed, you will be at the stage at which a reprotect phase can be run, and you can consider a failback to the original Protected Site. Before issuing the reprotect plan it's perhaps worth thinking about the realities of a true disaster. If the disaster destroyed your storage layer at the Protected Site, and new storage has to be provisioned, it will need to be configured for replication. That volume of data may be beyond what is reasonable to synchronize across your site-to-site links. It's highly likely in this case that the new array for the Protected Site will need to be brought to the DR location so that it can be synchronized locally first, before being shipped to the Protected Site locale.

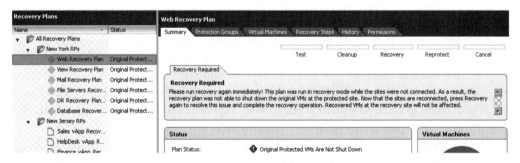

Figure 14.29   As SRM was unable to gracefully shut down VMs in the Protected Site, these are marked as not being shut down.

Summary

As you have seen, the actual process of running a plan does not differ that greatly from running a test. The implications of executing a Recovery Plan are so immense that I can hardly find the words to describe them. Clearly, a planned failover and failback is much easier to manage than one caused by a true failure. I've spent some time on this topic because this is chiefly why you buy the product, and perhaps if you are lucky you will never have to do this for real.

Despite this, if you look back through the chapter, most of what I have written is about failback, not failover. This improved automation will be very welcome by some of the big companies that use SRM. I know of certain banks, financial institutions, and big pharmaceuticals which test their DR strategies rigorously—some to the degree of invoking them for real once per quarter, despite not actually experiencing a real disaster. The idea behind this is twofold. First, the only way to know if your DR plan will work is if you use it. Think of it like a UPS system—there's nothing like pulling the power supply to see if a UPS actually works. Second, it means the IT staff is constantly preparing and testing the strategy, and improving and updating it as the Protected Site changes. For large organizations the lack of an automated failback process was a significant pain point in the previous releases of the SRM product.

Perhaps this will be a good opportunity to move on to another chapter. I'm a firm believer in having a Plan B in case Plan A doesn't work out. At the very least, you could abandon SRM and do everything we have done so far manually. Perhaps the next chapter will finally give you the perspective to understand the benefits of the SRM product. One of the frequent cries I hear about SRM is folks saying, "Well, we could script all that." Of course, these people are right; they could more or less cook up a home-brewed DR solution using scripting tools. What they forget is that this needs to be constantly maintained and kept up-to-date. Our industry is somewhat notorious for people building their own solutions, and then poorly documenting them. If I could say one thing about home-brewed scripting solutions it would be this: "There used to be this clever guy called Bob, who built this excellent scripted solution. Anyway, he left the company about six months ago, and now I'm in charge…"

Chapter 15

Scripting Site Recovery

One of the interesting ironies or paradoxes that came to my mind when writing this book was what if, at the point of requiring my DR plan, VMware's Site Recovery Manager failed or was unavailable? Put another way, what's our Recovery Plan for SRM? Joking aside, it's a serious issue worth considering; there's little point in using any technology without a Plan B if Plan A doesn't pan out as we expected.[1]

Given that the key to any Recovery Plan is replication of data to a Recovery Site, at the heart of the issue the most important element is taken care of by your storage array, not by VMware's SRM. Remember, all that SRM is doing is automating a very manual process. Of course, this is not the case if you are using vSphere Replication (VR). So there are really two main agendas behind this chapter: Show how to do everything SRM does manually in case our Plan A doesn't work out, and show how incredibly useful SRM is in

---

1. I would like to give a special acknowledgment to four individuals who helped directly with this chapter, with specific reference to the PowerShell aspect. Thank you to Carter Shanklin of VMware, who was happy to answer my emails when he was product manager for VMware PowerShell. Additionally, thank you to Hal Rottenberg, whom I first met via the VMware Community Forum. Hal is the author of *Managing VMware Infrastructure with PowerShell*. If you wish to learn more about the power of PowerShell I recommend watching and joining the VMware VMTN Community Forum, and purchasing Hal's book. Thank you to Luc Dekens of the PowerShell forum who was especially helpful in explaining how to create a virtual switch with PowerShell. Finally, thank you to Alan Renouf of VMware, whom I have known for some time through the London User Group. Alan has been especially helpful in this edition of my book on SRM both in this chapter and in Chapter 11, Custom Recovery Plans. Alan and Luc, together with Glen Sizemore, Arnim van Lieshout, and John Medd, recently collaborated to produce *VMware vSphere PowerCLI Reference: Automating vSphere Administration*, a book which sits on my bookshelf and which I highly recommend you read.

automating this process. Hopefully you will see in this chapter how hard life is without SRM. Like any automated or scripted process, you don't really see the advantages until you know what the manual process is like.

With that in mind, I could have started the book with this chapter as Chapter 1 or 2, but I figured you would want to dive deep into SRM, which is the topic of this book, and save this content for the end. I also figured that structuring the chapters the way I have would give you an idea of what SRM is doing in the background to make your life much easier. The big advantage of SRM to me is that it grows and reacts to changes in the Protected Site, something a manual process would need much higher levels of maintenance to achieve.

As part of my preparation for writing this chapter, I decided to delete the Protection Groups and Recovery Plans associated with our bidirectional configuration from my Recovery Site (New Jersey). I did this to create a scenario where it appeared there was no SRM configuration in the Recovery Site. The manual recovery of virtual machines will require some storage management, stopping the current cycle of replication, and making the remote volume a primary volume and read-writable. While SRM does this automatically for you using the SRA from your storage vendor, in a manual recovery you will have to do this yourself. This is assuming you still have access to the array at the Protected Site, as with a planned execution of your DR plan. Additionally, once the replication has been stopped, you will have to grant the ESX hosts in the Recovery Site access to the last good snapshot that was taken.

Once the ESX hosts are granted access to the volumes, they will have to be manually rescanned to make sure the VMFS volume has been displayed. Based on our requirements and the visibility of the LUN, we will have the option either to not resignature or to force a resignature of the VMFS volume. After we have handled the storage side of things, we will have to edit the VMX file of each virtual machine and map it to the correct network. Then we will be able to start adding each virtual machine into the Recovery Site, each time telling the vSphere client which cluster, folder, and resource pool to use. In an ideal world, some of this virtual machine management could be scripted using VMware's various SDKs, such as the Perl Scripting ToolKit, the PowerCLI, or the vCenter SDK with some language of your choice—VB, C#, and so on. I intend to use PowerCLI for VMware as an example. As you will see, with scripting, the process is laborious and deeply tedious. Critically, it's quite slow as well, and this will impact the speed of your recovery process. Think of all those RTOs and RPOs...

There are many ways to script a recovery process—as many ways as there are system administrators. But the basics remain the same: At some stage, storage must be presented to the hosts at the Recovery Site, and VMs must be registered and powered on. I've seen many different examples of doing this. One interesting example was presented at the London User Group in 2011. Our guest, Gabrie Van Zantan, presented a solution he built using PowerCLI that would export the current configuration of an existing site (clusters, resource pools, folders, and VM names) to a .csv file, and then at the DR location this would be "imported" to the system, effectively creating a mirror image of the production location. I thought this was a very interesting approach to take. In this chapter, I won't try to emulate Gabrie's configuration; I mention it as an example of how many different approaches there are to this issue. Instead, I will be focusing on the core basics that allow for recovery to take place.

Scripted Recovery for a Test

One of the main tasks to consider if you are planning for a totally scripted DR solution concerns handling storage. The backbone of all DR work is replication, and if your ESXi hosts cannot access the storage and register a VM to the system, your manual DR plan will fail at the first hurdle. With ESXi's rich support for different types of storage, this adds a layer of complexity, especially if you are using all three storage protocols that are supported.

Managing the Storage

Without an SRA, we will have to engage more with the vendor's tools for controlling snapshots and replication. This area is very vendor-specific, so I refer you to your vendor's documentation. In general terms, this means taking a snapshot at the Recovery Site array of the LUNs/volumes currently being protected, and then presenting that snapshot volume to the ESX hosts. In the case of block-based storage, the ESX hosts would need to have their HBA rescanned and the VMFS volume resignatured to make it accessible to the ESX hosts. In the case of NFS, it would merely be the process of making sure the snapshot was an NFS export and accessible to the hosts, and then mounting the NFS export to the hosts. In terms of this book, it would be too much to explain how this is done for each storage vendor I have available in my lab. But as an example, on a Dell EqualLogic system this would be achieved by taking a clone of the most recent replica (see Figure 15.1).

When the clone volume replica wizard runs, you assign the replica a new name and allow access to it from the ESX hosts (see Figure 15.2).

At this stage, the storage management is dealt with and the next step is to allow the ESX hosts to see the storage. Of course, there is always the possibility that storage vendors provide their own PowerShell or remote CLI utilities that will allow you to automate this stage as well.

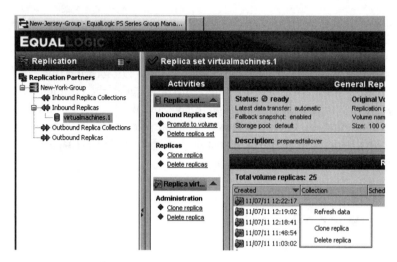

Figure 15.1 Taking a clone of the most recent replica on a Dell EqualLogic system

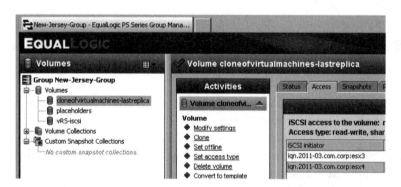

Figure 15.2 Modifying the ACL on the Access tab of the volume to allow access to the replica from the ESX hosts

Rescanning ESX Hosts

You should be more than aware of how to do a rescan of an ESX host either from the GUI or from the CLI, but what you are looking for is a new VMFS volume to appear. This rescan has to be done once per affected ESX host, and it would be quite laborious to do this via the vSphere client (and again, if you made a mistake with the storage layer). Of course, you could log in with PuTTy and use esxcfg-rescan or the vCLI's esxcfg-rescan.pl script. Personally, I prefer to use PowerCLI. The following snippet of

PowerCLI rescans all the ESX hosts in vCenter, which is much more efficient from a scripting perspective:

```
connect-viserver vcnj.corp.com -user corp\administrator -password vmware
get-vmhost | get-vmhoststorage -rescanallhba
```

The syntax of the above snippet of PowerShell is relatively easy to explain. `Get-vmhost` retrieves all the names of the ESX hosts in the vCenter that you authenticated to, and this is piped to the command `get-vmhoststorage`, to then rescan all the ESX hosts. `Get-vmhoststorage` supports a `-rescanALLhba` switch, which does exactly what you think it does.

Resignaturing VMFS Volumes

Now we need to mount the VMFS volume to the ESX hosts. From a PowerCLI perspective, no cmdlets currently exist to carry out a resignature of a VMFS volume. However, it is possible to dive into the SDK. As we saw in earlier chapters, we can use the Add Storage Wizard to resignature VMFS volumes, and both the Service Console and vCLI contain `esxcfg-volume` and `vicfg-volume` commands which allow you to list LUNs/volumes that contain snapshots or replicated data. From the vCLI you can use the following command to list LUNs/volumes that are snapshots or replicas:

```
vicfg-volume.pl -l --server=vcnj.corp.com --username=corp\administrator
  --password=vmware --vihost=esx3.corp.com
```

This will produce the following output:

```
VMFS UUID/label: 4da70540-50ec1cd9-843d-0015600ea5bc/dell-eql-virtualmachines
Can mount: Yes
Can resignature: Yes
Extent name: naa.6006048c68e415b4d1c49e2aac2d4b4a:1    range: 0 - 100095 (MB)
```

With the `escfg-volume` and `vicfg-volume` commands you have the choice of either mounting the VMFS volume under its original name, or resignaturing it. To mount the volume *without* a resignature you would use:

```
vicfg-volume.pl -m 4b6d8fc2-339977f3-d2cb-001560aa6f7c
  dell-eql-virtualmachines --server=vcnj.corp.com
  --username=corp\administrator --password=vmware --vihost=esx3.corp.com
```

If you did want to carry out a resignature you would simply replace the –m switch to mount with the –r switch, like so:

```
vicfg-volume.pl -r  4b6d8fc2-339977f3-d2cb-001560aa6f7c
  dell-eql-virtualmachines --server=vcnj.corp.com
  --username=corp\administrator --password=vmware --vihost=esx3.corp.com
```

If you want to rename the VMFS volume as SRM does after a resignature you can use this piece of PowerShell. In this case, the PowerCLI searches for my resignatured volume called "snap-17ab25ce-dell-eql-virtualmachines," and renames it to "dell-virtualmachines-copy":

```
set-datastore -datastore (get-datastore *dell-eql-virtualmachines) - name
   dell-virtualmachines-copy
```

Mounting NFS Exports

Of course, your environment might not be using block-based storage and VMFS; you may be using NFS instead. To some degree, automating this is much easier because you do not have the issue of potentially resignaturing VMFS volumes. In the example below I use the get-vmhost cmdlet to retrieve all the hosts in the vCenter, and then use the foreach-object cmdlet to say that for each ESX host ($vmhost) found in the array, carry out the NFS mounting process using the new-datastore –nfs cmdlet:

```
connect-viserver vcnj.corp.com -user corp\administrator -password vmware
foreach-object ($vmhost in (get-vmhost))
        {
new-datastore -nfs -vmhost $vmhost -nfshost 172.168.3.89 -path  /vol/
   cloneofreplica-virtualmachines -name virtualmachines
        }
```

Creating an Internal Network for the Test

It is part of my standard configuration on all my ESX hosts that I create a port group called "internal" which is on a dedicated switch with no physical NIC uplinked to it. However, you might wish to more closely emulate the way SRM does its tests of Recovery Plans, and create a "testbubble" network. Creating virtual switches in PowerCLI is very easy, and again we can use the logic of foreach-object to apply this to all the ESX hosts.

```
connect-viserver vcnj.corp.com -username corp\administrator -password
   vmware
foreach-object ($vmhost in (get-vmhost))
{
$vs =  new-virtualswitch -vmhost $vmhost -name "recovery-vswitch1"
$internal =  new-virtualportgroup -virtualswitch $vs -name "testbubble-1
   group"
}
```

IMPORTANT NOTE

Remember, when you're dealing with port groups on Standard vSwitches (SvSwitches) the label in this case, "testbubble-1 group," is case-sensitive.

Adding Virtual Machines to the Inventory

The next stage involves interrogating the datastores that were mounted earlier in this exercise. If you were doing this manually, it would involve browsing the datastores and looking for the VM directories that contain .vmx files, and then right-clicking each one and adding it to the inventory. While using the Add to Inventory Wizard, you would need to select a vSphere cluster, ESX host, and folder and resource pool location for the VM. Remember, you would have to repeat these steps for every virtual machine that needs to be recovered. This is made more complicated by the fact that there is no "inventory mapping" as there is in SRM, so you will be forced to register the VMs to the correct resource pool and folder. I think it's in this area where Gabrie's approach becomes interesting. If we had a record of all the VMs from the Protected Site, a .csv file that listed all the VMs together with their correct resource pool and folder location, life would be much simpler. Essentially, this .csv file would become not unlike the SRM database that holds the inventory mapping data.

It is possible to automate the process of adding a virtual machine to an ESX host (not a cluster) using the command-line ESX host tool called vmware-cmd; unfortunately, this tool cannot handle vCenter metadata, such as folder location and resource pools. Perhaps a better approach is to use some PowerCLI. Once we know the path to the VM, we can think about trying to register a VM. There is a New-VM cmdlet which we can use to handle the full registration process, including the ESX host, resource pool, and folder location in the vCenter inventory, like so:

```
connect-viserver vcnj.corp.com -username corp\administrator -password
  vmware
new-vm -vmhost esx3.corp.com -vmfilepath "[dell-virtualmachines-copy]
  fs05/fs05.vmx" -resourcepool "file servers" -location "file servers"
```

Remember, this registration process would have to be repeated for every VMFS volume, for every VM needing recovery. That would be very time-consuming, given the time it would take to complete every registration. A better method is to use PowerCLI's ability to query datastores for files ending with ".vmx" and then pipelining the results to the new-vm cmdlet.

```
connect-viserver vcnj.corp.com -username corp\administrator -password
   vmware
dir 'vmstores:\vcnj.corp.com@443\nj datacenter\dell-virtualmachines-
   copy\*\*.vmx' | % {new-vm -host $vmhost -vmfilepath $_.datastorefullpath}
```

If your datastore and VM placement were more discrete the same command could contain the -resource pool and –location parameters as well:

```
connect-viserver vcnj.corp.com -username corp\administrator -password
   vmware
dir 'vmstores:\vcnj.corp.com@443\nj datacenter\db-copy\*\*.vmx' | %
   {new-vm -host $vmhost -vmfilepath $_.datastorefullpath -resourcepool "DB"
   -location "DB"}
```

Of course, there are many ways to approach this complex registration process. For example, Luc Dekens has a rather good function called Register-VMX which he explains in detail on his site:

www.lucd.info/2009/12/02/raiders-of-the-lost-vmx/

You might find that you have a blend of different VMs in the same datastore, but different VMs need to be located in the correct resource pool and folder. If that's the case, you could register the VMs first, and then move them with:

```
connect-viserver vcnj.corp.com -username corp\administrator -password
   vmware
move-vm -vm db* -destination (get-folder -name db)
move-vm -vm db* -destination (get-resourcepool -name db)
move-vm -vm fs* -destination (get-folder -name "file servers")
move-vm -vm db* -destination (get-resourcepool -name "file servers")
```

Fixing VMX Files for the Network

One of the critical tasks SRM automates is the mapping of the VM to the correct network port group on a vSwitch. If you add your virtual machine into the vCenter first (our next task) you can automate the property change (as I mentioned previously) with PowerShell for VMware. The commands required to achieve this depend very much on whether you are working with SvSwitches or Distributed vSwitches (DvSwitches). With SvSwitches it is merely an issue of searching for the VMs that have a certain port group label, such as "vlan11," and replacing them with the desired port group—say, "testbubble-1 group":

```
get-vm | get-networkadapter | sort-object -property "networkname" | where
   {'vlan11' -contains $_.networkname} | set-networkadapter -networkname
   "testbubble-1 group" -confirm:$false
```

If, on the other hand, you are working with the DvSwitch, it is a little bit trickier. Currently, there is a gap between the functionality of the cmdlets for SvSwitches and DvSwitches. The piece of PowerCLI shown above simply won't work currently for a manually recovered VM which was configured for a DvSwitch from a different vCenter, because a VM that is configured for a DvSwitch holds unique identifiers for the DvSwitch at the Protected Site, and these simply don't exist at the Recovery Site. When this VM is manually recovered without SRM because no inventory mapping process is in place, the VM will lose its connection to the DvSwitch as it now resides in a new vSwitch. Essentially, the VM becomes orphaned from its network configuration. This shows itself as an "invalid backing" for the network adapter.

You might be interested to know that the aforementioned Luc Dekens (of http://lucd.info/ fame) has a whole series of articles on handling DvSwitches using PowerCLI. He's even gone so far as to write his functions (which behave just like regular cmdlets) to address this functionality gap in the PowerCLI. I wouldn't be surprised if there are new cmdlets in the next release of the PowerCLI to address this limitation. For the moment, unfortunately, it's perhaps simpler to have one vCenter for both sites. In this case, the ESX hosts in the DR site would share the same switch configuration as the ESX hosts in the primary site. However, a word of warning: Such a configuration runs entirely counter to the structure of VMware SRM that demands two different vCenters for every Protected and Recovery Site. So, if you cook up your manually scripted solution and you later decide to adopt SRM, you will have a great deal of pruning and grafting to do to meet the SRM requirements.

Specifically, Luc has been working on DvSwitch equivalents of the SvSwitch cmdlets called `get-networkadapter` and `set-networkadapter`. Luc's `get-dvswnetworkadapter` and `set-dvswnetworkadapter` functions are much easier to use. To use his functions, create or open your preferred PowerShell profile. If you don't know what PowerShell profiles are or how to create them, this Microsoft Web page is a good starting point:

   http://msdn.microsoft.com/en-us/library/bb613488%28VS.85%29.aspx

Next, visit Luc's website at the location below and then copy and paste his functions into the profile:

   http://lucd.info/?p=1871

Using these functions, you can run commands such as the example below to set every VM that begins with `ss0*` to use `vlan55`:

```
get-dvswnetworkadapter (get-vm ss0*) | set-dvswnetworkadapter -networkname
  "vlan55" -StartConnected:$true
```

I'm sure Luc will carry on improving and extending the features of his functions, and I heartily recommend his series of articles on PowerCLI and DvSwitches.

Summary

As you can see, the manual process is very labor-intensive, which is to be expected by the use of the word *manual*. You might have gotten the impression that this issue can be fixed by some whiz-bang PowerShell scripts. You might even have thought, "This sucks; why do I need SRM if I have these PowerShell scripts?" However, it's not as simple as that, for two main reasons. First, there's no real support for this home-brewed DR, and second, you can test your scripts all you want, but then your environment will change and those scripts will go out of date and will need endless reengineering and retesting.

In fact, the real reason I wanted to write this chapter is to show how painful the manual process is, to give you a real feel for the true benefits of SRM. I know there are some big corporations that have decided to go down this route, primarily because of a number of factors. First, they have the time, the people, and the resources to manage it—and do it well. Second, they were probably doing this manually even before SRM came on the scene. At first glance their manual process probably looked more sophisticated than the SRM 1.0 product; they might feel that way about SRM 4.0. Personally, I think as SRM evolves and improves it will become increasingly harder to justify a home-brewed configuration. I think that tipping point will probably come with SRM 5.0.

Chapter 16

Upgrading from SRM 4.1 to SRM 5.0

Throughout my career I've been asked this one question over and over again: "What works best—an upgrade or a clean install?" Without fail the folks asking this question nearly always know the answer. What they really are asking me is whether I think the upgrade process is robust enough to justify its use. I've always been happy to upgrade within releases—say, from 3.0, 3.1, 3.5, and so on. My personal rule has always been to carry out a clean installation when the version's major number changes—from Windows 2003 to Windows 2008, for example. With that in mind, I think it's perfectly feasible to have a combination of upgrades and clean installs. It makes sense that VMware customers would want to upgrade their vCenter environment. Even with a relatively small environment it takes some time to add all the hosts, create clusters, potentially configure resource pools, and create folders. When it comes to other components like ESX hosts, I just don't see why people would want to upgrade a hypervisor. In an ideal world, there should be no data that isn't reproducible. I speak as someone who has invested a lot of time in scripted installations for both ESX and PowerCLI scripts for vCenter. In the course of a year, my labs are endlessly rebuilt and it makes no sense to do that work constantly by hand. So when I am asked that question, I often respond, "Why do you ask me a question you already know the answer to?" The fact is that clean installations are destined to always provide a high ratio of success since there is no existing configuration data to be ported to a new environment. Given the complexity and flexibility available in most technologies, it seems inevitable that more complications are likely to arise from upgrades than from clean installs, but to say so seems to be both a truism and rather trite. Personally, I'm one of those loony guys who upgrades as soon as a new release comes out. For example, I upgraded from Mac OS X Leopard to Lion on the very day Apple shipped the new version of its OS. I do this largely from an academic interest in knowing about pitfalls and perils long before any of my customers embark on the same path some months (and in some cases years!) later. I regard this as a foolhardy approach from a production environment where upgrades must be carried out cautiously and judiciously. This chapter is not intended to be a thoroughly comprehensive guide to upgrading from vSphere 4 to vSphere 5; for that I recommend you consult other literature that covers this process in more detail. Nonetheless, it would be difficult to explain the SRM upgrade process properly without also covering the vSphere 4 to vSphere 5 upgrade path. As you know, SRM 5.0 requires vSphere 5, and if you were previously a customer of SRM 4.1 you would need to carry out both a platform upgrade as well as an upgrade to SRM 5.0 to be on the latest release. A successful upgrade begins with a backup of your entire vSphere environment, including components such as SRM, View, and vCloud Director. Your upgrade plan should also include a rollback routine should the upgrade process falter—and I recommend taking snapshots and backups along the way so that you can roll back in stages during the upgrade. I make regular use of VMware snapshots in my upgrade processes; that's because everything I do is based on virtual machines. In some cases I will take the extra precaution of taking hot clones of critical VMs just in case there is an issue with the snapshot once it has been reverted.

Like all upgrades, the process follows a particular order. Many steps are mandatory, and some are optional, and they must be undertaken in the right order to ensure that the requisites for the upgrade are successful. You might also want to consider the possibility that a clean installation may actually be the fastest route to your goal. So, if you need SRM for a particular project, and lead-in times are narrow, you might find a fresh install meets your needs more directly. It's also worth stating that individual steps in the upgrade process may not necessarily require or support an in-place upgrade. For instance, many of my customers prefer to evacuate an ESX host of all its VMs using maintenance mode, and then execute a clean scripted installation of the ESX server software. Most of these customers have invested a lot of time and effort in automating their ESX host builds. This pays off in a number of places: consistency, rebuilding hosts if they fail, and upgrading ESX from one release to another. As for this chapter, you will find that I will take the in-place approach wherever possible—although in the real world an upgrade process might actually use a combination of methods.

As stated previously, a successful upgrade begins with a backup and carrying out the steps in the correct manner. If you want to back up your existing SRM 4.1 you can do this by backing up the SQL database that backs the installation, together with the vmware.xml file that defines some of the core configuration settings. You should also consider a backup of any scripts from the SRM server, together with any ancillary files that make the current solution work—for example, you may have a .csv file that you use for the re-IP of your VMs. You should also thoroughly test that your existing Recovery Plans and Protection Groups work correctly, because only the Protection Groups and Recovery Plans that are in a valid state are saved during the upgrade. If they are not in a valid state they are discarded.

Below is a checklist that outlines the stages that are required. I've marked some as optional, which means they can be skipped and returned to later. I would have to say that my attitude regarding what is optional and what is required is a very personal one. For instance, some people regard an upgrade of VMware Tools as required, while others would see it as optional, as VMs will continue to function normally even when they are out of date. The way I look at upgrades is that in the main, customers want to install the upgrade in the shortest possible time. If there are any nonmandatory steps, they can defer the upgrade until a later date, and perhaps roll out over a longer period. This stealthier approach to upgrades limits the steps to just the bare minimum required to become functional.

1. Run the vCenter Host Agent Pre-Upgrade Checker (optional).

2. Upgrade vCenter.

3. Upgrade the vSphere client.

4. Upgrade the vCenter Update Manager.

5. Upgrade the Update Manager plug-in.

6. Upgrade third-party plug-ins (optional).

7. Upgrade ESX hosts.

8. Upgrade SRM.

9. Upgrade VMware Tools (optional).

10. Upgrade the virtual hardware (optional).

11. Upgrade the VMFS volumes (optional).

12. Upgrade Distributed vSwitches (optional).

Upgrading vSphere

The first stage in upgrading SRM is to upgrade vSphere from version 4 to version 5. In all of my upgrades throughout my career I've always ensured that I was just one version revision away from the new release and upgrade release. It follows that the closer the revisions the greater your chance of success. There are two reasons for this. First, the deviation of difference between the releases is kept to a minimum, and in my experience vendors plough most of their testing efforts against upgrading from the immediate release prior to the new release; the farther back your platform is from the new release the greater the chance that problems can occur. Second, if you keep on top of patches and mainte-nance of vSphere 4 you won't face a double-upgrade—in other words, having to upgrade vSphere 4.0 to vSphere 4.1, for example, before upgrading to vSphere 5. As soon as your build lags massively behind the current release this can be a compelling reason to cut to the chase and opt for a clean installation.

I would begin the upgrade process at the Protected Site, and complete those tasks there initially. After you have upgraded vCenter from version 4 to version 5, you will find the SRM 4.1 service will no longer start or function as SRM 4.1 is not forward-compatible with vCenter 5. If the Protected Site experiences an unexpected disaster, you would still have a valid vCenter 4.1/SRM 4.1 configuration at the Recovery Site from which you could still run a Recovery Plan. The Protected and Recovery Sites would not be able to communicate to each other because of this version mismatch, and the pairing between the sites would be lost, with the Protected Site marked as "Not Responding" in the SRM interface (see Figure 16.1).

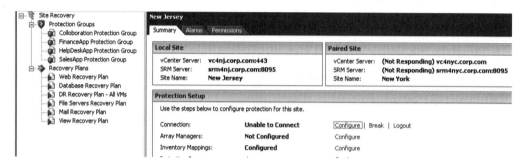

Figure 16.1   The New Jersey site, based on SRM 4.1, cannot connect with the New York site, which was upgraded to vSphere 5 and SRM 5.

Step 1: Run the vCenter Host Agent Pre-Upgrade Checker

Before embarking on a vCenter upgrade I heartily recommend running the upgrade checker that ships on the .iso file for vCenter. The utility actually updates itself from VMware.com and as such keeps track of new upgrade issues as they are discovered. Run the utility before you start the vCenter/ESX portion of the upgrade. When the utility has run you will be asked to select the DSN used to connect the vCenter together with the database credentials. Once this has passed, the checker interrogates the vSphere environment, including the ESX hosts (see Figure 16.2).

Step 2: Upgrade vCenter

Before upgrading vCenter you should uninstall the Guided Consolidation feature of vCenter if you have installed it. Guided Consolidation has been deprecated in the

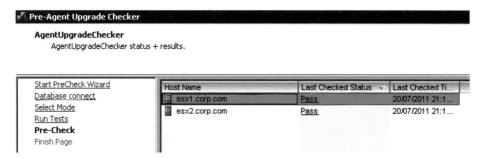

Figure 16.2 A successful outcome from the upgrade checker utility

vSphere 5 release, and upgrades will not proceed if it is installed in the current vCenter. There's a very good chance that this will not be the case; for some reason the Guided Consolidation feature didn't catch on among my customers or peer group. I think this was largely because many had already P2V'd their environments some time ago. This has been an issue for some time and did affect some vSphere 4.1 upgrades. In fact, I had problems uninstalling the Guided Consolidation feature from my test vCenter 4 environment that I created for this chapter. I had to refer to VMware KB1025657 (http://kb.vmware.com/kb/1025657) to correctly remove it from the system. During my build of my vCenter environment I had to change the Windows drive letter used for the DVD/CD from D: to E:. I found that the easiest way to resolve this issue was to swap the drive letters around on the vCenter, and then the uninstall of Guided Consolidation worked perfectly without a problem.

The other issue you will need to consider is what user account to use for the vCenter upgrade. vCenter 4 introduced full support for Windows Authentication to Microsoft SQL—something I've wanted for some time—so you may wish to remind yourself of how vCenter was installed initially so that you use the same service account for the upgrade. In my case, I created an account called vcdbuser-nyc, and gave that account local administrator rights on the vCenter server. This same account was used to create the Microsoft SQL DSN configuration using Windows Authentication. So, before mounting the vSphere 5 .iso file, I logged in to the same account I had used for my initial installation.

Once you have worked your way through the usual layers of the media UI, you should see a message indicating that the installer has found that a previous release of the vCenter Server software is installed (see Figure 16.3).

Work your way through the usual suspects of the EULA and so forth, and you will have an opportunity to input your vCenter 5 license key. It is possible to carry on with the upgrade without this license key; without a license key your vCenter 5 system will be in evaluation mode for 60 days. After accepting the default settings for the database options, you will

Figure 16.3   The vCenter 5.0 installer has detected that vCenter 4.1 is already installed.

receive a warning indicating that the installed version of Update Manager is not compatible with vCenter 5, and will itself need upgrading at some later stage (see Figure 16.4).

Once this warning is confirmed, the system will ask you for confirmation that you wish to upgrade the vCenter database from one suitable for version 4 to one suitable for version 5 (see Figure 16.5). If you have ever carried out an intermediary upgrade of vCenter from one subrelease to another you should recognize this dialog box, as it has been present in vCenter upgrades for some time. Once this is confirmed, you will be asked if you would like the system to automatically upgrade the vCenter Agent that is installed in every ESX host managed by vCenter (see Figure 16.6).

Next, you will be asked for the password of the service account used to start vCenter (see Figure 16.7). If you use Windows Authentication with Microsoft SQL, this will be the same account used to create the DSN and start the upgrade. If you're using Microsoft

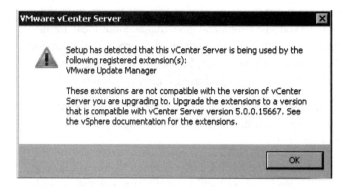

Figure 16.4   The vCenter 5 installer detects that other vCenter services are incompatible with it, and will also need upgrading.

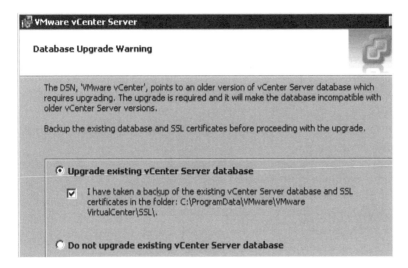

Figure 16.5 vCenter will not only upgrade the vCenter software, but the database back end as well.

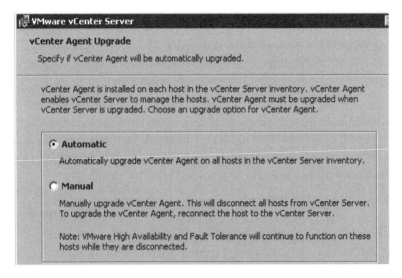

Figure 16.6 The vCenter upgrade process also upgrades the VPX agent on ESX 4.1 hosts, allowing them to be managed by the new vCenter.

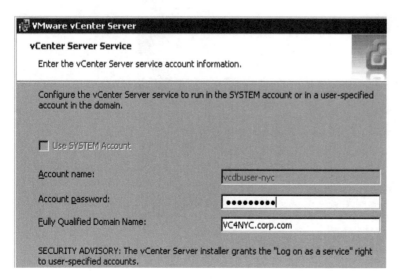

Figure 16.7   My upgrade was triggered using the vcdbuser-nyc account that will use Windows Authentication to the SQL server, and will also be the service account for the vCenter Server Services.

SQL Authentication you may need to provide separate database and service account credentials to complete this process. All in all, Windows Authentication is much simpler and more secure, and I switched to it as soon as VMware fully supported it.

At this stage you may receive an error stating "The fully qualified domain name cannot be resolved." At the time of this writing, there is a small bug in the vSphere 5 release candidate that is generating this error message, and hopefully it will be resolved by the time of GA. I found that vCenter could indeed resolve the FQDN via both ping and nslookup tests, so I took this to be a benign error that would not affect the upgrade.

Next, you will be asked to set the path for both the vCenter Server software and the new inventory service. Once these paths are set, you can accept the defaults for the TCP port numbers for both the vCenter and Inventory Service, respectively. I've never had to change these defaults, but you may need to review them in light of your datacenter security practices. At the end of the upgrade wizard you can set the amount of memory to allocate to Java Virtual Machine (JVM) memory. This control was introduced in vSphere 4.1 and allows the administrator to scale the amount of RAM allocated to the JVM system. Select the radio button that reflects the scale of your environment; this parameter can be changed after the installation, if necessary (see Figure 16.8).

Finally, you will be asked if you want to "bump" (increase) the ephemeral ports value. This somewhat cryptic dialog box is all about the default settings for ephemeral ports used on

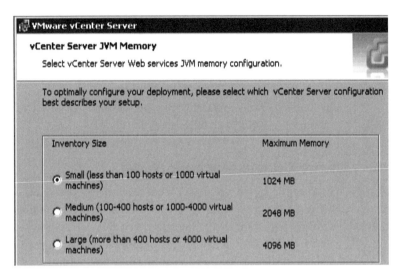

Figure 16.8 Since vCenter 4.1, the administrator can allocate a portion of memory to the JVM relative to the scale of the vCenter deployment.

Distributed vSwitches (DvSwitches). Ephemeral ports are a type of port group setting that allows a VM to grab a port on a DvSwitch, and then hand it back to the "pool" of ports when it is powered down. These ports are created on demand, and when used in the context of vCloud Director it can take time for them to be created and assigned if you have a significant number of vApps created simultaneously. "Bumping" the configuration allows vCloud Director to use ephemeral ports quickly, efficiently, and with scale. My general recommendation is that if you have no intention to deploy vCloud Director in your environment, just ignore the dialog box.

Step 3: Upgrade the vCenter Client

After the upgrade of vCenter you will need to update the vSphere client. This can be triggered in two main ways: from the install media .iso file, or by merely logging on to the vCenter with an existing client and acknowledging the update message. I've had issues with the latter process in previous releases, mainly because I once canceled the update process midway through and my vSphere client was broken from that point onward. It is also possible to download the vSphere client from the vCenter Welcome Web page, but remember that the client is no longer on the ESX host locally. If you use an ESX host to download the client you will be downloading it via the Internet and VMware.com. The client isn't a small .exe file; it's 300MB in size. I think the upgrade of the vSphere client is trivial and isn't worth documenting beyond the points I've made above. One final statement I would make is that if you are working in a hybrid environment of mixed versions of vSphere 4 and vSphere 5 you will end up with multiple versions of the vSphere client installed. If you think this is likely, it is a good idea to download the ThinApp version of the vSphere client from the VMware Flings website to reduce the number of client installs and updates you have to do. If you are licensed for VMware ThinApp or some other third-party application virtualization software, it's a good idea to do that for the vSphere 5 client as well.

Step 4: Upgrade the VMware Update Manager (VUM)

It seems like a curious phrase—to update the Update Manager—but nonetheless you can upgrade the very tool that will allow you to upgrade the rest of your infrastructure, including ESX hosts, VMware Tools, and VMware hardware levels. There are a couple of changes around VUM that you should be aware of. First, VUM no longer supports the patching of VMs. In early versions, VUM would communicate to the popular Shavlik.com website as an independent source of patch updates for Windows and Linux guests. This feature has been deprecated and is no longer used, probably because patch management is often carried out with third-party tools that don't care if Windows is physical or virtual. Historically, VUM only ever patched VMs, which is understandable given its remit. VUM allows for upgrades from ESX/ESXi 4.x to ESXi 5.0 only. It cannot be used to upgrade ESX/ESXi 3 hosts to ESX/ESXi 4 or ESXi 5.0. I think this is a classic case where if you were using a platform that was two generations behind (in this case, ESX 3) a clean install would be more appropriate than an upgrade. Finally, you should know that, unlike the vCenter 5 upgrade where no reboot is required at the end of the process, VUM requires a reboot. If, like me, you run your VUM instance on the same system as your vCenter, you will need to plan for a maintenance window. If you run VUM on a dedicated Windows instance, you should be able to tolerate this temporary outage. With that said, the reboot is not called by the installation, and I was able to ignore the reboot and it did not cause a problem.

When you run the installer for VMware VUM, just as with vCenter, the system will recognize that the previous installation is present (see Figure 16.9).

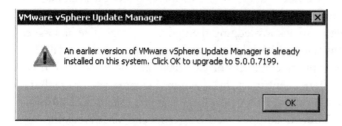

Figure 16.9 The install of Update Manager 5.0 detects the previous release of the product.

You will also be given some controls and a warning about the upgrade process with respect to what's supported and unsupported (see Figure 16.10).

After this warning, you will need to provide the name, port number, and username/password credentials to allow VUM to register with vCenter. In most cases you should find all the dialog box fields will be completed, and all you will need to supply is the password to authenticate with vCenter. VUM is still a 32-bit application that, although it can run a 64-bit platform, still requires a 32-bit DSN in the Microsoft ODBC configuration. Additionally, it does not officially support Windows Authentication to the Microsoft SQL server; as such you will need to provide the database password values during the upgrade (see Figure 16.11). In this case, you will find that the username field is already filled in from the previous installation of VUM on vSphere 4, and all you will need to provide is your password for the database user. As with the vCenter upgrade, you will be asked to confirm that you want to upgrade the database that backs VUM (see Figure 16.12).

Step 5: Upgrade the VUM Plug-in

Once the new version of VUM has been installed you should be able to install the new plug-in for it using the Plug-in Manager windows available from the Plug-ins menu. You might notice that the vCenter SRM 4.1 plug-in is listed there as well (see Figure 16.13). You can ignore this plug-in as we will not need it in our upgrade from SRM 4.1 to SRM 5.0.

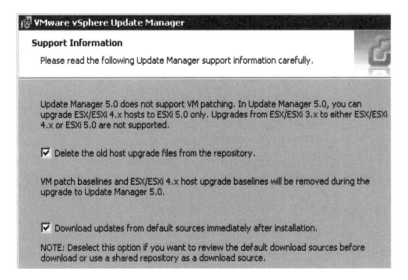

Figure 16.10   Update Manager explains the new support rules. Critically, VMware has deprecated patching of virtual machines.

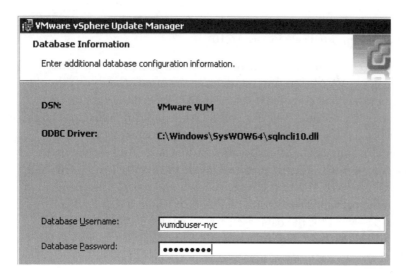

Figure 16.11   Update Manager only supports SQL Authentication and requires a 32-bit DSN, but it will only install to a 64-bit edition of Windows.

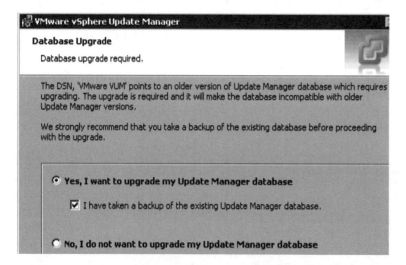

Figure 16.12   VUM's back-end database is upgraded. Back up the VUM database and take a server snapshot if you run VUM and SQL in a VM.

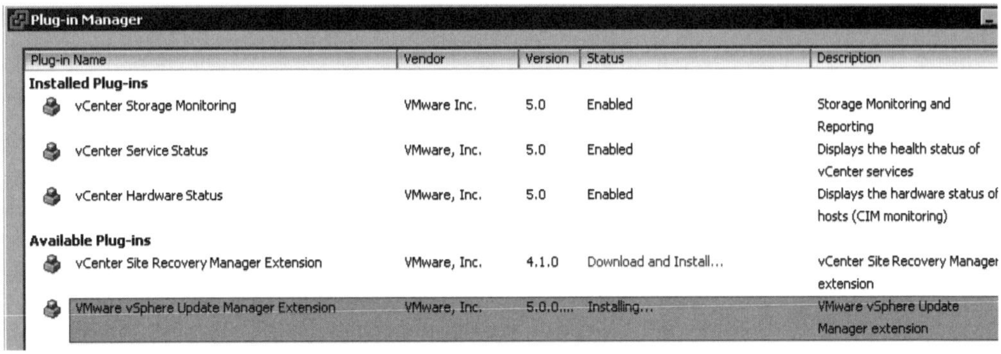

Figure 16.13   As vCenter and VUM are upgraded, new client plug-ins are required, and this is also true of SRM.

Step 6: Upgrade Third-Party Plug-ins (Optional)

As a regular user of the vSphere client I make extensive use of third-party plug-ins from many vendors. It's highly likely that the old vCenter 4 plug-ins will not be certified for use with vCenter 5, and therefore they are most likely due for an upgrade. My top plug-ins come from my main storage vendors that I use on a daily basis, including Dell, EMC, and NetApp. With that said, I don't consider these plug-ins to be a vital or essential part of my upgrade process. In short, they are nice to have rather than must-haves. That's why I consider this step as being "optional" as it could be deferred to the end of the process. Nonetheless, if you are not in a hurry, now would be a good time to review these plug-ins given that we are handing over extensions to vCenter from VMware.

Step 7: Upgrade the ESX Hosts

From a technical standpoint, SRM 5.0 has no dependencies from an ESX version perspective. It will work with ESX 4.1 and ESX 5.0 added into the same vCenter. Of course, you would need to be careful not to mix ESX 4 and ESX 5 in the same cluster because they are incompatible with each other. But if your goal is to upgrade SRM and get to a functional state such that you can carry out failovers and failbacks at will you could actually bypass this step. However, historically VMware has always placed this stage after the upgrade of the management system, and it's for this reason that I placed this step in this location. One anomaly I have seen is when an ESX 4.1 host is added to vCenter 4 before its iSCSI configuration has been set up. I found I could not even see the iSCSI software adapter from vCenter 5. Instead, I had to open the vSphere client directly on the host, and configure it there. This was an experience I had in the early beta and release candidates, which I assume will be resolved by the time of the GA.

It's worth saying that VMware's VUM is not your only option for an upgrade process. It is possible to have an interactive upgrade from ESX 4 to ESX 5 using the ESX 5 DVD installer. There is also the option of using the esxcli utility to upgrade using an offline patch bundle, which might appeal to you if you need to perform so-called "headless" upgrades. Finally, there's an option to use the new Auto Deploy functionality that loads ESXi across the network into memory; of course, this isn't really an upgrade process but a redeploy process. I will focus on the VUM method as I believe this is the most nonintrusive method from the perspective of maximizing the uptime of your VMs, and reducing the steps required to get to a new version of ESX while retaining the existing configuration as much as possible. Before you begin with an upgrade you might like to carry out another scan of your ESX 4.1 host to make sure it is patched to the hilt, and fully compliant from a VUM baseline perspective. As you can see, I have two ESX 4.1 hosts being managed by vCenter 5 that are fully compliant after having the default Critical Host Patches and Non-Critical Host Patches assigned to them (see Figure 16.14).

The first stage in the upgrade process is to import the ESX 5.0 image into the Update Manager repository. You can do this by using the Import ESXi Image link in the ESXi Images tab (see Figure 16.15).

In the wizard you can browse for the .iso image of the ESX 5.0 build. After you select it, it will be imported into the VUM storage location (see Figure 16.16), and you will be prompted to create a baseline. After completing this import process you should have an ESX 5.0 build in the ESXi Images tab, as well as an upgrade baseline in the Baselines and Groups tab. A baseline is merely a collection of agreed-upon patches that can be used as

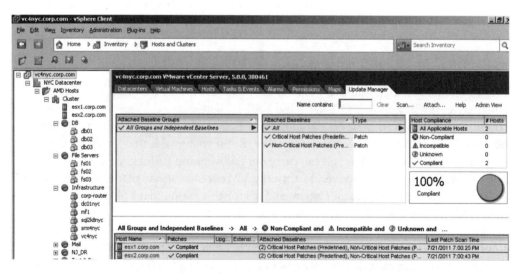

Figure 16.14   A successful scan of two ESXi 4 hosts using vCenter 5 and VUM 5, indicating they are fully patched prior to the upgrade

Figure 16.15 Using the Import ESXi Image link to bring the ESXi 5 image into the VUM scope

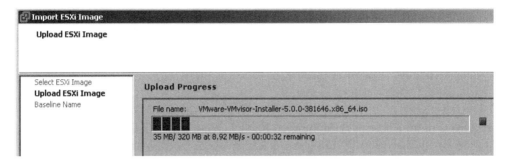

Figure 16.16 The progress bar showing the import of the ESXi image held within the DVD .iso file

a barometer of whether a host is compliant when scanned, or as the list of patches to be applied during the remediation process (see Figure 16.17).

The next stage is to attach the baseline to the ESX host or a cluster (see Figure 16.18). You do this by switching to the Hosts & Clusters view, selecting the Update Manager tab, and using the Attach link to assign the desired baseline. The VUM baseline that contains

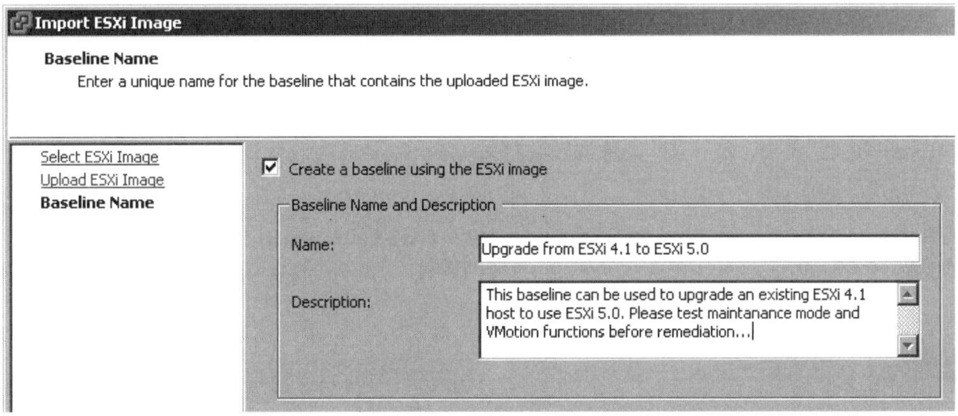

Figure 16.17 Once the import is successful a VUM baseline can be created.

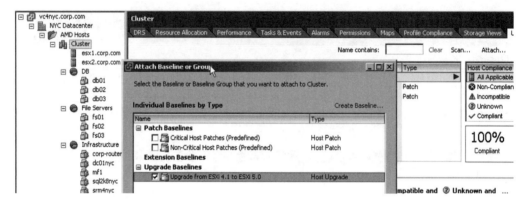

Figure 16.18   Attaching the baseline to the ESX host or a cluster

the requirement for a host to be running on ESXi 5 can be attached to a cluster. The administrator can then ask VUM to scan the host to check its compliance, and then issue a "remediate" command.

If a scan was carried out at this stage the status of the ESX hosts would change from green to yellow, and the hosts would be marked as "incompatible" with the baseline from an upgrade perspective (see Figure 16.19). This is because we have yet to actually push out the upgrade to the hosts.

The remediation process comes in two parts: a stage process and a remediate process (see Figure 16.20). The stage process pushes the update down to the host but does not trigger the remediation, whereas the remediation process both pushes the update down to the host and triggers the remediation process at the same time. I prefer to stage up the hosts, especially when I have a lot of them. I also like the confidence that successful staging of the

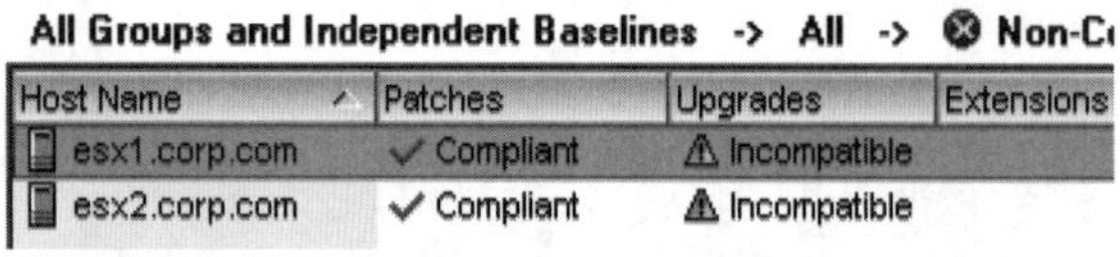

All Groups and Independent Baselines -> All -> ✖ Non-C

Host Name	Patches	Upgrades	Extensions
esx1.corp.com	✔ Compliant	⚠ Incompatible	
esx2.corp.com	✔ Compliant	⚠ Incompatible	

Figure 16.19   After a scan using an ESXi 5 baseline, the ESXi 4 hosts are shown to be incompatible, and in need of remediation.

Figure 16.20   Prestaging an upgrade or patch process allows the host to be operational for the longest period of time.

hosts gives me, as I feel the "all or nothing" approach of just clicking the Remediate button is somewhat risky. Additionally, it means I can keep the ESX hosts up for the maximum time, using the current uptime to drive the update down to the ESX hosts, before requesting that the update be applied.

Before you carry out a remediation, you should confirm a few features: first, whether vMotion is working successfully, and second, whether maintenance mode executes without errors. VUM relies heavily on these two features. If they fail for any reason, you will find that the remediation process will stall, and you will be required to resolve that problem manually. Third, I recommend setting your DRS cluster to be fully automated as this will allow the remediation process to continue without waiting for an administrator to be involved. When I run the remediation process I generally start with just one ESX host within the cluster, and I confirm that the upgrade process works for one host. In a small cluster I will tend to do the remediation on a host-by-host basis, especially if the cluster is heavily loaded and cannot tolerate a huge amount of maintenance mode activity. In large clusters, once I have one ESX upgraded, I will tend to run the remediation on the entire cluster. Whether you do the remediation on a host-by-host or a cluster-by-cluster basis a lot depends on how much confidence you have in Update Manager, and the time you have. When you click the Remediate button, you must select the right type of baseline to apply (in our case, Upgrade Baseline) and the baseline you created at the end of the ESX 5.0 image import process (see Figure 16.21).

A significant number of settings appear in the wizard (see Figure 16.22), and I feel most of these fall squarely into the zone of "common sense," but I would like to draw your attention to a couple of options that could greatly increase the success of the upgrade process. First, I recommend enabling the option labeled "Disable any removable media devices connected to the virtual machines on the host" in the Maintenance Mode page. Connected floppy and DVD/CD-ROM devices are known to cause problems with

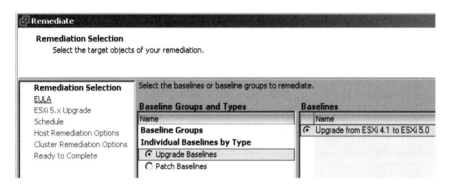

Figure 16.21 The Remediation Selection Wizard where the upgrade baseline created earlier can be applied

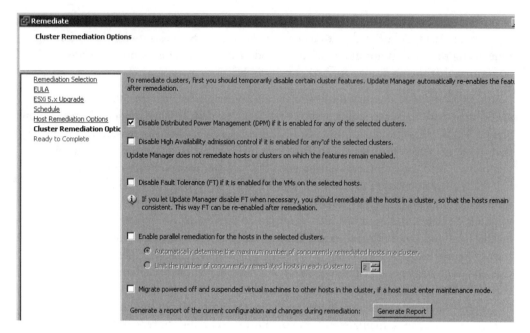

Figure 16.22 VUM supports many options. The important factor is how many simultaneous remediations can be carried out.

vMotion, and as a consequence, with maintenance mode as well. Additionally, I would enable as many of the options within the Cluster Remediation Options section as possible.

Let me take each of these in turn and explain how I think they could improve the experience of using VUM. I will assign each option a number, with the first option (Disable Distributed Power Management…) as #1 and the last option (Migrate powered off and suspended virtual machines…) as #5, so that I do not have to reproduce the long descriptions of each option.

1. DPM puts ESX hosts in a powered-off or "standby" state when it deems you have more hosts powered on than are really necessary. The more hosts you have online during the remediation the more "slots" exist for moving VMs off the ESX hosts. The net effect should be to reduce the strain the cluster is put under with hosts going in and coming out of maintenance mode.

2. It is possible for ESX to refuse to enter maintenance mode due to a general lack of resources in the cluster. HA has strict admission control rules that prevent VMs from being powered on if it thinks there are insufficient resources in terms of capacity.

You will see this with small clusters that are heavily loaded which, for various reasons, have calculated a large slot size. Turning this option on relaxes admission control and makes it more likely that the VMs will be evacuated from the host in a graceful manner through a combination of vMotion and maintenance mode, all orchestrated by Update Manager.

3. Temporarily disabling FT during the remediation process does introduce a slight risk: What if the host where the primary FT VM was running failed? There would be no FT protection for that VM. However, by turning off FT you increase the number of possible targets for vMotion, since the primary and secondary pairs in FT can never be on the same host.

4. I think this setting is common sense. The more simultaneous remediation you can carry out the faster the whole process is completed. Of course, on my two-node cluster the setting is rather meaningless, because I simply don't have enough physical hosts in my lab to configure my preferred minimum—at least three ESX hosts or more in any VMware cluster are necessary.

5. This option will ensure that VMs are located on other ESX hosts during the remediation. The same effect can be achieved by enabling the Fully Automated setting on a DRS cluster.

Once the remediation has completed you will need to relicense the host; until you do this it will be in evaluation mode.

Upgrading Site Recovery Manager

After all that, we are finally in a position to carry out an upgrade of SRM. We could actually continue with the vSphere 5 upgrade process if we wished, but as this book is essentially about SRM I want to get into the SRM upgrade as soon as possible. If you have gotten this far in the upgrade process, you might like to consider taking a snapshot of your environment. I've been doing that all along in the process. The actual upgrade of SRM 5.0 is more akin to a clean install than an in-place upgrade. The only real difference is that you have to establish a database or DSN configuration prior to running the setup. During the upgrade the installer will preserve your configuration held in the vmware-dr.xml file, which can be imported back into the system once the repair and array configuration steps have been carried out. Before embarking on the upgrade I recommend manually backing up any scripts and .csv files you have to another location as an additional precaution.

Step 8: Upgrade SRM

During the installation you will be asked to reinput the vCenter user account and password used to register the SRM extensions. At this point the SRM 5.0 installer will recognize the previous registration made by SRM 4.1; to continue you will need to click the Yes button, to overwrite the existing registration (see Figure 16.23).

Alongside this authentication process you will need to resupply the original SRM database user account and password. As with vCenter and VUM, successful authentication will result in SRM 5.0 discovering an existing SRM database, and you will get the opportunity to upgrade it to be compatible with the new release (see Figure 16.24). Despite the lack of a warning about backing up the SRM database which we saw previously, again I recommend a backup and snapshot of the SRM server and SQL systems where possible.

At the end of the upgrade you will be given a prompt indicating the next stages: updating the storage configuration and repairing the sites. The storage configuration option essentially opens a Web page that is a report of the array configuration prior to the upgrade (see Figure 16.25). In this case, I used NetApp as the storage vendor.

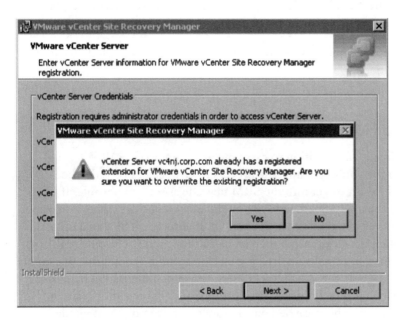

Figure 16.23   The SRM 5.0 installer recognizes a previous extension based on SRM 4.1, and lets you overwrite it with the newer version.

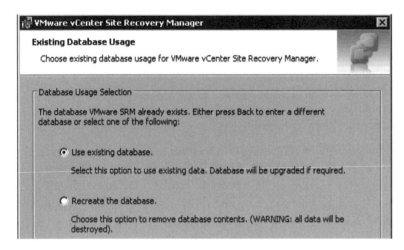

Figure 16.24 As with vCenter and VUM, the SRM installer can upgrade the database.

SRM Array Manager Configuration Report   VMware vCenter Site Recovery Manager

SRM Site: New Jersey
SRM Version: 5.0.0
Date: 07/22/2011 03:29 (UTC 401+01)

This report contains information about your array manager configuration. To complete the upgrade process, you must pair the SRM sites, then configure the array managers using the information below, and then run the SRM migration utility.

Protection Configuration

NOTE: Connection parameters may change with each version of the SRA. Refer to the SRA documentation for information about how to map the values listed below to new parameters.

Array Manager	SRA	Connection Parameters		Arrays
Array Manager for New Jersey	ONTAP	IP Address:	172.168.4.89	new-jersey-filer1, FAS2040, FAS2040
		NFS IP Addresses:	172.168.4.89	

This report contains information about your array manager configuration. To complete the upgrade process, you must pair the SRM sites, then configure the array managers using the information below, and then run the SRM migration utility.

Recovery Configuration

Note: Connection parameters may change with each version of the SRA. Refer to the SRA documentation for information

Figure 16.25 Post-upgrade information reports on the current SRA configuration

Clearly, using an SRA from the previous release that lacks the advanced functionality that SRM 5.0 offers isn't going to get us very far. So the next stage is to uninstall all the SRAs that were deployed with SRM 4.1 and install the new versions that ship with SRM 5.0. I had variable success with uninstalling SRAs; some would uninstall and some would not. Of course, I did not have the opportunity to install every SRA and check the uninstall routine. But I generally recommend the removal of old software before installing the new software to prevent any situation where SRM accidentally discovers an old and out-of-date SRA.

Once the SRA software has been upgraded we are in a position to install the new SRM plug-in, and complete the upgrade. Occasionally, I've found that the Plug-ins Manager allows me to download the SRM 5.0 plug-in. It is possible to bypass the download and install link in the Plug-ins Manager, and download and install the plug-in directly from the SRM 5.0 server using this URL:

http://srm4nyc:8096/VMware-srmplugin.exe

A word of warning here: At first sight, it will look as though the upgrade has completely clobbered the original configuration. Even after repairing the site and configuring the array managers, the Recovery Plans and Protection Groups do not auto-magically appear in SRM. Instead, they have to be restored from the backup taken by SRM 5.0 during the upgrade. Installing the SRM 5.0 plug-in, re-pairing the site, and creating an array manager configuration are all topics I covered in Chapter 7, Installing VMware SRM, and I don't feel it would be beneficial to repeat that again here. Different vendors have different approaches to managing the SRA component, but most require an uninstall of their old SRA prior to installation of the new SRA. I heartily recommend that once the SRA has been configured you confirm that it returns all the LUNs/volumes you expect to be replicated. Occasionally, I've had to "refresh" the SRA to ensure that all volumes are marked as being replicated.

Once the pairing and array configuration is in place you can open a command prompt on the SRM server. It doesn't matter which SRM server you connect to run the `srm-migrate` command. To run the following command you will need to be in the C:\Program Files (x86) \VMware \VMware vCenter Site Recovery Manager \bin path:

```
srm-migration.exe -cmd importConfig -cfg ..\config\vmware-dr.xml -lcl-usr
  corp\administrator -rem-usr corp\administrator
```

The `srm-migrate` command also supports `-lcl-csv-file` and `-rem-csv-file` switches that allow you to import the dr-ip-exporter files from the SRM 4.1 release. As you can see, the srm-migration tool requires you to supply the username of the SRM administrator account of the SRM server you connect to, to run the command (`-lcl-user`), as well as the account of the remote SRM server (`-rem-usr`). The utility then completes quite lengthy output as it re-creates the Protection Groups and Recovery Plans. In my tests, running this command stopped the SRM service on the SRM server on which it was run, and I needed to restart the service in order to connect.

Step 9: Upgrade VMware Tools (Optional)

> **WARNING**
>
> The upgrade of VMware Tools and virtual hardware has been known to create a brand-new local area connection within Windows. This results in the "loss" of your static IP addresses as the new network interface defaults to using DHCP. Ensure that you back up your VM and make a note of its current IP configuration before embarking on this step of the upgrade process. I found with Windows 2008 R2 64-bit an update of VMware Tools and virtual hardware did not remove my NIC settings. A VMware Tools upgrade initiated via Update Manager does trigger a reboot.

After an upgrade of ESX from version 4.1 to 5.0 you will find that your VM's internal VMware Tools package will be out of date. To determine which VMs need their tools updated, from vCenter you can add an additional column to the Virtual Machines tab, called VMware Tools Status (see Figure 16.26). You can then sort it to display all the VMs whose VMware Tools package is out of date.

Alternatively, if you prefer you can use VMware PowerCLI to see a definitive report of the VMs whose VMware Tools are in a troublesome state, such as "Not running" or "Out of date." Although it's a bit torturous to look at, this PowerCLI one-liner will produce the report:

```
Get-VM | Get-View | Select-Object
  @{N="Name";E={$_.Name}},@{Name="ToolsStatus";E={$_.Guest.ToolsStatus}}
```

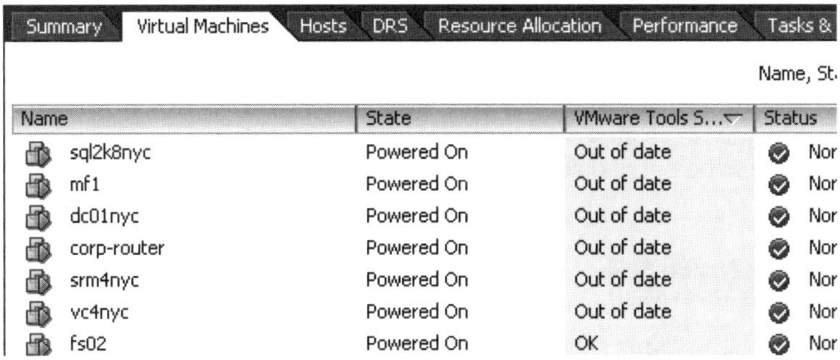

Figure 16.26 This tab shows that some VMs are in need of a VMware Tools upgrade.

This report also returns information about your placeholder VMs, so you may wish to filter out those with your PowerCLI commands.

You might find some VMs have already had their VMware Tools automatically updated. This is because toward the end of vSphere 4, VMware introduced new settings that enable the VM to check its tools status on boot-up, and if it discovers its VMware Tools are out of date, to automatically upgrade them (see Figure 16.27).

This setting is not a default for all VMs, but fortunately VUM can assist in enabling it for large numbers of VMs, with the need to resort to PowerCLI. In the VMs and Templates view on the Update Manager tab of the vCenter, datacenter, or folder of VMs, you should see a "VMware Tools upgrade settings" button next to the Remediate button (see Figure 16.28).

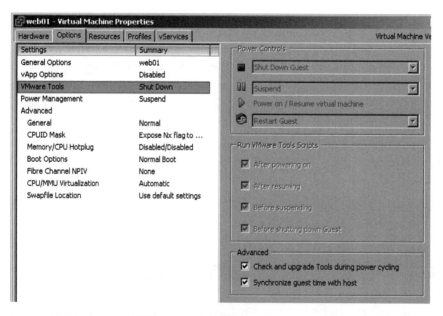

Figure 16.27   It is possible to have the status of VMware Tools checked on next power on and upgraded if found to be out of date.

Figure 16.28   The "VMware Tools upgrade settings" button allows you to control how VMware Tools is upgraded.

Clicking this button will bring up a dialog box that will allow you to select which VMs will have this option enabled, including templates.

Ideally, any upgrade should avoid the need to shut down VMs, so it's likely that the vast majority of your VMs will not be up to date.

It's possible to upgrade VMware Tools via many methods.

- Individually, by right-clicking a VM, selecting Guest, and choosing Install/Upgrade VMware Tools. This option allows for an interactive or automatic tools upgrade.

- In bulk, using the preceding method if you multiselect affected VMs in the Virtual Machines tab.

- Via PowerCLI, through the Update Tools option which will apply the VMware Tools update package to nominated VMs, like so:

  ```
  Get-ResourcePool Web | Get-VM | Update-Tools -NoReboot
  ```

- Via Update Manager, using the same method we used to upgrade the ESX hosts with VMware Update.

Different people in the VMware community have different approaches to the VMware Tools update. Some use the "Check and Upgrade Tools during power cycling" option, and just assume that over a period of time VMware Tools will eventually be updated, as part of a normal patch management schedule that frequently will require a reboot anyway as part of the process. Others prefer the PowerCLI method because it allows them to use very tailored filters to apply the update to the right VMs at the right time; critically, it also allows the administrator to suppress the default reboot of VMware Tools to Windows guests. Yet other administrators prefer the consistency of using one management system— in our case, VMware Update Manager—to manage the entire process. Whatever you prefer, there are some important caveats to remember. For instance, if you are using the PowerCLI method, the -NoReboot option when using Update Tools in PowerCLI *only* applies to Windows guest operating systems. There is no 100% guarantee that the reboot will not happen even if you use the -NoReboot option, though; a lot depends on the version of the tools installed, and the version of ESX/vCenter you are using. Additionally, in a non-Windows-based operating system you may find that all Update Tools does is mount the VMware Tools .iso file to the guest operating system, leaving it to you to extract the .tgz file or install the .rpm file in the case of some Linux distributions. If this is the case you might prefer to use your own in-house methods of pushing out software updates, instead of using VMware's. I prefer using VMware Update Manager as it has a sophisticated way of applying the update, while at the same time offering the VMware administrator a method to validate whether the update was successful.

Step 10: Upgrade Virtual Hardware (Optional)

Alongside a VMware Tools update you may also want to carry out a virtual machine hardware upgrade. You will be pleased to learn that upgrading the VM hardware doesn't require any anti-static discharge precautions or run the risk of losing fiddly screws down the crevices of badly finished cases that cut you to ribbons! VMware has its own unique version system for VM hardware levels that increment across the various virtualization platforms it produces (Workstation, Fusion, Player, and ESX). ESXi 5 raises the VMware hardware level from version 7 (also supported on ESX 4) to VM version 8. You can see these hardware levels in the vSphere client when you create a brand-new VM using the custom options (see Figure 16.29).

You will find the VM version using the same changes to the GUI I showed in the previous section. The Virtual Machines tab also supports the addition of a VM Version column (see Figure 16.30).

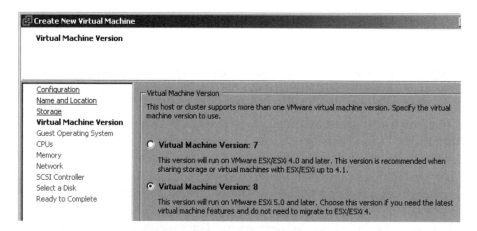

Figure 16.29   Upgrading the VM version requires a power off of the VM. Remember, a VM with hardware level 8 cannot run on an ESX4 host.

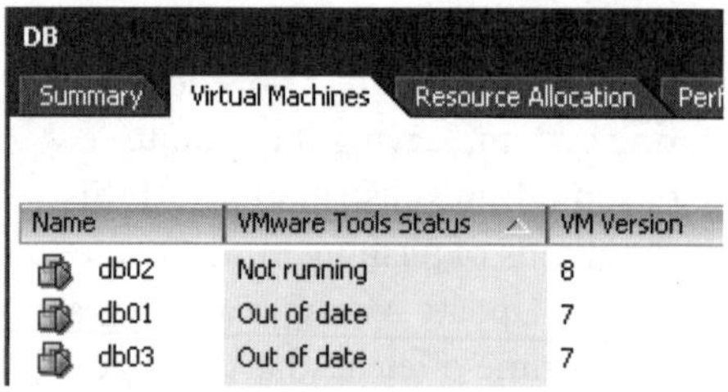

Name	VMware Tools Status	VM Version
db02	Not running	8
db01	Out of date	7
db03	Out of date	7

Figure 16.30   The VM Version column indicates the hardware level of the VM.

Again there's is a PowerCLI "one-liner" that will list all your VMs with their VM version, like so:

```
Get-VM | ForEach-Object {Get-View $_.ID} | ForEach-Object {Write-Host
  $_.Name $_.Config.Version} | sort
```

Unlike VMware Tools upgrades where a reboot can sometimes be suppressed or deferred, virtual hardware upgrades require a reboot. Additionally, these upgrades are nonreversible, so once a VM is upgraded from VM version 7 to VM version 8 it will no longer run on ESX 4.0. Therefore, the decision to upgrade the virtual machine hardware level is not to be undertaken lightly if you plan to undertake your upgrade process in a gradual and stealthy manner where you are running a hybrid model in which vCenter 5 manages both ESX 4 and ESX 5 clusters. I like the idea of doing the VMware Tools and hardware level upgrade in one fell swoop. It gets the whole unpleasant business out of the way, and again I prefer to do this via VUM. However, as with VMware Tools there are a number of different methods for you to choose from.

- Individually, by right-clicking a VM when it is powered off and selecting the Upgrade Virtual Hardware option.

- In bulk, by multiselecting affected VMs in the Virtual Machines tab. Remember, the selected VMs must be powered off first.

- Via PowerCLI, using the following command:

  ```
  Get-VM web* | Get-View | % { $_.UpgradeVM($null) }
  ```

  I recommend looking at these scripts from Arne Fokkema's ict-freak.nl site. Although these were developed from the perspective of an upgrade from ESX 3 to ESX 4, there is no reason they could not be used for an upgrade from ESX 4 to ESX 5:

  http://ict-freak.nl/2009/06/27/powercli-upgrading-vhardware-to-vsphere-part-1-templates/

  http://ict-freak.nl/2009/07/15/powercli-upgrading-vhardware-to-vsphere-part-2-vms/

- Via Update Manager, using the same method we used to upgrade the ESX hosts with VMware Update.

As I stated earlier, I prefer to use Update Manager, as I think it's nice to be consistent with other methods used. By default, VUM ships with two built-in baselines: one for upgrading VMware Tools and one for upgrading the VM version. This can be seen under the Baselines and Groups tab by clicking the VMs/VAs button (see Figure 16.31).

Figure 16.31 While there are many ways to upgrade both VMware Tools and virtual hardware, I prefer to use VUM for consistency.

These baselines can be attached to any object in the VMs & Templates view. However, there's one big downside. Although multiple baselines can be *attached* to the VMs, only one can be applied to VMs at any one time (see Figure 16.32).

Step 11: Upgrade VMFS Volumes (Optional)

As you probably know, VMFS has been updated from version 3 to version 5. The last time there was an upgrade to the VMware file system was when people transitioned from ESX 2 to ESX 3. When ESX 4 was released VMware chose not to change the file system and this offered an easy upgrade path from one release to another. Changing a file system is a big undertaking for any vendor and it's not unusual for this to be done only when absolutely necessary. Fortunately, our lives will be made easier by the fact that VMware has made it possible to upgrade VMFS even when there are VMs that are powered on. Previous upgrades require Storage vMotion or a power off of all VMs to unlock the file system ready for an upgrade.

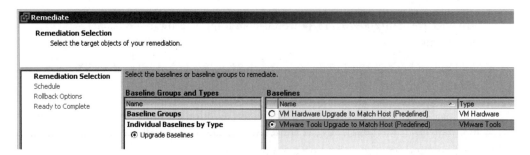

Figure 16.32 Sadly, it appears that one cannot simultaneously upgrade both the VMware Tools and virtual hardware in one fell swoop.

In an ideal world you would create a brand-new LUN/volume and format that cleanly with VMFS-5, the reason being that although VMFS-3 volumes can be upgraded to VMFS-5, doing this preserves some of the original limitations surrounding VMFS-3. I think Cormac Hogan of VMware has one of the best roundups of VMFS-5 and the upgrade process online:

> http://blogs.vmware.com/vsphere/2011/07/new-vsphere-50-storage-features-part-1-vmfs-5.html

Here is a list of some of the old properties that are still present when an in-place upgrade has been made of VMFS.

- VMFS-5 upgraded from VMFS-3 continues to use the previous file block size which may be larger than the unified 1MB file block size.

- VMFS-5 upgraded from VMFS-3 continues to use 64KB sub-blocks and not new 8K sub-blocks.

- VMFS-5 upgraded from VMFS-3 continues to have a file limit of 30,720 rather than a new file limit of > 100,000 for the newly created VMFS-5.

- VMFS-5 upgraded from VMFS-3 continues to use the Master Boot Record (MBR) partition type; when the VMFS-5 volume grows larger than 2TB, it automatically and seamlessly switches from MBR to GUID Partition Table (GPT) with no impact to the running VMs.

- VMFS-5 upgraded from VMFS-3 continues to have its partition starting on sector 128; newly created VMFS-5 partitions will have their partition starting at sector 2048.

Whether these "lost" features are significant to you is moot. For me the big change is the move away from MBR to GPT. It opens the door to allow VMware to have virtual disks and RDMs that break through the 2TB size barrier. It's worth remembering that currently in ESX 5, despite the improvements in the VMFS file system and VMkernel, the maximum size of any .vmdk file and RDM is still only 2TB. This is in spite of the fact that many modern guest operating systems can address single partitions that are much larger than this, with them moving to GPT some time ago.

So, what is the alternative if you feel a desperate urge to have your VMFS partitions start at sector 2048 rather than 128? Well, you could create a new LUN/volume, format it natively with VMFS-5, and then use Storage vMotion to move your VMFS from the old file system to the new one. Depending on the size of the VMs and the performance of your storage array, that could take some time. This new LUN/volume would have to be configured for replication if it was to be used by Site Recovery Manager. It's perhaps worth remembering that SRM doesn't really handle Storage vMotion very seamlessly.

If I was going to embark on this approach I would make my two datastores part of the *same* Protection Group. In this configuration, Storage vMotion works like a charm. Nonetheless, the extra administrator time to complete the process is something you might want to balance against the perceived "benefits" of cleanly installed VMFS volumes. Of course, customers who use NFS don't have to worry about this issue in the slightest—a fact that has not escaped the attention of many of my customers. To carry out an in-place upgrade of the VMFS file system, locate the VMFS volume in the inventory and click the link to Upgrade to VMFS-5 (see Figure 16.33).

Step 12: Upgrade Distributed vSwitches (Optional)

vSphere 5 introduces enhancements to the VMware Distributed vSwitch, and it is possible to upgrade to the new version 5 switch (see Figure 16.34). The upgrade process is seamless to the vSphere and does not affect virtual machines. To carry out the upgrade, switch to the Networking view, select the DvSwitch, and click the Upgrade link.

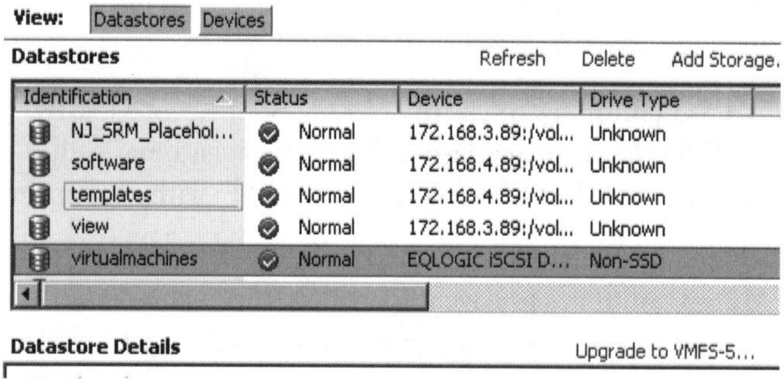

View:	Datastores	Devices			
Datastores			Refresh	Delete	Add Storage.

Identification	Status	Device	Drive Type
NJ_SRM_Placehol...	Normal	172.168.3.89:/vol...	Unknown
software	Normal	172.168.4.89:/vol...	Unknown
templates	Normal	172.168.4.89:/vol...	Unknown
view	Normal	172.168.3.89:/vol...	Unknown
virtualmachines	Normal	EQLOGIC iSCSI D...	Non-SSD

Datastore Details   Upgrade to VMFS-5...

Figure 16.33   The Upgrade to VMFS-5 link on the properties of a VMFS volume

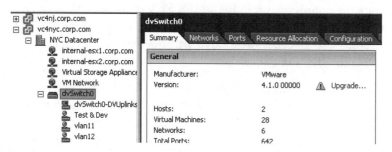

Figure 16.34   vSphere 5 introduces a new distributed virtual switch format.

Summary

This concludes the upgrade process, but of course, given your use of VMware technologies, the upgrade process might not end here. For example, you may need to update your VMware View deployment as well. As you can see, the upgrade process is a highly automated and relatively smooth process, but care should be taken to minimize downtime wherever possible. As virtualization platforms increasingly mature, it is possible to upgrade the vSphere and associated layers seamlessly without much interruption to the guest operating systems that provide the applications and service upon which your users depend. I think VMware has done a good job of planning and staging the vSphere 5 aligned releases so that there is not a large lead-in time between the platform release (vSphere 5) and the associated add-ons like SRM that complement it.

Well, this is the end of the book, and I would like to use these last few paragraphs to make some final conclusions and observations about VMware Site Recovery Manager and VMware generally. I first started working with VMware products in late 2003. In fact, it wasn't until 2004 that I seriously became involved with VMware ESX and VirtualCenter. So I see that we are all on a huge learning curve because even our so-called experts, gurus, and evangelists are relatively new to virtualization. But as ever in our industry, there are some extremely sharp people who work out in the field who reacted brilliantly to the seismic shift that I saw coming when I saw my first vMotion demonstration.

There's been a lot of talk about how hypervisors will or are becoming a commodity. I still think we are a little bit away from that, as VMware licensing shows—there is still a premium to be charged on the virtualization layer. The marketplace is forever changing and VMware's competitors will try to catch up, but I think that will take much longer than many pundits think. These pundits don't realize that VMware isn't going to stay still while others advance. Companies thrive when they have a market to either create or defend. As the virtualization layer becomes increasingly commoditized, for me that means management is now where the money has moved to, and SRM is firmly in that camp.

But I see another shift that is equally seismic and that is a revolution in our management tools because, quite simply, the old management tools simply don't cut the mustard. They aren't VM-aware. VMware is creating these VM-aware products (Site Recovery Manager, vCloud Director View, and others) now, not in some far-flung future. So, if you are a VMware shop, don't wait around—get on and play with these technologies now, as I have done, because they are "the next big thing" that you have been looking for in your career. As the years roll by, expect to see the *R* in *SRM* disappear—and with the advent of cloud computing, VMware Site Manager will be as much a cloud management tool as it is a disaster recovery tool. I imagine Site Manager will also integrate seamlessly with the new developments in long-distance vMotion, allowing you to orchestrate the planned move of VMs from one site to another without the VMs being powered off. In the future, I can imagine using the technology that currently sits behind SRM being used to move virtual machines from an internal private cloud to an external public cloud—and from one cloud provider to another.

Index

G

H

Q

Qtree Details page, Create Mirror Wizard, 152

R

RAID groups
  defined, 78
  EMC CLARiiON, 44
  EMC LUN, 78–80
  LUNs for reserved LUN pool, 76
RAM, reduce in recovery process, 316–321
Rate of Change Rule of Thumb (RCRT), 165–166
Raw device/disk mappings (RDMs), 204, 348–350
RCRT (Rate of Change Rule of Thumb), 165–166
RDMs (raw device/disk mappings), 204, 348–350
Re-IP process, improved in SRM 5.0, 4–5
Reboot
  change in ESX iSCSI stack, 31, 56
  ESXi host access to NetApp iSCSI target, 146
  HIT-VE configuration, 40–41
  virtual hardware upgrade, 459
  VMware Tool upgrade, 457
  VMware Update Manager, 442
Reciprocity, pairing process, 227
RecoverPoint technology, EMC, 119
Recovery button, 399, 402
Recovery Plans
  basic full-site, 269–273
  bidirectional configurations, 381
  clean up after test, 283–285
  control and troubleshoot, 285–291
  create, 262–266

disable power-on function of VMs, 383
order of configuration of SRM, 343
pause, resume and cancel, 285–287
remove when decommissioning site, 394
reprotect process. *See* Reprotect process
run after unplanned failover from loss of Protected Site, 415–417
run multiple simultaneous, 276
SRM 5.0 protection for, 10
storage array vendors and, 291–294
test, basic steps, 277–281
test, exercise, 281–283
test storage configuration, 273–275
test, understanding, 275–276
test with Protection Groups, 257–262
view Recovery Steps, 397–398
Recovery Plans, custom
  add command steps, 313–314
  add command steps with VMware PowerCLI, 315–321
  add prompt steps, 309–312
  add VM dependencies, 302–305
  configure IP address changes for Recovery VMs, 329–337
  configure priorities for recovered VMs, 299–302
  configure start-up and shutdown options, 305–307
  control how VMs power on, 299
  lost Repair Array Managers button, 354
  manage changes at Protected Site. *See* Protected Site, managing changes at
  manage PowerCLI authentication and variables, 321–327
  multiple datastores, 350–351
  multiple Protection Groups, 351
  multiple Recovery Plans, 352–354
  overview of, 297–298
  review summary, 354–355
  suspend VMs at Recovery Site, 308–309

W

Y

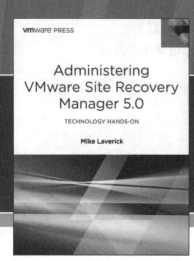

FREE Online Edition

Your purchase of *Administering VMware Site Recovery Manager 5.0* includes access to a free online edition for 45 days through the **Safari Books Online** subscription service. Nearly every VMware Press book is available online through **Safari Books Online**, along with thousands of books and videos from publishers such as Addison-Wesley Professional, Cisco Press, Exam Cram, IBM Press, O'Reilly Media, Prentice Hall, Que, and Sams.

Safari Books Online is a digital library providing searchable, on-demand access to thousands of technology, digital media, and professional development books and videos from leading publishers. With one monthly or yearly subscription price, you get unlimited access to learning tools and information on topics including mobile app and software development, tips and tricks on using your favorite gadgets, networking, project management, graphic design, and much more.

Activate your FREE Online Edition at
informit.com/safarifree

STEP 1: Enter the coupon code: FQSBXAA.

STEP 2: New Safari users, complete the brief registration form. Safari subscribers, just log in.

If you have difficulty registering on Safari or accessing the online edition, please e-mail customer-service@safaribooksonline.com